READINGS IN READING INSTRUCTION
ITS HISTORY, THEORY, AND DEVELOPMENT

RICHARD D. ROBINSON

University of Missouri–Columbia

PEARSON

Boston ■ *New York* ■ *San Francisco*
Mexico City ■ *Montreal* ■ *Toronto* ■ *London* ■ *Madrid* ■ *Munich* ■ *Paris*
Hong Kong ■ *Singapore* ■ *Tokyo* ■ *Cape Town* ■ *Sydney*

Senior Series Editor: Aurora Martínez-Ramos
Editorial Assistant: Erin Beatty
Executive Marketing Manager: Amy Cronin Jordan
Editorial-Production Administrator: Anna Socrates
Editorial-Production Service: Omegatype Typography, Inc.
Manufacturing Buyer: Andrew Turso
Composition and Prepress Buyer: Linda Cox
Cover Administrator: Joel Gendron
Electronic Composition: Omegatype Typography, Inc.

For related titles and support materials, visit our online catalog at www.ablongman.com.

Between the time Website information is gathered and then published, it is not unusual for some sites to have closed. Also, the transcription of URLs can result in unintended typographical errors. The publisher would appreciate notification where these errors occur so that they may be corrected in subsequent editions.

Library of Congress Cataloging-in-Publication Data

Readings in reading instruction : its history, theory, and development / [edited by] Richard D. Robinson.
    p.   cm.
    Includes bibliographical references and index.
    ISBN 0-205-41058-8
    1. Reading.   I. Robinson, Richard David, 1940–

LB1050.R4335 2005
418.4—dc22

                                                                    2004054726

Printed in the United States of America

10 9 8 7 6 5 4 3 2 1   09 08 07 06 05 04

If we see further today, it is simply because we stand on the shoulders of giants.

—Isaac Newton

This book is dedicated to those educators of the past who have shaped the literacy practices and beliefs of today's teachers.

*We believe that the teacher must use any [reading]
method that seems to meet the needs of the child,
and that one teacher may give her pupil the power
of gaining thought and help him to form habits in
reading in one way, while another teacher may do
the same thing by an entirely different method.*
—Edmund Huey
The Psychology and Pedagogy of Reading (1908)

CONTENTS

Reading maketh a full man; conference a ready man; writing an exact man.
—Francis Bacon
Essays: Of Studies (1579)

The art of reading is in great part that of acquiring a better understanding of life from one's encounter with it in a book.
—Andre Maurois
The Art of Living (1973)

Learning to read is an essential foundation for success in our society.
—President George W. Bush
No Child Left Behind (2003)

To be able to read is one of mankind's greatest accomplishments. As Edmund Huey noted, "Reading as a psycho-physiological process is almost as good as a miracle." Because reading has always been considered so important, educators have long been vitally interested in the effective teaching of literacy skills. From the earliest times there have been those who have written with skill and insight about the teaching of reading. Many of these writings, despite their age, often read as remarkably current and relevant to today's teaching of reading.

No facet of literacy is an isolated moment in time. Each concept or idea has had a unique developmental history that represents a wide range of opinion and definition. What we believe today is in reality the end result of a rich and diverse process of historical thought and change. Issues such as the phonics controversy, the use of various types of reading assessment, and the teaching of reading comprehension are typical of reoccurring themes in reading education. Yet in many literacy areas, a historical perspective quite clearly reveals positive progression of ideas and thoughts. A review of the literature on a given topic in reading shows, as is true in all learning, investigations and work that were both fruitful and less than effective.

The primary purpose of this book is to provide the reader with an understanding of the development of a number of significant issues in the field of literacy education. This is not a history of reading books but rather one that uses historical resources to show how current reading practices have developed over time. Emphasis in the selection process of this material has been placed on the evolution of these ideas across time as well as in terms of pedagogical development.

There are a number of reasons awareness of the development of current literacy practices is important for today's teachers. For example, educators are often restricted to a parochial view of reading instruction when they limit their opportunity of experiencing the breadth and depth of understanding provided by a wide knowledge of the past work in a particular area in literacy education. Unfortunately, many in today's educational world are often heavily influenced by the current fads and foibles of reading education. The classics in reading education will hopefully become a solid foundation or benchmark from which current reading teachers can experiment with ideas and practices, clearly knowing that they have a reliable basis for determining the effectiveness of the new ventures.

Moreover, even a cursory exploration of classic books and articles reveals that their authors typically reached conclusions that have been confirmed, not refuted, by subsequent research and actual practice. Perhaps the most critical reason to have an understanding of reading's past history is simply that many of these writers saw and understood the reading process with great individual insight and understanding. Rather than being of only passing historical interest, these classic readings are invariably relevant and important for today's reading teacher. They have clearly withstood the test of time, and because of their enduring quality, contain much to inspire current teachers to carefully address their most fundamental beliefs and practices in reading education.

In this book, the articles were selected carefully with the purpose of illustrating the developing nature of literacy education. A number of noteworthy authors are represented here, including in some instances past educators who may not be as commonly known to modern audiences. In this latter group, despite their relative obscurity, are writers who have made important contributions to reading educators of today. The dialogue of these authors represents an ongoing discussion of some of the most important issues in the field of literacy education from the past to the present. It is hoped that the readers of this book will feel a part of this enduring conversation and want to add to future developments in these literacy areas.

To adequately know and understand where we are today in the teaching of reading requires a sound knowledge of where we have been in the past.

ORGANIZATION OF THIS BOOK

Each of the chapters in this book is organized into four sections: (1) introductory discussion of the topic, (2) the articles, (3) an annotated bibliography related to the primary topic, and (4) suggestions for further involvement.

Chapter Introductions

The introductions are designed to provide an overview of the chapter topic with special emphasis on the importance of this material both in terms of its historical and current educational value. These discussions will be centered on the development of significant questions, common themes, and related answers for each of the literacy areas.

Articles

The articles in this book are arranged chronologically in terms of the historical development of the topic, except for the contents of Chapters 1 and 10. An explanation for these changes is provided in each of these two chapters. Preceding each of the articles is a brief overview of what readers need to be aware of in terms of the contributions to literacy instruction of each reference.

Annotated Bibliographies

The purpose of the annotated bibliography is to encourage further reading on each of the chapter topics. These references include related materials that illustrate various historical or educational developments associated with the primary theme being discussed.

You Become Involved

The final section of each chapter is designed to help the reader formulate his or her own views of the literacy topic by engaging in activities that encourage independent thought. For each chapter, a range of possibilities is presented.

ACKNOWLEDGMENTS

I would like to gratefully acknowledge the reviewers of this book: Sarah Ann Beach, University of Oklahoma; Thomas A. Caron, Marshall University Graduate College; Annemarie Francois, University of California, Los Angeles; Douglas K. Hartman, University of Pittsburgh; Sharon M. Peck, SUNY Geneseo; Patricia B. Schmidt, LeMoyne College; and April Whatley, University of New Orleans.

READING RESEARCH

The more extensive the research on reading, the more complex the process seems to be.

—Arthur I. Gates
NSSE Yearbook (1949)

A major task, the real frontier in reading research, and one that needs constant attention, is putting research to work in the classroom.

—Theodore Clymer
The Reading Teacher (1958)

In the endeavor of reading research, we, as observers of the phenomenon of reading, all begin and end with the same problem, the problem of how to define reading.

—Peter Mosenthal
51st Yearbook of the National Reading Conference (2002)

Almost from the beginning of literacy instruction, there has been interest and debate as to the best methods and materials for the effective teaching of reading. In attempting to resolve the many issues that developed in literacy education, there quickly began related research and study (Smith, 1934). What started with relatively few investigations in the early 1900s rapidly became a dominant aspect of the total research done in the field of education. Reading researchers such as Gray (1925), Betts (1934), and Strang (1939) reported this growing interest in the study of various aspects of reading research. In fact, Betts and Betts (1945), near the midpoint of the previous century, referenced over 8,200 studies that had been done in the field of literacy education in a little less than fifty years. Later reviews of literacy research such as those done by Traxler (1941, 1946, 1955) and Summers (1969) show the continued interest in the study of reading. Of particular note has been the publication of the three volumes of the *Handbook of Reading Research* (Pearson et al., 1984; Barr et al., 1991; Kamil et al., 2000). Each of these comprehensive publications contains extensive reviews of literacy research and study on many of the most important issues and trends in this field.

Any attempt to be cognizant of all of the available research and writing on even a small aspect of literacy education is virtually impossible when faced with the large number of possible studies to be considered. With this difficulty in mind, this chapter highlights four important studies that illustrate the scope of research from a historical viewpoint. All of the authors of these four references are noted reading researchers and represent research that best illustrates the thinking of the period in which it was done. Reading this material should give you a good overview of what has been done in the past and should be a good introduction to further reading and study of the field of literacy education.

AS YOU READ

The following four articles are a historical overview of the important studies done in literacy research. In your reading of this material, you might compare and contrast the differing views of literacy research as represented by these authors. What are some current themes that seem to appear repeatedly over time? Which themes seem to be unique to a specific time period?

Reading Research That Makes a Difference

DAVID H. RUSSELL

The first article, by David Russell (1961), serves to introduce reading research from a historical perspective. Russell was a prominent literacy educator of the last century. He is perhaps best known for his work related to children's language and its relation to cognition. His article identifies what he considered to be the ten reading research articles that had the most influence on the teaching of reading through 1961. As you read this article note especially how current many of the ideas these writers had about the teaching of reading are.

It is a peculiarly American custom to select "the best ten" or "one hundred best" or "most likely to succeed" individuals or products. Since we select the "All-Americans" in football or "Most Valuable Player" in baseball the idea may be extended to education. More specifically, it may be applied to research in reading.

This article selects "the best ten" examples of reading research, not because they are most valuable in all situations, but in response to the challenge of a superintendent of schools. Some

time ago he said something like this to me, "You university people are always talking about ways research should influence teaching. Teachers teach the way they were taught, with some modification for the demands of their community. When did research ever influence the teaching of reading?"

At that time, my answer to the skeptical superintendent was not as complete as I should have liked, so as a result of thinking over his challenge, I list here more fully ten studies which have widely influenced reading instruction over the years. Because most of the researches are well known, I describe their method and results only briefly, but some characteristics of these influential studies are given with an attempt to analyze why they have so powerfully affected the curriculum in reading and related areas.

The first of the classic studies in reading that comes to mind is the series of investigations by Buswell and Judd (2, 7) on the reading process made at the University of Chicago around 1920. These are examples of "basic" research in education—studies which may be considered as "pure," as discovery of knowledge for its own sake, but studies nevertheless which had great influence in showing the advantages of silent over oral reading and which illustrated the differential nature of the reading act. The analyses of the act of reading destroyed, once and for all, the notion that reading is a unitary activity. Instead, they suggested that reading skills differ with different purposes and materials. Accordingly, wise teachers began to help the child learn to read for a variety of purposes and using different kinds of printed matter.

A second memorable study was the investigation of errors in paragraph comprehension made by Thorndike in 1917 (12). This was an example of applied research. In an area which took oral teaching of reading for granted, Thorndike clearly showed differences between mouthing words and understanding meaning. He likened the process of reading a paragraph to that of solving a problem or combining dispersed ideas into a related whole. By illustrating the wide variety of errors children make in the comprehension of a relatively simple paragraph, he demonstrated the need for instruction in getting meaning from the printed page. He also raised the issue of causes of misunderstanding and attributed it in part to the over-potency of certain words, thus foreshadowing some recent psychological work on individual perceptions.

A third classic publication related to Thorndike's study was a teaching study which helped provide teachers with concrete materials they could use in place of the common oral attack of that day. This was the investigation described in Gates' *New Methods in Primary Reading* (3). In it Gates did not toss phonics out the window, as sometimes claimed, but he did show the importance of visual techniques and a method he called "intrinsic" in getting meanings of words and sentences. Such a study led directly to a revolution in teaching materials and in methods which combined a variety of ways for children to recognize words.

Like his study of primary methods and materials, Gates' *The Improvement of Reading* (4) is a report of the number of experiments and try-outs of diagnostic material. It represents not only a fresh concept in the scientific study of reading but was among the first major investigations in a long list of researches on diagnostic and remedial activities. One outgrowth of the measurement movement was the attempt to get at specific factors and causes of low educational achievement. The point of view in *The Improvement of Reading* is that most reading retardation and disability are not explained by vague, blanket terms such as "laziness" or "low intelligence" or "bad attitude" but, rather, are the resultant of a group or syndrome of specific, related factors which must be diagnosed exactly. The first and subsequent editions of *The Improvement of Reading* contained a battery of diagnostic tests which have been extended in other tests by different authors and in numerous books and articles on diagnostic and remedial activities. The present-day reading clinic is one example of the influence of the diagnostic approach to educational problems, a concept exemplified in Gates' pioneer work.

A fifth classic in the field of reading investigation was the Terman and Lima book (11) on children's reading interests. Reinforced by some of the educational theories of the day, it helped provide a basis for the concept of developmental reading. Terman and Lima discovered the typical interests of boys and girls at various age levels and showed how these changed from preschool through early adolescent years. Accordingly, they not only provided some basis for the selection of children's literature at various ages, but they also helped evolve a dynamic concept of children's reading.

The sixth study is an example of the historical method of research. Smith's *American Reading Instruction* (8) illustrates the long gradual development of methods and practice which are a basis for what teachers do in classrooms today. For nearly three hundred years, and dating back at least to the alphabet method and theological content of the *New England Primer,* devoted teachers have worked to help their students read accurately and efficiently. Smith's historical survey has given supervisors, instructors of professional classes, and teachers themselves considerable confidence in what they advocate and do in teaching reading. The methods and materials used in classrooms today are not based on the personal opinion of some textbook author or school principal, nor on the whim of an individual teacher. Rather, they are the resultant of generations of trial in classrooms from Colonial to modern times. Smith's study, which should be projected into the last twenty-five years, can and does provide a background against which current criticisms of teaching can be measured and a basis established for continued research in methods and materials.

A seventh study opened up a new field for evaluation of reading materials rather than influencing methods of teaching of reading in the classroom. This was Gray and Leary's *What Makes A Book Readable* (6). Their formula for measuring the level of difficulty of printed materials has since been simplified by Lorge and other useful formulas developed by Dale-Chall, Flesch, and Spache. Problems of ease or difficulty of stories were studied quantitatively as early as 1923 by Lively and Pressy (14) but the more recent work, summarized by Chall (13), clearly shows the influence of the pioneer work of Gray and Leary in trying to get at objective measures of the difficulty of books or passages. Such work still requires extension into the measures of concept difficulty and density. It is influencing the writing of textbooks and other materials and makes

possible some matching of pupil ability and reading materials to challenge it.

The space given to discussion of the role of phonics in reading instruction suggests that research on the topic should be included in any list of "best ten." Unfortunately, no investigation in this area can be labelled "definitive." At least thirty experimental or applied researches have been carefully done but they all have some limitations in scope or technique. One of several worthy of mention is the Agnew (1) study made in 1939, not because it answered all questions about phonics, but because it combined several methods of attack and because it attempted to tackle a complex instructional problem, one that some researchers, prophets, and charlatans have attempted to oversimplify since. The Agnew study may be important just because it left certain questions about phonics unanswered. In general, it suggests that there are both advantages and disadvantages in emphasizing phonics methods. More detailed and comprehensive studies of the most valuable phonics techniques in relation to individual differences among children remain to be done. The Agnew study is included, therefore, as a representative of a group of studies which gave careful leads to the use of phonics.

The ninth study on the list is hard to select. Names of persons who have published valuable work come easily to mind—Betts, Bond, Dale, Dearborn, DeBoer, Durrell, Harris, McKee, Robinson, Dora V. Smith, Witty, and others should surely be on any "must" list. Important areas of reading research such as reading readiness, the sociology of reading, critical and creative reading, and the effects of reading have not been mentioned. In terms of impact, however, perhaps the vote should go to Strang for a series of studies and publications which clearly pointed to the need for developmental reading instruction in secondary schools and in colleges. Her first edition of *Problems in the Improvement of Reading in High School and College* (10) collated the scattered work in the field up to 1937 and other articles and studies, notably *Explorations in Reading Patterns* (9), extended the interest in reading habits from adolescence into adulthood. Strang's work helped develop the strong current interest in reading in the post-elementary school years and, in the second book mentioned, began some study of the relationships of reading interests to other patterns of response to reading materials, an area in which the research is only beginning. Despite the dearth of solid data, teachers are becoming more concerned about the effects of reading upon children and adolescents, one phase of mental hygiene which has been one of Strang's interests.

The last study in the list of ten is easy to select, not because its impact has yet been great, but because it points the way to important future developments. The investigation is Gray's (5) survey, done for UNESCO in 1956, of methods of instruction in reading and writing around the world. Our methods of study in comparative education are not well developed but the Gray description points to world-wide problems in literacy, in types of language, and in adaptation of instruction to the nature of the language.

As we project into possible future research, let us note a few points about these ten studies which have, with the possible exception of the recent survey by Gray, so thoroughly influenced instruction in reading. First, the studies are of different research design. One is a laboratory study, one a diagnostic study, one a teaching investigation, another a survey of large numbers of children, one a collection of case studies, each design fitting the explicit purposes of the investigator. The continued attack on problems of instruction in the language arts can be a varied one.

We may note, secondly, that each of the studies was closely connected to the problems of its day. For example, the laboratory studies by Buswell and Judd gave basic data about a little known process in the days psychology was beginning as a science. The impact of the Thorndike and Gates studies can be understood only when one realizes that reading instruction of that day was almost completely oral. The Terman study coincided with some phases of the Progressive Education movement. The Agnew study dealt with a problem which is still concerning primary-

and intermediate-grade teachers and the Gray survey, whose impact is still to be felt, came in a day when the United States was beginning to take an interest in the social and educational welfare of the under-developed nations of the world. Each of these ten studies had impact because they were closely related to the context in which they were made. As we look to the future we must also ask: What is relevant and pressing?

A third mark of these classic studies is their simplicity of design and statistical analysis. My friends in statistics tell me that simplicity is desirable, that good planning at the beginning can eliminate the necessity for intricate statistical analysis. As we look to the future, then, we can emulate the older studies by careful planning, but along with such planning we can be aware of more sophisticated models of investigations and the utilization of new resources such as machines and computers. The researcher in English is not usually acquainted with all new technical developments and so the team approach, especially at the planning and analysis stages of the study, would seem to be desirable today. I believe that some of our best research is done by individuals, but today individual researchers in the language arts field should usually consult other experts.

A fourth characteristic of these studies is that they were concerned with very different problems of reading. They help represent the tremendous scope of the reading field and the even greater possibilities for the future in the whole area of the language arts. They involve eye movements, teachers' methods, clinical procedures, children's motivations, the emotional and personality concomitants of reading, and the problems of reading and language all over the world. Horizons unlimited!

These four and other characteristics must be borne in mind as we evaluate current and future research. Perhaps some of the studies that will go into a "twenty best" list have already been done and are awaiting recognition. Many more still need to be done. We hear much these days of providing for gifted youngsters in mathematics or science, but what about giftedness in the

English language arts? We read of differences among individuals but what about the neglected area of intra-individual differences? In reading instruction there is the study of basal versus individualized versus language arts approaches to reading now being done in San Diego County, California. Many teachers are interested in the current reassessment of reading readiness, in the work in beginning reading and team learning around Boston and Harvard, in the concern with creativity which is spreading from psychological laboratories to classrooms. The whole area of do-it-yourself in language has hundreds of possibilities to be tried and tested. All this and many more! We don't do enough of it, and use enough of it, but research in reading has influenced, and will influence practice. Research can "make a difference."

REFERENCES

1. Agnew, D. C., *The Effect of Varied Accounts of Phonetic Drill on Primary Reading*. Duke University Press, 1939.
2. Buswell, G. T., "An Experimental Study of the Eye-Voice Span in Reading," *Supplementary Educational Monographs*, No. 17 University of Chicago, 1920.
3. Gates, A. I., *New Methods in Primary Reading*. Bureau of Publications, Teachers College, Columbia University, 1928.
4. Gates, A. A., *The Improvement of Reading*. Macmillan Co., 1927.
5. Gray, W. S., *The Teaching of Reading and Writing*. An International Survey. UNESCO. Scott, Foresman, 1958.
6. Gray, W. S., and Bernice Leary, *What Makes a Book Readable*. University of Chicago Press, 1935.
7. Judd, C. H., and G. T. Buswell, *Silent Reading: A Study of the Various Types*. Supplementary Educational Monographs, No. 23. University of Chicago Press, 1922.
8. Smith, Nila B., *American Reading Instruction*, Silver Burdett, 1934.
9. Strang, Ruth, *Explorations in Reading Patterns*, University of Chicago Press, 1942.
10. Strang, Ruth, *Problems in the Improvement of Reading in High School and College*. Lancaster, Pa.: The Science Press, 1938.
11. Terman, L. M., and Margaret Lima, *Children's Reading*. Appleton & Co., 1929.
12. Thorndike, E. L., "Reading as Reasoning: A Study of Mistakes in Paragraph Reading," *Journal of Educational Psychology*, 8:323–332, June, 1917.
13. Chall, Jeanne S. *Readability: An Appraisal of Research and Application*. Bureau of Educational Research Monograph No. 24 Ohio State University, 1958.
14. Lively, Bertha A., and S. L. Pressey. "A Method for Measuring the Vocabulary Burden of Textbooks," *Educational Administration and Supervision*. 9:389–398, October, 1923.

Research That Should Have Made a Difference

HARRY SINGER

The two articles by Harry Singer (1970; 1978) continue this discussion of literacy research and, along with Russell's piece, provide a historical overview of the subject. Singer selects those reading research studies that he believed should have made a significant difference in the teaching of literacy education. As you read this material do you agree or disagree with his selection and his rationale for their inclusion in his articles?

Some research in reading has made a difference in reading instruction. In the judgment of Russell (1961), the ten "best" or widely influential studies had the following consequences: (1) a change in the definition and consequent teaching of reading from a process of just sounding out words to getting meaning from the printed page through reasoning or problem solving processes (Thorndike, 1917); (2) a shift in emphasis from oral to silent reading and use of different kinds of materials to teach children to read for a variety of purposes (Buswell, 1920; Judd and Buswell, 1922); (3) development and use of concrete materials and techniques for teaching various ways of recognizing words in silent reading (Gates, 1928); (4) construction and value of tests for diagnosing reading, providing the basis for the eventual establishment of reading clinics (Gates, 1927); (5) selection of children's literature according to developmental changes in children's interests (Terman and Lima, 1929); (6) appreciation of the evolution of current reading methods and materials (Smith, 1934); (7) objective measurement of levels of difficulty of reading materials (Gray and Leary, 1935); (8) insight into some advantages and disadvantages of phonics instruction (Agnew, 1939); (9) the foundation of and concern for postelementary instruction in reading (Strang, 1938; 1942); and (10) establishment of the need for adapting reading instruction to the language of a country and appraisal of world wide problems in literacy (Gary, 1956).

However, there are other studies that should have made a difference, but did not. From the studies which fit into this category, I have selected a handful for review. Undoubtedly other researchers in reading might select another set. However, the studies I have selected have significant implications for objectives, evaluation of teaching and research, reading readiness, word recognition training, and the round-robin or reading circle type of instruction.

Review of Research

In 1921, Gates (1921) administered a battery of tests to assess oral and silent reading (speed and comprehension), vocabulary knowledge, and intelligence (group and individual) in grades 3 through 8. From analysis of the resulting correlation matrix, he concluded that "the results do not justify the conclusion that we have, in reading, a group of functions, bound by some general factor." Furthermore, he found that there is a "useful distinction between 'ability to comprehend' and 'rate of reading' " (p. 310).

Although these conclusions led Gates to construct his *Reading Survey Test for Grades 3 to 8* to assess separately speed and level of comprehension, his study did not have any widespread effect upon objectives or evaluation of reading instruction. Even today schools do not attempt systematically to develop or to assess both speed and comprehension, particularly at the elementary level, perhaps because of a primary concern with development of accuracy in reading, but, I also suspect because of a lack of awareness of the importance of or a need to develop speed of reading. Although, under present instructional procedures, individuals do improve their subabilities and processes for attaining speed of reading as they progress through the grades (Singer, 1965), systematic instruction might accelerate the rate of development of speed of reading. Since there are some factors common to speed and comprehension or power of reading, improvement in speed of reading is also likely to have salutary effects upon power of reading. Elsewhere, I have suggested that:

> . . . *individuals . . . need to mobilize some different subsystems as they shift from Speed to Power, and viceversa. Perhaps these subsystems may be developed more effectively by alternating instruction from accuracy to speed of response. For example, after an individual has been taught by an analytical method to arrive at an accurate recognition of a word, he can be given practice in a variety of ways for perceiving the word accurately* and *quickly. An individual could, therefore, learn to be* effective and efficient *in solving his reading tasks. Analogous to the rate, accuracy, and processes necessary for mature development in arithmetic (Brownell, 1961), an individual by alternately developing subsystems necessary for speed and power of reading could make progress towards maturity in both reading components. Thus, the curriculum would*

emphasize the necessary subsystems in the context of appropriate purposes in order to promote individuals' developments of speed and power of reading to their highest potential (Singer, 1965, p. 47). . . .

Corroborating Gates's conclusions that reading is not a general, unitary factor, McCullough (1957) found that the intercorrelations of comprehension scores for tests of main ideas, details, sequence, and creative reading at the second grade level were low, ranging from .26 to .50 with a median of .45. Second graders could, therefore, score high on one type of comprehension and low on another, and vice-versa. Hence, if a single type of comprehension measure were used and teachers did not teach for this type of comprehension, the results might be misleading. Although this pitfall in assessing comprehension could be avoided by selecting or constructing tests that are relevant to the curriculum, we find that in practice the criterion of curricular validity for tests does not tend to be satisfied.

Because of the high degree of pupil and teacher mobility in the United States, not only from one state to another but also within the state, curricular validity for standardized tests is difficult to obtain. For example, California, a state with a high mobility index has been receiving about 1,000 arrivals from other states each day for the past 20 years. Also, one of four of its residents is estimated to move each year, mostly within the state. Furthermore, one third of its teachers have been trained and have taught in other states (Stone and Hempstead, 1968). Teachers new to a school district are, of course, unfamiliar with its curriculum, and pupils who transfer into a school district from out of state or from another school district within the state are likely to have experienced a different curriculum. Under these conditions, it is understandable why California is encountering difficulties in adopting a standardized test, particularly for the primary grades, that would be valid for all of its locally controlled school districts.

The relative specificity of different kinds of comprehension tasks in the primary grades also has implications for methodological studies. For example, in the Research Program in First Grade Reading Instruction, only one test of reading comprehension was utilized for comparing the 27 methodological studies, probably for the same reason that schools limit their testing program to a single test—lack of time. Consequently, the result that "Wide differences in mean achievement of classrooms were found for all the programs" (Bond and Dykstra, 1967, p. 121) may, in part, be due to degree of congruency between types of comprehension questions in the reading achievement test and those types stressed in the various classrooms.

Whether or not a particular variable is predictive of reading achievement, especially at the end of the first year of instruction, depends to some degree upon the common elements among the predictor variable, the evaluation instruments, *and* the method of instruction. This conclusion was reached by Gates, Bond, and Russell (1939) who assessed four average first grade classes in New York City on 62 variables at the beginning of the year and then correlated these variables with the Gates and Stanford Reading Achievement Tests at three periods during the year. They found that at the top of the list of predictive measures were tests of word and letter recognition and phonic combinations.

Because variations in correlations accompanied methodological differences, they recommended:

> *Reading readiness tests, therefore, must be chosen to fit the teaching method. In other words one should test the reading abilities which the teaching program will attempt to develop in order to determine the needs of each pupil before instruction is begun and to predict the pupil's likelihood of becoming a successful reader. (p. 43)*

However, the Gates, Bond, and Russell study did not have a wide influence on reading instruction because, as Chall (1967) explains, the study with its environmental emphasis went against the "conventional wisdom" of its day, which Durkin (1988) points out had a maturational bias.

Instead, a study which had a significant and long lasting effect, but shouldn't have, was the study by Morphett and Washburne (1931). They recommended that "a child would gain considerably in speed of learning if beginning reading was postponed until the child had attained a mental age of six years and six months" on the Detroit First Grade Intelligence Test or *seven years and six months* on the Stanford Binet Test of Intelligence. Their recommendation was based on the finding that of the children who had attained a mental age of six years and six months on the Detroit Test, 78 percent made satisfactory general progress, that is, progressed through at least 13 steps of the Winnetka program and had learned a minimum of 37 sight words by February. Even though the Morphett and Washburne recommendation was based upon a particular test of intelligence and a particular method of instruction, "conventional wisdom" generalized their recommendation to all tests of intelligence, programs of instruction, and evaluation instruments. Instead, perhaps in consonance with the conventional wisdom of our day, with its emphasis on not just *matching* instruction to individual capacities but on designing curricula to *stimulate* the development of such capacities, we have recommended that "since children are at various stages of readiness for instruction in reading during kindergarten . . . that provision should be made for such individual differences by adapting the teaching strategy of a differentiated curriculum" (Singer, Balow, and Dahms, 1968, p. 467)

The widespread impact of Cattell's study (1886) was also not justifiable since his conclusions based on adult readers were applied to instruction of beginning readers. Cattell adduced evidence that adults or *mature* readers could perceive meaningful sentences or words more rapidly than unrelated groups of letters or words. This finding, along with other experimental data (Erdmann and Dodge, 1898), was interpreted as indicating that readers perceived whole words by means of their configuration. Perhaps unaware of developmental changes in perception as individuals learned to read, the whole word method with its emphasis on word configuration as a primary cue for word recognition was used for teaching *beginning* readers how to read. Even after Buswell (1922) had demonstrated that readers on the average took two fixations per word in the *initial* stages of learning to read, progressed through developmental changes in word perception, and at *maturity* in reading perceived on the average one and a quarter words per fixation, children were still taught to use configuration as a cue.

Even if configuration cues were appropriate for beginning readers, word frequency control with selection and presentation of high frequency words that are uniformly similar in appearance would tend to preclude use of such cues in the initial stages of reading. Yet, as Chall (1967) has pointed out, basal readers in the early 1960's had actually increased the use of word frequency control over previous basal readers and were still advocating teaching beginning readers the whole word method as "the prime means of word recognition" and to utilize configuration as a cue to perceive them (Chall, 1967, p. 214).

The finding in the Gates, Bond, and Russell (1939) study that perception of printed words and letters is among the best predictors of subsequent reading achievement is consistent with reports over the past 40 years. Some time ago, Gates (1926) found that perception is not a unitary function because the intercorrelations among perception of numbers, geometric symbols, and printed words were quite low; the average intercorrelation correlation among these stimuli for grades 1 through 6 was only .35. Because of the specificity of perception, he suggested that "differences in reading ability may depend considerably upon the specific skills pupils have of perceiving a certain kind of material, namely, *printed words*. . . ." (p. 438) Balow (1963) and Barrett (1965) have also found that perception of visual representations of verbal stimuli, not ability to respond accurately to pictures or geometric objects, is the best predictor in a reading readiness battery for subsequent achievement at the end of first grade. Moreover, discrimination training given on printed words, particularly those that will be met later in the reading program, is likely to lead to positive transfer for recognition of these words (Staats, Staats, and Schutz, 1962). The implication from these studies appears to be that perceptual training on materials other than printed words is not as likely to develop the ability to perceive printed words nor is such training as likely to be related to reading achievement. Despite the implication, we still find materials produced and instructional programs pursued which purport to prepare children for reading with such titles as *We Read Pictures* and *We Read More Pictures* (Gray, Monroe, and Artley, 1956) or which claim to remedy word perception difficulties by training pupils to perceive non-verbal stimuli (Frostig and Horne, 1964) or by having them engage in motor exercises designed to correct their laterality (Delacato, 1959). Instead, the research evidence implies that to the extent that perceptual improvement is needed in reading readiness or in remedial reading programs, emphasis should be on visual perception and discrimination of printed words. If these printed words occur in close temporal and spatial contiguity to referent objects and actions, it would be possible to develop not only perceptual but also conceptual responses to printed words (Singer, 1966).

A device which purports to improve speed and span of perception and hence increase speed of reading is the tachistoscope. Advertisements for the tachistoscope appeal to American values of efficiency and economy of time. Moreover, in consonance with the spirit of the Industrial Revolution, there is ready acceptance among educational decision-makers of machines as a way of reducing costs of education. With the increased availability of funds, particularly federal funds, school districts have purchased abundant amounts of equipment, such as tachistoscopes.

However, the evidence indicates that there is only a correlation of about .06 between the tachistoscopic speed of perception and rate of reading easy prose. To determine why the relationship is low, Gilbert (1959a, b, c, and d) conducted a series of studies of speed of processing visual stimuli. Using college students and a motion picture technique for separating and measuring the components of duration of fixation or pause time, he was able to demonstrate that the average adult fixation time of a quarter of a second could be separated into three parts. The parts, each about two twenty-fourths of a second in duration, consisted of seeing time, central processing time, and eye movement stabilizing time. Gilbert's results seem to explain why students who improve their speed of perception in tachistoscopic training fail to transfer their improved perceptual speed to normal reading. The explanation appears to be that tachistoscopic training is aimed at only *one* of the three components of the fixation pause, seeing time. But, in normal reading, eye movement stabilizing time occurs and is a necessary source of interference in speed of perception (Holmes and Singer, 1964). One implication from Gilbert's studies is that evaluation of improvement in speed of reading necessitates measurement of all three components of the fixation pause. It is possible that reduction in one of the components, such as seeing time, may be compensated by an increase in another component, such as processing time or eye movement stabilizing time.

TRANSLATING RESEARCH RESULTS INTO CLASSROOM PRACTICES

Obstacles

If we ask why the studies reviewed in this paper have not yet had widespread impact upon teaching reading, we would give several major reasons, some of which have already been cited in the text. On this list would be inattention or even ideological resistance to research results (Moynihan, 1968), findings contrary to "conventional wisdom" (Chall, 1967), acceptability of only those research findings that are in accord with the prevailing maturational-environmental bias (Durkin, 1958), susceptibilities of educational decision makers to commercial propaganda, and variation in adequacy of dissemination of findings (Chall, 1967).

Strategy

To the above I would add one more reason, gleaned from an experience I had in translating basic research results into classroom practice: for basic research findings to make a difference in classroom practice, they have to go through several developmental steps before they are in a form that can be used in the classroom. In this translation experience, I used a study reported by Gilbert (1940) on the disruption of eye movement behavior in reading that occurs when a poor reader is trying to follow the oral reading of a good reader, and vice-versa. Essentially, the poor reader is frustrated in trying to keep up with the good reader; in turn, the good reader is annoyed in having to adapt to the poor reader's pattern of reading behavior. Although this study was done about thirty years ago, primary grade teachers still follow the practice of having pupils learn to read by taking turns reading aloud while the rest of the group with their eyes locked into step with the pupil reading aloud tries to follow along, reading silently. The learning theory for such instruction is that each pupil in the group who sees the word and hears the correct or corrected response is having his own silent or oral response to the stimulus word reinforced. However, observation of such instruction reveals that the children do not have their eye movements locked into step. The good reader might be reading ahead when he is supposed to be following the poor reader, while the poor reader, in turn, might lag behind the good reader or do something else, such as look out the window. Since this behavior is apparent to teachers, why don't they do something else? Spache (1964) believes that teachers find that this mode of instruction is the easiest to use, but another answer is possible: teachers do not have an alternate method.

To provide an alternative to what I have called the "lock-eyed" strategy for teaching read-

ing, I suggested that the teacher have one pupil read aloud while the other pupils close their books or not even have books and just listen to the pupil who is reading aloud. An experienced and competent teacher in one of my advanced courses in teaching reading decided to try this alternative out on her class of first grade pupils. She informed me that the strategy seemed to work, but the pupils who were listening appeared to be bored. I then suggested that she make the listening purposeful by giving them questions about the story or that she develop *active* listeners by having the pupils learn to formulate their *own* questions about the story and listen for answers as each pupil read aloud in turn. As a result of this modification, the teaching strategy was quite effective: children in the reading group were an attentive audience; they could not use the "vulture technique" of raising their hands to be called upon by the teacher as soon as the oral reader made an error in reading, and the teacher did not have to use conformity procedures to keep all eyes locked in step.

Although I heartily recommend the stepwise procedure described above for translating basic research findings into classroom practice, I am not advocating that teachers should limit themselves to the use of a purposeful listening strategy for teaching reading. However, I believe that teachers should understand the effects of various instructional procedures, such as the "lock-eyed" vs. the "purposeful listening" strategy, and that teachers should have a variety of methods and techniques in their repertoire. They are then more able and more likely to adapt teaching methods and modes to instructional needs of their pupils and to use their teaching methods and strategies to solve instructional problems and enhance reading achievement.

Conclusion

In the past some research has not had the impact upon practice that it should have. However, in the future, translation of basic research findings into classroom practice is more likely to occur and in a more systematic way. New educational institutions have been organized by the U.S. Office of Education, such as the research and development centers in universities, computer storage and retrieval of educational information centers, regional laboratories, supplementary instructional centers in public schools, and institutes for teachers. As these institutions begin to mesh with each other and with established educational institutions, such as school systems and teacher education and research programs in universities and colleges, and as school districts employ more specialized personnel, which they are already beginning to do, the probability will be greater that research which should make a difference, will.

REFERENCES

Agnew, Donald C. *The Effect of Varied Amounts of Phonetic Drill on Primary Reading.* Duke University Press, 1939.

Balow, Irving H., "Sex Differences in First Grade Reading." *Elementary English,* 40 (1963) 303–306; 320.

Barrett, Thomas C. "The Relationship Between Measures of Prereading Visual Discrimination and First Grade Reading Achievement: A Review of the Literature." *Reading Research Quarterly,* 1 (1965) 51–76.

Bond, Guy L. and Dykstra, Robert. "The Cooperative Research Program in First-Grade Reading Instruction." *Reading Research Quarterly,* 2 (1967), 5–142.

Brownell, William A. "Rate, Accuracy, and Processes in Learning." Abridged by T. L. Harris and W. E. Schwahn (Editors), *Selected Readings on the Learning Process.* New York: Oxford University Press, 1961. Pp. 388–400.

Buswell, Guy T. "An Experimental Study of the Eye-Voice Span in Reading." *Supplementary Educational Monographs,* No. 17, University of Chicago Press, 1920.

Buswell, Guy T. "Fundamental Reading Habits: A Study of Their Development." *Supplementary Educational Monographs,* No. 21, University of Chicago Press, 1922.

Cattell, James McKeen. "The Time it Takes to See and Name Objects." *Mind,* 11 (1886) 63–65.

Chall, Jeanne. *Learning to Read.* New York: McGraw-Hill, 1967.

Delacato, Carl H. *The Treatment and Prevention of Reading Problems.* Springfield, Illinois: Charles C. Thomas, 1959.

Durkin, Dolores. When Should Children Begin to Read." In Helen M. Robinson (Editor), *Innovation and Change in Reading Instruction,* The Sixty-Seventh Yearbook of the National Society for the Study of Education, Part II. Chicago: University of Chicago, 1988. Pp. 30–71.

Erdmann, B. and Dodge, R. *Psychologische Untersuchungen über dos Lesen und Experimenteller Grundlage.* Halle: Neimeyer, 1898. Reviewed in Irving H. Anderson and Walter F. Dearborn (Editors), *The Psychology of Reading.* New York: Ronald Press, 1952.

Frostig, Marianne, and Horne, David. *The Frostig Program for the Development of Visual Perception.* Chicago: Follett, 1964.

Gates, Arthur I. "An Experimental and Statistical Study of Reading and Reading Tests." *Journal of Educational Psychology,* 12 (1921) 303–314.

Gates, Arthur I. "A Study of the Role of Visual Perception, Intelligence and Certain Associative Processes in Reading and Spelling." *Journal of Educational Psychology,* 17 (1926) 433–445.

Gates, Arthur I. *The Improvement of Reading:* New York: Macmillan, 1927.

Gates, Arthur I. *New Methods in Primary Reading.* New York: Bureau of Publications, Teachers College, Columbia University, 1928.

Gates, Arthur I.; Bond, G. L.; and Russell, D. H. *Methods of Determining Reading Readiness.* New York: Bureau of Publications, Teachers College, Columbia University, 1939.

Gilbert, Luther C. "The Effect on Silent Reading of Attempting to Follow Oral Reading." *Elementary School Journal,* 40 (1940) 614–621.

Gilbert, Luther C. "Genetic Study of Eye Movements in Reading." *Elementary School Journal,* 59 (1959) 328–335. (a)

Gilbert, Luther C. "Influence of Interfering Stimuli on Perception of Meaningful Material." *California Journal of Educational Research,* 10, (1959) 15–23. (b)

Gilbert, Luther C. "Saccadic Movements as a Factor in Visual Perception in Reading." *Journal of Educational Psychology,* 50 (1959) 15–19. (c)

Gilbert, Luther C. "Speed of Processing Visual Stimuli and Its Relation to Reading." *Journal of Educational Psychology,* 50 (1959) 8–14. (d).

Gray, William S. *The Teaching of Reading and Writing.* An International Survey, UNESCO. Scott, Foresman, 1956.

Gray, William S., and Leary, Bernice. *What Makes a Book Readable.* University of Chicago Press, 1935.

Gray, William S., Monroe, Marion, and Artley, A. Sterl. *We Read Pictures, We Read More Pictures,* and *Before We Read.* Chicago: Scott, Foresman, 1956.

Judd, Charles H., and Guy T. Buswell. *Silent Reading: A Study of the Various Types.* Supplementary Educational Monographs, No. 23, University of Chicago Press, 1922.

Holmes, Jack A. and Singer, Harry. "Theoretical Models and Trends Toward More Basic Research in Reading." *Review of Educational Research,* 34 (1964) 127–155.

McCullough, Constance M. "Responses of Elementary School Children to Common Types of Reading Comprehension Questions." *Journal of Educational Research,* 51 (1957) 65–70.

Morphett, Mabel and Washburne, Carlton. "When Should Children Begin to Read." *Elementary School Journal,* 31 (1931) 496–503.

Moynihan, Daniel P. "Sources of Resistance to the Coleman Report." *Harvard Educational Review,* 38 (1968) 23–36.

Russell, David C. "Reading Research That Makes a Difference." *Elementary English,* 38 (1961) 74–78.

Singer, Harry. "A Developmental Model for Speed of Reading in Grades Three Through Six." *Reading Research Quarterly,* 1 (1965) 29–49.

Singer, Harry. "An Instructional Strategy for Developing Conceptual Responses in Reading Readiness." In J. A. Figurel (Editor), *Vistas in Reading.* Proceedings of the Eleventh Annual Convention, International Reading Association, 11 Part I (1966) 425–431.

Singer, Harry, Balow, Irving H., and Dahms, Patricia. "A Continuum of Teaching Strategies for Developing Readiness at the Kindergarten Level." In J. A. Figurel (Editor), *Forging Ahead in Reading,* Proceedings of the Twelfth Annual Convention of the International Reading Association, 12 (1968) 463–468.

Smith, Nila B. *American Reading Instruction.* New Jersey: Silver Burdett, 1934.

Spache, George S. *Reading in the Elementary School.* Boston: Allyn and Bacon, 1964.

Staats, Carolyn K.; Staats, Arthur W.; and Schutz, Richard E. "The Effects of Discrimination Pretraining on Textual Behavior." *Journal of Educational Psychology,* 53 (1962) 32–37.

Stone, James C. and Hempstead, R. Ross. *California Education Today.* New York: Thomas Y. Crowell, 1968.

Strang, Ruth. *Problems in the Improvement of Reading in High School and College.* Lancaster, Pa.: The Science Press, 1938.

Strang, Ruth. *Explorations in Reading Patterns.* University of Chicago Press, 1942.

Terman, L. M., and Margaret Lima. *Children's Reading.* New York: Appleton, 1929.

Thorndike, Edward. "Reading as Reasoning: A Study of Mistakes in Paragraph Reading." *Journal of Educational Psychology,* 8 (1917) 323–332.

Research in Reading That Should Make a Difference in Classroom Instruction

HARRY SINGER

Some research in reading has made a difference in reading instruction (Russell, 1961). Other research that should have made a difference, hasn't; while some research that did make a difference, shouldn't have (Singer, 1970).

CONDITIONS DETERMINING WHETHER STUDIES WILL MAKE A DIFFERENCE

Russell believed that studies he cited made a difference because they focused upon significant issues in reading and were based upon simple designs and easily understood statistical techniques. However, the investigations that should have made a difference also fit these criteria. Consequently, additional explanations have to be adduced to understand why these studies did not make a difference. On the list of possible explanations are ideological resistance to research results (Moynihan, 1968), findings contrary to "conventional wisdom" (Chall, 1967), acceptability of only those research findings that are in accord with prevailing maturational-environmental bias (Durkin, 1968), variation in adequacy of dissemination of findings (Chall, 1967), susceptibilities of educational decision-makers to commercial propaganda, and maintenance of vested interest. Although I am aware of the pitfalls between research results and changes in practice based upon them, I am nevertheless hopeful that dissemination of research results with implications clearly drawn for practice will have an impact upon reading instruction.

Reading Research That Makes a Difference

Russell's ten "best" or most widely influential studies had the following consequences.

1. **Thorndike, 1917**   A change in the definition and subsequent teaching of reading from a process of just sounding out words to getting meaning from the printed page through reasoning or problem solving processes.
2. **Buswell, 1920; Judd and Buswell, 1922**   A shift in emphasis from oral to silent reading and use of different kinds of materials to teach children to read for a variety of purposes.
3. **Gates, 1928**   Development and use of concrete materials and techniques for teaching various ways of recognizing words in silent reading.

4. **Gates, 1927**   Construction and value of tests for diagnosing reading, providing the basis for the eventual establishment of reading clinics.
5. **Terman and Lima, 1929**   Selection of children's literature according to developmental changes in children's interests.
6. **Smith, 1934**   Appreciation of the evolution of current reading methods and materials.
7. **Gray and Leary, 1935**   Objective measurement of levels of difficulty of reading materials.[1]
8. **Agnew, 1939**   Insight into some advantages and disadvantages of phonics instruction.
9. **Strang, 1938; 1942**   The foundation of and concern for postelementary instruction in reading.
10. **Gray, 1956**   Establishment of the need for adapting reading instruction to the language of a country and appraisal of worldwide problems in literacy.

Research That Should Have Made a Difference

Singer's list of significant research studies in reading and their implications for instruction.

1. **1921, Gates**   There is a "useful distinction between 'ability to comprehend' and 'rate of reading.'" Hence, schools should test for speed and for comprehension of reading to diagnose and evaluate student progress.
2. **1957, McCullough**   Correlations of comprehension scores for tests of main ideas, details, sequence, and creative reading at the second grade level range from .26 to .50 with a median of .45. Comprehension in primary grades is a function of the type of test administered and comprehension tends to be specific. Therefore, use a comprehension test that has curricular validity.
3. **1939, Gates, Bond, and Russell**   Whether or not a variable is predictive of reading achievement, especially at the end of the first year of instruction, depends to some degree upon the

common elements among the predictor variable, the evaluation instruments, *and* the method of instruction. Hence, determine whether readiness test fits the program of instruction.

4. 1926, Gates   Perception is not a unitary function. Correlations among perception of numbers, geometric symbols and printed words were quite low, averaging only .35. Hence, training in laterality, tracing lines, matching block designs, or motor activities is not likely to transfer to perception of printed words. What is most effective is training on discrimination and perception of printed words.

5. 1940, Gilbert   Eye-movement behavior is disrupted when good reader tries to follow poor reader, and vice-versa. Hence, reading in a circle, using the lock-eyed method of instruction is inappropriate. Have children *listen actively* while one student is reading aloud to audience of other children and teacher is diagnosing the oral reader.

Research That Made a Difference, but Shouldn't Have

6. 1931, Morphett and Washburne   This study had a significant and long-lasting effect, but shouldn't have because reading readiness does not depend solely on a mental age of 6 years, 6 months.

7. 1886, Cattell   This study also had an unjustifiably widespread impact: configuration, based on research with adults, is not a clue for word identification in beginning readers, especially when words taught in primary grades are short and similar in appearance.

In order for the studies I review to make a difference, I know that teachers or educational decision-makers will first have to become aware of the research and decide to act on the results; then they will have to transform the implications into teaching procedures and plans and, in some instances, persuade other faculty members, supervisors or specialists, and administrators to let them put their research-based instructional changes into practice. If teachers undertake this developmental process, then the research reviewed below will make a difference in reading instruction.

The studies which I believe should make a difference, supplement the research listed previously. I have organized them into a developmental sequence. While I could have included other studies—undoubtedly other researchers could construct their own list of studies that should make a difference—the studies included here concentrate on significant aspects of reading instruction: 1) research on the relation between IQ and reading, 2) pacing instruction, 3) teaching word recognition, 4) type and timing of supplementary instruction, 5) impact of a comprehensive instructional program on reading achievement, and 6) an hypothesis on a schoolwide program for the improvement of reading.

RELATIONSHIP BETWEEN IQ AND READING

IQ tests have been much maligned, partly because they have not been used and interpreted properly. In the field of reading, researchers have usually only reported that IQ has an increasing relationship with reading as students progress through the grades, for example, as Durkin (1966) has done. She reported that the correlation coefficient between IQ and reading increased steadily from .40 at grade 1 to .79 at grade 5. If these results alone are considered, they might be misinterpreted. The implication that might be incorrectly drawn from them is that a child has to be bright to learn to read. Indeed, Morphett and Washburne (1931) are frequently quoted, even today, as having proven that a mental age of six years and six months is necessary for beginning reading instruction. Their criterion (based upon research that shouldn't have made a difference) is still applied on a widespread basis, despite demonstrations that a "talking typewriter" can be used to teach three-year-olds to being learning to read successfully (O.K. Moor in H. Rowan, 1961) or that four-year-olds through the normal range of mental ability from IQ about 70, on up, can learn some sight words at age four (Davidson, 1931). Indeed, the age when instruction can be initiated is a function of a number of variables, including a criterion of what constitutes successful instruction over a given period of time and a student-teacher ratio that is correlated with age of the students (Holmes, 1962). Indeed, Gates and Bond (1936) judged that the age for initiating reading instruction was not a function of biological (maturation) nor a psychological (readiness) criterion but, instead, was determined by a social criterion. Thus, if society considered that it is socially useful to begin teaching children under age five to learn to read, we would do so. Moreover, research has indicated we could do so, provided, of course, the criterion for success is changed and a lower teacher-student ratio is funded.

In fact, IQ for a group of children in the normal range of mental ability (IQ about 70 and above) has a *decreasing* relationship with learning to read, while IQ for the same group of children has an *increasing* relationship to reading achievement or ability to learn from text as the group progresses through school (Singer, 1977a). The reason for this seemingly paradoxical relationship is that reading has two overlapping phases of development which we shall refer to as 1) learning to read or reading acquisition behavior and 2) learning from text or gaining information from text (Singer et al., 1973–1974; Singer and Rhodes, 1976; Singer and Donlan, 1978).

Learning to read consists of acquiring responses to printed words and learning to integrate these responses with previously developed language processes, particularly semantic and syntactic processes. This phase of reading, consisting of close-ended objectives that require convergent thinking, can be mastered by 95 percent of the population (Bloom, 1971), probably by a large percent of the student population prior to grades six to eight. As a group of students begins to master reading acquisition behavior (or, indeed, any phase of instruction), the group's range of individual differences in the particular phase of instruction decreases. Hence, the corre-

lation between achievement in the particular phase of instruction and IQ scores decreases.

The second phase of reading goes beyond the first phase. It also includes use of "materials and processes of thinking" (Russell, 1956) to gain information from text. The materials of thinking consist of percepts, images, memories, associations, and concepts, while the processes of thinking involve discrimination, abstraction, generalization, concept formation, inference, interpretation, problem-solving, and critical and creative thinking. These materials and processes of thinking are open-ended and are never mastered. Consequently, the range of individual differences on these cognitive abilities and processes increases as a group of students goes through school because individuals differ in their rate of learning and level of cognitive capability. Moreover, reading achievement tests are made more difficult from grade to grade, mostly by using more complex syntax and more abstract vocabulary. IQ tests also become weighted with more abstract vocabulary at successive age levels. Consequently, these two tests become more alike. As they do so, it is not surprising to find their correlations increasing at successive age levels.

However, we must try to measure these two aspects of reading separately and keep their implications independent in our thinking and educational planning, even though we cannot completely separate the two components. Nevertheless, we can better approximate their separate assessment by repeatedly using the achievement test administered at the end of each grade, starting with grade one, until students have demonstrated mastery of the test at that grade level. We can also continue to administer reading achievement tests standardized for each grade. The repeatedly administered grade level test can then be called a test of learning to read. The results of repeated testing will demonstrate that students are learning to read and that they are progressing towards mastery of this phase of reading. Typical year-end reading achievement tests can be referred to as tests of ability to read and learn from text or printed materials. Scores on this type of test will reveal how well students, in comparison with their peer group, are able to gain information from text. The results will also show that the range of individual differences in reading achievement or ability to read and learn from text increases through the grades (Singer, 1977b).

Figure 1 depicts a plan for measuring changes in individual differences that occur in both phases of reading development as students progress through the grades. Note that as students master reading acquisition behavior at one grade level, they can go on to repeated testing at another grade level until they demonstrate mastery of reading acquisition behavior at that grade level, too. The implications of these two types of measurement are:

1. All students in the normal range of intelligence can learn to read, given adequate instruc-

tion and time for learning. Therefore, schools should allow for varying rates in mastery of reading acquisition behavior through repeated testing and continuity of instruction over the grades.

2. Students differ increasingly in their ability to gain information from text as they progress through the grades. Furthermore, this increase in variability is normal. Consequently, teachers should adapt instruction to this increasing range of individual differences.

If schools do initiate repeated testing, we would find that teachers, students, parents, administrators, and the community in general would realize that students are mastering reading acquisition behavior while also increasing in variability of ability to gain information over the grades. Therefore, these two measures could serve as suitable indices for accountability of

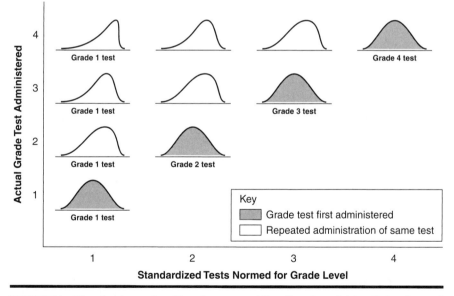

FIGURE 1   Plan for Assessing Development of Reading Acquisition Behavior and Ability to Gain Information from Test. The figure shows that the standardized test for grade 1, which is repeatedly administered in grades 2, 3, 4, and 5, decreases in variability as increasing numbers of students master it, while grade level standardized tests administered at the end of each grade level (diagonal curve) increase in variability across the grades as students differ more and more in progressive grade levels on their ability to learn or gain information from printed materials.

schools and, perhaps, resolve a perennial conflict between what the school can accomplish and what the community expects and even demands that schools achieve. Schools could reasonably be held accountable for *decreasing* variability in reading acquisition behavior and *increasing* variability of students to gain information from text.

PACING READING INSTRUCTION

Since students vary in rate of acquisition in both phases of reading development, teachers must learn to pace students appropriately. Barr (1972) reported data, however, which indicated that the two schools in her study varied in the rate at which students were paced in reading instruction, even though the students appeared to be comparable in socioeconomic level and, presumably, in ability.

An implication from Barr's study is that rate of learning to read is partially a function of how teachers pace their students. Consequently, expectancy criteria, to determine appropriate pacing rates, should be devised. Although such expectancy criteria have been developed and are in use, they are not infallible. California, for example, employs a complex set of criteria (Law, 1975). Moreover, they do not indicate the range of individual difference in expectancy levels within a classroom. Consequently, teachers must also depend upon their own observations, including use of criterion-referenced tests and their own judgment to determine adequacy of instructional pacing of students. The criterion should be the maximum rate at which students can learn. Through experimentation such as observing the rate at which individual students master lessons (for example, recognition of sight words or acquisition of grapheme-phoneme correspondences), teachers can arrive at their students' most effective learning rates. An example of a more formal type of learning rate test consists of teaching and measuring over several trials a student's acquisition of a group of sight words, grapheme-phoneme relationships, or some other aspect of word recognition (Singer

and Beasley, 1970). By applying their knowledge of students' learning rates to pacing students properly, teachers can not only stimulate maximum cumulative reading development but also prevent cumulative reading failure.

Helpful for determining students' rate of learning and also for establishing student motivation for learning is a procedure for putting rate of learning under the control of the student. This procedure, which can be called a *motivational graph method*, consists of having pupils participate in setting their own achievement goals, giving students adequate time to progress towards their goals, and plotting the results on a cumulative graph. This procedure proved to be very effective in motivating a seriously disabled reader and may be even more effective in developmental instruction (Singer and Beasley, 1970).

WORD RECOGNITION STRATEGIES

Important in pacing and motivating pupils is not only rate at which students are taught and amount of instructional time, but also how pupils are taught to recognize printed words. While various cues can be used to help pupils identify words, including context and picture clues, pupils must eventually acquire responses to the printed words themselves. Singer, Samuels, and Spiroff (1973–1974) have demonstrated that elimination of external cues, such as context and/or pictures, and focusing attention on the printed words themselves is a more efficient procedure for learning sight word recognition. Although students tend to make more rapid initial progress through the use of external cues, the cues are no longer sufficient when similar words appear or when synonyms occur or when students are asked to transfer their word recognition ability to novel words (Samuels, 1976).

In general, what appears to facilitate and affect word recognition ability is training in perception of printed letters, phoneme-grapheme correspondences, functional units such as blends and digraphs, and ability to blend these constituents of a word together. Students must also learn to use their language abilities, including syntactic and semantic processes, for formulating expectancies on word identification in the process of reading (Samuels, 1973). Furthermore, they must also develop automaticity of word recognition, particularly for high frequency words, so that they can concentrate their attention on comprehending or gaining information from text (LaBerge and Samuels, 1976). However, some students who do not make expected progress in classroom instruction alone can frequently benefit from supplemental instruction.

SUPPLEMENTAL READING INSTRUCTION

As more aides enter the classroom and as more specialists are trained to assist the classroom teacher, the questions asked are: "When should supplemental instruction be given?" and "What content should be used in this supplemental instruction?" The answers can be gleaned from two research studies. Gates and Bond (1936) found that those pupils who were making least progress in reading made "marked" improvement after three weeks of special instruction while still in first grade. They also pointed out that in this supplemental instruction the "techniques and materials of reading can be adjusted to teach children successfully . . . " (p. 685). More recently, Ellson et al. (1968) confirmed Gates and Bond's earlier results that supplemental instruction in the primary grades using the same content taught in the classroom enhances reading achievement. Both of these studies support a theory of school learning which emphasizes, in part, that aptitude is inversely related to time to learn and that quality of instruction is a function of the degree to which tasks have been properly sequenced, presented, and adapted to the learner (Carroll, 1963).

Hence, supplemental instruction that provides students who have lower aptitude with additional time to learn, and paces students properly through the sequence of tasks, will tend to be beneficial. Furthermore, supplemental instruction on materials used in the class can significantly improve the reading achievement of first graders. Since Ellson et al. had used programed tutoring, it appears that the instructional strategies of programed instruction with its careful directions, systematic sequencing, step-by-step feedback, individually determined rate and progress, and variable time for learning, which are consistent with a theory of school learning, are effective supplemental procedures for enhancing reading instruction.

Intervention programs based on a *change* in curriculum do not satisfy the aptitude and the quality of instruction criteria. Instead, they *add* to the learning burden. In short, the best intervention for low achieving students should come during the first grade and should supplement classroom instruction. But in some schools supplemental instruction alone is not enough, particularly where there is significant disparity between average rate of reading development for boys and girls.

DIFFERENCES BETWEEN BOYS AND GIRLS IN RATE OF READING DEVELOPMENT

Boys are usually slower than girls in rate of reading development (Balow, 1963; Singer, 1964), but under certain cultural conditions boys can be superior. For example, in Germany, boys had superior reading achievement to girls (Preston, 1962). However, even in the United States where cultural conditions are presumably favorable to reading achievement for girls, instructional conditions can be devised which eliminate sex differences in rate of reading acquisition. These conditions, constructed by McNeil and Keislar (1964), not only provide strong evidence for a cultural explanation of sex differences in reading achievement but also provide insight into instructional dynamics that lead to sex differences in achievement in American elementary schools which, unlike German schools, are dominated by female teachers.

In their experiment, McNeil and Keislar, using a programed autoinstructional device to teach kindergarteners, found that boys and girls acquired sight word recognition at an equal rate, even though girls had higher reading readiness scores. But, after instruction in a typical first grade classroom, the girls began to achieve at a faster rate of acquisition. An interview with the boys and girls provided insight into the acquisition gap. To the question, "Who in your group does the teacher most often call upon to read?" the answer usually was "a girl" but when asked, "To whom does the teacher say 'Sit up!' 'Turn around!' 'Pay attention!'" the answer was most often "boys." In general, girls tended to receive *reading instruction* while boys got *behavioral modification.*

Similar differences in behavior have been reported for high and low reading achievement groups: the high group cooperated with their teacher to maximize reading instruction while the low achievers and their teacher used a variety of "misbehavior" to minimize reading instruction (McDermott, 1976). A possible interpretation is that the students and their teacher were consciously or unconsciously avoiding a difficult and embarrassing situation of learning to read.

The implications from these two studies are clear: 1) create an environment more appropriate to boys, perhaps through use of more male teachers in primary grades; 2) use instructional aides to help manage the class while reading instruction is given; 3) attempt to prevent embarrassment in oral reading, perhaps through emphasis on silent reading before oral reading or through group oral reading; 4) intervene as early as possible, for example, in follow-up lessons for any students not making expected progress, which Gates and Bond (1936) and more recently Ellson et al. (1968) found were salutary provided the follow-up instruction, given by aides or by specialists, supported and reinforced ongoing instruction; and 5) adapt the pace of instruction to stimulate maximum positive and cumulative reading development while minimizing a negative accumulation of errors (Barr, 1972).

In some schools, however, it is not enough to eliminate sex differences through a change in the culture and improve the class's reading development through supplemental instruction. In these schools, the total quality of instruction may have to be improved.

COMPREHENSIVE INSTRUCTIONAL PROGRAM

Over the short run, a narrowly based instructional program can be successful because the load on learning is reduced and the criterion for achievement is narrower. Consequently, the time to learn can be shorter. Over the long haul, however, the more comprehensive program (which, of course, requires more time to learn) can be more successful because it contains the necessary components for a broader criterion and more mature level of reading achievement. The evidence for this conclusion comes from a two-year, longitudinal study conducted by Ruddell (1968). He compared four programs: programed instruction emphasizing phoneme-grapheme correspondence was compared with a basal reader program stressing, initially, whole word recognition; two other programs consisted of supplementing the programed instruction and basal reader programs with instruction that taught students meaning of printed morphemes and use of syntax in reading. At the end of the first year, the narrower-based, supplemented programed instruction resulted in superior achievement, but at the end of the second year the supplemented basal reader instruction yielded significantly higher reading achievement.

The supplemented basal reader not only had all the necessary subskills components in its sequence of instruction but also was devised to maximize, in the process of reading, the use of all the subskills taught in the program. Developmental instruction in reading skills is not complete unless students are taught to integrate the subskills into the process of reading. Like the swimming instructor, the reading teacher should analogously direct students: "Now that you have learned this skill, jump into your reading material and use it." More specifically, after first graders have learned a grapheme-phoneme correspondence for an initial consonant, the teacher can direct them to read a story and each time they come across the initial consonant and respond with the corresponding phoneme they should signal silently that they had done so by crooking their finger or some other appropriate silent motion. Thus, students will be intentionally mobilizing their new skill in the process of reading and integrating it into their repertoire of skills for attaining reading achievement.

Although a classroom teacher can make a difference in students' reading achievement in the classroom during the year, what makes a cumulative difference in a school is not the classroom teacher alone but a schoolwide approach to improving reading development. Essentially, we have to modify the hypothesis that the teacher alone makes the difference in reading instruction and substitute a broader hypothesis for improving a school's reading achievement.

HYPOTHESIS FOR IMPROVING
READING ACHIEVEMENT

Although Ruddell found that a comprehensive program, consistently applied, made a significant difference in reading achievement, the conclusion drawn from the results of all the First Grade Studies is that the variation in reading achievement within a method was greater than the variation in achievement among the methods (Bond and Dykstra, 1967). Since classes taught by some teachers attained high reading achievement while classes with comparable students taught by other teachers had relatively low achievement with the same method in the First Grade Studies—which attempted to compare all methods (e.g., basal vs. programed instruction vs. initial teaching alphabet)—an hypothesis was formulated to explain the results. The hypothesis, which is still untested, is that it is not the method, nor the program, but the teacher who makes the difference in reading achievement. An implication would be that each teacher in a school could adopt any

method or program of instruction and yet attain high achievement.

While particular teachers might be successful, if each teacher at successive grade levels in a school used a different program, the overall achievement of the school would not likely be high. The reason for this apparent paradoxical conclusion is that students in the school would not have a cumulative program that would pace them appropriately and provide for their individual differences in aptitude and in time needed for learning. Indeed, in case studies of three schools which had different programs but were alike in faculties trained and committed to the same instructional program, reading achievement in all three schools was significantly above average (Singer, 1977c). Hence, the modified hypothesis for schoolwide achievement is that while a teacher can make a difference in reading achievement in a given year, what makes for a cumulative difference in a school's reading achievement is a coherent and systematic program throughout the grades to which the faculty is committed.

CONCLUSION

In a coherent and systematic program a school can employ repeated testing that is currically valid and demonstrate that students are progressing in both phases of reading development. Teachers can then be trained to use techniques that will promote necessary skills required in the program. Those students whose aptitudes require supplemental instruction can receive it from aides or specialists familiar with the school's program. But contrary to conventional wisdom, a comprehensive program over the long haul yields more superior results than does a narrower program. If the hypothesis concerning a coherent and systematic application of a schoolwide reading program is tested, together with the implications drawn from research reviewed above, then we are likely to find that research in reading that should make a difference, will.

NOTES

1. For a current review of computational readability formulae, see Klare (1974–1975); for a noncomputational technique, see Singer (1975).

2. A more recent study that had a wide impact contained the hypothesis that dialect interfered with comprehension (Goodman, 1965); the hypothesis was subsequently found to be false (Goodman and Buck, 1973). However, a more recent investigation indicated that dialect, only in its syntactic component, may have merely a transitory effect upon oral reading achievement (Lucas and Singer, 1975).

REFERENCES

Agnew, Donald C. *The Effect of Varied Amounts of Phonetic Drill on Primary Reading.* Duke University Press, 1939.

Barr, Rebecca C. "The Influence of Instructional Conditions on Word Recognition Errors," *Reading Research Quarterly,* 7 (1972), 509–529.

Balow, Irving H. "Sex Differences in First Grade Reading" *Elementary English,* 40 (1963) 303–806, 320.

Bloom, Benjamin S. "Mastery Learning and Its Implications for Curriculum Development," in Elliot W. Eisner (Ed.), *Confronting Curriculum Reform.* Boston: Little, Brown, 1971, 17–49.

Bond, Guy L., and Robert Dykstra. "The Cooperative Research Program in First Grade Reading Instruction," *Reading Research Quarterly,* 2 (1967), 5–142.

Buswell, Guy T. "An Experimental Study of the Eye-Voice Span in Reading," *Supplementary Educational Monographs,* No. 17, University of Chicago Press, 1920.

Carroll, John B. "A Model of School Learning," *Teachers College Record,* 64 (1963), 723–733.

Cattell, James McKeen. "The Time it Takes to See and Name Objects," *Mind,* 11 (1886), 63–65.

Chall, Jeanne. *Learning to Read: The Great Debate.* New York: McGraw-Hill, 1967.

Chall, Jeanne. *Reading and Development,* Keynote Address, Twentieth Annual Convention. Newark, Delaware: International Reading Association, 1976.

Davidson, Helen P. "An Experimental Study of Bright, Average, and Dull Children at the Four Year Mental Level," *Genetic Psychology Monographs,* 9 (1931), 119–289.

Durkin, Dolores. *Children Who Read Early.* New York: Columbia University, Teachers College Press, 1966.

Durkin, Dolores. "When Should Children Begin to Read?" in Helen M. Robinson (Ed.), *Innovation and Change in Reading Instruction,* the Sixty-Seventh Yearbook of the National Society for the Study of Education, Part II. Chicago: University of Chicago, 1968, 30–71.

Ellson, D. G., P. Harris, and L. Barber. "A Full Test of Programed and Directed Tutoring," *Reading Research Quarterly,* 3 (1968), 307–367.

Gates, Arthur I. "An Experimental and Statistical Study of Reading and Reading Tests," *Journal of Educational Psychology,* 12 (1921), 303–314.

Gates, Arthur I. "A Study of the Role of Visual Perception, Intelligence, and Certain Associative Processes in Reading and Spelling," *Journal of Educational Psychology,* 17 (1928), 433–445.

Gates, Arthur I. *The Improvement of Reading.* New York: Macmillan, 1927.

Gates, Arthur I. *New Methods in Primary Reading.* New York: Bureau of Publications, Teachers College, Columbia University, 1928.

Gates, Arthur I., and Guy L Bond. "Reading Readiness: A Study of Factors Determining Success and Failure in Beginning Reading," *Teachers College Record,* 37 (1936), 679–685.

Gates, Arthur, G. L. Bond, and D. H. Russell. *Method of Determining Reading Readiness.* New York: Bureau of Publications, Teachers College, Columbia University, 1939.

Gilbert, Luther C. "The Effect on Silent Reading of Attempting to Follow Oral Reading," *Elementary School Journal,* 40 (1940), 614–621.

Goodman, Kenneth S. "Dialect Barriers to Reading Comprehension," *Elementary English,* 42 (1965), 853–860.

Goodman, Kenneth S., and Catherine Buck. "Dialect Barriers to Reading Comprehension Revisited," *Reading Teacher,* 27 (1973), 6–12.

Gray, William S. *The Teaching of Reading and Writing.* An International Survey, UNESCO. Glenview, Illinois: Scott, Foresman, 1956.

Gray, William S., and Bernice Leary. *What Makes a Book Readable?* Chicago: University of Chicago Press, 1935.

Holmes, Jack A. Research proposal submitted to and funded by the Carnegie Corporation, New York, 1959.

Holmes, Jack A. "When Should and Could Johnny Learn to Read?" in J. Allen Figurel (Ed.), *Challenge and Experiment in Reading,* Proceedings of the International Reading Association, 7, 1962. New York: Scholastic Magazines. 237–241.

Judd, Charles H., and Guy T. Buswell. *Silent Reading. A Study of the Various Types.* Supplementary Educational Monographs, No. 23, University of Chicago Press, 1922.

Klare, George R. "Assessing Readability," *Reading Research Quarterly,* 10 (1974–1975), 62–102.

LaBerge, David, and S. Jay Samuels. "Toward a Theory of Automatic Information Processing in Reading," in H. Singer and R. B. Ruddell (Eds.), *Theoretical Models and Processes of Reading,* Second Edition. Newark, Delaware: International Reading Association, 1976.

Law, Alexander. *Student Achievement in California Schools: 1974–1975,* Annual Report, California Assessment Program. Sacramento: California State Department of Education, 1975.

Lucas, Marilyn S., and Harry Singer. "Dialect in Relation to Oral Reading Achievement: Recoding, Encoding, or Merely a Code?" *Journal of Reading Behavior,* 7 (1975), 137–148.

McCullough, Constance M. "Responses of Elementary School Children to Common Types of Reading Comprehension Questions," *Journal of Educational Research,* 51 (1967), 65–70.

McDermott, R. P. "Achieving School Failure: An Anthropological Approach to Illiteracy and Social Stratification," in H. Singer and R. B. Ruddell (Eds.), *Theoretical Models and Processes of Reading,* Second Edition. Newark, Delaware: International Reading Association, 1976, 389–428.

McNeil, John D., and Evan R. Keislar. Cooperative Research Project No. 1413, U.S. Office of Education. Reported by John D. McNeil, "Programed Instruction Versus Usual Classroom Procedures in Teaching Boys to Read," *American Educational Research Journal,* 1 (1964). 113–119.

Moore, Omar K. In Helen Rowan, " 'Tis Time He Should Begin to Read," *Carnegie Corporation of New York Quarterly,* 9 (1961). 1–3.

Morphett, Mabel, and Carlton Washburne. "When Should Children Begin to Read?" *Elementary School Journal,* 31 (1931). 496–603.

Moynihan, Daniel P. "Sources of Resistance to the Coleman Report," *Harvard Educational Review,* 38 (1968), 23–36.

Otto, Wayne. "Developing a Skill Based Approach to Reading Comprehension," Proceedings of the National Reading Conference, 1976 (in press).

Preston, Ralph C. "Reading Achievement of German and American Children," *School and Society,* 90 (1962). 350–354.

Ruddell, Robert B. "A Longitudinal Study of Four Programs of Reading Instruction Varying in Emphasis on Regularity of Grapheme-Phoneme Correspondences and Language Structure on Reading Achievement in Grades Two and Three," Final Report, Project Nos. 3099 and 78085. Berkeley: University of California, 1968.

Russell, David. *Children's Thinking.* Boston: Ginn, 1956.

Russell, David G. "Reading Research that Makes a Difference," *Elementary English,* 38 (1961), 74–78.

Samuels, S. J. "The Technology of Reading: A Current View," Technological Report No. 2. University of Minnesota: Minnesota Reading Research Project, 1973.

Samuels, S. J. "Modes of Word Recognition," in H. Singer and R. Ruddell (Eds.), *Theoretical Models and Processes of Reading,* Second Edition. Newark, Delaware: International Reading Association, 1976.

Singer, Harry. "Substrata Factor Theory of Reading: Grade and Sex Differences in Reading at the Elementary School Level," in J. A Figurel (Ed.), *Improvement of Reading through Classroom Practice,* Proceedings of the International Reading Association, 9, 1964. Newark, Delaware: International Reading Association, 313–320.

Singer, Harry. "Research that Should Have Made a Difference," *Elementary English,* 47 (1970), 27–34.

Singer, Harry, "IQ Is and Is Not Related to Reading," in S. Wanat (Ed.), *Issues in Evaluating Instruction.* Arlington, Virginia: Center for Applied Linguistics, 1977a, 43–63.

Singer, Harry, "The SEER Technique: A Noncomputational Procedure for Quickly Estimating Readability Level," *Journal of Reading Behavior,* 7 (1975), 255–267.

Singer, Harry. "Measurement of Early Reading Ability," in W. G. McCarthy (Guest Editor), *Contemporary Education,* 48 (1977b), 3, 145–150.

Singer, Harry. "Resolving Curricular Conflicts in the 1970s: Modifying the Hypothesis, It's the Teacher who Makes the Difference in Reading Achievement," *Language Arts,* 54 (1977c), 158–163.

Singer, Harry, and Sherrel Beasley. "Motivating a Disabled Reader," *Thirty-seventh Yearbook of the Claremont Reading Conference.* California: Claremont College, 1970, 141–160.

Singer, Harry and Dan Donlan. *Reading and Learning from Text.* In preparation, 1978.

Singer, Harry, and Alan Rhodes. "Problems, Prescriptions, and Possibilities in High School Reading," in W. Otto, C. Peters, and N. Peters (Eds.), *Perspective on Reading Problems.* New York: Allyn and Bacon, 1977.

Singer, Harry, S. J. Samuels, and Jean Spiroff. "Effect of Pictures and Context on Learning Sight Words, *Reading Research Quarterly,* 9 (1973–1974), 555–667.

Smith, Nila B. *American Reading Instruction.* Morristown, New Jersey: Silver Burdett, 1934.

Strang, Ruth. *Problems in the Improvement of Reading in High School and College.* Ephrata, Pennsylvania: Science Press, 1938.

Strang, Ruth. *Explorations in Reading Patterns.* Chicago: University of Chicago Press, 1942.

Terman, L. M., and Margaret Lima. *Children's Reading.* New York: Appleton, 1929.

Thorndike, Edward. "Reading as Reasoning: A Study of Mistakes in Paragraph Reading," *Journal of Educational Psychology,* 8 (1917), 323–332.

Literacy Research That Makes a Difference

TIMOTHY SHANAHAN AND SUSAN B. NEUMAN

The last article, by Shanahan and Neuman (1997), is an important discussion of literacy research studies that have had influence on instructional practice in literacy education. Of particular note here is the detailed discussion of the history of literacy research and its historical effect, both positive and negative, on classroom practices in reading. As you read this article, observe the detailed process the authors followed in their selection of influential studies completed since 1961.

In 1961, David H. Russell. published an article entitled, "Reading Research that Makes a Difference." In it, he chronicled 10 studies that he claimed had significantly influenced the "curriculum in reading and related areas" (p. 74). He also explained why these studies had been significant. Later, Harry Singer (1970, 1976) published two rejoinders to this article. He neither challenged Russell's original premise—that research could or should influence teaching—nor argued with the specific choices of studies. Instead, he challenged Russell's explanation of why some studies mattered. He presented two lists in support of his position: influential studies that misdirected practice, and positive studies that, though they met Russell's criteria, failed to have any discernible sway.

As we write this article, 35 years after Russell's, more than 50,000 new studies on literacy have appeared. Which studies have changed how we teach literacy? What are the fundamental characteristics of studies that make a difference? At the invitation of the Editors of *Reading Research Quarterly,* we have carried on a stimulating, and at times contentious, conversation exploring these issues. Here, we will propose a list of studies that have influenced instructional practice and consider the role of research in instruction.

HOW WE WORKED

We have never written together before, though we have served together on professional committees and have become friends during the past few years. We share a deep and abiding interest in family literacy and in the literacy learning of poor children. Susan is interested, also, in preschool development, how children's play supports learning, and the role of media—particularly television—in literacy learning. Tim's other research interests include beginning reading development, the connections between learning to read and write, and the use of classroom assessment to inform teachers' decisions.

We live and work in different regions of the U.S. so we carried on our conversation over electronic mail. Sometimes we exchanged several notes in a single day, a brief sustained conversation of a specific point. Often a single note would be sent one day with a response the next, while at other times there were long delays. In all, we exchanged more than 80 e-mail notes, some several pages long. We often disagreed about which studies mattered or even as to what should count as a study.

The discussion of the practical influence of research has been too rare in the public discourse of our field, such topics usually being relegated to the safety of graduate seminars. This is unfortunate as such discussion, we found, requires nothing less than a construction of the state of the field: power and authority, the current state of practice, the nature and source of knowledge, and even whether education is improving or declining. These issues are entailed in the imaginative narrative history of the changing classroom that each of us conjures. We believe that open discussion of these issues can expose and correct bias and illogic in our perceptions of the status of our field.

Lest readers think this to be overstated, consider one recent example from public discussions

of reading achievement. Such discussions have often been based on the premise that reading instruction has changed, and that, consequently, reading achievement has declined. As a result, more than a dozen U.S. states are exploring legislation to better regulate reading instruction, despite the fact that national achievement data do not support an achievement decline.

Although we often disagreed, the quality of discussion was high, and mutual respect was always evident. No matter how formidable the disagreement, we always assumed the possibility of persuasion through information and logic. We sometimes found to our consternation that our conversational partner wasn't the one who lacked sufficient knowledge on a particular point. We strove to agree on a single list of studies rather than to argue for two separate, personal lists, as we hoped that this approach would make it easier for others to join the conversation.

Our first task was actually the most difficult: how to define *influence*. Citation rates, we agreed, were an inadequate measure. Although they give us some idea of *impact*, they tend to reflect interest rather than importance. Tim noted the example of cloze—among the hottest research topics during the 1950s through the 1970s. Yet neither Russell nor Singer even mention cloze. Why not? "Might have been that it was a well-researched topic, but not particularly important," Tim said.

Further, rather than one study, "isn't it a body of work, like schema-theory, that really makes an influence on practice?" Susan wondered. "The body of work idea is one that we need to think about," Tim said. "We could highlight two or three studies in a section." Returning again to Russell and Singer's efforts, however, we decided to "bite the bullet." Tim suggested, "Let's point to the important work done by various people in an area, but select and highlight one that stands out and explain why. If we don't point to single studies no one can argue with us, and that goes against the real idea of the article."

Likewise, we chose to consider empirical studies only; that is, investigations in which the researcher collected or analyzed data. There are many integrative literature reviews, theoretical treatises, and practical recommendations available concerning literacy education. As valuable as these are, they are not primary research and, thus, were not considered. This approach required the omission of influential literature reviews such as Chall's (1967) and Adams's (1990) analyses of phonics, Hiebert's (1983) review on ability grouping, Stanovich's (1986) on phonological awareness, Hillocks's (1986) on composition instruction, and some reviews in the *Handbook of Reading Research* (Barr, Kamil, Mosenthal, & Pearson, 1991; Pearson, 1984). These syntheses used research to suggest valuable directions for instruction. However, Russell's original purpose was to show how particular empirical studies altered practice, and we stayed true to this despite our own misgivings. Moreover, we see it as a sign of the growing sophistication of the field that accumulations of studies have become so influential.

We limited ourselves to those works published since Russell's article appeared. And, of course, there was the recency effect. "Doesn't it take time to have influence?" Susan asked. "No question about it," Tim said. "Work done in the 1960s has a greater chance of having a stronger impact than something done in the 1990s." But given our contrary nature and reluctance to neglect newer work, we agreed to "not hesitate to make a mistake."

Finally, we broadened Russell's criteria to reflect the important conceptual changes that have taken place within the field. We have considered *literacy* research as opposed to reading research. Thus, work on writing and spelling, for instance, could be considered. We also did not limit ourselves to elementary and secondary school considerations. Russell noted with great satisfaction that reading research had expanded the scope of reading instruction into high school. The broader enfranchisement for literacy teaching has continued since then and now includes preschoolers and adults. These changes are reflected in our selections.

Our first approach was straightforward. We proposed studies, traded lists, and added more studies. We were not yet attempting to make our cases, so these proposals were made without explanation or challenge. As we discussed the relative merits of these, however, it became apparent that we were on the wrong track. For example, studies like Heath's (1983) *Ways with Words* or Scribner and Cole's (1981) *The Psychology of Literacy* powerfully influenced cultural theory and methodology. Susan argued that Heath popularized ethnography as a research strategy. "If you look at the *NRC (National Reading Conference) Yearbook,* it is amazing how many ethnographic or qualitative studies there are in comparison to good ol' quantitative studies. These methodological changes essentially led to a broadened definition of what literate behavior might be." Tim responded, "You raise some interesting issues, but I think you are ranging too wide. The issue that we are revisiting is research that has made a difference to practice. Many of the studies that we have been discussing have been important in changing our research conceptions, but have they had any practical significance? We've got to stick to what made a difference in classroom practice: who is taught, what is taught, and how it is taught."

Practical influence had to be the hallmark for inclusion. We did not consider quality, value, citation rate, or any other way of appraising research. We agreed that our list should not reveal much about changes we hope will take place or about current practices that we abhor. Our task would have been easier if we could have focused on our favorite studies, model research, or those that have influenced our own thinking. Russell established this standard, but he failed to honor it entirely. Curiously, some of the studies that he proposed had not influenced practice, even in his own opinion. In his article, Russell included Nila Banton Smith's chronicle of U.S. reading instruction "as an example of the historical method of research" (1956, p. 75), and a study by William S. Gray "not because its impact has yet been great, but because it points the way to important future developments" (1934, p. 77). We tried to avoid such inconsistency. However, by thinking "from studies to practice," we were neglecting many important changes that had taken place in literacy instruction.

We began to think more about how literacy instruction has changed. Fortunately, Austin and Morrison's survey, *The First R* (1963), provides a useful baseline description of classroom practices at that time. Our perceptions of current practices, however, were still often in disagreement. Each of us is a prisoner of experience, and instructional practices can differ by grade level, socioeconomic status, recency of teacher education, district policies, and even regional concerns. The status of reading achievement has been monitored for decades, but instruction has not. The most recent national examinations of classroom instructional practice are Applebee's (1993) analysis of secondary literature instruction, and the National Assessment of Educational Progress's (NAEP) descriptions of classroom practice (Mullis, Campbell, & Farstrup, 1993). Unfortunately, the NAEP information is sketchy, and Applebee's considers only one area of instruction. Thus, there is little normative empirical data about classroom practices against which to test our own perceptions.

HOW HAS LITERACY INSTRUCTION CHANGED?

We, nevertheless, constructed our own shared personal portrait of the changes that have taken place in literacy instruction since the early 1960s. This rather impressionistic sketch became the basis for additional brainstorming of potential studies, and it guided our final selection. The major features of that sketch are as follows:

Literacy is taught both earlier (kindergarten and preschool) and later (adult literacy) than before. Readiness activities once so ubiquitous in kindergartens and the first half of first grade have generally disappeared and have been replaced with reading instruction. Ability grouping has probably declined, especially in the

primary grades where it had been so popular. Remedial reading in the U.S. grew dramatically through Chapter/Title I programs since the mid 1960s, but these have begun to be supplanted or supplemented with early interventions such as Reading Recovery.

Elementary instruction became increasingly eclectic, but the past decade witnessed the rise of a new factionalism with regard to instructional methods. Phonemic awareness, fluency instruction, and the use of invented spelling have all become part of the literacy curriculum. Self-selected reading in elementary classrooms is more likely to take place now. Worksheets became popular, though we discern some recent decline in their use. Management systems, in which collections of discrete skills are tested and taught, appeared, gained wide use, and have largely disappeared again. The minilesson and the literacy club have emerged as popular instructional activities.

The books used to teach elementary literacy have changed rather dramatically in content and style. Such books, whether referred to as basals or literary anthologies, are probably used less now than even a decade ago. Initially, basal stories were written specifically to be used for teaching reading. Later, these were replaced with adaptations of more widely known trade books. More recently, the mainstay of textbooks has been nonadapted original trade book selections, though publishers continue to alter the graphic aspects of these. Reading textbooks no longer use careful vocabulary controls; these have been replaced by a predictable or patterned style of writing in the beginning levels. These changes have elevated the quality of what children read but might be making it more difficult to teach and learn reading. Textbooks and trade books have become more reflective of diversity in the U.S., so minority children in 1996 read stories more reflective of their racial and ethnic heritages. Textbook use may be down, but the growth of trade book availability, both in and out of schools, has been remarkable, and this growth is reflected in the expansion of children's book clubs and bookstores. Readability controls are used less often than before in reading textbooks. This shift is particularly intriguing as such controls became commonplace around the time of Russell's article, and he praised them as an important advance.

Elementary writing instruction, after decades of neglect, has become the norm in U.S. schools. Children, even those in kindergarten, now usually receive some writing instruction. Preservice and inservice teachers learn more about the teaching of writing than in 1961, and the writing achievement of their elementary and secondary students will probably be tested now. Textbooks of all kinds now stress the value of writing activities and instruction.

There is more instruction devoted to reading comprehension than before, and certainly such instruction is more varied than when its scope was governed mainly by the questions to be asked. Ideas like strategic comprehension and metacognition have become widespread since the mid 1970s—though still probably not the norm—and related instructional practices like ReQuest, DRTA (Directed Reading-Thinking Activity), mapping, story structure summaries, and other related techniques have greatly expanded the instructional repertoires of many teachers.

Teachers are more likely to use informal assessments such as portfolios, and student achievement now is widely and publicly evaluated with large-scale assessment tests. Parents in the 1990s receive more encouragement to help their children with academic work. Different kinds of literacy are now recognized—at least beyond the K–12 curricula—through family literacy and workplace literacy programs. The canon certainly remains, but it has broadened a bit to include more recently published pieces, especially those by women or racial/ethnic minorities. Inclusion of such authors is evident in elementary materials as well. Media and technology, still limited in most schools, are far beyond what was available in 1961. The focus of technology in literacy instruction seems to have changed, too, from machines that teach reading to teaching children to use literacy with various technological tools (word processors, CD-ROM reference materials, hypercards, Internet). Teachers are better educated with regard to reading, literature, and writing, and teacher research has grown.

This brief sketch became the basis for considering a wider range of studies in our conversation. For some changes, it was easy to select an appropriate influential investigation, while others did not seem to develop directly from research findings.

THE ROLE OF RESEARCH IN INSTRUCTIONAL CHANGE

In fact, many changes that have occurred in literacy instruction have been due less to research than other factors. Worksheet use in reading is a case in point. We could find no research antecedent to this. It occurred more because of the development of the photocopier and decline of bulk paper prices than because of research. Similarly, many of the changes noted in large-scale assessment or textbook design have been due to economic, political, and social factors. This is not to say that research has not been used to develop such measures or that these tests have not been used to generate worthwhile data. The point is simply that large-scale assessments are not used *because* some influential research study found this to be helpful. Accountability is a political issue, not an educational one, and this has driven the expanded use of large-scale assessments. Similarly, the growth in availability of children's trade books has been fueled more by demographic and economic changes outside of school than by school actions instigated by research.

Research does play a role in educational change, but it might be more like the view of history implied by Singer than by Russell. Russell apparently subscribed to so-called "Great Man" theories of history (or, in this case, a "great study" theory). According to such views, history is determined by the actions of a particularly forceful individual. For Russell, simply designed, well-written, utilitarian studies are influential by dint of their quality, utility, and simplicity. Singer made it clear that more is going on here than just well-executed research. The features of research highlighted by Russell are more important than the methodology used, but possibly no study will have much impact if it does not match the Zeitgeist. Certainly, it is rare that research sets or reverses major practical trends in education. The idea is not that studies are just material objects in space with no force, but that this force is necessarily mediated by other, possibly more fundamental, forces.

In both Russell and Singer, there is a strong sense that research can and should influence instructional practice. Certainly, such views are held by many researchers and policymakers. Our view is more conflicted. We hope our studies will influence practice, but we recognize the real limits on the applicability of most findings. Research is complicated, and the results of a single study can be woefully wrong and misleading. Attempts to apply research too quickly can do harm. Also, as valuable as research can be, there are important epistemological, social, and economic forces at worst in determining the nature of instruction in schools and how research is used.

Our previous examples of economic and social forces should suffice, though the value of teacher autonomy and professionalism deserves note. How research findings are applied must be determined, in part, by the professional who has to apply them. Views of research as *the* determining factor in educational history supposes a hierarchical field in which researchers, at the top of the pyramid, make decisions about how teachers, lower in status, will conduct their work. Teaching is difficult, and research is only one source of information used along with teacher lore, community values, and experience (Shanahan, 1994).

Research findings should be viewed as a powerful, but partial, form of rhetoric. The idea that any study can provide sufficient perspective on which to determine practice is naive. Research is one of our most useful tools for constructing knowledge. However, a basic part of the research process is to conduct multiple studies of the same phenomenon using different conceptualizations of the problem, samples of participants, measures of success, and so on. Practitioners and policymakers are frustrated by the messiness of this process, as it often leads to conflicting results. However, research discourse through which such differences are analyzed, argued over, and, eventually, understood is a major part of what research brings to practice. To us, the determinants should not be individual studies, but the accumulation of knowledge across lines of research.

Educational research can be thought of as a process that develops transportable technologies that can be applied easily and homogeneously. Alternatively, it can be seen as a reasoning process in which empirical data are used to help formulate more useful conceptualizations of the world. Though we have disagreed about the premises underlying these fundamental notions, we both are aware that individual studies influence practice, and we both hope for an application process that would be considered, deliberate, and reliant on larger collections of studies.

THE STUDIES THAT HAVE INFLUENCED PRACTICE

By these different approaches we actively considered about 40 studies. We narrowed the field, from there, by logical discussion. In a number of cases, the process was easy, and one interchange sufficed. Other times we argued. Which studies have influenced practice the most? Russell proposed a top 10, but our conversations led us to what we hope is a "thoughtful 13." Although a top 10 list would have been more consistent with Russell's original plan, we allowed the list to grow a bit longer as we were reviewing a larger and more varied corpus of studies that had been produced over a shorter period of time. Descriptions of the 13 most influential studies since 1961 follow and appear chronologically in the accompanying list.

A Chronological List of the 13 Most Influential Literacy Studies Since 1961

Goodman, K. S. (1965). A linguistic study of cues and miscues in reading. *Elementary English, 42,* 639–643.

Durkin, D. (1966). *Children who read early.* New York: Teachers College Press.

Bond, G. L, & Dykstra, R. (1967). The cooperative research program in first-grade reading instruction. *Reading Research Quarterly, 2,* 5–142.

Children's Television Workshop. (1969). *Sesame Street.* New York: Public Broadcasting System.

Freire, P. (1970). *Pedagogy of the oppressed* (Trans. M. B. Ramos). New York: Herder & Herder.

Read, C. (1971). Preschool children's knowledge of English phonology. *Harvard Educational Review, 41,* 1–34.

Sticht, T. G., Caylor, J. S., Kern, R. P., & Fox, L. C. (1972). Project REALISTIC: Determination of adult functional literacy skill levels. *Reading Research Quarterly, 7,* 424–465.

Pichert, J. W., & Anderson, R. C. (1977). Taking different perspectives on a story. *Journal of Educational Psychology, 69,* 309–315.

Stein, N. L., & Glenn, C. G. (1977). An analysis of story comprehension in elementary school children. In R. Freedle (Ed.), *New directions in discourse processing: Vol. 2. Advances in discourse processing* (pp. 53–120). Norwood, NJ: Abler.

Durkin, D. (1978–79). What classroom observations reveal about reading-comprehension instruction. *Reading Research Quarterly, 14,* 481–533.

Clay, M. M. (1979, 1985). *The early detection of reading difficulties.* Auckland, New Zealand: Heinemann.

Graves, D. H. (1981). *A case study observing the development of primary children's composing, spelling, and motor behaviors during the writing process.* Final report. NIE Grant No. G-78–0174. Durham, NH: University of New Hampshire. (ERIC Document Reproduction Service No. 218 653)

Atwell, N. (1987). *In the middle.* Portsmouth, NH: Boynton/Cook, Heinemann.

Most research usually ends up as a paper or book, but in the case of our first selection the research culminated in an ongoing television program for children. Now more than a quarter of a century old, *Sesame Street* (Children's Television Workshop, 1969), the educational and entertainment program for preschoolers, is an exemplar of a successful research experiment: the collaboration of educational advisors and professional researchers with TV production. Susan had to argue strenuously for this one. "But is it research?" Tim had challenged. Her response, and, indeed, the history of the project, proved persuasive. "Research usually ends up as a paper or book, but here the 'treatment' and the 'effect' is actually a TV show for children." From its inception—under the brilliant leadership of Joan Ganz Cooney along with her colleagues, Director of Research Ed Palmer and Chairperson of the Board of Advisors Gerry Lesser—the show was designed as an experimental research project. Together, this team refined child watching to an art form. Prior to broadcasting, researchers estimated what children knew about a topic; program materials were created and tested on target audiences for appeal, comprehensibility, and educational value; researchers then reported back to producers who modified or discarded materials based on these continuous reports from the field. This approach proved highly beneficial for the beginning literacy development of Sesame Street viewers as revealed in summative analysis (Ball & Bogatz; 1970) and led to the creation of a new model for **educational television production.** This innovative experiment proved beyond doubt, the potential of television as an educational asset in the lives of young children. As a result of Sesame Street, beginning reading curricula in schools began to assume greater literacy knowledge among young children.

No study has so successfully influenced remedial reading instruction as Marie Clay's *Reading Recovery* program, described in her book, *The Early Detection of Reading Difficulties* (1979, 1985). In a series of studies conducted over a 5-year period, Clay examined the effects of her innovative **one-on-one tutorial program to intervene early in reading failure.** Up to then, remediation was usually delayed until students were in the fourth grade, as it was assumed that they might catch up on their own. Clay intervened, often successfully, after only 1 year of instruction. Unlike traditional remedial programs, Clay emphasized instruction in the context of real reading, observation as a key assessment technique, high-quality teacher education as a fundamental part of the intervention, and individualized instruction that would raise student achievement to the average level of class performance. The program began in New Zealand but rapidly spread to Australia, England, Canada, and the United States.

Another influential study of early literacy learning was conducted by Charles Read (1971). Read studied how young children understood the phonemic aspects of English as related to the spelling system. His analysis of the attempted spellings of preschool children showed that they were able to use their tacit knowledge of phonological relations and could make sense of highly abstract principles of spelling even without formal instruction. Initially, this work exerted little impact on instruction as it was assumed that Read's subjects were particularly gifted. However, work by Carol Chomsky (1971) and Ed Henderson and his students at the University of Virginia (Henderson & Beers, 1980) showed the relevance of Read's findings to more typical school settings. As a result, we no longer assume that children enter school with little knowledge of the phonological-orthographic features of lan-

guage, and **invented spelling** has become a popular instructional activity that allows earlier writing and provides children a venue to explore the orthography of their language.

Paulo Freire's (1970) concept of literacy for liberation, beautifully articulated in *Pedagogy of the Oppressed,* is another highly influential study. Working with Brazilian peasants, Freire recognized that literacy was not merely a technical skill, but one that was rooted in the histories, cultures, and day-to-day experiences of learners. His notion of **emancipatory literacy** argued against a *banking* concept of education in which teachers simply deposited information into learners. In its place, he successfully tried a *problem-posing education* in which ideas take shape and change as the learners critically think about their lives and the conditions of state and society. For Freire, literacy was essentially a political act in which individuals assert their rights and responsibilities not only to read, but also to restructure their relationship with society. His work has had a transforming influence in adult literacy education. Today, programs using a Freirian approach focus on collaborative relationships among learners and teachers and involve participants in curriculum development that is centered on their own characteristics, aspirations, backgrounds, and needs.

Another influential study in adult literacy is Tom Sticht's work on literacy in work training and job performance (Sticht, Caylor, Kem, & Fox, 1972). Working with military personnel, he developed an innovative approach that continues to influence **workplace literacy.** He reasoned that effective reading strategies could be taught using job-related materials so that students would learn both skills and the technical content of the job. He based his approach on a functional-context principle—that new knowledge must build on old knowledge, and that literacy instruction could be made more meaningful by using *real life* situations, tasks, and materials. Intertwining transferable processing skills and situation-specific job and career knowledge, his research on functional contexts for literacy and technical training evolved into the concept of workplace literacy used in industry training programs across the U.S. This approach has been extended conceptually into other functional approaches such as family literacy and health literacy.

One of the most ambitious ventures in reading research, the U.S. Cooperative First-Grade Studies, remains a classic in research collaboration as well as literacy education. Written by Guy Bond and Robert Dykstra (1967), the study represented a compilation of data from 27 individual studies examining the effects of instructional approaches on beginning reading and spelling achievement. The study was set up by Donald Durrell, and the list of project directors reads like a Who's Who of Reading Research (Jeanne Chall, Donald L. Cleland, Edward B. Fry, Albert J. Harris, Arthur W. Heilman, Thomas D. Horn, John C. Manning, Helen Murphy, Olive S. Niles, Robert B. Ruddell, William D. Sheldon, George D. Spache, Russell G. Stauffer, and others). Programs studied included phonics, linguistic readers, basals, initial teaching alphabet, individualized reading, the language experience approach, and various grouping schemes and combinations of instruction. These studies found that no instructional method was superior to the others for students at either high or low levels of readiness. Susan was troubled by this choice, as she felt that much of its influence was based upon false warrants—it had not actually found that teachers made a difference, only that instructional method had not. Tim was able to win the argument by noting that this study did more than highlight "teacher effects"; it also demonstrated that although no single method proved best, combinations of methods were associated with the highest achievement. In other words, it encouraged greater **methodological eclecticism** in elementary instruction than had previously existed. Although no study has successfully challenged these basic findings, eclecticism has been under renewed attack recently. Increasingly rancorous arguments about the superiority of various instructional approaches are evident, and some members of the research community have again become involved in the search for best method. An enduring legacy of this study has

been a greater focus on teacher and learning situation characteristics rather than on methods and materials.

The next two classic studies, both conducted by Dolores Durkin, have powerfully influenced reading instruction. Recognizing the incongruity between what early precocious readers knew and what first-grade programs offered, Durkin's studies of *Children Who Read Early* (1966) raised questions about reading readiness. Both of us thought this belonged on the list, but we were concerned that the findings of the study did not line up with the outcome we have attributed to it. Durkin conducted longitudinal studies of precocious readers in California and New York and reported findings that challenged the prevailing view that early readers would suffer problems in school. She found quite the opposite. Early readers maintained their achievement lead. Children who read early typically showed early interest in reading, were read to regularly by parents or siblings, and their parents believed themselves to be their young children's teachers. Although in this study Durkin did not show benefits of earlier school instruction—she hadn't even studied that—she did show that children could learn to read successfully without delay, and this was a critical reason for the eventual **demise of reading readiness programs.** More than any other study, this highlighted the role of parents in literacy learning and set the stage for later emergent literacy views.

Durkin (1978–79) also helped to focus needed attention on reading comprehension. Relatively little work on reading comprehension was done until the 1970s. Durkin, on the basis of a carefully conducted observational study that examined classrooms under nearly ideal conditions, concluded that virtually no reading comprehension instruction was taking place in U.S. classrooms. Her findings indicated that most comprehension instruction took the form of questioning students about what they had read. Durkin's unflattering portrait of instructional neglect set off a series of efforts in research, material development, and teacher training. After Durkin's stark portrait of **reading comprehension instruction** appeared, it became increasingly difficult to ignore this critical area of concern.

This was not the only major influence on reading comprehension instruction, however. Pichert and Anderson (1977) demonstrated convincingly that a reader's perspective influences comprehension and recall. Although they worked from a framework first proposed by Bartlett in 1932, and other notable researchers were conducting similar studies (such as John Bransford's fine work), this study was particularly persuasive because of its ingenious design. They asked participants to read a complete story from one of two perspectives, that of a home buyer or a thief, and found that these pretend perspectives affected what was remembered. This study became a cornerstone in the literature on schema theory and led to a **greater emphasis on instructional techniques that activate prior knowledge** as part of the comprehension process.

Cognitive psychologists wondered what makes a story a story, and how people remember and create narratives; the idea of **story grammar** emerged from this work. A story grammar is a set of tacit rules that determines the essential parts or structures of a story and how these parts relate. Researchers such as Mandler and Johnson (1977) and Stein and Glenn (1977) developed story construction rules, on the basis of analyses of children's recall of story elements and experiments that showed what readers do when particular elements are omitted or disorganized. This was a difficult choice. Susan pointed out that Mandler and Johnson seemed to be cited most often by researchers, but Tim suggested that "if you look at teacher journals, basals, or magazines, they propose activities that are more like the Stein and Glenn's categories." Thus, though both grammars have been widely used by the research community, we think Stein and Glenn's work has been more directly influential on instructional practice. Their grammar, probably as a result of its simpler categories and more parsimonious description of relationships, has become the basis of a number of story mapping and summarizing techniques that are now a mainstay of narrative instruction in U.S. schools.

Before Donald Graves's research (1981), elementary writing, if taught at all, was dominated by grammar, spelling, and usage. Influenced by Donald Murray, Graves, along with his students Lucy Calkins, Mary Ellen Giaccobe, and Susan Sowers, carefully observed what children did within the writing process. Graves's thoughtful instructional recommendations and keen observations of elementary school writers showed that children could successfully engage in writing activities similar to those used by professional writers. His **writing conference method** of instruction emphasized revision processes especially, in which students would write and rewrite drafts with teacher and peer feedback. At a time when many teachers were wondering what to do with this long neglected aspect of the curriculum, Graves's research dramatically created an attractive approach to elementary writing instruction. Although Graves's research has been criticized in terms of methodological adequacy, the effects of his work are seen widely in classrooms throughout the U.S., as well as in many other countries.

Graves helped to bring about another trend, best exemplified by the influential work of Nancie Atwell (1987). Atwell's *In the Middle* describes how the writing workshop in Boothbay, Maine, developed into a complete, and very progressive, approach to the teaching of middle school literacy. Using yearlong case studies, logs of observations, and portfolios, this classic of teacher research demonstrated how a responsive classroom literacy context could be created. Together, she and her students tried out and tested their beliefs about written language, creating solutions grounded in their particular experiences and not in a prescribed curriculum. Her **full-immersion approach to reading and writing,** including minilessons and status reports, has been used in classrooms across the U.S. Most enduring, perhaps, will be the possibilities that her work suggests to future teacher researchers. Written from the inside, Atwell's compelling research details the principles, complexities, and practicalities that define literacy teaching.

Kenneth Goodman's (1965) study of oral reading miscues has been central to what eventually became known as the **whole language** movement. At the time of his study, instructional practices in reading often emphasized word recognition in isolation from meaningful contexts. Goodman argued, from a psycholinguistic perspective, that reading involves the use of multiple cue systems rather than only the cues within printed words. Investigating the role of decoding skill in isolation and context, he examined primary students' ability to read words in lists and texts. He found that children could recognize words in context that they could not in isolation, and that this ability increased with age. Children had used syntactic and semantic cues to better anticipate and recognize unfamiliar words. From this, Goodman and his colleagues challenged oral reading, phonics drills, word lists, and, other skills-based approaches that take words out of context. The findings of this study have been severely challenged and certainly much of what has been inferred from it exceeds the actual limits of the study. Nevertheless, there is little doubt that it has been influential on instructional practice.

A SUMMING UP

What are the common bonds of these studies? First, they tend to address what could be characterized as *important* issues—all of them set out to answer genuine questions rather than simply to add items to somebody's vita. They often reflected efforts to reconsider current practices or views of learning in new, refreshing, and unique ways. Second, these studies were strongly driven by theory. In some, the authors proposed new theoretical principles, while in others there were clear attempts to extend theory into issues of practice; in each case, it meant that the fruits of the studies could be brought to bear on a set of issues that exceeded those directly addressed by the single investigation alone. Third, each was rhetorically powerful, and simply—perhaps even elegantly—executed. Finally, the researchers were not timid; they boldly speculated on broad issues of learning, teaching, and instruction, drawing fully on the implications of their findings.

Nevertheless, though we were able to arrive at a single list, we could not entirely agree on the true source of power that these studies exerted. Research is influential, according to Susan, when it is creative, tied to important ideas, and sensible to practitioners. Consequently, the researcher is in the saddle and can choose, to some extent, whether or not to be influential. Contrarily, Tim noted that each of these studies somehow matched the social, political, and economic tenor of its times. In other words, studies that demonstrate something that the field or society apparently wanted to believe at a given moment are the ones that matter. According to this view, research will be most influential not necessarily when it provides the right answers, but the answers that we most hope to hear. This disagreement has not been resolved. Let the conversation continue. . . .

REFERENCES

Adams, M. J. (1990). *Beginning to read: Thinking and learning about print.* Cambridge, MA: MIT Press.

Applebee, A. N. (1993). *Literature in the secondary school: Studies of curriculum and instruction in the U.S.* (ERIC Document Reproduction Service No. 357 370)

Austin, M. C., & Morrison, C. (1963). *The first R.* New York: Macmillan.

Ball, S., & Bogatz, G. A. (1970). *A summary of the major findings in the first year of Sesame Street: An evaluation.* (ERIC Document Reproduction Service No. 122 799)

Barr, R., Kamil M. L. Mosenthal, P., & Pearson, P. D. (Eds.). (1991). *Handbook of reading research, Volume II.* New York: Longman.

Bartlett, F. C. (1932). *Remembering.* Cambridge, England: Cambridge University Press.

Chall, J. S. (1967). *Learning to read: The great debate.* New York: McGraw-Hill.

Chomsky, C. (1971). Approaching reading through invented spelling. In L. Resnick & P. Waver (Eds.), *Theory and practice of early reading* (Vol. 2, pp. 43–65). Hillsdale, NJ: Erlbaum.

Gray, W. S. (1956). *The teaching of reading and writing.* Glenview, IL: UNESCO and Scott, Foresman.

Heath, S. B. (1983). *Ways with words.* New York: Cambridge University Press.

Henderson, E. H., & Beers. J. W. (Eds.). (1980). *Developmental and cognitive aspects of learning to spell.* Newark, DE: International Reading Association.

Hiebert, E. H. (1983). An examination of ability grouping for reading instruction. *Reading Research Quarterly, 18,* 231–255.

Hillocks, G., JR. *(1986). Research on written composition.* Urbana, IL: National Conference on Research in English.

Mandler, J. M., & Johnson, N. S. (1977). Remembrance of things parsed: Story structure and recall. *Cognitive Psychology, 9,* 111–151.

Mullis, I. V. S., Campbell. J. R., & Farstrup, A. E. (1993). *NAEP 1992 reading report card for the nation and the states.* Princeton, NJ: Educational Testing Service.

Pearson, P. D. (Ed.). (1984). *Handbook of reading research.* New York: Longman.

Russell, D. H. (1961). Reading research that makes a difference. *Elementary English, 38,* 64–68.

Scribner, S., & Cole, M. (1981). *The psychology of literacy.* Cambridge, MA: Harvard University Press.

Shanahan, T. (1994). (Ed.). *Teachers thinking, teachers knowing.* Urbana, IL: National Conference on Research in English & National Council of Teachers of English.

Singer, H. (1970). Research in reading that should have made a difference. *Elementary English, 47,* 27–34.

Singer, H. (1978). Research in reading that should make a difference in classroom instruction. In S. J. Samuels (Ed.), *What research has to say about reading instruction,* (pp. 57–71). Newark, DE: International Reading Association.

Smith, N. B. (1934). *American reading instruction.* New York: Silver Burdett.

Stanovich, K. E. (1986). Matthew effects in reading: Some consequences of individual differences in the acquisition of literacy. *Reading Research Quarterly, 21,* 360–407.

CHAPTER REFERENCES

Barr, R., Kamil, M. L., Mosenthal, P., & Pearson, P. D. (1991). *Handbook of reading research: Volume II.* White Plains, NY: Longman.

Betts, E. A. (1934). *Bibliography on the problems related to the analysis, prevention, and correction of reading difficulties.* Meadville, PA: Keystone View Company.

Betts, E. A. (1945). *An index to professional literature on reading and related topics.* New York: American Book.

Gray, W. S. (1925). *Summary of investigations related to reading* (Supplemental Educational Monographs, No. 28). Chicago: University of Chicago Press.

Kamil, M. L., Mosenthal, P., Pearson, P. D., & Barr, R. (2000). *Handbook of reading research: Volume III.* Mahwah, NJ: Earlbaum.

Pearson, P. D., Barr, R., Kamil, M. L., & Mosenthal, P. (1984). *Handbook of reading research.* New York: Longman.

Russell, D. H. (1961). Reading research that makes a difference. *Elementary English, 38,* 74–78.

Shanahan, T., & Neuman S. B. (1997). Literacy research that makes a difference. *Reading Research Quarterly, 32,* 202–210.

Singer, H. (1970). Research that should have made a difference. *Elementary English, 47,* 27–34.

Singer, H. (1978). Research in reading that should make a difference in classroom instruction. I. S. J. Samuels (Ed.), *What reading research has to say about reading instruction* (pp. 57–71). Newark, DE: International Reading Association.

Smith, N. B. (1934). *American reading instruction: Its development and its significance in gaining a perspective on current practices in reading.* New York: Silver Burdett.

Strang, R. (1939). *Bibliography relating to reading on the high school and college level.* New York: Bureau of Publications. Teachers College, Columbia University.

Summers, E. D. (1969). *20 year annotated index to The Reading Teacher.* Newark, DE: International Reading Association.

Traxler, A. E. (1941). *Ten years of research in reading* (No. 32). New York: Educational Records Bureau.

Traxler, A. E. (1946). *Another five years of research in reading* (No. 46). New York: Educational Records Bureau.

Traxler, A. E. (1955). *Eight more years of research in reading* (No. 64). New York: Educational Records Bureau.

_____ ANNOTATED BIBLIOGRAPHY OF RELATED REFERENCES _____

Barr, R., Kamil, M. L., Mosenthal, P., & Pearson, P. D. (1991). *Handbook of reading research, Volume 2.* White Plains, NY: Longman.

Contains extensive reviews of reading research and practices divided into 30 literacy topics (*see also* Pearson et al., [1984] and Kamil et al., [2000] for additional volumes in this series).

Betts, E. A. (1934). *Bibliography on the problems related to the analysis, prevention, and correction of reading difficulties.* Meadville, PA: Keystone View Company.

This reference of 1,200 historical studies on research and practice related to the diagnosis and remediation of reading difficulties constitutes the most complete record of research on these topics.

Betts, E. A., & Betts, T. M. (1945). *An index to professional literature on reading and related topics.* New York: American Book.

One of the most complete bibliographies on reading practices and research available. The authors reference 8,200 articles, books, and other studies in the field of literacy in general and research related materials in particular.

Giordano, G. (2000). *Twentieth-century reading education: Understanding practices of today in terms of patterns of the past.* Stamford, CT: JAI Press.

A detailed discussion of several of the important trends and issues in the history of literacy education. In contrast to many other such texts, the material is organized by topic rather than chronology.

Kamil, M. L., Mosenthal, P., Pearson, P. D., & Barr, R. (2000). *Handbook of Reading Research: Volume III.* Mahwah, NJ: Erlbaum.

The contents of this volume are divided into the following four sections: "Literacy Research Around the World," "Methods of Literacy Research," "Literacy Processes," and "Literacy Policies." The three volumes in this series (*see also* Barr et al. [1991] and Pearson et al. [1984] in this Annotated Bibliography) provide the most complete review of current research in literacy available.

Pearson, P. D., Barr, R., Kamil, M. L., & Mosenthal, P. (1984). *Handbook of reading research.* New York: Longman.

This volume, along with Volumes II and III in this series (*see* Barr et al. [1991] and Kamil et al. [2000]), constitutes one of the most complete references of research in reading education.

Robinson, H. A. (1977). Reading instruction and research: An historical perspective. In H. A. Robinson (Ed.), *Reading and writing instruction in the United States: Historical trends* (pp. 44–58). Newark, DE: International Reading Association.

An extensive historical description of the history of reading instruction with particular emphasis on important related reading research.

Robinson, R. D. (2000). *Historical sources in U.S. reading education 1900–1970: An annotated bibliography.* Newark, DE: International Reading Association.

An annotated listing of important historical research references of the last century arranged according to fifteen categories related to various aspects of literacy history and instruction.

_____ YOU BECOME INVOLVED _____

This initial chapter presents information on the history of reading research. After you have read this material consider the following questions regarding this discussion.

• Compare and contrast the various research studies that are discussed in this chapter on reading investigations.

• Do you notice any general trends in this literacy research from a historical viewpoint from Russell (1961) through the two articles by Singer (1970; 1976) and the final one by Shanahan and Neuman (1997)?

• Why do you think there has been so much controversy on the teaching of reading, despite the amount of research done in this field?

CHAPTER 2

READING ASSESSMENT

The typical reading test which yields a single gross score can scarcely measure general reading skill since no single ability exists. Scores from such tests fail to reveal many aspects of reading technique which are of prime importance as a guide to instruction. Even if an elaborate test did measure general reading ability, the mere information that a pupil or class is, in general, good or average or poor would be much less useful to the teacher than a knowledge of strengths and weaknesses in particular types of reading techniques.

—Arthur I. Gates

The Improvement of Reading (1929)

Effective [reading] instruction is based on two fundamental principles: first, attainment of a thorough understanding of learner strength and weaknesses; second, provision for guidance in terms of individual needs. In short, the basic notion is that the teacher should learn, or know, the child before attempting to teach him.

—Emmett Betts

Foundations of Reading Instruction (1946)

Assessing children's reading development is more important than ever—not just because test scores are visible indices of educational accountability that are reported in newspapers but because teachers use many types of assessment to inform their daily instruction.

—Scott Paris and Robert Carpenter

FAQs About IRIs (2003)

Edmund Huey in his classic book on reading, *The Psychology and Pedagogy of Reading* (1908), noted, "So to completely analyze [assess] what we do when we read would almost be the acme of a psychologist's achievement, for it would be to describe very many of the most intricate workings of the human mind, as well as to unravel the tangled story of the most remarkable specific performance that civilization has learned in all its history" (p. 6). The need for educators to better understand the reading process is one that has been of primary importance almost from the beginning of literacy instruction (Smith, 2002). Historically, assessment procedures have ranged widely from a multitude of informal approaches to various forms of formal "paper and pencil" tests, to the state and national testing programs of today. Because reading is such a complex, subtle process, the effectiveness of these assessment procedures has often been open to question as to the usefulness of their results.

Literacy tests have been used for many purposes beyond simply the measurement of reading ability. The results of these tests have traditionally been used to place students in groups, aid in the selection of reading materials, and measure teacher performance. In addition, literacy assessment has also become a political statement that school districts and government leaders have used to support various types of school reform and change. Each of these various uses of reading test results has had important effects on the classroom literacy curriculum of today. The articles selected for this chapter on literacy assessment reflect this long tradition of interest in the measurement of reading ability.

AS YOU READ

As you read the material in this section on reading assessment, you need to consider how many of the issues in this area have been debated and discussed from the earliest period of U.S. literacy research. Fundamental concerns have included the primary role of literacy tests, their construction and format, and the effectiveness of the results of these procedures.

Reading Tests

CHARLES H. JUDD

The first article in this chapter, by Judd (1914), is an excellent introduction to many of the issues in the field of literacy assessment. Despite the fact that this material was written over ninety years ago, it addresses many of the concerns in the testing of reading ability that still face educators today. In this interesting article, Judd addresses many topics, including teachers' attitudes toward testing; measurement of individual performance compared with whole-class performance; evaluations of one school versus another based on individual student performances; differences between silent and oral reading; and the development of a national test of reading ability.

Many teachers are prejudiced against the measurement of school work because they assume that such measurement means the imposition of arbitrary outside standards on their pupils. They assume that someone believes that he has a definite yardstick by which he can determine the efficiency of all the children in the United States in their reading or arithmetic. Such prejudices would disappear entirely if the distinction between social standards and physical standards of measurement were clearly apprehended.

The fact is that every teacher is employing standards in judging the efficiency of various children in his or her class. If a given boy in the fourth grade reads poorly as compared with the other members of the class, if he shows no ability to understand the passage which the other members of the class easily understand, the teacher grades this boy as inefficient in the work of the class. In this case the boy has been measured by comparison with other members of his own class. The standard to which he has been subjected is a social standard. It is not held by his teacher that he ought to have the mental ability of an older boy, and the teacher would not be satisfied with this fourth-grade boy on the ground that he shows great efficiency in reading the primer used by the first grade. In other words, the boy must prove himself to be like the other members of the group with which he is associated. If he can do this he is judged to be efficient; if he cannot he is judged to be in some sense deficient.

The kind of comparison which the teacher is able to make within the limits of her own class ought to be extended in such a way that the class as a whole may be compared to larger units of school organization. That is, the efficiency of a fourth-grade class can be determined by comparing it with classes above and below, exactly as the efficiency of a single boy can be determined by comparing him with the other members of his class; or a fourth grade in one school building can be compared with similar grades in other school buildings, or other school systems. This comparing of one class with another is also a common fact in school experience. A certain boy comes to a given school, transferred from a neighboring school. We have no hesitation whatever in condemning the school from which he comes if this product of the school does not succeed in taking his place with the class which he enters. In other words, we judge schools by their products, and we formulate our judgment in detail by comparing one product with another product. In the same way the students who come to a given high school from several neighboring elementary schools are all compared with each other and judgments are formed by the high-school teacher regarding the efficiency or deficiency of the various elementary schools which contribute their students to the high school. Here again standards are social standards rather than absolute standards.

Even when the child's ability is measured by what seems to be an absolute standard, as by his actual solving of certain problems which are set for him, there are certain variable characteristics of the standard which must be taken into consideration. Thus the difficulty of solving the problems chosen is an important consideration in any case. If, for example, the ten problems set are very easy, the child who fails in one of these problems is not as efficient as the child who fails in several problems of a difficult set. In other words, the level at which the work is done becomes a matter of importance, and the level which is expected is determined by comparison, not by some absolute measure. Other considerations are, of course, of equal importance. How long were the children allowed to work on the problems? Was their preparation immediately before the test directed toward this particular examination or was it general in character? In other words, though a test seems at the outset to be an absolute test of the child's ability, it turns out on analysis to contain many elements which differ with the social setting in which the pupil works, and the absolute character of the standard is seen to be a mere fiction. The standard is in reality a social standard and its value depends upon comparison with other school situations and with other groups of individuals who are undertaking similar work.

With this definition of the meaning of standards in mind, let us consider some of the comparative problems which are of importance in the teaching of reading in the elementary school. In the first place, it is obvious that a comparison of different grades in the same school system is a matter of great importance. If the child shows adequate progress as he passes from the second to the third grade, from the third to the fourth grade, and so on, we may be satisfied that the school is doing efficient work even if the ability to read at any given point is in the absolute not great. Or, to put the matter in another way, the grade which is steadily improving shows a higher degree of efficiency than a grade which is improving less rapidly, even though the grade which is improving less rapidly shows a fair degree of ability. In preparing our test, therefore, we should aim to determine the rate of improvement during the different grades.

Second, there are two fundamentally different types of reading. There is reading which is oral and reading which is silent. If one notes the sharp contrast between little children and adults, he finds that oral reading is the common mode of reading among little children and the very exceptional form of reading in adult life. The ordinary adult finds it so much more convenient and easy to read to himself that he does not read aloud except under the most unusual circumstances. This distinction between oral and silent reading is not one which has been clearly recognized in school work. School work has for the most part dealt with oral reading. A comparison of the two types of reading will soon convince even the casual observer that oral reading is a rather slow and inconvenient form of reading as compared with silent reading. Furthermore, oral reading does not exhibit the highest training given in the schools, therefore a comparison of oral and silent reading will help in making a systematic comparison of the mental development of children at different stages of school work.

Third, reading is after all merely a secondary form of activity. What we want primarily in the reading class is ability to understand the passages which are read. In the lower grades the mastery of words is itself so difficult a problem that the child is able only very slowly to take in information from the passage which he reads. In the upper grades, on the other hand, the comprehension of the passage is so fully developed that the chief value of reading in these later grades is the information which it gives. Little or no time is required in the upper grades for the formal process of pronouncing words or mastering sentence forms. The mechanics of reading, if we may use that phrase to distinguish the process of reading from the process of understanding, are mastered and the whole attention may now be concentrated on the significance of the passage. We have here an important contrast between pupils in different stages of advancement. If the little child expends most of his mental energy in reading the sentence and the older child expends most of his mental energy in getting the significance of the passage, we may, therefore, test the various children in different grades by inquiring into their ability to get the meaning of the passages which they read. We shall have to choose passages with different kinds of ideas and with different degrees of complexity; simple ideas and ideas which are easy to formulate will be given in the lower grades; more complex and difficult ideas in the upper grades. It would indeed be possible in some cases to use exactly the same passage all through the school for the purpose of finding out how the ability to get at the meaning progresses at different stages in education, but it will usually be found to be more practical to arrange an overlapping series of tests so that comparisons between the extremes may be made indirectly through intermediate tests which are applied only to smaller units of the school population. For example, we may make a comparison of the first three grades with each other. Then compare the third, fourth, and fifth grades with each other, and finally the fifth, sixth, and seventh grades. The overlapping of the third and fifth grades, each appearing in two groups, will make it possible to get an idea of the relative ability of the first and eighth grades, or any other two grades in the series.

Another type of variation in the reading matter to be used is suggested by a consideration of the changing interests of children. There is a period in the intermediate grades when children exhibit a marked interest in the things in the physical world about them as contrasted with the people who go to make up the social world. Later in the adolescent period the social interests are renewed, and there is a marked interest in romantic or social literature. By testing the ability of children to get the meaning of different kinds of reading matter we gain some insight into the kinds of reading matter best suited to different stages of development. Children at one stage will get the meaning of one kind of reading matter most easily, while children at another stage of development will take up readily a totally different type of matter.

It would undoubtedly be advantageous in the interests of direct comparison if tests could be made all over the United States with the same material, that is, if the same passage could be presented to every third grade in the United States and the results carefully tabulated. We should then have a very illuminating study of the whole American school system. The disadvantage with such an effort at absolute unifor-mity is that while the passage itself might be the same, it would undoubtedly relate itself to the preparation of the different third grades in very different ways. It is conceivable that a third grade otherwise relatively inefficient would have just the preparation in words and ideas that would make it possible for that particular third grade to stand well in the test on the passage selected. Conceivably a third grade which had had an entirely different type of training might show very little ability with the particular passage chosen. We shall accordingly lose little by foregoing the use of a single passage. Each school system may select its own material, provided only the material is thoroughly analyzed and the results accompanied in every case by a statement of the material thus employed. After a number of tests of this sort within single school systems have been carried out, we shall perhaps be prepared to undertake a more systematic and unified test of many school systems. . . .

General Principles of Diagnosis of Reading Disabilities

MARION MONROE

The second article, by Monroe (1937), is a discussion of general principles of reading diagnosis as developed by one of the pioneers in this aspect of literacy education. This discussion clearly indicates that most reading disabilities are the result of a number of causes rather than a single one.

To be effective, remedial instruction in reading must be preceded by careful diagnosis. The remedial teacher must first discover the nature of the child's difficulty, search for causes and then set up a specific program to treatment that will either remove the causes, or if that is impossible, will at least enable the child to read as well as his limitations permit. The very complexity of the reading process makes diagnosis difficult. So many condi-tions and factors which affect reading have been brought to light by recent investigations with such divergent interpretations that the remedial reading teacher may find herself in a state of uncertainty and confusion in trying to reconcile conflicting theories and points of view. A few general principles of procedure and a classification of causes may assist the teacher in making a diagnosis of the difficulties of children who cannot read.

MULTIPLE CAUSATION
OF READING DISABILITIES

Reading disabilities are usually the result of several contributing factors rather than one isolated cause. Studies of the causes of reading disabilities reveal no clear-cut factors which occur only in poor readers and never in good readers. Some children who possess the impeding factors appear to be able to read in spite of them. For example, poor vision occurs as a factor in a certain percentage of reading-disability cases and undoubtedly impedes reading; yet some good readers are found who also have poor vision. A similar state of affairs occurs in the studies of almost every discovered cause of reading disability. A few good readers are found who have poor vision, poor hearing, emotional instability, who come from environments detrimental to reading, and who have had inferior teaching. Even among mental defectives are found occasional children who have acquired a glib skill in the mechanics of reading even though unable to comprehend much of the content read. We may conclude that in most cases, one factor alone is not sufficient to inhibit the act of reading, if compensating abilities are present and if the child's reaction to the difficulty is a favorable one. This fact should not, however, serve to minimize the importance of any difficulty. Occasionally a simple difficulty, so easily overcome in the majority of cases as to appear unimportant, may be the direct reason for setting up in a certain child a number of emotional inhibitions to further learning. The reading diagnostician must, therefore, investigate each case with the hope of locating as many contributing factors as possible, study the interrelationships of these factors and weigh their importance in the light of the child's reactions to the difficulties. Individuals vary greatly in their experiences and in the number and combinations of factors contributing to the problem: only a thorough acquaintance with each child can lead to a complete understanding of his reading disability.

It is not essential, however, for every cause to be located before beginning remedial work.

This would delay the remedial instruction unnecessarily. A first "working-hypothesis" may be set up after the initial tests and the remedial teacher may begin treatment with those factors which are best understood. The diagnosis then continues as the remedial work gives further opportunities for observation and testing of hypotheses, and opens new leads for investigation. Diagnosis and treatment, therefore, go hand in hand—the treatment being based on the first tentative diagnosis, and the diagnosis being modified or confirmed on the basis of the outcomes of remedial instruction.

DIAGNOSTIC PROCEDURES

The diagnosis of reading disabilities should contain two types of analysis: (1) descriptive and (2) causative. In the descriptive analysis the examiner details as completely as possible the nature of the child's reading disability. Both subjective observation and objective test data are included in this type of analysis. The descriptive analysis should answer the following questions:

a. *What reading level has this child reached?* This question is answered by data from standardized reading tests, usually in terms of reading grade, and varies from total non-reading to almost any grade level of reading.

b. *How far below expectation is this reading level?* This question is answered by comparing the child's reading-grade with his actual grade placement, his chronological age, his mental age, the number of years he has attended school, and his achievements in other non-reading subjects. Here again almost any degree of retardation may be present. This relationship between reading and other abilities may be expressed as a reading index or an achievement quotient.

c. *Are all types of reading equally retarded?* This question is answered by comparing grade scores on different types of reading tests: that is, oral, silent, word-recognition, vocabulary, reading for particular types of comprehension, reading rate, etc. Many variations may be found: the accurate oral reader who gets no meaning from his reading; the speedy silent reader who stumbles orally; the generally poor reader in all types; or the child who is up to grade in the mechanics of reading but who lacks interest or desire to read.

d. *What are the particular characteristics of the child's reading?* This question is answered by analysis and description of his reading errors, the most frequent types, how his errors compare with typical errors at his own reading level, how his eyes move in reading across the page, how he articulates and phrases in oral reading, what mannerisms and peculiarities he shows while reading, and what methods of self-help he employs (such as spelling, sounding, pointing, etc.). Photographs of eye-movements assist in analyzing the characteristics of his reading.

e. *How does the child respond to his reading difficulty?* This question is answered by a description of his reactions to reading such as aggressive dislike, withdrawal, compensatory activities, discouragement, apathy, etc. The examiner tries to discover what the reading disability means to the child in his social relationships.

f. *What is the child like as an individual, apart from reading?* This question is answered by a general description of the child, his personality, his physical appearance and physical condition, his social response, his spontaneous language and comments. The examiner tries to discover the interests and motivating drives in his behavior.

g. *What have been this child's experiences?* This question is answered by conversation with the parents and teachers in which the examiner obtains a personal, social, and school history of the child. Family relationships are often helpful in understanding the child's difficulty, particularly if he is compared unfavorably with siblings, or if he feels insecure in his personal relationships.

From the descriptive analysis of the child the examiner forms his opinion as to what are the causal factors in the disability. The questions now to be answered are: *Why has this child failed to learn to read? Why does he show these particular characteristics and mannerisms in reading and why has he chosen these particular reactions to failure?* The examiner now is set searching for reasons and explanations. Perhaps it will not be possible to answer these questions for every case. Researches on reading disabilities are fairly recent; most of our knowledge in this field dates within the past ten or fifteen years. Some of the causes of reading disabilities have already received fairly intensive and critical study; others have been merely suggested as possibilities from case studies without having been put to experimental tests. Still other causes, as yet unrecognized, may come to light with increased knowledge. Granting the limitations of our present knowledge, the examiner will find it helpful to state the causes of the difficulties in so far as can be determined.

Values and Limitations of Standardized Reading Tests

Arthur E. Traxler

The third article, by Traxler (1958), reflects the progression of thinking about literacy assessment in the middle of the previous century. Although many of the same concerns are expressed in this discussion as were present in the previous article by Judd, there are notable differences. Traxler is much more specific in describing the inherent limitations of most reading tests as well as the positive values of reading assessment. Note especially the discussion regarding the value of using a variety of tests as opposed to a single assessment procedure.

In discussing my topic, I am going to reverse the key words in the title and consider the limitations first and the values second. This reversal does not mean that I believe the limitations are more important than the values, but there are certain limitations which are inherent in the reading process and which logically ought to be considered first of all.

LIMITATIONS

The *first kind of limitation* is to be found in the nature of the reading act, and this limitation can never be entirely resolved. If reading were wholly, or even mainly, a mechanical process, as is implied in some theoretical discussions and some methods for the teaching of reading, then measurement would be comparatively simple. An observable manifestation of the mechanics of reading is found in eye movements, which are measurable and, in fact, have been measured precisely for many years.

But learning to read is much more than learning the mechanical aspects, as every teacher knows from experience and as Gates,[1] Gray,[2] and other reading specialists have frequently emphasized. Reading is a complex, unified, continuous activity which does not naturally fall into subdivisions or measurable units. In this respect, reading differs from other basic skills, such as arithmetic and spelling. You can take a problem in multiplication or a set of such problems, or you can take a list of spelling words representing, let us say, the *i-e e-i rule,* and study pupils' achievement on these in isolation. But reading is a process which flows past as you try to appraise it. You can arrest the flow to examine some aspect, but then it ceases to be reading.

Moreover, reading which is at all mature is an associative thinking process deep within the recesses of the mind. There is no way for an observer to be sure at a given moment whether a subject reading silently is gleaning facts or gathering main ideas or evaluating the writer or gaining aesthetic satisfaction or, in fact, whether he is really putting his mind to the printed page at all.

Much can be inferred about the person's ability by having him read aloud. An oral reading test is undoubtedly one of the best ways of appraising the reading ability of a pupil but, since it must be administered individually, this kind of measure requires too much time for extensive use with large numbers of pupils.

Since, except for a superficial estimate of speed, no aspect of silent reading can be measured without interrupting the process, we customarily resort to a kind of addendum to the reading process itself. We ask a series of questions when the reading is finished and hope that the answers to these will indicate the quality of the comprehension which took place while the reading was being done. This isn't as good as we would like it to be, but it is about the best we can do, and, as will be indicated later, this rather clumsy procedure does yield valuable information about reading comprehension.

Since we cannot measure reading "all of a piece" while the act is taking place, we usually have recourse to some artificial and presumably logical analyses of the process and then build our tests upon the elements into which reading was analyzed. These analyses are likely to be somewhat different, depending upon the predilections of the persons doing the analysis. As I reported in an earlier one of this series of conferences, a survey of twenty-eight published reading tests showed that attempts were being made to measure forty-nine different aspects of reading ability, although some of these differed little except in the names assigned to them by the test authors[3]

Factors analysis is of some help in identifying the fundamental areas of reading which ought to be measured. For instance, Davis[4] carried on a factor analysis of the Cooperative Reading Comprehension Test some years ago and reported that most of the variance was accounted for by two factors—word knowledge and reasoning in reading. However, the components of reading logically identified by reading specialists may differ considerably from those based on statistical analysis.

There is considerable agreement among those who have constructed reading tests based upon logical analysis of the reading process that three broad aspects of reading on which information is needed are speed, vocabulary, and comprehension. But if these are accepted as the main components toward which measurement should be directed, a *second kind of limitation* arises because of the complex nature of the subdivisions.

For instance, the measurement of rate of reading is not the simple procedure it may at first seem to be. There is not just one rate of reading for an individual; there are innumerable rates depending upon the nature of the material and the purposes of the reader. The speed at which a good reader covers an exciting novel may be several times as fast as his rate of reading a research article in a professional journal. The more mature the reader, the more his speed will vary. If a rate score of three hundred words a minute is obtained for a pupil on a reading test, one cannot say that this is his normal reading rate; one can say only that this was his rate on the material used in the test and under the kind of motivation which the test provided.

Most individuals, however, maintain somewhat similar *relative* reading speeds in different reading situations. So a pupil's standard score or percentile rating is likely to be fairly stable from one reading test to another, provided the test is long enough to yield reliable results. In some reading tests an attempt is made to obtain a speed score in just one minute of reading time. This is much too short an interval. Three minutes of reading time is the minimum for a reliable rate score, and at least five minutes of reading time would be preferable.[5]

Similarly, the measurement of reading vocabulary is complicated by a number of variables. There is not only a general reading vocabulary; there are also vocabularies of special fields. An individual's standing within a norm group will be affected to some extent by the relative weight given in the vocabulary test to the different special fields. If a major proportion of the test words happen to come from the fields of

mathematics and science, pupils with special reading facility in the humanities and social studies will be handicapped, and vice versa. Nevertheless, a reading vocabulary test which is carefully and scientifically prepared is one of the most reliable and valid of all tests for use in placing an individual in a norm group.

The anomalous nature of part scores on reading tests is nowhere more evident than it is in the case of reading comprehension tests. The kinds of questions used and the manner of responding to the questions differ widely. In some comprehension tests the subject may refer back to the reading material while answering the questions, whereas in others he must recall what he has read. Some comprehension tests consist largely of factual questions, others stress main ideas, and still others attempt to measure critical thinking, inferences, or appreciation stimulated by the reading passage.

When the comprehension score is broken down into part scores, the variety of the scores may be inferred from the names of some of the parts. These include, among others, paragraph comprehension, main ideas, fact material, directed reading, level of comprehension, general significance of a passage, use of references, relevant and irrelevant statements, true and false deductions, and ability to perceive relationships.

Yet research indicates that attempts by testmakers to differentiate among various aspects of comprehension have not usually been very successful. The intercorrelations of the subscores, when corrected for attenuation, tend to be so high that they suggest that almost the same thing is measured by the different subtests.[6] This seems to be something closely akin to what Davis called reasoning in reading, or something very similar to that broad area of general intelligence which is measured by paper-and-pencil group tests of mental ability.

This brings us to a *third limitation of reading tests*—the lack of clear differentiation between measurement of reading comprehension and measurement of intelligence. In a sense, the better and more searching the reading test is, the greater this limitation becomes. It was pointed out earlier in this paper that reading, particularly high-level reading, is actually a form of thinking. But thinking is the process through which intelligence is manifested. So, when we give a reading test that really probes ability to think about the reading material, are we measuring reading or intelligence? The answer is that scores on this kind of test represent a composite of both intelligence and ability to read. Hence, it is very difficult to predict how much the scores of individuals who are low on such a test may be improved by teaching. For some individuals the possibilities of improvement are considerable; for others the main determiner of low reading comprehension scores is low verbal intelligence, and the prognosis for significant improvement is not favorable. Teachers need to recognize this failure of even the best reading tests to differentiate between reading comprehension and intelligence and to be prepared to accept the fact that not every pupil with a low reading score is capable of much improvement. But it is almost impossible to predict in advance which pupils with low reading scores are capable of improvement and which ones are not, unless scores are also available on such measures as an individual intelligence test and a listening comprehension test.

A *fourth limitation of reading tests* is the time-consuming nature of the measurement of reading, particularly reading comprehension. Vocabulary test items can be done quickly, but reading comprehension tests are not efficient because of the necessity of covering both reading passages and questions based on them. It is not unusual for a reading test to require the reading of a paragraph of two hundred words or so in order for the pupil to be able to answer four or five questions. Since many schools demand tests which can be administered within forty minutes, the number of comprehension questions used is likely to be too small for high reliability. If attempts are made to subdivide the comprehension test into parts measuring different aspects of comprehension, as is true of some reading tests, and if the comprehension test, along with a vocabulary test and a speed test, is squeezed into a forty-minute period, one may expect the subtest scores to be almost valueless for the study of individuals, although of some use in the study of groups.

This limitation of reading tests can readily be removed if schools will agree to devote a period of two or three hours to the measurement of reading instead of forty minutes or less.

VALUES

Notwithstanding the limitations of standardized reading tests, it would be next to impossible to plan and carry on a modern reading program without them. They have a number of positive values for instruction in reading in all schools. Some of these were referred to in connection with the discussion of limitations.

Perhaps the *most important value* of a reading test, or any other standardized test, is that it lends a certain amount of definiteness to our thinking about the achievement of a pupil or a group. Without reading tests it is possible to say in a vague or general way "Here is a pupil who appears to be a good reader; here is another who doesn't read well; and here is another who doesn't seem able to read at all." But we cannot be very confident about our classification when it is done simply on a subjective basis.

Reading tests enable us to speak about reading ability in quantitative terms with considerable confidence, provided we keep in mind that every test score contains an error of measurement and that we recognize the unimportance of small differences in score.

A reading test may be given to a seventh-grade class, and then it is possible to say, "That pupil reads about as well as the average ninth grader; this pupil is approximately at the fifth-grade level in reading ability; and here is a very retarded pupil whose reading is still on the level of Grade II." Moreover, if the test yields part scores, we can make such further quantitative statements as "In comparison with the norms for his grade, John has a rate of reading percentile of 96; a vocabulary percentile of 52, but a comprehension percentile of only 15."

These kinds of information lend definiteness and direction to the planning of reading instruction for both groups and individuals. They provide a reasonably firm basis for developmental, corrective, and remedial programs, even though teachers need to remind themselves occasionally that the basis is not quite so solid and dependable as the bald, bold figures suggest, because of the limitations of reading tests already mentioned.

A *second value* of reading tests is for the appraisal of growth of individuals and groups in a developmental reading program. Is the total reading program of the school well designed to bring about normal or better growth of pupils at all grade levels and levels of ability? If not, where do the weaknesses exist? Such questions as these cannot be answered simply through the use of observation and teacher judgment. But if different forms of tests yielding comparable scores are used annually, and if the results are carefully studied, a constant check can be kept on the reading program as a whole and on the rate of reading growth of individual pupils.

A *third value* of reading tests lies in diagnosis of the strengths and weaknesses of groups and individuals as a starting point for corrective or remedial work. However, it should be kept in mind that reading tests are not in themselves diagnostic. They yield worthwhile information for diagnosis only when someone attempts to relate the results to other kinds of information about the pupil.

Still another value of reading tests lies in the early identification of gifted pupils. Nearly all gifted pupils read well, particularly in the field of their greatest ability and interest. Not infrequently, one of the first indications of unusually high mental ability is the tendency of a young child to begin reading on his own a year or two before he reaches the age of school entrance. When he enters school, his reading ability may be beyond the usual reading test designed for the lower primary grades, and a more difficult test may be needed in order to measure his actual achievement. It is desirable to supplement the school's regular testing program with reading tests appropriate to the ability level of very superior children so that suitable activities may be planned for them. Too often attempts to identify the gifted are delayed until the junior or senior high school level. This is frequently too late, for by that time many potentially outstanding children will have fallen into habits of an easy mediocrity in reading, as well as in other school activities.

VALUES AND LIMITATIONS OF DIFFERENT KINDS OF READING TESTS

Now I should like to comment briefly on the values and limitations of several types of reading tests.

One kind is that which yields only one total score. Forty or fifty years ago, when the first objective tests appeared, a number of reading tests were one-score tests, but tests of this kind almost disappeared from the scene until 1957, when the Sequential Tests of Educational Progress (Educational Testing Service, 1957), or STEP, were published. At each level, the reading test of this series is a seventy-minute test yielding only one over-all score. The STEP Reading Test is a most carefully constructed test, but it is difficult to see how it will be of much value in a reading program if used alone.

However, there is also in the STEP series a Listening Comprehension Test. It is believed that a listening test is one of the best measures of potential reading ability, although more research evidence is needed on this point. In any event, the STEP Listening Test and the STEP Reading Test, when used together, should furnish some information having broad diagnostic value.

At the other extreme, there is the kind of reading test in which an attempt is made to obtain within a class period a large number of part scores for purposes of diagnosis. This type of test is well illustrated by the Iowa Silent Reading Tests (World) and the California Reading Tests (California Test Bureau). Such tests, in which the time limits for the parts are very brief, either will have a large speed component in all scores, or the number of questions in each part will be so small that the scores will be low in reliability, or both. The total scores on these tests are often highly reliable, but it is more appropriate to use the part scores on tests of this kind for the study of groups than for individual diagnosis.

A third kind of reading test is aimed at the measurement of three aspects of reading believed to be especially important, such as rate, vocabulary, and power of comprehension. Fairly reliable measures of these aspects may be obtained within a class period, although the reliability of the comprehension score tends to be somewhat low.

In the primary grades the measurement of three or more aspects of reading ability within the same class period presents difficulties because of the short attention span of young children. Gates met this problem by having his Primary Reading Tests (Bureau of Publications, Teachers College) printed separately—one each for word recognition, sentence reading, and paragraph reading. The Gates tests continue to be among the most satisfactory reading tests at this level.

The most logical way of meeting the needs for a quickly administered survey test and dependable diagnostic scores would seem to be through a coordinated battery in which the survey test would be given first, to be followed by diagnostic tests appropriate to the weaknesses indicated on an individual or small-group basis. Thus far, the only tests of this kind are the Diagnostic Reading Tests (Committee on Diagnostic Reading Tests, Inc.). The committee has also undertaken to provide teaching materials for use in overcoming the weaknesses revealed by the diagnosis.

As already suggested, reading tests furnish only a portion of the information needed in carrying on a school reading evaluation program. So far as is possible, these tests should be used in conjunction with individual tests of mental ability, listening ability, achievement tests in the content areas, measures of interests, and inventories of personal qualities. Standardized reading tests have a limitation, in addition to those mentioned earlier, in that they furnish no direct information about interests or personality. As all teachers know, the sources of reading difficulty are not always to be found in the learning area; they often originate in the pupil's home, in his social group, in health and physical handicaps, or in his general adjustment to the environment of the school.

Reading test scores reach their greatest meaning and usefulness when they fall into place in a comprehensive individual cumulative record.

NOTES

1. Arthur I. Gates, "Character and Purposes of the Yearbook," *Reading in the Elementary School*, p. 3. Forty-eighth Yearbook of the National Society for the Study of Education, Part II. Chicago: University of Chicago Press, 1949.

2. William S. Gray, "Essential Objectives of Instruction in Reading," *Report of the National Committee on Reading*, p. 16. Twenty-fourth Yearbook of the National Society for the Study of Education, Part I. Bloomington, Ill.: Public School Publishing Co., 1925.

3. Arthur E. Traxler, "Critical Survey of Tests for Identifying Difficulties in Interpreting What Is Read," *Promoting Growth toward Maturity in Interpreting What Is Read*, p. 196. Ed. William S. Gray. Supplementary Educational Monographs No. 74. Chicago: University of Chicago Press, 1951.

4. Frederick B. Davis, "Fundamental Factors of Comprehension in Reading," *Psychometrika*, IX (September, 1944), 185–97.

5. Arthur E. Traxler, "The Relationship between the Length and the Reliability of a Test of Rate of Reading," *Journal of Educational Research*, XXXII (September, 1938), 1–2.

6. Arthur E. Traxler, "A Study of the Van Wagenen-Dvorak Diagnostic Examination of Silent Reading Abilities," *1940 Fall Testing Program in Independent Schools and Supplementary Studies*, pp. 33–41. Educational Records Bulletin No. 31. New York: Educational Records Bureau, 1941.

How Will Literacy Be Assessed in the Next Millennium?

Robert J. Tierney

The fourth article (Tierney, Moore, Valencia, & Johnston, 2000) in this series on reading assessment is a set of four position statements on the future of how literacy might be measured in the new millennium. As you read these comments reflect on what you have read in the previous articles in this section and consider whether you agree or disagree with what is predicted for the future of literacy assessment.

As we make the transition to a new millennium, I would encourage educators to look for approaches to assessment that are both just and empowering and that assess the literacies of learners richly and in all their complexities, without fear of what is not quantifiable or uniform. I look for assessments that consider the quality and usefulness of information that is gleaned for teachers and learners—descriptions and possibilities versus numbers and crude labels. Mostly, I look for a future that views evidence from assessments as conversation starters that engage the learners as decision makers with the support of teachers, parents, and others. If standards are to be pursued, I concur with Carini (1994) that our goal should be standards and assessment with the following characteristics:

> active, fresh, emergent in work and works, arising in the midst of persons whose lives and works are mutually influencing, who argue and jostle or challenge each other. (p. 40)

We need to judge the quality of assessment in terms that are based upon a meaningful partnership that allows for dialogue, a consideration of different sources of information, and multiple interpretations.

My goals for evaluation and assessment befit the following tenets:

- Evaluation as a social construction that is continuous, recursive, and a divergent process (raising more questions than answers).

- Evaluation as an emergent process that cannot be fully designed in advance.
- Evaluation as a process for sharing accountability rather than assigning it.
- Evaluation as a *joint face-to-face* process that requires, at a minimum, the clarification of competing constructions and that is an *educative and empowering* activity for all.
- Evaluation that respects diversity more than standardization and verifiability and possible interpretations over consistency or traditional notions of reliability and reverence for scores.
- Evaluation intent on affording students opportunities to engage with teachers, caregivers, and stakeholders in meaningful partnerships involving genuine decision making.

I see the new millennium as marking a more enduring shift toward learner-centered assessment, encompassing a shift in why assessments are pursued as well as how and who pursues them.

My position contrasts sharply with what I see at the end of the 1990s, when politicians and, in turn, psychometricians seem intent on holding students' and teachers' feet to the fire, using high-stakes testing to do so. In the late 1990s, politicians and educators seemed to rally around calls for increased standards while ignoring the likelihood that high-stakes testing restricts access for students who have been historically denied educational opportunities. Indeed, high-stakes testing has a history of making underrepresented students a casualty of the system, increasing the likelihood that they will drop out (Ellwein, Glass, & Smith, 1988; Tierney, 1998). The approach might be seen to privilege some and not others, ensuring the liberties of some and the regulation of others. Politicians on both sides of the aisle seem to be touting what the past United States Secretary of Education William J. Bennett and his assistant Chester Finn (1999) are suggesting—namely, schools need to meet a certain grade or be "thrown back into the regulatory briar patch" (p. A9).

Politicians would suggest that the shift responds to the public appeal for improving education, pressures from industry for better prepared employees, an aversion to social promotion, a discrediting of the qualities of teachers, and a desire to make schools accountable. Yet it is important to also note that testmakers have carefully orchestrated tests to align with the letter of the law to ensure the legal defensibility of their measures (Phillips, 1993). Indeed, they limit the recourse or options of teachers and parents while increasing the government's license to compare and discriminate. Furthermore, they leverage curriculum control by aligning teaching to tests.

While most educators seem to be acquiescing and realigning their curricula in a manner that could be characterized as test driven (Madaus, 1988), I suspect that we will see growing criticism and increased opposition. Indeed, I think we are seeing the start of such.

In New Zealand, for example, the introduction of national testing was recently challenged by academicians and others and, as a result, was not supported by the parliament. In Greece there has been wide-scale rioting by teachers and students in response to increasing the amount of national testing. In pockets across the United States, parents in several states have mounted campaigns opposed to the increased emphasis upon tests used for these purposes. For example, Bayles (1999) reported that a boycott against the Michigan Educational Assessment Program reached 90% in some school districts, despite the promise of college tuition assistance for students who pass the state exam.

Chicago area students and parents, angered over the time spent preparing for three assessment tests, have begun campaigning against testing. One group, the Organized Students of Chicago, recently staged a demonstration outside the Board of Education offices. Parents in Massachusetts and Virginia have mounted campaigns against the use of high-stakes testing, which has prompted a reconsideration of the tests and their use by legislators. A joint committee of Wisconsin legislators voted to end funding of a statewide high school graduation test after a lobbying campaign by parents. New York City's Board of Education canceled a citywide reading test for second graders after parents and principals complained that the children were tested too much. In some states the campaigns have been less successful to date.

Some educators have suggested that teachers may need to go underground, so that they give the illusion of compliance, but in their classrooms (i.e., behind closed doors) they will find ways to partition their approaches so that two forms of assessment occur in the same space. Perhaps, as Sheehy (1999) has proposed, teachers should recognize that the spaces within which they work are rented rather than owned and that they should pursue their desired engagements in the cracks or spaces within the system.

Some have attempted to pursue waivers from these impositions and developed their own renditions of testing—simultaneously meeting state guidelines and the principles governing learner-centered assessment. In Massachusetts, for example, the Parker School has engaged in the use of portfolios that seem to serve both sets of principles. Without compromising the richness and diversity of portfolio content, the school staff ensure that their assessments of portfolios are calibrated by using qualified outsiders to audit the teachers' and schools' determination of the quality of student learning. At the same time, they are careful to ensure that what they do is aligned with legally defensible guidelines states eschew.

In some instances, the tenets undergirding such testing have been challenged. For example, Mark Dressman's (1999) recent discussion entitled "On the Use and Misuse of Research Evidence: Decoding Two States' Reading Initiatives" questioned the selective use of certain research findings to give the impression of compelling evidence when the information provided is selected to serve a certain political agenda—one that excludes alternative perspectives, certain studies, and alternative interpretations. As he suggested, studies cited in support of claims need to be examined in terms of the reasons and assumptions (including views of society, language, and reading) that, in turn, shape the research used to lace the reports that serve narrow purpose—tacitly or otherwise.

The high-stakes literacy assessment movement is a powerful political move with problematic educational results—especially in matters of social justice (House, 1991; Johnston, 1993). Whereas psychometricians may see this development as a shift in the balance from formative assessment toward summative evaluation—a shift that has been the subject of considerable debate over the past 30 years (Cronbach, 1963; Scriven, 1967)—I see high-stakes testing as one step forward for traditional testing and centralized curriculum control and two steps backwards for teachers, students, and ethics that aspire to respect for diversity, opportunities and access for all, and judicious decision making based upon the teachers' knowledge, the learners' experience, and participation by the various stakeholders.

REFERENCES

Bayles, F. (1999, June 1). Standardized exams coming under fire: Protests decry "proficiency test madness." *USA Today,* p. 10A.

Bennett, W., & Finn, C. (1999, June 29). GOP's bold education package. *Cape Cod Times,* p. A9.

Carini, P. F. (1994). Dear Sister Bess—An essay on standards, judgment, and writing. *Assessing Writing, 1*(1), 29–65.

Cronbach, L. (1963). Course improvement through evaluation. *Teachers College Record, 64,* 672–683.

Dressman, M. (1999). On the use and misuse of research evidence: Decoding two states' reading initiatives. *Reading Research Quarterly, 34,* 258–285.

Ellwein, M. C., Glass, G. V., & Smith, M. L. (1988). Standards of competence in educational reform. *Educational Researcher, 17*(8), 4–9.

House, E. R. (1981). Evaluation and social justice: Where are we? In M. W. McLaughlin & D. C. Phillips (Eds.). *Evaluation and education at quarter century.* 19th yearbook of the National Society for the Study of Education (p. 233–247). Chicago: National Society for the Study of Education.

Johnston, P. (1983). Assessment as social practice. In D. J. Leu & C. K. Kinzer (Eds.). *Examining central issues in literacy research, theory and practice.* 42nd yearbook of the National Reading Conference (pp. 11–24). Chicago: National Reading Conference.

Madaus, G. F. (1988). The influence of testing on the curriculum. In L. N. Tanner (Ed.), *Critical issues in curriculum.* 87th yearbook of the National Society for the Study of Education (pp. 83–121). Chicago: National Society for the Study of Education.

Phillips, S. (1993). *Legal implications of high stakes assessment: What states should know.* Oak Brook, IL: North Central Regional Educational Laboratory.

Scriven, M. (1987). The methodology of evaluation. In R. Stake (Ed.), *Perspectives on curriculum evaluation* (AERA Monograph Series on Curriculum Evaluation, No. 1. pp. 39–83). Chicago: Rand McNally.

Sheehy, M. (1999). *Un/making place: A topological analysis of time and space representation in an urban Appalachian seventh grade civics project.* Unpublished dissertation, Ohio State University, Columbus.

Tierney, R. J. (1998). Testing for the greater good: Social injustice and the conspiracy of the proficiency standards. *The Council Chronicle, 8*(2), 16–20.

David W. Moore

Even the most cursory review of the social history of literacy shows that reading and writing assessments link with their times. Remember that the oral examinations predominant in U.S. schools during the early years were patterned after the European system previously known to the colonists. Students stood collectively as a class and responded individually to questions such as "What does the book say of Job?" The comprehension task in this system, verbatim recall, fit expectations of the time for a wholly mimetic style of teaching and learning.

The written assessments that emerged during the middle 1800s corresponded with increasing expectations for literacy. During this time the U.S. society changed from a rural to an urban setting with newly developed industrial, market, and judicial systems. Assessments that added a writing component to silent reading paralleled these changes. Furthermore, school reformers disdained oral examinations that deviated from school to school in favor of written examinations that were more consistent. Written examinations enabled all students to respond simultaneously to identical passages and directives, offering a somewhat comparable basis for decisions about school administration.

Standardized reading comprehension tests suited the new social settings and searches for the best, most efficient schooling of the early 1900s. For the first time, these reading assessments required students to indicate their comprehension by answering unpracticed questions about passages never before encountered. This increase in cognitive demand fit the increasing demands for literate workers, consumers, and citizens. Also for the first time, standardized tests required students to mark multiple-choice items, a convenient and inexpensive procedure that became even more so with machine scoring. By rigorous specification of testing conditions and scoring procedures, standardized exams produced scores that could be compared more acceptably than written exam outcomes. The establishment in 1901 of the U.S. National Bureau of Standards, an agency charged with facilitating common systems of measurement for industry and commerce, suggests the assessment milieu that embedded the standardization of reading tests.

The state standards-based assessments of the 1990s are related to concerns about U.S. economic competitiveness and public and political perceptions of the public school ethos. Reformers of this era specified concrete reading and writing attainments, supplying educators and students particular goals and assessments. Some of these assessments have students employ reading and writing to perform complex real-world inquiry tasks, a feature many prefer over standardized contrivances. These assessments have high stakes, helping to determine schools' curriculums, students' promotion and graduation, and educators' job security. State standards-based assessments continue exerting standardized assessments' legacy of bureaucratic control because they are designed outside the classroom, independent of particular teachers' efforts.

As can be seen in the capsule review just presented, U.S. school literacy assessments were products of and produced educational reforms that corresponded with societal structures such as urbanization, industrialization, bureaucratization, and public dissatisfaction with schools. Because educators of the past devised literacy assessments amid the conditions of their times, educators of the future can be expected to do the same. Consequently, predicting how literacy will be assessed in the new millennium means predicting what will happen at the confluence of future educational reforms and societal structures.

Rapidly changing technological systems constitute one societal structure that probably will last far into the future and be enmeshed with educational reform. It seems obvious that the somewhat innovative technologically enhanced communication practices of 1999 such as distance learning, producing documents collaboratively through the Internet, compiling multigenre presentations through Power Point, and interacting with a computer through voice recognition soon will be common. What is unclear is exactly how these and related innovations will be connected with educational reforms and literacy assessments.

Globalization is another societal structure many foresee being present in the distant future. As business, culture, and communication flow more and more readily through state and national boundaries, educational policies probably will decease their emphases on local issues. Practices in 1999 to monitor education at the national level, such as the U.S. National Assessment of Educational Progress, will be enhanced and joined with those of other nations for comparative purposes. Teachers and students will have countless opportunities to engage people throughout the world in educational activities. Again, exactly how globalization will relate to educational reforms and literacy assessments is yet to be determined.

In closing, only a few pages were available here for responding to an extremely knotty question, so calling attention to what else deserves consideration seems to be an appropriate conclusion. My response emphasized formal assessments of reading comprehension typically conducted in school settings to guide policy makers. The following also deserve attention: (a) dimensions of literacy such as deciphering the alphabetic code, writing particular genres, choosing to read and write, and valuing particular genres; (b) settings for literacy defined by social markers such as race, income, gender, immigrant status, and age; (c) functions of literacy such as performing jobs, running households, acting as citizens, and leading personal lives; and (d) purposes for assessment such as guiding classroom instruction and advancing scientific and theoretical insights. I am confident these aspects of literacy assessment will link with the social conditions of the new millennium too.

SHEILA W. VALENCIA

Assessment has shifted as dramatically in the last 2 decades as it has in the last century. Although we have seen many good new ideas take hold, others have failed to hit the mark. And we have watched the pendulum swing back and forth in record time, making it difficult to predict where, or if, it will stop. What is clear, however, is that the future of assessment is as much about politics as it is about meaningful outcomes for children and teachers' instructional practice. As a result, I approach this topic as a realist, not a romantic.

One future trend that seems most certain is that high-stakes, large-scale assessment will continue to dominate the assessment scene. External audiences need easily interpretable, reliable, inexpensive information that is most readily provided by large-scale group tests. At the same time, the press for accountability in the U.S. using national comparisons is being demanded by both conservative and liberal policy makers as well as the public at large. Just witness the renewed interest in state-by-state National Assessment of Educational Progress (NAEP), the Voluntary National Test (VNT) in reading, and the upcoming international literacy assessment scheduled for 2001. To that, add more than 44 states in the U.S. that now conduct some form of statewide literacy assessment. It is inconceivable that these testing programs will disappear or that our obsession with comparisons across schools, students, and time will fade. In fact, I predict *more* school district assessment at grade levels leading to the targeted state testing grades. Districts don't want to be surprised; they want to identify and intervene with struggling students before they take the high-stakes test. As a result of this emphasis on large-scale, high-stakes assessment, certain forms of assessment are likely to gain prominence and others are likely to drop away, especially when they compete for resources and for teachers' and students' time.

With large-scale, high-stakes assessments in the picture, the next question is what form these assessments will take. Here is where I believe we will see a swing back from full-blown authentic performance assessments to more moderated definitions of authenticity and performance. California and Arizona are examples of states that have been there and done that. California was forward looking in the 1980s with its literature-based language arts framework and innovative performance assessment. Although the assessment had been successfully implemented and validated (at great expense and teacher effort), it was recently abandoned and replaced with a norm-referenced standardized test. The reasons for the backlash in California are difficult to pinpoint, but a combination of factors—cost, time, psychometric issues, equity concerns, conservative politics, and poor performance on NAEP— all likely contributed. Arizona experienced a similar backlash (although there the shift can be traced largely to a change in state leadership), while other states such as Wisconsin and Indiana never implemented performance assessments they had in the works.

Interestingly, the criticisms of performance assessment for large-scale, high-stakes assessment are coming from both traditional and progressive perspectives. Questions about utility, generalizability, reliability, and validity of performance assessments have raised concerns about using test results to make high-stakes decisions about individual students. But even among those who support the concept of performance assessment, there are questions about the narrow range of tasks, specific scoring rubrics, and tightly constrained contexts in which performance assessments are administered. Some argue that, similar to norm-referenced tests, these conditions may restrict teaching and learning and fail to provide useful instructional information. Others argue that large-scale performance assessments resemble neither the high-quality performance assessments teachers do in their classrooms nor the rigor of standardized tests— they are some sort of strange hybrid that don't succeed at either aim.

Overall, the future of performance assessment for large-scale use is dim. Nevertheless, it is unlikely most large-scale tests will regress to the formats and content of the 1960s. There is too much attention to new content standards and to the importance of critical literacy skills to revert back to the old ways. I believe there will be at least a nod to the intellectual quality of high-stakes assessments. In reading we will see medium-length reading passages and a mix of predominantly multiple-choice items, some short constructed responses, and perhaps a few extended constructed response items similar to NAEP and the VNT (states do not want to find themselves doing poorly on state-by-state comparisons). Several norm-referenced reading tests and state assessments have already struck this middle ground. In writing, I predict we will stay with direct writing assessment. Although some questions of generalizability and reliability have been raised, many of the problems have been worked out over the years, and there seem to be fewer acceptable fallback formats for assessing students' writing. In many ways, because reading comprehension assessments, performance-based or multiple choice, have always been proxies for the real thing, fighting the performance assessment battle seems to be less compelling in reading than in writing.

A second future trend I predict is the strengthening of classroom-based assessment, much of it in the form of performance assessment. Researchers from every arena have identified problems with using large-scale, high-stakes assessment as a reform strategy; its power to influence classroom instruction has been oversold. Although this research cannot counter the press for accountability, it does suggest an alternative path to improving instruction and learning: the teacher. Teachers who understand and focus on content standards, and who make links between instruction and classroom assessment, are more likely to be effective. Another line of support for classroom assessment comes from the recent emphasis on early literacy and early intervention. Running records, informal reading inventories, and other individualized administered performance assessments are now widely used at the early grade levels. And, even with the current emphasis on phonemic awareness and phonics skills, the power of classroom assessment to yield more useful instructional information seems to be fairly well established. Several states (e.g., Vermont, Washington) have even introduced statewide assessments at the early grades that require classroom-based assessments. A final line of support for classroom assessment comes from the local accountability it affords. It provides timely, concrete evidence of students' learning that can support or refute high-stakes assessments. More importantly, it provides the evidence behind grades.

How well classroom assessment fares in the face of high-stakes tests will be a function of the support available for teachers' professional development, both inservice and preservice, and the value placed on the information it provides. Clearly, the power behind classroom assessment comes from teacher knowledge, not from administering one more assessment. At the inservice level, resources for professional development will have to compete with resources needed for high-stakes test implementation. Effective professional development is more expensive than purchasing a test, yet I think most teachers, parents, administrators, and policy makers realize the long-term benefits of investing in professional development. At the preservice level, teacher education programs may need to be revised or restructured to provide additional preparation in diagnostic teaching and classroom assessment. The other factor that will influence the fate of classroom assessment is the extent to which school districts use shelf-tests to test at grades off the state cycle. As described above, districts don't want to be surprised by student performance at the targeted testing grades, so they will certainly implement some form of assessment at the other grades. If they value the information and professional development that come with classroom assessment, and if they believe the information is sufficiently reliable and valid to help them identify students who might experience difficulty on upcoming state assessments, then classroom assessment will be supported. Conversely, if school districts don't have resources to support professional development or if they don't trust or value teacher judgment, classroom assessment may fade from the assessment scene.

The wildcard in the scenario I've described is the implementation of the new Title I legisla-tion. This legislation requires states to evaluate student progress using their regular assessments; this ensures that Title I students are included in the same assessments as other students in the state. Furthermore, the state assessment must be aligned with the state content outcomes, thereby ensuring that Title I students have access to the same curriculum as other students. Because so many Title I programs target early literacy learners and most state assessment programs don't begin until third or fourth grade, new assessments will need to be developed for the lower grades. There will be debates about whether Title I assessments should be classroom based or large scale, performance based or multiple choice, and norm referenced or standards based. The way states address these challenges is certain to have implications for the balance between large-scale and classroom-based assessments.

Although I have taken a realistic approach, I close by arguing that we cannot sit back and watch as the assessment drama unfolds. We must step forward as advocates for assessments that foster better teaching practice, insist on curricular rigor, and value worthwhile student learning and engagement—all the while respecting the public mandate for accountability. Envisioning what is good for students and teachers led to remarkable changes in assessment in the 1990s. As we cross the millennial marker, vision won't suffice. Tenacity and the willingness to both read and respond to politics are needed too. Imagination, hard work, and a big dose of reality will make the difference.

Peter Johnston

I have always found predicting what will happen tomorrow difficult, so it is with some caution that I predict shifts in assessment in the next century. But I had a dream recently involving one of my children in the next century getting his 3-year-old to log on to the computer (whose hardware was the size of a matchbox in his pocket, and the screen was projected onto his glasses). The computer in a few minutes of games figured out that the child was going to have trouble learning to read because of her lack of phonological knowledge and that she should engage in particular activities on the computer to remediate the problem. The computer chastised my son for not previously using the genetic test, which would have located the gene causing the problem, which could then have been replaced through gene therapy. The computer added that if my grandchild followed the exercises then her preparedness for reading would move from the 30th percentile to the 80th percentile (above the Jones's child next door)—guaranteed (because the computer would keep records of the child's use of the exercises). I did not sleep well.

The dream was inspired by recent online articles and advertising. New tests do exist that operate on these premises (except the gene repair part, but it's only a matter of time). My dream is also consistent with the trend for earlier and earlier assessment of literacy. The roots of literacy malfunction are increasingly assessed as small cognitive and perceptual units and even particular genes. So this is the edge of the present, and although it is technically more sophisticated, in principle, it is not much different from assessments seen earlier in the century.

Historically, changes in assessment practices have primarily been technical, in spite of changes in theory. Thus, I suspect that changes in assessment will continue to be predominantly technical in nature, for reasons I shall note presently. Nonetheless, there is little doubt that computers will figure more prominently in literacy assessment (for better and worse). For example:

1. It has apparently become possible for computers to score essay exams reliably, albeit narrowly and conventionally.
2. Because speech recognition is developing apace, it is probably technically possible for a computer to take and analyze a record of a child's oral reading, possibly including continuous alteration of text difficulty.

3. Increasing storage capacity of computers makes it possible for children to build accessible and manageable portfolios of their literate development.
4. Assessment instruments can be brought into the classroom (and the home) through the Internet, including a potentially wide array of different tasks selected for personal and cultural appropriateness.
5. The size and flexibility of computers make it easier for teachers to make ongoing records as they move about the classroom.

It is certainly possible to assess children's reading on computer screens by examining the process—the direction of gaze, order of strategy use, and so forth, a kind of assessment that until recently would have been considered not authentic since it might not transfer to books. Its authenticity, however, increases daily as the computer becomes a more common text source than the book. Indeed, the literacies we are assessing are constantly changing. Many adolescents who spend their free time (and official school time) surfing the Internet are literate in ways barely imagined by their parents. They filter and simultaneously analyze, respond to, and integrate a wide (almost unlimited) array of images, words, and sounds. This is, and will be, the real-world literacy of information, leisure, and commerce, which schools must help students manage and critically analyze. In other words, technology potentially opens a range of interesting assessment options just as it opens an array of different literacies.

Changes in assessment theory also open possibilities. For example, the notion of consequential validity—the idea that the value of an assessment practice cannot be examined without considering its consequences—has reached the assessment mainstream, albeit some 15 years after similar issues became mainstream in educational research. This shift balances attention to technical improvements for measurement accuracy, theoretically making it possible to reconsider the validity of high-stakes testing practices in the light of their destructive effects. However, in the face of this, the trend to use literacy assessment as a tool for management and control and as a gatekeeping device continues to expand. It is increasingly common to have grade-by-grade retention policies enforced by literacy tests. I expect such practices to continue along with the expanding difference between rich and poor.

So much of what we already know about productive and unproductive assessment practices cannot be acted on for cultural or political reasons. We know that program monitoring is best accomplished with careful matrix sampling. However, such systems do not enable the control functions of assessment and are thus eschewed in favor of more expensive and less productive approaches.

The substantial changes in how we understand what it means to be literate—particularly the shift from the autonomous model to the social or ideological—suggest that we should not continue to pursue assessment practices premised on autonomous literacy. Similarly, changes in our understanding of what it means to comprehend and the role of language, culture, and experience in sense making should make multiple-choice testing practices singularly suspect. But putting these understandings into practice in assessment would limit the ever-increasing control function of assessment and increase the legal coats of maintaining the assessment gatekeeping system. It is the accuracy view of literacy (featuring reliability) that will continue to prevail in the courts,

which is why there are such concerns about portfolio and other performance assessment approaches in high-stakes situations and retreats from initially productive implementations.

We can expect high-stakes assessment to continue because the already extreme differences between rich and poor in the United States (and many other countries) continue to escalate. In this context, the combination of a competitive individualism and a meritocracy places tests as the gatekeepers to wealth and opportunity. Tests, particularly literacy tests, are the means of bloodlessly maintaining class differences. Consequently, although the ways teachers and students assess development will remain the most significant assessments, they will continue to attract less interest and fewer resources than technical advances and marketing of testing instruments.

Though my predictions so far seem pessimistic, there is always some ebb and flow in social evolution. I am optimistic that our increased understanding of the social and contextual nature of literacy and learning will compel us to transform some assessment practices. For example, classroom assessment will, I believe, come to include not just what the child knows and can do, but the classroom circumstances in which children, individually and collaboratively, know and do literate acts. But for this to happen, cultural beliefs and values—the conversations within which assessments are generated—must change. It might also be necessary to change the stakes.

CHAPTER REFERENCES

Huey, E. (1908). *The psychology and pedagogy of reading.* New York: Macmillan.

Judd, C. H. (1914). Reading tests. *Elementary School Journal, 14*, 365–373.

Monroe, M. (1937). General principles of diagnosis of reading disability. *Remedial reading.* Boston: Houghton Mifflin, pp. 12–17.

Smith, N. B. (2002). *American reading instruction.* Newark, DE: International Reading Association. (Original work published 1934)

Tierney, R. J., Moore, D. W., Valencia, S. W., & Johnston, P. (2000). How will literacy be measured in the next millennium? *Reading Research Quarterly, 35*, 244–250.

Traxler, A. E. (1958). Values and limitations of standardized reading tests. In H. M. Robinson (Ed.), *Evaluation of Reading* (pp. 111–117). Chicago: University of Chicago Press.

ANNOTATED BIBLIOGRAPHY

Calfree, R., & Hiebert, E. (1990). Classroom assessment of reading. In R. Barr, M. L., Kamil, P. Mosenthal, & P. D. Pearson (Eds.), *Handbook of reading research, volume II* (pp. 281–309). White Plains, NY: Longman.

Details the early development of the measurement of reading tests with particular emphasis on the use of various types of tests in the classroom setting.

Durrell, D. D. (1935). Tests and corrective procedures for reading disabilities. *The Elementary English Review, 12,* 91–95.

Discusses not only the assessment of reading skills using formal and informal approaches, but also includes information on related results based on various types of test results.

Farr, R. (1970). The fallacies of testing. (ERIC Document Reproduction Service No. ED040020).

Details three major questions in reading assessment, namely: (1) What are the demands for reading assessment and how have these demands increased?; (2) How adequately do present standardized reading tests meet these demands?; and (3) What possible approaches exist for developing assessment procedures that meet these demands?

Gray, W. S. (1916). Methods of testing reading. *Elementary School Journal, 16,* 231–246; 281–298.

An extensive discussion of the assessment of reading ability, divided into sections related to silent and oral reading and the speed of reading.

Gray, W. S. (1920). Value of informal tests of reading accomplishment. *Journal of Educational Research, 1,* 103–111.

Written by one of the leading literacy educators of the previous century, describes the role of informal

assessment of reading, noting the important strengths of this approach.

Jorgensen, A. N. (1932). Use of diagnostic tests in teaching silent reading. *The Elementary English Review, 9,* 86–88; 107.

Suggests in various ways how diagnostic reading tests can be used as a means for effective teaching, especially as they relate to silent reading.

Kirkpatrick, E. A. (1907). A vocabulary test. *Popular Science, 70,* 157–164.

An important article in the development and use of one of the first tests of vocabulary knowledge.

Robinson, H. M. (1946). *Why pupils fail in reading: A study of causes and remedial treatment.* Chicago: University of Chicago Press.

Considered a landmark work in the history of the diagnosis and remediation of reading difficulties. Of particular note is the extensive discussion of the effective use of a variety of assessment procedures to better understand reading problems.

Shiel, G., & Cosgrove, J. (2002). International assessment of reading literacy. *The Reading Teacher, 55,* 690–692.

A discussion of the role of international assessment in various countries, noting in particular what is measured and how the results of these tests are used.

Whipple, G. M. (1908). Vocabulary and word building tests. *The Psychological Review, 15,* 94–105.

An early article on the assessment of reading ability, particularly as it relates to vocabulary development.

YOU BECOME INVOLVED

Many issues in the area of reading assessment have been of concern from early in the history of U.S. literacy education. Based on the articles in this chapter you might consider the following points for thought.

The first article by Judd (1914) identifies a number of issues related to literacy assessment that for the most part remain unanswered even today.

- This article discusses a number of fundamental concerns in literacy assessment. Why do you think that after almost one hundred years many

of these assessment problems remain unanswered today?

- What do you think are some implications of Judd's article for your current views and uses of various types of reading assessment in your classroom literacy program?

Monroe (1937) stresses the fact that in most instances reading disability is the result of a number of causes.

- Why do many current literacy assessment programs tend to be based on the belief that students' reading problems are primarily the result of one or a limited number of causes?
- Based on your teaching experiences, what do you believe are some of the primary causes of reading disability? Have these causes changed dramatically over time or are they similar to those identified by Monroe?

Traxler (1958) notes a number of problems with the use of standardized reading assessment procedures.

- What are some of the specific problems and limitations of standardized reading tests identified in this article? In your opinion have these problems changed or are they basically the same for today's literacy testing?
- Have any of these problems associated with the testing of reading, as identified by Traxler, influenced your current teaching of reading? If so, in what ways have you tried to deal with these assessment concerns in your use of the results of standardized reading tests?

The final article by Tierney, Moore, Valencia, and Johnson (2000) represents a current collective view of the field of reading assessment.

- What do these authors identify as being some of the major issues facing teachers today in the use of various types of reading assessment?

- What are some of the suggestions made in these articles for how teachers can use the results of reading tests in an effective classroom reading program?
- Based on your reading of these four opinions, what do you see as some specific applications of these ideas in your own teaching of reading?

In summary, after reading the articles in this chapter on literacy assessment what are some of the important issues that remain unresolved, even since the beginning of reading instruction? For instance,

- How have the purposes and procedures of literacy testing changed from its beginning through today?
- What have been some of the specific purposes for reading assessment in the past and how have they changed today?
- What have been some of the outcomes of literacy assessment, both in the past and today? Examples beyond the testing of student reading achievement might include the measurement of teacher performance, the effectiveness of specific reading programs and materials, and comparison of school and state reading excellence. How do you feel about these uses of literacy tests?

CHAPTER 3

PHONICS

To teach reading as mere combination of letters which do not teach anything, which are often unintelligible to young persons and which leave minds in states of listless curiosity and total ignorance is a waste of time.

—David Blair
The Class Book (1806)

The fact that instruction in phonics has endured through all these years attests to its value. The fact that it has undergone so many changes attests to the open-mindedness of school people, their willingness to modify practices, and their continuous quest for improvement. . . .

—Nila Banton Smith
Phonics in Beginning Reading (1955)

There is in fact, no evidence—in the NRP Report [National Reading Report] or elsewhere—that children must develop phonemic awareness or phonics before they begin to read.

—Joanne Yatvin, Constance Weaver, Elaine Garan
"Reading First: Cautions and Recommendations" *Language Arts* (2003)

The debate related to phonics instruction has been a center of attention for both educators and the general public throughout most of the history of literacy education. Questions have prevailed as to the role of phonics in an effective reading program, the use of appropriate teaching techniques and materials, and even the basic definition of what is meant by the term *phonics*. In response to these concerns, educators have developed a great variety of approaches and programs that have ranged from total immersion to no phonics at all. Educators with either of these extreme views, as well as those of more moderate persuasion, have generated countless books, papers, and professional debates advocating their particular positions on phonics and its role in literacy education.

From a historical perspective it is interesting to note how little the debates on phonics concerns have expanded beyond relatively few central issues. Issues of importance to educators about the role of phonics in the reading process fifty or even one hundred years ago are in many instances still unresolved and debated today. These dominant questions about phonics instruction can be summarized as follows.

- What does the term *phonics* mean?
- What are the basic components of an effective phonics program?
- If and when should phonics be taught in the typical classroom literacy program?
- What are the most useful phonics materials for basic instruction?
- How can phonics knowledge best be measured—through formal or informal assessment procedures?

DIVERSITY IN THE TEACHING OF PHONICS SKILLS

The following historical statements from two of the leaders in the field of reading education clearly illustrate the wide diversity of opinion that has existed on the use of phonics in the teaching of reading (Lohmann, 1930).

Edmund Huey in his classic book *Psychology and Pedagogy of Reading* (1908) notes the following related to phonics.

> Studies in the psychology and physiology of speech indicate that any but the most incidental analysis of spoken language, such as phonics, is dangerous before the age of eight or nine and in my opinion the necessities of reading do not demand it before the latter age at the earliest. (p. 352)

William S. Gray (1920), perhaps the leading literacy researcher of the last century, takes a different view of the teaching of phonics.

> Independence in the recognition of words should be developed in the early grades by means of word study and phonetic analysis. . . . Phonic analysis should be introduced in special drill periods after the pupils have begun to note similarities and differences in the words which they have learned in reading exercises. It is the judgment of the writer that detailed studies of words should be made during drill periods set aside for this purpose. If such studies are made during the regular reading period there is danger that attention will shift from the content of what is read to the study of individual words. If the basic training in the analysis of words is given during drill periods, the information and skill thus secured can be applied quickly and effectively during reading exercises without withdrawing attention from the content of what is read. (pp. 32–33)

AS YOU READ

The following articles represent a sampling of viewpoints related to the long history of the controversy related to the role of phonics in classroom literacy programs. These papers have been selected not because they necessarily take a particular viewpoint on the teaching of phonics, but rather to illustrate the historical development of thinking on this aspect of reading education. Note in particular the continuing emphasis placed by these various authors on balance in the effective use of phonics.

Phonics or No Phonics?

LILLIAN BEATRICE CURRIER AND OLIVE C. DUGUID

The first article, a brief one by Currier and Duguid (1916), is included for several reasons. It is one of the first references in literacy research to the discussion of the primary role of phonics in reading. It is also an article that is often referenced by subsequent literacy researchers and writers. Finally the title of this article, "Phonics or No Phonics?" expresses what is perhaps the central theme repeated throughout much of the subsequent work in this area.

Many are doubtless endeavoring to decide as to the most efficient method of teaching primary reading, whether through phonetic drills or otherwise.

To those who are interested in determining the value of phonics as related to primary reading, this test may prove helpful.

The experiment was carried on in the first and second grades. In each grade two classes of equal size and equal average ability were formed, and in each one division was given through phonetic drills. All words were developed phonetically. The other classes had no knowledge whatever of phonics. Words were developed by quick-perception and sense-content methods.

During the year the following observations were made in both grades.

The phonic classes so concentrated upon letter sounds that the attention was diverted from the sense of the paragraph to word pronunciation. This brought about lack of interest and fatigue and destroyed the pleasure which the story should yield. The reading was generally less smooth, slower, and the idea confused.

The classes having no phonics were found to enjoy reading for the sake of the study. From the story they got the sense-content. They were less careful and less correct than the phonic classes in regard to word pronunciation. Keeping the sense in mind, they often substituted words from their own vocabulary for difficult or unfamiliar words in the text. They read more swiftly and with more expression. Fatigue was reduced, because curiosity in the story held the interest and caused the attention to be focused upon the outcome of the story.

From time to time stories with which the children were unfamiliar were assigned for them to read silently, entirely unassisted. At a signal, books were closed and the pupils were asked to reproduce what they had read. Many of the children of the phonic classes, although very accurate in word pronunciation, were almost helpless when this reproduction was required. Those in the nonphonic classes were, in most cases, able to give clear ideas of the contents.

As a final test in June, the superintendent gave to all classes books which they had never before seen, and stories were chosen which were also new.

No words were developed in preparation for any class. The ability of the classes in attacking new words was found to be about the same, although the class having no phonics read more rapidly, more expressively, but less accurately.

In special cases these observations were made, which have proved valuable: Foreign children, those having impediments of speech, and those who had previously formed bad habits of pronunciation were greatly benefited through the phonetic drills. Certain hesitant, expressionless, and habitually slow readers were gently helped in overcoming these faults by the rapid work required in the quick-perception and sense-content methods.

The Present Situation in Phonics

NILA BANTON SMITH

The second article, by the noted literacy historian Nila Banton Smith (1927), discusses the fundamental question of whether phonics should be taught in reading instruction. The author's response to this important query is simply to take a "common sense middle course." Note the emphasis placed on the importance of meaning as a part of effective phonics instruction.

Probably there is no other subject in the school curriculum which is the topic of greater controversy than that of phonics. The varying and diverse opinions on this subject could be arranged in a perfect scale beginning at one extreme with those who believe that no phonics at all should be taught, and ranging up to the other extreme represented by those who are convinced that the teaching of phonics should dominate all other subjects in the field of primary instruction. It is unfortunate that so many angles of this important problem should be left to *opinion,* but until more extensive investigations have been made, this must necessarily be the case. In the meantime, teachers are much perplexed as to what course to pursue in their classrooms, and one constantly hears them asking such questions as these: Shall we teach phonics? If so, *when* shall we teach them? *What* processes and elements shall we teach? *How* shall we teach them?

Each of these points will be discussed briefly in this article. Conclusions will be drawn from the results of scientific research in connection with phases of the problem which have been investigated. In the absence of such evidence, generalizations and interpretations will be based upon classroom observations and diagnosis resulting from supervisory contact with the many types of children and teachers which one finds present in a representative city system. However, the writer has no thought of making any *final* decisions in this matter. The article is written only in the hope of setting up some *temporary* guide posts for those who have not had the time or opportunity to pursue recent developments in this field, and to challenge additional research on the part of those who are in a position to conduct such studies.

SHALL WE TEACH WORD ANALYSIS?

Many different investigations have been conducted for the purpose of trying to find an answer to this question. The results of these investigations have been so varied that on the face of things, it would seem we are as far from an answer as ever. However, when all angles of the different situations are properly interpreted and the results amalgamated the conclusions drawn from these investigations lose much of the contradictory aspect which they assume at first appearance.

Some investigators have shown that as the pupils *sight-word* vocabulary increases in size and complexity that some sort of analysis of words is necessary in order that periods of confusion be avoided. They show further that most pupils require definite assistance in learning economical methods of attacking new words if they are to become independent readers.

A second group of educators believes that phonic training is positively harmful. They have shown that over-emphasis of phonics early in the child's reading experiences has led to such serious difficulties as: habit of progressing in very small units, thereby inhibiting development of speed; habit of too explicit articulation, thus retarding speed; habit of looking directly at each word during the process of pronunciation, thus encouraging a very narrow eye-voice span; habit of reacting primarily to the pronunciation stimulation, and disregarding comprehension. While these investigators have proved that such habits will become fixed and almost impossible to eradicate when phonics are over-emphasized for a long period of time to the exclusion of training in thought-getting and speed, others have proved that when phonics are taught moderately and the other phases of reading are also emphasized, that these undesirable habits will be only temporary ones.

A third group of investigators has evidence that children do not need phonics at all, in that they naturally and unconsciously generalize sounds and make use of phonic analysis from the beginning without having received any training whatever along this line. The investigators who have drawn these conclusions, however, have used for the material of their experimentation, only one or two small groups of children, one or both of which were composed of the select type which one finds in a college training school. The writer's experiments with the general rank and file of pupils which one finds in the large city school system, reveals the fact that cases in which first grade children learn to generalize and blend sounds without training are very much in the minority. A survey of 10,000 first grade children in Detroit showed that only two percent of them possessed this natural phonetic sense which they developed and applied unaided.

In case a child does develop this natural ability to solve new words independently, it is, of course, a waste of time to teach phonics to him. He might better be excused from such practice and be provided with various types of instruction designed to develop important reading abilities, other than that of word recognition.

On the other hand, since the ability to recognize words is so basic that all other reading abilities are to a large extent dependent upon it, and since, so far as we know at present, training in word analysis is the best method of developing this power, it would seem highly advantageous to provide such training to the great mass of children who do not possess this natural phonetic sense.

Of course, the formal phonetic methods which subordinated practice in all other reading abilities to that of skillful juggling with word elements should not be countenanced in modern teaching. I refer to those methods in which even the content of the readers was written for the sole purpose of giving practice in phonics, all of the early reading consisting of sentences of this type, "Kate ate a date," "Nan ran for the fan," etc.

While it is true that there is much to be condemned in these formal phonetic methods, it is equally true that we have not sufficient evidence at the present time to warrant us in going to the other extreme of providing no training whatever in word analysis. Perhaps there are more effective ways of developing ability to attack new words than those which we already know, but at any rate, such methods have not yet been practically formulated even by those who are strongest in denouncing our present methods. In the meantime, we must remember that thousands of children are passing through our schools each semester and must be given the best training which we know how to give them at the present time. Consequently, we should not hastily discard those methods with which we are already familiar, of developing ability to attack new words until we have something better with which to replace them.

Rather than go either to the extreme of giving phonics precedence over all other phases of reading instruction or to the other extreme of teaching no phonics at all, let us take our place for the time being midway in the scale of advocates and promote a common sense middle course. Let us select the best from our present methods and instruct those pupils who would profit by such methods, but at the same time take care never to sacrifice vital, interesting content, and definite, specific training designed to develop other fundamental reading habits.

It is with this attitude toward a middle course for the time being that the recommendations in the remainder of this article are made.

WHEN SHALL WE TEACH WORD ANALYSIS?

After having decided to teach word analysis, the question arises, "*When* shall we begin this important study?" The general tendency is to defer such training until after the early stages of beginning reading, rather than start it at the very beginning of the term as was the practice a few years ago. Let us consider the specific reasons for this delay.

WHY SHOULD WORD ANALYSIS BE DELAYED?

1. Children should first acquire a large enough reading vocabulary of word wholes to represent the letter sounds which are later to be taught, so that they may generalize from known words those sounds needed in unlocking new words. For example, if we are to teach the consonant *f,* the child should previously have had experience in recognizing a few words beginning with *f,* such as *fox, fat, for.*

2. Children should acquire the attitude of reading for *meanings* in word and sentence wholes, before directing their attention to the analysis of words—an activity which is likely to distract temporarily from their learning meaning concepts.

3. It is important to make a start in the type of reading which is conducive to the establishment of good eye habits, before causing the children to concentrate on the smaller units within words.

4. The complex activity of mastering the early mechanics of reading is too heavy for both teacher and children if the additional subjects of phonics is introduced during the first few weeks.

WHEN ARE CHILDREN READY FOR PRACTICE IN THE WORD-GETTING PROCESSES?

Granted that it is advisable to defer the teaching of phonics at the beginning of the term, just when then are children ready for such practice? It would seem that the best guides which we can use at the present time in determining this point are those listed below:

1. When the child has developed a desire to read,

2. When he has mastered the very early mechanics of reading,

3. When he has mastered a reading vocabulary large enough to represent the most common sound. (Such a vocabulary gives him a basis from which he may generalize sounds needed in unlocking new words.)

4. When he has had practice in reading a quantity of narrative material,

5. When he has enjoyed Mother Goose rhymes and other simple poems which cause his ear to be sensitive to rhyme words,

6. When he, of his own accord, begins to notice likenesses and differences in words.

WHAT CONTENT AND PROCESSES SHALL WE TEACH?

Having determined at what time it is desirable to begin teaching word analysis, the question immediately arises as to what processes and content should be taught. Fortunately we have scientific evidence which enables us to give a definite answer to this question.

WHAT PROCESSES SHALL WE TEACH?

Every primary teacher has noticed that some pupils have the natural phonetic sense mentioned above, in other words, they seem to have some special aptitude for successfully attacking new words without having had phonetic training. In considering this point, two questions arose in the mind of the writer: "What are the natural methods of attack developed and used by the children themselves?" And then, "Would the children who have no methods of their own develop more rapidly if given training through methods naturally used by other children, rather than through artificial methods devised by an adult who makes up a scheme because it seems logical from his point of view?"

In an attempt to answer the first question, an investigation was carried on with four hundred Detroit children who had finished reading Picture-Story material, Series I, and were reading out of other primers, without having had any training at all in word analysis.

As a child read orally, the teacher carefully observed his behavior when attacking a new word, and after he had solved it, she questioned him minutely to ascertain his exact method of attack. Then she recorded the method on a blank provided for that purpose.

The result of this investigation revealed the following methods of attack and their frequencies:

Methods of Attack

PUPILS SOLVED THE NEW WORDS BY:	CASES
1. Fitting them into the context of the sentence	68
2. Looking at an accompanying picture	67
3. Analyzing or synthesizing compound words.	43
4. Analyzing a known word to get a smaller unknown word within	40
5. Comparing the new word with the rhyme word	39
6. Combining a generalized consonant with a letter group	24
7. Applying a vowel sound after generalizing it from a familiar word	19
8. Sounding syllables	7
9. Spelling word	3
10. Sounding letters	2

The method of sounding syllables, spelling, and sounding letters occurred with such a small frequency that the children who used these methods were further investigated and it was found that they were "repeaters" who had phonetic training the previous term; so these cannot be counted as natural methods of attack.

In the light of this investigation it is quite obvious that we have not been putting sufficient emphasis upon methods of attack other than learning the sounds of letters and letter groups. To be sure, good teachers have always called attention to these other methods of attack incidentally, but the findings of this study justify us in the belief that the system which would be most effective in developing power in the word-getting processes is one in which all these methods of attack are taught systematically and thoroughly as needed. . . .

The Utility of Phonic Generalizations in the Primary Grades

THEODORE CLYMER

The next article, by Clymer (1963), is considered by many reading authorities to be a classic in the field of literacy education. The author discusses the value of a number of often taught phonic generalizations and finds that many have limited usefulness. As you read this article you might consider how many of these rules you may have learned as a student or have taught as a teacher.

The origins of this study go back to Kenneth, an extraordinary elementary pupil. Prior to my encounter with Kenneth I had completed a reading methods course in a small teachers college, which provided a background in the principles of teaching reading as well as a good introduction to techniques. Among these techniques were procedures to develop phonic generalizations and also *the* list (not *a* list) of the most valuable generalizations to develop. (To those of you who might like copies of the list, I am sad to report that somehow through the years it has been lost.)

Difficulties with Kenneth began as the class reviewed phonic generalizations at the start of the school year. Our procedures were like those used in many classrooms: Groups of words were presented, and the class analyzed their likenesses and differences with a view toward deriving a generalization about relationships between certain letters and sounds or the position and pronunciation of vowels.

Throughout these exercises, following the dictum of my reading methods teacher, we were careful not to call the generalizations "rules," for all our statements had a number of exceptions. As the class finally formulated a generalization regarding the relationships of letters, letter position, and sounds, such defensive phrasing as "most of the time," "usually," and "often" appeared as protective measures. We also spent time listing some of the exceptions to our generalizations.

At this point Kenneth entered the discussion. While the class was busily engaged in developing the generalization, Kenneth had skimmed his dictionary, locating long lists of exceptions to the generalization. In fact, he often located more exceptions than I could list applications. When I protested—somewhat weakly—that the dictionary contained many unusual words, Kenneth continued his role as an educational scientist. He turned to the basic reader word list in the back of his text and produced nearly similar results. Today, of course, Kenneth's behavior would be rated as "gifted," "talented," or "creative"—although I remember discussing him in other terms as I sat in the teachers' lounge.

As Kenneth had provided a memorable and even a "rich" learning experience for me, he furnished the impetus for a series of studies which will attempt to answer three questions: (1) What phonic generalizations are being taught in basic reading programs for the primary grades? (2) To what extent are these generalizations useful in having a "reasonable" degree of application to words commonly met in primary grade material? (3) Which of the generalizations that stand the test of question 2 can be learned and successfully applied to unknown words by primary children?

WHAT GENERALIZATIONS ARE TAUGHT?

Four widely used sets of readers were selected to determine the phonic generalizations being taught in the primary grades. After a preliminary study of the manuals, workbooks, and readers, the manuals were selected as the source of the generalizations. The manuals presented the generalizations in three ways: (1) statements to be taught to the pupils, (2) statements to be derived by the pupils after inductive teaching, and (3) statements with no clear indication as to what was to be done. Generalizations presented by all three means were included in the analysis.

Five general types of generalizations emerged from the study of the teachers' manuals. These types dealt with (1) vowels, (2) consonants, (3) endings, (4) syllabication, and (5) miscellaneous relationships. Arbitrary decisions were made in assigning some generalizations to one or another of the five types since certain statements might easily be classified under two or more headings.

If we eliminate from our consideration the miscellaneous type of generalization, a total of 121 different statements were located. There were 50 vowel generalizations, 15 consonant generalizations, and 28 generalizations in each of the ending and syllabication groups. In evaluating these figures it should be kept in mind that any statement was considered a separate generalization when its phrasing excluded or included different sets of words than another statement.

For example, the generalization, "When there are two vowels side by side, the long sound of the first is heard and the second one is usually silent" and "When *ea* come together in a word, the first letter is long and the second is silent" were counted as two separate generalizations, although the second statement is a special application of the first.

While not directly related to our discussion here, note should be made of the wide variation of grade level of introduction, emphasis, and phrasing of the generalizations. Of the 50 different vowel generalizations, only 11 were common to all four series. None of these 11 was presented initially at the same half-year grade level in all four series. Some series gave a much greater emphasis to the generalizations than did other series. One publisher introduced only 33 of the 121 generalizations, while another presented 68. These comments are not meant to detract from the usefulness of basic materials, but simply to point out some of their differences. These differences do call for careful adjustments in the classroom when pupils are moved from one set of materials to another. The teacher who changes from series X to series Y may need to make some important revisions in his word recognition program. These findings may indicate also the need for further experimentation on emphasis and the developmental aspects of our word recognition program.

WHICH GENERALIZATIONS ARE USEFUL?

Forty-five of the generalizations given in the manuals were selected for further study. The selection of these was somewhat arbitrary. The main criterion was to ask, "Is the generalization stated specifically enough so that it can be said to aid or hinder in the pronunciation of a particular word?" An example or two will make our criterion clear. The generalization, "Long *o* makes a sound like its name," is undoubtedly a valuable generalization, but it was not specific enough to meet our criterion. On the other hand, the statement, "When a vowel is in the middle of a one syllable word, the vowel is short," was included because we could judge by reference to a word list how often one syllable words with a vowel in the middle do in fact have a short vowel sound.

Our next problem was to develop a word list on which we could test the generalizations. A reasonable approach seemed to be that of making up a composite list of all the words introduced in the four basic series from which the generalizations were drawn, plus the words from the Gates Reading Vocabulary for the Primary Grades. Once this list of some twenty-six hundred words was prepared, the following steps were taken:

1. The phonetic respelling and the syllabic division of all words were recorded. Webster's *New Collegiate Dictionary* was used as the authority for this information.

2. Each phonic generalization was checked against the words in the composite list to determine (a) the words which were pronounced as the generalization claimed and (b) the words which were exceptions to the generalization.

3. A "percent of utility" was computed for each generalization by dividing the number of words pronounced as the generalization claimed by the total number of words to which the generalization could be expected to apply. For example, if the generalization claimed that "When the letters *oa* are together in a word, *o* always gives its long sound and the *a* is silent," all words containing *oa* were located in the list. The number of these words was the total number of words to which the generalization should apply. Then the phonetic spellings of these words were examined to see how many words containing *oa* actually did have the long *o* followed by the silent *a*. In this case thirty words were located which contained *oa*. Twenty-nine of these were pronounced as the generalization claimed; one was not. The percent of utility became 29/30 or 97. This procedure was followed for all generalizations.

When the percent of utility was completed for each generalization, we set two criteria as to what constituted a "reasonable" degree of application. We have no scientific evidence to demonstrate that these criteria are valid; it can only be said that they seemed reasonable to us.

The first criterion was that the composite word list must contain a minimum of twenty words to which the generalization might apply. Generalizations with lower frequencies of application do not seem to merit instructional time.

The second criterion was a percent of utility of at least 75. To state the matter another way, if the pupil applied the generalization to twenty words, it should aid him in getting the correct pronunciation in fifteen of the twenty words.

The table gives the results of our analysis of the forty-five phonic generalizations. An inspection of the data leaves me somewhat confused as to the value of generalizations. Some time-honored customs in the teaching of reading may be in need of revision.

Certain generalizations apply to large numbers of words and are rather constant in providing the correct pronunciation of words. (See, for example, generalizations 19, 35, and 36.)

A group of generalizations seem to be useful only after the pupil can pronounce the word. Generalizations which specify vowel pronunciation in stressed syllables require that the pupil know the pronunciation of the word before he can apply the generalization. (See, for example, generalization 33.) This criticism assumes, of course, that the purpose of a generalization is to help the child unlock the pronunciation of *unknown* words.

The usefulness of certain generalizations depends upon regional pronunciations. While following Webster's markings, generalization 34 is rejected. Midwestern pronunciation makes this generalization rather useful, although we reject it because we used Webster as the authority. Such problems are natural, and we should not hold it against Mr. Webster that he came from New England.

If we adhere to the criteria set up at the beginning of the study, of the forty-five generalizations only eighteen, numbers 5, 8, 10, 16, 20, 21, 22, 23, 25, 28, 29, 30, 31, 32, 40, 41, 44, and 45 are useful. Some of the generalizations which failed to meet our criteria might be useful if stated in different terms or if restricted to certain types of words. We are studying these problems at the present time. We are also examining other generalizations which we did not test in this study.

CONCLUSION

In evaluating this initial venture in testing the utility of phonic generalizations, it seems quite clear that many generalizations which are commonly taught are of limited value. Certainly the study indicates that we should give careful attention to pointing out the many exceptions to most of the generalizations that we teach. Current "extrinsic" phonics programs which present large numbers of generalizations are open to question on the basis of this study.

This study does not, of course, answer the question of which generalizations primary children can apply in working out the pronunciation of unknown words. The answer to the question of the primary child's ability to apply these and other generalizations will come only through classroom experimentation. Also, this study does not establish the percent of utility required for a generalization to be useful. The percentage suggested here (75) may be too high. Classroom research might reveal that generalizations with lower percentages of utility should be taught because they encourage children to examine words for sound and letter relationships.

The most disturbing fact to come from the study may be the rather dismal failure of generalization 1 to provide the correct pronunciation even 50 percent of the time. As one teacher remarked when this study was presented to a reading methods class, "Mr. Clymer, for years I've been teaching 'When two vowels go walking, the first one does the talking.' You're ruining the romance in the teaching of reading!"

The Utility of Forty-Five Phonic Generalizations

*GENERALIZATION	NO. OF WORDS CONFORMING	NO. OF EXCEPTIONS	PERCENT OF UTILITY
1. When there are two vowels side by side, the long sound of the first one is heard and the second is usually silent.	309 (bead)†	377 (chief)†	45
2. When a vowel is in the middle of a one syllable word, the vowel is short.	408	249	62
middle letter	191 (dress)	84 (scold)	69
one of the middle two letters in a word of four letters	191 (rest)	135 (told)	59
one vowel *within* a word of more than four letters	26 (splash)	30 (fight)	46
3. If the only vowel letter is at the end of a word, the letter usually stands for a long sound.	23 (he)	8 (to)	74
4. When there are two vowels, one of which is final *e*, the first vowel is long and the *e* is silent.	180 (bone)	108 (done)	63
*5. The *r* gives the preceding vowel a sound that is neither long nor short.	484 (horn)	134 (wire)	78
6. The first vowel is usually long and the second silent in the digraphs *ai, ea, oa,* and *ui.*	179	92	66
ai	43 (nail)	24 (said)	64
ea	101 (bead)	51 (head)	66
oa	34 (boat)	1 (cupboard)	97
ui	1 (suit)	16 (build)	6
7. In the phonogram *ie,* the *i* is silent and the *e* has a long sound.	8 (field)	39 (friend)	17
*8. Words having double *e* usually have the long *e* sound.	85 (seem)	2 (been)	98
9. When words end with silent *e,* the preceding *a* or *i* is long.	164 (cake)	108 (have)	60
*10. In *ay* the *y* is silent and gives *a* its long sound.	36 (play)	10 (always)	78
11. When the letter *i* is followed by the letters *gh* the *i* usually stands for its long sound and the *gh* is silent.	22 (high)	9 (neighbor)	71
12. When *a* follows *w* in a word, it usually has the sound *a* as in *was.*	15 (watch)	32 (swam)	32
13. When *e* is followed by *w,* the vowel sound is the same as represented by *oo.*	9 (blew)	17 (sew)	35
14. The two letters *ow* make the long *o* sound.	50 (own)	35 (down)	59
15. W is sometimes a vowel and follows the vowel digraph rule.	50 (crow)	75 (threw)	40
*16. When *y* is the final letter in a word, it usually has a vowel sound.	169 (dry)	32 (tray)	84

† Words in parentheses are examples—either of words which conform or of exceptions, depending on the column.

* Generalizations marked with an asterisk were found "useful" according to the criteria.

The Utility of Forty-Five Phonic Generalizations *continued*

*GENERALIZATION	NO. OF WORDS CONFORMING	NO. OF EXCEPTIONS	PERCENT OF UTILITY
17. When *y* is used as a vowel in words, it sometimes has the sound of long *i*.	29 (fly)	170 (funny)	15
18. The letter *a* has the same sound (ô) when followed by *l*, *w*, and *u*.	61 (all)	65 (canal)	48
19. When *a* is followed by *r* and final *e*, we expect to hear the sound heard in *care*.	9 (dare)	1 (are)	90
*20. When *c* and *h* are next to each other, they make only one sound.	103 (peach)	0	100
*21. *Ch* is usually pronounced as it is in *kitchen*, *catch*, and *chair*, not like *sh*.	99 (catch)	5 (machine)	95
*22. When *c* is followed by *e* or *i*, the sound of *s* is likely to be heard.	66 (cent)	3 (ocean)	96
*23. When the letter *c* is followed by *o* or *a* the sound of *k* is likely to be heard.	143 (camp)	0	100
24. The letter *g* often has a sound similar to that of *j* in jump when it precedes the letter *i* or *e*.	49 (engine)	28 (give)	64
*25. When *ght* is seen in a word, gh is silent.	30 (fight)	0	100
26. When a word begins *kn*, the *k* is silent.	10 (knife)	0	100
27. When a word begins with *wr*, the *w* is silent.	8 (write)	0	100
*28. When two of the same consonants are side by side only one is heard.	334 (carry)	3 (suggest)	99
*29. When a word ends in *ck*, it has the same last sound as in *look*.	46 (brick)	0	100
*30. In most two-syllable words, the first syllable is accented.	828 (famous)	143 (polite)	85
*31. If *a*, *in*, *re*, *ex*, *de*, or *be* is the first syllable in a word, it is usually unaccented.	86 (belong)	13 (insect)	87
*32. In most two-syllable words that end in a consonant followed by *y*, the first syllable is accented and the last is unaccented.	101 (baby)	4 (supply)	96
33. One vowel letter in an accented syllable has its short sound.	547 (city)	356 (lady)	61
34. When *y* or *ey* is seen in the last syllable that is not accented, the long sound of *e* is heard.	0	157 (baby)	0
35. When *ture* is the final syllable in a word, it is unaccented.	4 (picture)	0	100
36. When *tion* is the final syllable in a word, it is unaccented.	5 (station)	0	100
37. In many two- and three-syllable words, the final *e* lengthens the vowel in the last syllable.	52 (invite)	62 (gasoline)	46
38. If the first vowel sound in a word is followed by two consonants, the first syllable usually ends with the first of the two consonants.	404 (bullet)	159 (singer)	72

† Words in parentheses are examples—either of words which conform or of exceptions, depending on the column.

* Generalizations marked with an asterisk were found "useful" according to the criteria.   *(continued)*

The Utility of Forty-Five Phonic Generalizations *continued*

*GENERALIZATIONS	NO. OF WORDS CONFORMING	NO. OF EXCEPTIONS	PERCENT OF UTILITY
39. If the first vowel sound in a word is followed by a single consonant, that consonant usually begins the second syllable.	190 (over)	237 (oven)	44
*40. If the last syllable of a word ends in *le*, the consonant preceding the *le* usually begins the last syllable.	62 (tumble)	2 (buckle)	97
*41. When the first vowel element in a word is followed by *th, ch,* or *sh,* these symbols are not broken when the word is divided into syllables and may go with either the first or second syllable.	30 (dishes)	0	100
42. In a word of more than one syllable, the letter *v* usually goes with the preceding vowel to form a syllable.	53 (cover)	20 (clover)	73
43. When a word has only one vowel letter, the vowel sound is likely to be short.	433 (hid)	322 (kind)	57
*44. When there is one *e* in a word that ends in a consonant, the *e* usually has a short sound.	85 (leg)	27 (blew)	76
*45. When the last syllable is the sound *r*, it is unaccented.	188 (butter)	9 (appear)	95

† Words in parentheses are examples—either of words which conform or of exceptions, depending on the column.

* Generalizations marked with an asterisk were found "useful" according to the criteria.

Phonics Revisited

A. Sterl Artley

Artley (1977) continues the discussion of the phonics issue, identifying those principles that seem to have the most effectiveness in the reading process. Here again the emphasis is on a balance in the teaching of phonics. Note how he builds on the work of both Smith and Clymer.

One needs only to walk through the exhibits at a meeting of the International Reading Association or to look through any professional journal dealing with reading instruction to note the emphasis being given to phonics. Tapes, records, films, and workbooks are on the market to give instruction, practice, and self-help in the application of phonic principles. Editorials, news articles, and reports advocate a "return" (as though it were not always present) to phonics as a means of preventing reading problems. Individuals, parent groups, and even a "foundation" have been vocal in advocating the early teaching of symbol-sound relations, sound blending, and patterned words. Reading programs and textual materials have been organized on the rationale of the "phonics approach" to instruction. More recently performance-based instruction and management systems have given additional impetus to phonics through narrowly stated learning objectives, many of which deal with phonic "rules." Roma Gans, in discussing the attention given to phonics instruction, quips, "It is easy to understand and accept baseball fans and sports-car enthusiasts, but phonics devotees tax one's comprehension" (1964, p. 46).

One can understand that emphasis given to phonics because its use in the act of reading appears to be so perfectly logical. Language is oral, so goes the reasoning, and writing is a graphic representation of the spoken word. Reading, then, is the act of turning the graphic representation into its spoken counterpart. Since letters and letter combinations (graphemes) stand for spoken sounds (phonemes), reading reverses the process by associating the proper sounds with the letters, thus enabling the reader to pronounce the word and, hence, reconstruct meaning—a deceptively simple process.

This concept of reading, with its related emphasis on phonics, was expressed in the frequently quoted statement from Flesch's *Why Johnny Can't Read:* "Reading means getting meaning from certain combinations of letters. Teach the child what each letter stands for and he can read" (1955, p. 2). Continuing, Flesch wrote, ". . . as soon as you switch to the common-sense method of teaching the sounds of letters, you can give them a little primer and then proceed immediately to anything from the *Reader's Digest to Treasure Island*" (p. 8). In short, Flesch was referring to the use of phonics as a *method* of teaching reading.

Though few people today could accept Flesch's dictum as a rational approach to reading instruction, phonic skills and understandings are

frequently taught as the primary method of word identification. Teachers admonish the reader, on coming to a word that cannot be identified by sight, to "sound it out." And perhaps unwittingly, phonics is still being considered the *method* of teaching reading instead of one of several cue systems that the informed reader has available to comprehend written language.

As the primary means to the identification of unfamiliar words, phonics has certain inherent limitations. In the first place phonic rules and understandings are difficult for many children to learn and apply. We might as well admit it. A programmed "word-attack" text that I have gives instruction for twenty-one "regular" consonants, twenty-five consonant "blends" in the initial and six in the final position, nine consonant digraphs, and thirteen "silent" consonants. For vowels, all the conventionally taught material is included—single vowels, digraphs, blends, vowel generalizations, plus rules for sounds for which vowel letters stand in multi-syllabic words. This is a massive load, even though instruction is spread over two or three years.

But the striking fact is that after all of this content has been taught, assuming that it can be, the symbol-sound relationships in English words are not sufficiently consistent to make it possible to use phonic generalizations with any degree of regularity. If our language were such that each symbol signified one sound, as was attempted in the Initial Teaching Alphabet, one could at least pronounce any word that could be written. But with the twenty-six letters of the alphabet having to stand for some forty different phonemes, real problems arise for the novice reader. Note, for example, the *ea* digraph in these words—*break (brāk), bread (brĕd), near (nǐr), beach (bēch).*

Clear evidence of the problem confronted by the reader who attempts to apply phonic generalizations to the identification of unfamiliar words was dramatized by a series of studies by Clymer (1963), Emans (1967), Bailey (1967), and Burmeister (1968). These studies showed what children discover for themselves—that many of the so-called phonic "rules" don't work. There are too many exceptions. Clymer's study, for example, shows that the commonly taught generalization, "when two vowels go walking . . ." applies to only forty-nine percent of the words frequently met in the primary grades. In fact, of forty-five phonic generalizations studied, Clymer found only eighteen to meet his criteria of usefulness. He concluded that many commonly-taught generalizations are of limited value.

Four years later Emans (1967) investigated the usefulness of Clymer's forty-five generalizations, but used words of intermediate grade level. Emans found that only sixteen rules now met the criteria of usefulness. Some of the generalizations cited by Clymer were no longer useful on levels above the fourth grade, whereas some found useful by Emans were not included on Clymer's list. Emans also pointed out that the utility of a generalization was no indication that it should be taught since some rules may be so complicated that children have difficulty in applying them. It is interesting to note, too, that the "two vowels walking" principle applied to only eighteen percent of the words studied by Emans. The English language is rich and beautiful, but because we have inherited it from so many different sources the grapheme-phoneme patterns are inconsistent and "unlawful."

While discussing phonic generalizations it is worthwhile to note that twenty-seven of the forty-five principles used by Clymer and Emans in their studies had to do with vowels. And it is on "vowel rules" that reading teachers spend the majority of their time teaching, drilling, and testing. Yet, vowels are the least important element to be concerned with in the identification of words. The following sentence with vowels omitted illustrates this fact:

Wh-n h-s s-st-r -p-n-d th- b--k sh- f--nd p-nc-l m-rks -ll -v-r th- p-g-s.

Vowel letters serve as bridges between consonants in spoken words, but serve a minor role in written words. One would have extreme difficulty pronouncing a word without vowels. Try it

for *smtm* (*sometime*) or *brng* (*bring*). Yet if one were to establish the convention that *brng* would be the written symbol signifying "to cause to come," one could use it to convey meaning the same as though it were written *bring*. Though the symbol could not be pronounced it would signify meaning. This illustrates the fact that certain elements included in phonic instruction may be less important than assumed.

The most serious limitation of phonics is yet to come, for regardless, of whether vowels are emphasized or deemphasized, whether generalizations are developed inductively or deductively, whether words are identified by sound blending or by wholes, the implication is that reading is essentially the act of turning printed symbols into speech which, in turn, conveys meaning. In the form of a formula it would be, printed symbol = spoken symbol = meaning. One says (subvocally) or at least thinks the meaning of each word, adds the separate meanings together, and in this manner arrives at the meaning of the sentence.

In the first place the fallacy of such a concept is readily apparent if one could imagine the meaning that a child might construct from reading the Gettysburg Address.

> *Forescore (a score is what we have after a baseball game is played) and seven years ago our fathers (our own and our step-fathers) brought forth on this continent (that's North America) a new nation (that's America or the United States, I think), conceived (I wonder what that means) in liberty (that's what a sailor gets), and dedicated (that's what they did to the building on the corner) to the proposition (that's what they voted on to give the teachers more money) that all men (what about the women?). . . . (Smith, 1983, p. 255)*

In the second place, and most important, psycholinguistic literature is showing very convincingly that reading is not the act of word-by-word identification. A full discussion of this significant insight into language is outside the province of this paper. Language teachers should familiarize themselves with the challenging ideas offered by Goodman and Fleming (1969),

Smith (1971, 1973), Hodges and Rudorf (1972), Wardaugh (1969), Goodman (1972) and others.

Briefly, such writers as these are saying that sentence comprehension, for example, is not the process of identifying the pronunciation and meaning of individual words, with word meaning added to word meaning. Meaning is more than the product of word identification, or in Kolers' words, "Reading is only incidentally visual" (1969, p. 8). Reading is, in fact, a complicated act of processing grammatical information which transcends individual words. Or, said still another way, readers are no more concerned with separate words in reading than they are concerned with separate words in speaking. In speaking, concern is with meaning conveyed as an utterance, not with individual words. As a result, reading instruction should shift emphasis from word perception to comprehension. Instead of stressing the skills involved in word perception, Goodman (1969) contends that more emphasis should be placed on silent reading, taught in such a way that the reader will learn to go from print directly to meaning without resorting to the implicit or explicit use of oral language.

In spite of this contention, the fact remains that there are words on the page with which the reader must deal. One cannot reconstruct meaning from a blank page. Readers do meet words that are not identified. Does phonics still have a place in the identification process?

Goodman (1971) explains how surface structure (writing) is processed into meaning through the use of syntactic, semantic, and graphophonic (phonic) language cues. A syntactic cue is one residing in the syntax and order of words in a sentence. In the sentence, "Bill went to the gas station to fill the tire with air," the reader's intuitive knowledge of word function and word order tells him how the words must fit together to make a logical construction. He knows that the sentence could not read *air the tire,* or *go the to.* A semantic cue is one growing out of the understanding that words in both spoken and written discourse must make sense. Though in the sentence above it would make sense to say, "Fill the

balloon with air," it would not convey meaning were it to read, "Fill the house with air." A phonic cue resides in the letters and letter groups standing for speech sounds. Consequently, if a child has been taught symbol-sound relations, and if the context cues are not adequate to enable the reader to predict the surface structure, there is at hand a very helpful cue. If the word *station* is not recognized immediately as a sight word in our example sentence, the reader's awareness that the word that tells where Bill went must begin with the "st" sound and end with the "n" sound, tells that the word would be *station* rather than *pump* or *house.* The fluent reader uses all three of these cues to reconstruct the writer's message. Because the reader is concerned with meaning or comprehension, the use of these cues is more properly referred to as comprehension strategies or techniques rather than word perception skills.

There is no question about the fact that phonic cues are important in the identification of unfamiliar words, not as the primary means of identification, but as a support to the other cue systems. If one is reading for meaning—and that is what reading is all about—one's intuitive knowledge of language, of the way words must "fit" and make sense, is usually all that is required to enable the reader to predict what the unidentified words must be. Where a choice must be made from among several words, each of which would fit and make sense, phonics becomes an invaluable aid. For example in the sentence, "The postman put a _____ in the mail box," the unknown word might be package, letter, or message. Noting, however, that the word begins with *p* and the "p sound" tells the reader that it would be *package* rather than *letter,* or *message.* "Sounding out" the word is cumbersome, time consuming, and unnecessary. Like the appendix, its usefulness is vestige of the past.

This being true, what should be included in the phonics program to make it a useful aid in word identification? Certainly consonant symbol-sound relationships are important, since words usually begin and/or end with consonants. Instruction would include, of course, the single consonants, consonant digraphs (*ch, th*, etc.) and consonant blends or clusters (*st, bl*, etc.). If one knows that the word begins with /*b*/, /*wh*/, or /*sw*/, this knowledge alone gives the reader a powerful leverage over unfamiliar words.

What about vowels? As was indicated earlier, vowel letters are not as necessary in word identification as we have been led to believe. Certainly children should be taught the difference between consonants and vowels and what it is about vowel letters that make them unique in the alphabet. But the twenty-seven vowel generalizations identified by Clymer would seem to be quite beyond what would be helpful or even necessary.

Artley (1976) in an analysis of the vowels in 644 high utility words met in early reading activities, found that sixty-eight percent of the total number were classified as either "long" or "short." When he added to this number the percentage of indeterminate sounds (ə) in polysyllabic words, the percentage rose to seventy-nine. One could say that in four out of five words met in early reading, the vowel letters will indicate either long or short sounds, as they are referred to, or the schwa, if the vowel letter is in an unstressed position. The above being true, it appears that if a teacher feels impelled to deal with vowel letters and sounds, the reader could be taught the long and short vowel symbol-sound relations, and, on coming to a new word, to try both sounds to discover which pronunciation makes a known word, which fits, and which makes sense in its contextual setting. Such a procedure is used in reference to the *oo's* in words, for example. There is no "rule" that tells the reader whether *oo* in *troop* will signify the sound in *boot* or *foot*.

One will have to try each to see which makes a familiar word. The same is done for the *th* in words. No rule indicates its voiced or unvoiced sound. Where it appears in an unfamiliar word, one must try both to see which makes a word the reader knows.

Following the suggestion above, for example, makes unnecessary the teaching of the rule that in a one-syllable word with a single vowel ending with *e*, the *e* is silent and the vowel will be short if the *e* is preceded by two consonants, and long, if preceded by one (even then *done* will have to be an exception). Rather than trying to remember and apply the "final e rule," the child on reading, "We had a good _____ at the party," will need only to try *tĭme* or *tīme* to see which makes a known word that makes sense in the sentence.

The other vowel principles commonly taught (the "consonant controllers," the two sounds for which the letters *c* and *g* stand, the diphthongs, and vowel digraphs)—those elements which all together constitute the twenty percent of the words surveyed by Artley—can be taught as deviations from the "either long or short" suggestion. The understandings may be developed informally and inductively from words which the child already knows.

The fact still remains that phonic cues are only aids to word identification and not a method of teaching reading. Furthermore, when reading is taught with an emphasis on meaning, contextual cues become preeminent and, as Heilman tersely writes, "In the final analysis, the *optimum* amount of phonics instruction for every child is the *minimum* that he needs to become an independent reader" (1972, p. 280).

REFERENCES

Artley, A. S. "Vowel Values in Early Reading Words." *The Reading Teacher,* in press.

Bailey, Mildred. "The Utility of Phonic Generalizations in Grades One through Six." *The Reading Teacher* 20 (1987): 415–418.

Burmeister, Lou. "Vowel Pairs." *The Reading Teacher* 21 (1968): 445–452.

Clymer, T. "The Utility of Phonic Generalizations in the Primary Grades." *The Reading Teacher* 16 (1963): 252–258.

Emans, R. "The Usefulness of Phonic Generalizations Above the Primary Grades." *The Reading Teacher* 20 (1967): 419–425.

Flesch, R. *Why Johnny Can't Read.* New York: Harper, 1955.

Gans, Roma. *Fact and Fiction About Phonics.* Indianapolis: Bobbs-Merrill, 1964.

Goodman, K. "Words and Morphemes in Reading." In *Psycholinguistics and The Teaching of Reading,* edited by K. Goodman and J. Fleming. Newark, Del: International Reading Association, 1968.

————. "The Search Called Reading." In *Coordinating Reading Instruction,* edited by H. Robinson. Glenview, Ill.: Scott, Foresman, 1971.

————. "The Reading Process: Theory and Practice." In *Language and Learning to Read,* edited by R. Hodges and E. Rudorf. New York: Houghton Mifflin, 1872.

Goodman, K. and Fleming, J. *Psycholinguistics and the Teaching of Reading.* Newark, Del.: International Reading Association, 1969.

Heilman, A. *Principles and Practices of Teaching Reading.* Columbus, Oh.: Charles Merrill, 1972.

Hodges, R. and Rudorf, E. *Language and Learning to Read.* New York: Houghton Mifflin, 1972.

Kolers, P. "Reading is Only Incidentally Visual." In *Psycholinguistics and the Teaching of Reading,* edited by K. Goodman and J. Fleming. Newark, Del.: International Reading Association, 1969.

Smith, F. *Understanding Reading.* New York: Holt, Rinehart and Winston, 1971.

————. *Psycholinguistics and Reading.* New York: Holt, Rinehart and Winston, 1973.

Smith, Nila B. *Reading Instruction for Today's Children.* Englewood Cliffs, N.J.: Prentice-Hall, 1963.

Wardaugh, R. *Reading: A Linguistic Perspective.* New York: Harcourt, Brace, 1969.

Phonics Instruction: Beyond the Debate

Susan Kidd Villaume and Edna Greene Brabham

The final article in this section, by Villaume and Brabham (2003), reflects the latest thinking on phonics methods used in instruction. Again, this material builds on previous research and practice on the effective use of phonics. The authors stress that there are multiple ways to use phonics in reading instruction. Emphasis is placed on the reader knowing and understanding how to use phonic information in the most appropriate manner for each text situation.

The RTEACHER electronic mailing list (listserv) periodically serves as a forum for teachers to discuss phonics instruction. During these online conversations, members often describe their own instructional practices, post the addresses of websites with information about and independent reviews of different phonics programs, and discuss diverse research findings and interpretations. As we visited archived electronic conversations and engaged in new ones with the listserv membership and other educators, we became convinced that most teachers have no desire to take sides in a reading war. They are not searching for an approach to phonics instruction that works equally well for every child, they do not want to set up residency in a "meaning-based" camp or a "code-emphasis" camp, and they do not want to participate in a debate about phonics and whole language. Because these teachers are committed to teaching *all* children to read, they aim for varied, flexible, and responsive phonics instruction. Their instructional belief is consistent with one of the most replicated findings in educational research: Teacher expertise, not teaching method, is the major contributor to student success.

In this month's column, we attempt to capture the complexity and thoughtfulness that permeate teachers' conversations about phonics instruction. These conversations reflect determined efforts to maneuver through research agendas, rise above political debates, and piece together a coherent view of effective phonics instruction. As in previous columns, we blend our thoughts with those of RTEACHER listserv members and the many teachers with whom we work as we explore this important topic.

WHAT IS THE GOAL OF PHONICS INSTRUCTION?

The goal of phonics instruction is to help students develop the alphabetic principle. Students who understand the alphabetic principle know that the sounds of spoken words are mapped onto written words in systematic ways. As students develop understandings of this principle, they become adept at using letter-sound correspondences to figure out unrecognized words. Command of the alphabetic principle is the foundation for accurate word recognition and a prerequisite for fluency—well-documented characteristics of skillful readers. These attributes are critical because they enable readers to invest their energies in the real business of reading—comprehension.

Listserv members agreed that phonics instruction is an essential component of beginning reading instruction. However, participants offered several important reminders: Students' knowledge of the alphabetic system is related in dynamic ways to their knowledge of letter names and their awareness that spoken words consist of sounds or phonemes; the application of the alphabetic principle includes the use of individual letter-sound correspondences as well

as consolidated units of letters recognized as patterns; and knowledge of the alphabetic principle enables readers to approximate pronunciations that they check against words in their oral vocabularies. Listserv members also pointed out that the intention of beginning reading instruction is not only to help students gain control of the alphabetic principle but also to promote an active stance toward learning, foster self-regulating behaviors, and nurture a love of reading. In addition, they emphasized that reading is more than word recognition and that phonics instruction should not crowd out literature- and language-rich instruction.

Inquiry about instructional purposes often launched listserv conversations about current calls for explicit and systematic phonics instruction. As we studied these electronic conversations and revisited professional literature, we noticed inconsistencies in how the terms *explicit* and *systematic* were used. We invited listserv members and the teachers with whom we work to help unravel the multiple uses for these terms in the context of phonics instruction. The ensuing discussions reflected open-minded and probing explorations of how to provide all children with the reading instruction that they need. These conversations also focused on how to provide all teachers with the instructional support that they need.

HOW IS THE TERM *EXPLICIT* USED IN THE CONTEXT OF PHONICS INSTRUCTION?

Dictionary definitions indicate that the word *explicit* may refer to precise, fully developed, clearly expressed instruction. Our explorations revealed two different but related uses for the phrase "explicit phonics instruction." Sometimes the phrase is used to describe the precise, fully developed, and clearly expressed instructions provided to teachers in scripted phonics programs. These programs make it perfectly clear what teachers are to say and do. At other times, explicit phonics instruction is used to describe precise and clearly expressed information about letter-sound correspondences that teachers explain to students—information that may or may not be scripted for teachers. Both of these uses are common. However, dictionary definitions also reveal that *explicit* can be used in reference to precise, fully developed, and well-formulated knowledge. Although references to explicit phonics knowledge are less common than references to explicit phonics instruction, discussions about how to help students develop explicit knowledge of the alphabetic principle bring into focus the goal of phonics instruction.

Explicit Instruction for Teachers

A substantial body of research has attempted to determine whether non-scripted phonics instruction or scripted phonics programs with explicit instruction for teachers lead to greater student achievement. Results of these studies have been inconclusive. Listserv members were not surprised by the conflicting results, but they were perplexed by research efforts that attempted to screen out the contributions of teacher expertise. Many teachers pointed out that scripted instruction may be beneficial in some instructional contexts and constraining in others. For example, some listserv members suggested that explicit, fully developed, and scripted instruction is helpful for some teachers, particularly those in the early stages of their professional development who may not have acquired the requisite expertise to offer more flexible and responsive instruction. In addition, they mentioned that fully developed lessons are instructional assets because few teachers have time to create every lesson from scratch. They also reasoned, however, that scripts cannot capture the interactive and dynamic conversations expert teachers have with their students about the ways that words work.

A long-standing and growing body of research confirms that teacher expertise is a more significant factor in student reading achievement than teaching method. Studies of exemplary teaching identify instructional flexibility and responsiveness as hallmarks of accomplished teachers—teachers whose students consistently outperform their peers in reading achievement. (See pp. 83–84 for references and further readings.) This research describes how the most effective teachers recognize and address student confusion by quickly providing additional clarifying examples and how they notice and respond to a lack of student engagement by changing the pace of the lesson or modifying the activity.

Many listserv members expressed concerns that superficial understandings of the relationship between explicit directions for teachers and reading achievement have resulted in alarming misinterpretations and misapplications of research findings. A few made references to program "police" who appear periodically in their schools to ensure that all teachers are adhering to an instructional script. Other members described administrators who threatened that deviations from scripted programs would be interpreted as insubordination. Such procedures and policies contradict the research evidence demonstrating that exemplary teaching is more akin to masterful orchestration than technical compliance. Understandably, most teachers rail against mandates requiring them to adhere rigidly to directions offered by commercial programs when their own levels of expertise enable them to teach in more powerful ways. Many listserv members suggested that a one-size-fits-all mentality cannot be applied to the instructional supports used by teachers or to the instruction that teachers offer students.

Explicit Instruction for Students

Often the term *explicit* is used to refer to the phonics instruction that teachers offer students. Used in this way, explicit phonics instruction is typically synonymous with direct instruction. In this part-to-whole approach, teachers isolate letter-sound correspondences, teach students how to synthesize the sounds represented by letters, provide blending and spelling practice with words that contain the targeted letter-sound correspondence, and supervise application of this knowledge as students read connected text that is composed primarily of words with taught letter-sound correspondences (i.e., decodable texts).

Certainly, direct instruction in decoding has helped children gain control of the alphabetic principle and develop expertise in tackling unrecognized words. Although many teachers acknowledged the benefits of direct instruction, they did not view it is a panacea. Teachers shared concerns based on their own experiences and observations. These concerns included teachers proceeding through direct instruction lessons oblivious to students' lack of phonemic awareness, unwavering in their procedures even though student participation had become mechanical and passive, inattentive to students' confusions about examples (e.g., in much of the southeastern United States, the majority of students and teachers pronounce *hen* with a short *i* not a short *e*), or unaware that students already knew what was being taught. These observations help explain research results that show explicit phonics instruction is used by both more and less effective teachers. Listserv members and teachers with whom we work suggested that what matters most about instruction is that students develop explicit understandings of the alphabetic principle—understandings that are precise, fully developed, and well formulated.

Explicit Student Knowledge

Many teachers and researchers have observed that explicit understanding or cognitive clarity about the alphabetic principle emerges not from a single instructional approach but from instruction that integrates aspects of direct, part-to-whole instruction and embedded, whole-to-part-to-whole instruction. In embedded phonics instruction, teachers assist students in developing explicit understandings of the alphabetic principle through guided discovery and analysis. They draw students' attention to a targeted letter-sound correspondence found in a familiar text or a writing experience. Teachers engage students in reading and spelling words with the targeted letter-sound correspondence as they make words and break

them apart using a variety of materials such as dry erase boards, magnetic letters, or letter tiles. Teachers use carefully planned searching and sorting activities to monitor how well students understand a lesson's focus and to arouse students' curiosities about how words work. They also coach students in word recognition and spelling strategies during authentic reading and writing events. In addition, some teachers use word walls as visual reminders of accumulated phonics instruction, a resource for independent reading and spelling, and springboards for various reading and spelling activities.

Research on exemplary primary grade teachers confirms that the most accomplished teachers have moved beyond the instructional debate. These teachers have in-depth and explicit understandings of the phonological system; this knowledge enables them to integrate direct and embedded approaches with minimal instructional support. Their instruction features aspects of direct instruction that include teacher explanations, isolation of sounds in words, blending of sounds into words, and supervised practice in reading and spelling words. However, these teachers' practices also feature aspects of embedded instruction that include coaching the application of word attack strategies in authentic reading and writing events as well as guiding the discovery of unfamiliar or unusual letter-sound correspondences (e.g., the medial letter-sound correspondence in *said*). This integration of instruction provides multiple and varied opportunities for students to develop clear understandings of the alphabetic principle, fosters an active learning stance, promotes self-regulating behaviors, and engenders a fascination for uncovering phonics patterns.

We are not so naive that we view an integrated approach to phonics instruction as a silver bullet. We have noted how high levels of engagement, thinking, and learning mark the integrated lessons of expert teachers, but effective combinations of direct and embedded instruction require well-honed conversational and management skills. Observations of preservice teachers in education programs remind us that teacher expertise is critical. For example, novice teachers vary greatly in their abilities to rescue students from confusing examples that emerge during word searches and to create appropriate word lists for making and breaking apart words. Interestingly, many seasoned teachers commented that their abilities to teach phonics flexibly and responsively were grounded in experiences they had as novices working with reading programs that featured a systematic phonics component. Such conversations caused us to think about multiple dimensions of systematic instruction and to consider how the structure of commercial phonics programs can create a foundation for the flexible and responsive phonics instruction characterizing exemplary reading instruction.

HOW IS THE TERM *SYSTEMATIC* USED IN THE CONTEXT OF PHONICS INSTRUCTION?

Dictionary definitions indicate that *systematic* means orderly, planned, and coordinated. In the context of phonics instruction, *systematic* is used sometimes to refer to instructional progression, sometimes to a set of activities and materials, and sometimes to the schedule of instruction. Although our conversations explored different dimensions of systematic phonics instruction, they also included discussions of what it means for students to develop systematic knowledge of the alphabetic principle.

A Systematic Instructional Progression

At times *systematic* is used in reference to a systematic or orderly progression for introducing letter-sound correspondences. Teachers typically make use of an instructional sequence outlined in a commercial program or in a district curriculum guide. Although these progressions or sequences may vary slightly, listserv members suggested that teachers within a school need to operate from an agreed-upon progression that maps out the teaching of letter-sound correspondences across the early grades. However, listserv members also noted that they are not slaves to

the sequence. They commented on the flexible ways they use these progressions—speeding up the progression when they determine that the students already know what is on the agenda, slowing down when students seem confused, and deviating from the progression when students notice and ask about other letter-sound correspondences. Their adaptive practices mirror the findings from research on exemplary primary-grade teachers.

A Systematic Set of Activities and Materials

Logically, effective phonics instruction features systematic activities and materials that are designed so that teachers can introduce a targeted letter-sound correspondence. Then they engage students in coordinated activities with materials that ensure sufficient practice in reading and spelling words with the targeted correspondence. Some research findings suggest that students are best served when teachers follow programs that provide coordinated activities and materials; however, listserv participants explained how they modified, added, or omitted activities in commercial programs as they monitored the understandings and engagement of their students. In addition, they described how they supplemented or substituted texts as they carefully matched texts and readers, basing decisions on their assessments of students' instructional needs and on their knowledge of the different types of leveled texts available for beginning readers (e.g., texts with varying degrees of decodability and predictability). In addition, listserv members argued that effective beginning reading instruction includes increasing students' volume of reading far beyond the coordinated set of activities and materials found in any commercial reading program.

A Systematic Schedule for Phonics Instruction

A systematic, planned schedule for phonics lessons is an important feature of effective phonics instruction. All the primary-grade teachers we know concur: Phonics instruction is too critical to leave to chance. However, listserv participants argued that the most powerful learning is situated in both planned and spontaneous instruction. We agree. Research on exemplary teachers suggests that the most effective teachers possess remarkable talents for supplementing scheduled phonics instruction with opportunistic and incidental teaching moments. Such teachers are experts at orchestrating a day packed with literacy activities. Their effectiveness, however, is grounded in an explicit knowledge of phonics and a great deal of expertise in managing and motivating student learning that results in systematic understandings.

Systematic Student Knowledge

Every primary-grade teacher intends for phonics instruction to assist students in developing understandings of the alphabetic principle that are explicit (i.e., fully developed and well formulated) and systematic (i.e., orderly and coordinated). However, we have become increasingly skeptical of a simplistic link between the implementation of systematic instruction and the development of systematic knowledge. For example, many primary-grade teachers noted that when students become aware that spoken words consist of separate sounds or phonemes, become familiar with a few letter names, and learn a few letter-sound correspondences, their knowledge of letter names and letter-sound correspondences often increases greatly, as does their fascination for "sounding out words" in the surrounding world of print. What these students learn continues to be linked to what is taught, but it is also fueled by newly awakened sensitivities to the ways that words work. They begin "seeing" printed words in new ways; these perceptions lead them to wonder why the names Carletta and Charlie begin with the same letter but different sounds and why the word *they* has a long *a* sound but is not spelled with the letter *a*.

Our experiences, and those of many teachers, suggest that once students are phonemically aware and have a grasp of the alphabetic principle they begin organizing knowledge of letter names and letter-sound correspondences in coherent and systematic ways. This systematizing of knowledge may not correspond to the neat, additive phonics progression described in a reading program, and it may proceed at a pace that lags behind or outruns the progression's suggested time frame. We argue that students are at risk of developing superficial and piecemeal understandings rather than coherent and orderly knowledge of the alphabetic principle if teachers impose systematic phonics instruction without monitoring how students organize this information. Similarly, we reason that students are at risk of becoming disenchanted with the world of print if teachers require them to spend significant time in activities that reinforce what they already know but stimulate few, if any, additional insights.

The Ongoing Challenge

We propose that the real challenge is to dispense with debates about what type of instruction to use and engage in serious deliberations and discussions about how multiple approaches to phonics instruction help children develop explicit and systematic knowledge of the alphabetic principle. This line of inquiry must include questions about how phonics instruction can be planned, prepared, and delivered to arouse students' curiosities about words, foster self-extending and even accelerated learning, and promote a love of reading. Such an inquiry must also include serious commitments to systematic progress monitoring that reveals when instructional adjustments are necessary.

As we embrace a broader band of purposes for phonics instruction, we are compelled to develop greater expertise for integrating aspects of direct and embedded instruction in ways that benefit all students. The most exemplary teachers have figured out how to do this. We submit that the professional journeys of teachers must feature instructional supports that are aligned with their levels of expertise, that awaken their sensitivities to how students are making sense of the alphabetic principle, and that foster varied, flexible, responsive, and self-regulating instructional practices. To do otherwise is to ignore what we have learned from the teachers who have been most successful in teaching all their students to read.

CHAPTER REFERENCES

Artley, A. S. (1977). Phonics revisited. *Language Arts, 54,* 121–126.

Clymer, T. (1963). The utility of phonics generalizations in the primary grades. *The Reading Teacher, 56,* 478–482.

Currier, L. B., & Dugid, O. C. (1916). Phonics or no phonics? *The Elementary School Journal, 4,* 209–210.

Gray, W. S. (1920). Principles of method in teaching reading, as derived from scientific investigations. In G. M. Whipple (Ed.), *The Eighteenth Yearbook of the National Society For the Study of Education: Part II* (pp. 36–51). Bloomington, IL: Public School Publishing.

Huey, E. (1908). *Psychology and pedagogy of reading.* New York: Macmillan.

Lohmann, E. (1930). Phonics as taught in our first grades throughout the United States. *Educational Administration and Supervision, 23,* 217–221.

Smith, N. B. (1927). The present situation in phonics. *The Elementary English Review, 4,* 278–281; 303–307.

Villaume, S. K., & Brabham, E. G. (2003). Phonics instruction: Beyond the debate. *The Reading Teacher, 56,* 478–452.

ANNOTATED BIBLIOGRAPHY OF RELATED REFERENCES

Adams, M. J. (1990). *Beginning to read: Thinking and learning about print.* Cambridge, MA: The MIT Press.

An extensive discussion of the role of phonics in the teaching of reading. Presents information on the development and history of phonics instruction. While controversial in the literacy community, Adams's work is often cited in recent research in the area of phonics.

Balmuth, M. (1982). *The roots of phonics: An historical introduction.* New York: McGraw-Hill.

An important reference in the study of the role of phonics in the teaching of reading. The author divides this scholarly work into four general categories: writing systems in general, the English writing system, spoken English, and English spelling patterns.

Chall, J. (1967). *Learning to read: The great debate.* New York: McGraw-Hill.

An important study in the debate on the role of phonics in the teaching of reading. Chall's work is often quoted in defense of a balanced approach to the use of phonics in the classroom reading program.

Cunningham, P. M., & Cunningham, J. W. (2002). What we know about the teaching of phonics. In A. E. Farstrup & S. Jay Samuels (Eds.), *What research has to say about the reading instruction* (pp. 87–109). Newark, DE: International Reading Association

This extensive, recent review of both research and classroom teaching of phonics represents current views on this aspect of reading instruction. Of particular note is the discussion of what is known about the role of phonics in reading instruction and how this knowledge can be used by the teacher in effective teaching.

Dickson, B. L. (1936). Trends in the teaching of reading. *California Journal of Elementary Education, 5,* 51–58.

A comprehensive discussion of the phonics practices used by contemporary classroom teachers. It also includes a review of related research on phonics in the first part of the previous century.

Dolch, E. W., & Bloomster, M. (1937). Phonic Readiness. *The Elementary School Journal, 38,* 201–205.

Ties the effectiveness of phonics instruction to a reader's mental maturity. It is typical of a number of articles during this period that emphasize the role of cognitive development and phonics training.

Garan, E. M. (2001). What does the report of the National Reading Panel really tell us about teaching phonics? *Language Arts, 79,* 61–71.

A critical review of the report of the National Reading Panel on the use of phonics in the teaching of reading. Contains a response to the author by Timothy Shanahan and Garan's rejoinder to Shanahan.

Gates, A. I. (1927). Studies of phonetic training in beginning reading. *The Journal of Educational Psychology, 18,* 217–226.

An important review of the contemporary research on phonetic methods being used by classroom teachers in the early teaching of reading.

Gray, W. S. (1948). *On their own in reading.* Chicago: Scott Foresman.

A key study of phonics and its role in an effective literacy program. This reference, written by one of the most important leaders in the history of reading education, provides an excellent overview of the different aspects of word analysis.

Judd, C. H. (1916). *Reading: Its nature and development* (Supplementary Educational Monographs, Vol. II, No. 4). Chicago: University of Chicago, 58–65.

This article, by one of the pioneers in literacy education, discusses the importance of phonics as a critical aspect of effective reading instruction.

Smith, N. B. (1943). Shall we teach phonics? *The Elementary English Review, 20,* 60–67.

Contains a historical review of the teaching of phonics from the Revolutionary War through the 1940s, with a summary of the arguments for and against the use of word analysis. See the Smith article included in this chapter for a parallel discussion by this literacy historian.

Spache, G. (1939). A phonics manual for primary and remedial teachers. *The Elementary English Review, 16,* 147–150, 156; 191–198.

An extensive discussion of the phonics knowledge that classroom teachers need to be effective literacy instructors. Particularly important for its lengthy bibliography of related phonics studies.

Vogel, M., Jaycox, E., & Washburne, C. (1923). A basic list of phonics for grades I and II. *Elementary School Journal, 23,* 436–443.

A listing of phonics generalizations and principles that these authors believe should be taught in the early elementary grades. This article is typical of many others of the period, summarizing what were considered to be effective phonics programs for elementary instruction.

Wheat, H. G. (1928). Examination analysis versus phonetic analysis in primary reading. *The Elementary School Journal, 39,* 256–266.

An early example of a study in which two approaches to reading instruction are compared and contrasted to determine their effectiveness in the teaching of early reading.

_____YOU BECOME INVOLVED_____

The role of phonics in reading instruction has had a long and often contentious history with ongoing heated debate and argument. Some questions to consider:

- Why do you think there has been so much controversy surrounding the topic of phonics instruction?
- What are some of the specific uses for phonics in literacy instruction as described by the articles in this chapter?
- After reading this material, what do you think should be the role of phonics in an effective classroom reading program?

Currier and Duguid's (1916) article is a very early discussion of the role of phonics in reading instruction.

- What were some of the issues faced by teachers in regards to the teaching of phonics as described in this article?
- Do you see some similarities between this early teaching of phonics and today's instruction in this area of literacy?

Nila Banton Smith (1927) continues this discussion of the role of phonics and effective reading instruction.

- What were some of the problems for teachers in the teaching of phonics in Smith's time? Do these differ from those faced by many of today's literacy teachers in their reading instruction?

- What suggestions does Smith make regarding the most effective manner of teaching phonics? Is there information provided here that would be helpful for your own teaching of phonics?
- What is Smith's answer to the basic question "Shall we teach word analysis?" How effective do you feel her answer is in terms of your current classroom reading instruction?

Based on your reading of the Clymer article (1963) consider the following points.

- What do you see as the most important conclusions of Clymer's research related to phonic generalizations? Based on this work, what do you see are the implications for your own classroom teaching of phonic generalizations?
- Are there some phonic generalizations that are much more applicable to effective reading than others? If so, why do you think some phonics instructional programs include all of these generalizations?

Artley's article (1977) discusses one perspective on the role of phonics in reading instruction.

- What does Artley mean when he suggests balance in the teaching of phonics as part of a total reading program?
- What are the implications of the conclusions of this article for your own teaching of phonics?

The final article in this chapter, by Villaume and Brabham (2003), reflects some of the most current thinking on phonics and reading.

- What is suggested as the primary goal of effective phonics instruction?
- How is "explicit phonics instruction" similar to or different from more traditional approaches to the teaching of this aspect of literacy? What is your personal opinion of explicit phonics instruction?
- In what ways might "systematic phonics instruction" be used in your own classroom reading instruction?

CHAPTER 4

READING COMPREHENSION

. . . the great object of [reading] which is to induce children to think and reflect on what they see.

—William & Robert Chambers
Infant Education (1836)

The only important thing in a book is the meaning it has for you.

—W. Somerset Maugham
Summing Up (1938)

The consequences of reading [comprehension] are also considered part of the reading activity and can include the knowledge that a reader has gained, the applications that a reader makes, and the level of engagement that a reader maintains while involved with a text. . . .

—Julie Corio
Exploring Literacy on the Internet (2003)

The ability to adequately understand what is being read has always been the foundation of what is considered to be successful reading. In one sense, comprehension of text is an easy concept to recognize; yet it is also one of the most complex and relatively unknown cognitive processes in the field of literacy education. There are still many issues and questions relative to reading comprehension that remain unanswered. In addressing the various issues related to reading comprehension, literacy researchers have a long history of investigations. Despite this legacy of educational research, it is still possible to identify a relatively small number of recurring themes. Examples of the most prominent concerns include the following issues.

Perhaps the most important question that has been investigated is the nature of reading comprehension itself. What does it mean to know and understand? For some it is simply the reconstruction of the author's original message. From this perspective, comprehension is simply being able to detail in various ways the basic intent of the original writer. While there may be various degrees of interpretation, the fundamental message of any particular text will be essentially the same. Others define understanding what is read in a much broader context, as comprehension based on each individual's unique background of knowledge and experience. Meaning for the individual reader is largely shaped by and filtered through his or her own distinctive experiences. In this case there is no single meaning for any text; often there can be a wide range of interpretations and understanding for each reader.

Closely related to a definition of reading comprehension is the question of how this particular aspect of literacy can be effectively taught. For instance, should reading comprehension be taught in terms of individual skills or is it better to have students view this process as a more unified strategy? Or is the use of both of these concepts appropriate depending on the text material and the type or degree of understanding required? Easy and specific solutions related to comprehension instruction are not readily forthcoming and many questions remain unanswered.

Throughout much of the past writing and thinking related to reading comprehension, the concern about adequate assessment of competence in this area is raised. Attempts at measuring specific degree of text understanding have ranged from the standardized reading test through various forms of informal measurement. Formats for these measurements have included reading a paragraph and answering the multiple-choice questions, classroom questioning techniques, and informal retelling procedures. Each of these assessment techniques has been justified in the past literature depending on the types of information needed about the reader's specific level and content of text understanding.

AS YOU READ

The articles that have been selected for this chapter represent the long history of interest in and investigations of the nature and content of reading comprehension. The goal is to introduce this field of inquiry with the intent of encouraging further study. References in the Annotated Bibliography that accompanies this material have been selected to clearly reflect some of the best writing on this topic by noted authorities in the field.

Annual Report of the Board of Education, Together with the Annual Report of the Secretary of the Board (1838)

HORACE MANN

Horace Mann, writing in 1838 as the Secretary of the Massachusetts Board of Education, made the following observations concerning reading comprehension. As you read this brief statement notice his discussion of what he believes constitutes real understanding of text.

I have devoted especial pains to learn, with some degree of numerical accuracy, how far the reading in our schools is an exercise of the mind in thinking and feeling, and how far it is a barren action of the organs of speech upon the atmosphere. My information is derived, principally, from the written statements of the school committees of the respective towns—gentlemen who are certainly exempt from all the temptation to disparage the schools they superintend. The result is, that more than eleven-twelfths of all the children in reading classes, in our schools, do not understand the meaning of the words they read; that they do not master the sense of the reading lessons, and that the ideas and feelings intended by the author to be conveyed to, and excited in, the reader's mind, still rest in the author's intention, never having yet reached the place of their destination. . . . It would hardly seem that the combined efforts of all persons engaged could have accomplished more in defeating the true objects of reading.

Reading as Reasoning: A Study
of Mistakes in Paragraph Reading

EDWARD L. THORNDIKE

The next article in this discussion of reading comprehension is one in a series of studies by E. L. Thorndike (1917; see Annotated Bibliography for additional references) done in the early part of the previous century. These articles, regardless of their age, reflect a depth of knowledge and insight into the reading process that has rarely been replicated. Issues such as the nature of comprehension, its precise definition, and the effective measurement of this aspect of reading were raised in these seminal articles and remain largely unanswered even today. Notice Thorndike's discussion of the responses made to the various comprehension questions and his comments concerning the dynamics existing between the reader and the text material during the reading process.

It seems to be a common opinion that reading (understanding the meaning of printed words) is a rather simple compounding of habits. Each word or phrase is supposed, if known to the reader, to call up its sound and meaning and the series of word or phrase meanings is supposed to be, or be easily transmuted into, the total thought. It is perhaps more exact to say that little attention has been paid to the dynamics whereby a series of words whose meanings are known singly produces knowledge of the meaning of a sentence or paragraph.

It will be the aim of this article to show that reading is a very elaborate procedure, involving a weighing of each of many elements in a sentence, their organization in the proper relations one to another, the selection of certain of their connotations and the rejection of others, and the cooperation of many forces to determine final response. In fact, we shall find that the act of answering simple questions about a simple paragraph like the one shown below includes all the features characteristic of typical reasonings.

J

Read this and then write the answers to 1, 2, 3, 4, 5, 6, and 7. Read it again as often as you need to.

In Franklin, attendance upon school is required of every child between the ages of seven and fourteen on every day when school is in session unless the child is so ill as to be unable to go to school, or some person in his house is ill with a contagious disease, or the roads are impassable.

1. What is the general topic of the paragraph?

2. On what day would a ten-year-old girl not be expected to attend school? _____

3. Between what years is attendance upon school compulsory in Franklin? _____

4. How many causes are stated which make absence excusable? _____

5. What kind of illness may permit a boy to stay away from school, even though he is not sick himself? _____

6. What condition in a pupil would justify his non-attendance? _____

7. At what age may a boy leave school to go to work in Franklin? _____

Consider first the following responses which were found among those made to Questions 1, 2, 5 and 6 above by two hundred pupils in Grade 6. (All are quoted exactly save that capitals are used at the beginning here regardless of whether the pupils used them.)

	PERCENTS	NUMBER PER THOUSAND
J 1. Unanswered	18	180
Franklin	4½	45
In Franklin	1	10
Franklin attendance	1	10
Franklin School	1½	15
Franklin attending school	1	10
Days of Franklin	½	5
School days of Franklin	½	5
Doings at Franklin	1	10
Pupils in Franklin	½	5
Franklin attends to his school	½	5
It is about a boy going to Franklin	½	5
It was a great inventor	½	5
Because its a great invention	½	5
The attendance of the children	½	5
The attendance in Franklin	½	5
School	7½	75
To tell about school	½	5
About school	4	40
What the school did when the boy was ill	½	5

(continued)

	PERCENTS	NUMBER PER THOUSAND
What the child should take	½	5
If the child is ill	2	20
How old a child should be	½	5
If the child is sick or contagious disease	½	5
Illness	1	10
On diseases	½	5
Very ill	3	30
An excuse	2	20
The roads are impassable	1	10
Even rods are impossible	½	5
A few sentences	½	5
Made of complete sentences	½	5
A sentence that made sense	½	5
A group of sentences making sense	½	5
A group of sentences	3	30
Subject and predicate	½	5
Subject	½	5
The sentence	½	5
A letter	½	5
Capital	5½	55
A capital letter	½	5
To begin with a capital	2	20
The first word	½	5
A general topic	½	5
Good topic	½	5
Leave half an inch space	2½	25
The heading	½	5
Period	½	5
An inch and a half	½	5
An inch and a half capital letter	½	5
The topic is civics	½	5
The answer	½	5
J 2. Unanswered	6	60
Unless the child is so ill as to be unable to go to school	41	410
Unless the child is unable to go to school	½	5
Unless she is ill or the roads are impassable	1	10
Roads are impassable	1	10
When his baby or brother have some kind of disease	1	10
When a parent is ill	½	5
If her father or mother died	½	5
On her birthday	6½	65
On her fourteenth birthday	½	5
On every day	4	40
On any day	½	5
Expected every day	1½	15
On Monday and for 5 days a week	½	5
On Monday	1	10

	PERCENTS	NUMBER PER THOUSAND
On Friday	1	10
When school is in session	1	10
The beginning of the term	½	5
Fourteen year	½	5
Age 11	½	5
She is allowed to go to school when 6 years	½	5
A very bad throat	½	5
When better	½	5
J 5. Unanswered	2	20
If mother is ill	5½	55
Headache, ill	½	5
A sore neck	½	5
Headache, toothache or earache	½	5
When a baby is sick	½	5
Playing sickness	½	5
Serious	½	5
When the roads cannot be used	½	5
Contagious disease, roads impassable	1½	15
He cannot pass the ball	½	5
A note	½	5
J 6. Unanswered	15	150
Ill with a contagious disease	5	50
Seven years old	½	5
By bringing a note	6	60
When going with his mother to his cousin	½	5
Is to go his mother	½	5
When he is well and strong	½	5
To have a certificate from a doctor that the disease is all over	½	5
Somebody else must have a bad disease	½	5
Torn shoes	½	5
Neat attendance	½	5
When he acts as if he is innocent	½	5
Being good	½	5
By being early	½	5
Get up early	½	5
Come to school	1½	15
Be at school every day	½	5
If he lost his lessons	½	5
Illness lateness or truancy	½	5
A bad boy	½	5
By not going to school	½	5
None	½	5
Not sick no condition and mother not ill	½	5
Not very good	½	5
When you come you get your attendance marked	½	5
Of being absent	½	5

(continued)

	PERCENTS	NUMBER PER THOUSAND
His attendance was fair	½	5
Truant	1	10
If someone at his house has a contagious disease	6½	65
When roads	½	5
If he was excused	½	5
Not smart	½	5
If his father or mother died	½	5
By not staying home or playing hookey	½	5

In general, in this and all similar tests of reading, the responses do not fall into a few clearly defined groups—correct, unanswered, error No. 1, error No. 2, and so on. On the contrary, they show a variety that threatens to baffle any explanation. We can, however, progress toward an explanation, by using the following facts and principles:

In correct reading (1) each word produces a correct meaning, (2) each such element of meaning is given a correct weight in comparison with the others, and (3) the resulting ideas are examined and validated to make sure that they satisfy the mental set or adjustment or purpose for whose sake the reading was done. Reading may be wrong or inadequate (1) because of wrong connections with the words singly, (2) because of over-potency or under-potency of elements, or (3) because of failure to treat the ideas produced by the reading as provisional, and so to inspect and welcome or reject them as they appear.

Everybody, of course, understands that (1) plays a part, but it is not so clearly understood that a word may produce all degrees of erroneous meaning for a given context, from a slight inadequacy to an extreme perversion.

Thus *Franklin* in the paragraph quoted (J) varies from its exact meaning as a local unit through degrees of vagueness to meaning a man's name (as in "Franklin attends to his school" as a response to question 1), or to meaning a particular personage (as in "It was a great inventor" as a response to question 1). Thus *contagious* in paragraph J permits responses to question 5 (What kind of illness may permit a boy to stay away from school, even though he is not sick himself?) ranging from "Scarlet fever, chicken pox, measles or diphtheria," through "Scarlet fever," "headache," "Serious," "Hay fever," "Pimple," to "Contagious or roads impassable," and "All kinds of disease." Thus *paragraph* in J 1 when over-potent produces responses ranging from "A group of sentences making sense" through "A group of sentences," and "A few sentences," to "The sentence," "Subject and predicate," "Begin with a capital," "A letter," and "Commas and periods."

In particular, the relational words, such as pronouns, conjunctions and prepositions, have meanings of many degrees of exactitude. They also vary in different individuals in the amount of force they exert. A pupil may know exactly what *though* means, but he may treat a sentence containing it much as he would treat the same sentence with *and* or *or* or *if* in place of the *though*.

The importance of the correct weighting of each element is less appreciated. It is very great, a very large percentage of the mistakes made being due to the over-potency of certain elements or the under-potency of others.

Consider first the over-potency of elements in the questions. The first question about paragraph J was, "What is the general topic of the paragraph?" A large group of answers show over-potency of *paragraph*. Such are those quoted above to show variation in the understanding of the word. We also find an over-potency of *top* (in topic) combined with that of paragraph, resulting in such responses as: "Leave a half-inch space," "An inch and a half," "An inch and a half capital letter," "The topic of paragraph is one inch in."

The second question was: "On what day would a ten-year-old girl not be expected to attend school?" We find under-potency of *not* resulting in answers like "When school is in session" or "Five days a week." We find under-potency of *day* resulting in responses like "She is allowed to go to school when 6 years," "Age 11," and "Fourteen years."

We find over-potency of *day* shown by "Monday," "Wednesday," and "Friday"; of *ten-year-old girl* in "The ten-year-old girl will be 5 a."

Ten-year-old is over-potent in an interesting way, namely, in the very large number of responses of "On her birthday." Over-potency, of *Attend school* seems to be one part of the causation of "To attendance with Franklin," "Ever morning at half past 8," "She should," and "Because he did learn."

Consider next over-potency and under-potency of the words or phrases in the paragraph. The following list of responses shows that each of ten words taken from the paragraph is over-potent so as to appear clearly influential in the response to each of the first three questions (and in seven of the cases to the fourth question as well). These occur within five hundred responses made by children within grades 5 to 8. Cases of under-potency would be still easier to collect.

The questions, I may remind the reader, were as follows:

1. What is the general topic of the paragraph?
2. On what day would a ten-year-old girl not be expected to attend school?
3. Between what years is attendance upon school compulsory in Franklin?
4. How many causes are stated which make absence excusable?

(The numbers refer to the question to which the words were the response.)

Franklin	1. Franklin. 1. Franklin and the diseases. 1. Franklin topic.
	2. Franklin.
	3. Because it is a small city. 3. Franklin was in school 141 years.
attendance	1. Attendance.
	2. To attendance with Franklin.
	3. In Franklin attendance upon school is required. Attending school 130 days.
school	1. School. 1. They must know their lessons.
	2. In the beginning of school.
	3. School in session. 3. In the years of school.
seven	1. Seven and fourteen. 1. How old a child should be.
	2. He should attend school at 7 years. 2. Between seven and fourteen.
	3. Seven years.
	4. Under seven.
fourteen	1. Every child between seven and fourteen. In Franklin how old they are.
	2. Fourteenth of everyday. 2. Fourteen years.
	3. Fourteen years. 3. Fourteen.
	4. 7 to 14.

every   1. Every child.
               2. Expected every day.   2. On every day.
               3. Every year.   3. Every child between fourteen or thirteen.
               4. Everyday.

ill   1. Illness.   1. Very ill.   1. If the child is ill.
               2. Ill.   2. A very bad throat.
               3. He cannot go to school unless ill.
               4. When child is ill.   4. Must be sick.

contagious   1. Contagious disease.
               2. If she is sick or has a contagious disease.
               3. Contagious disease.
               4. Contagious disease.

disease   1. Fever.   1. About disease.
               2. Often sick.
               3. Unless ill or contagious disease.   3. Disease.
               4. A terrible disease going out.   4. Because when a boy has disease.

impassable   1. The roads are impassable.   1. Snow.
               2. When roads are impassable.
               3. Seven to fourteen years or the roads are impassable.
               4. Or the roads are impassable.

To make a long story short, inspection of the mistakes shows that the potency of any word or word group in a question may be far above or far below its proper amount in relation to the rest of the question. The same holds for any word or word group in the paragraph. Understanding a paragraph implies keeping these respective weights in proper proportion from the start or varying their proportions until they together evoke a response which satisfies the purpose of the reading.

Understanding a paragraph is like solving a problem in mathematics. It consists of selecting the right elements of the situation and putting them together in the right relations, and also with the right amount of weight or influence or force for each. The mind is assailed as it were by every word in the paragraph. It must select, repress, soften, emphasize, correlate and organize, all under the influence of the right mental set or purpose or demand.

Consider the complexity of the task in even a very simple case such as answering question 6 on paragraph D, in the case of children of grades 6, 7, and 8 who well understand the question itself.

John had two brothers who were both tall. Their names were Will and Fred. John's sister, who was short, was named Mary. John liked Fred better than either of the others. All of these children except Will had red hair. He had brown hair.
6. Who had red hair?

The mind has to suppress a strong tendency for *Will had red hair* to act irrespective of the *except* which precedes it. It has to suppress a tendency for *all these children . . . had red hair* to act irrespective of the *except Will*. It has to suppress weaker tendencies for *John, Fred, Mary, John and Fred, Mary and Fred, Mary and Will, Mary Fred and Will*, and every other combination that could be a "Who," to act irrespective of the satisfying of the requirement "had red hair according to the paragraph." It has to suppress tendencies for John and Will or brown and red to exchange places in memory, for irrelevant ideas like *nobody* or *brothers* or *children* to arise. That it has to suppress them is shown by the failures to do so which occur. The *Will had red hair* in fact causes one-fifth of children in grades 6, 7, and 8 to answers wrongly,* and about two-fifths of children in grades 3, 4, and 5. Insufficient potency of *except Will** makes about one child in twenty in grades 6, 7, and 8 answer wrongly with "all the children," "all," or "Will Fred Mary and John."

Reading may be wrong or inadequate because of failure to treat the responses made as provisional and to inspect, welcome, and reject them as they appear. Many of the very pupils who gave wrong responses to the questions would respond correctly if confronted with them in the following form:

Is this foolish or is it not?
The day when a girl should *not* go to school
    is the day when school is in session.
The day when a girl should not go to school
    is the beginning of the term.
The day etc. . . . is Monday.
The day is fourteen years.
The day is age eleven.
The day is a very bad throat.
Impassable roads are a kind of illness.
He cannot pass the ball is a kind of illness.

They do not, however, of their own accord test their responses by thinking out their subtler or more remote implications. Even very gross violations against common sense are occasionally passed, such as letting Mary give Tom a blue dog, or giving "Thought the man fat out" as an answer to I 1. Usually, however, the irrelevance or inconsistency concerns something in the question or the paragraph and the failure to heed it is closely akin to the under-potency of certain elements.

I.

Nearly fifteen thousand of the city's workers joined in the parade on September seventh, and passed before the hundred thousand cheering spectators. There were workers of both sexes in the parade, though the men far out-numbered the women.

1. What is said about the number of persons who marched in the parade?

It thus appears that reading an explanatory or argumentative paragraph in his textbooks on geography or history or civics and (though to a less degree) reading a narrative or description involves the same sort of organization and analytic action of ideas as occur in thinking of supposedly, higher sorts. This view is supported by the high correlations between such reading and verbal completion tests, Binet-Simon tests, analogies tests and the like. These correlations, when corrected for attenuation, are probably, for children of the same age, as high as +.80.

It appears likely, therefore, that many children fail in certain features of these subjects not because they have understood and remembered the facts and principles but have been unable to organize and use them; or because they have understood them but have been unable to remember them; but because they never understood them.

It appears likely also that a pupil may read fluently and feel that the series of words are arousing appropriate thoughts without really understanding the paragraph. Many of the children who made notable mistakes would probably have said that they understood the paragraph and, upon reading the questions on it, would have said that they understood them. In such cases the reader finds satisfying solutions of those problems which he does raise and so feels mentally adequate; but he raises only a few of the problems which should be raised and makes only a few of the judgments which he should make. Thus one may read paragraph I with something like the following actual judgments:

Fifteen thousand did something—there was a parade—September seventh was the day—there were two hundred thousand something—there was cheering—workers were in the parade—both sexes in the parade—the men outnumbered the women.

---

*Some of these errors are due to essential ignorance of "except," though that should not be common in pupils of grades 6 or higher.

Contrast these with the following which may be in the mind of the expert reader:

Nearly fifteen thousand—not quite, but nearly—of the city's workers—people who worked for a living—joined in the parade—a big parade of nearly 15,000—on September seventh—the parade was in the fall—they passed before two thousand hundred cheering spectators—two hundred thousand saw the parade—they cheered it—they were workers of both sexes—there were men workers and women workers in the parade—the men far outnumbered the women. Many more men than women were in the parade.

In educational theory, then, we should not consider the reading of a textbook or reference as a mechanical, passive, undiscriminating task, on a totally different level from the task or evaluating or using what is read. While the work of judging and applying doubtless demands a more elaborate and inventive organization and control of mental connections, the demands of mere reading are also for the active selection which is typical of thought. It is not a small or unworthy task to learn "what the book says."

In school practice it appears likely that exercises in silent reading to find the answers to given questions, or to give a summary of the matter read, or to list the questions which it answers, should in large measure replace oral reading. The vice of the poor reader is to say the words to himself without actively making judgments concerning what they reveal. Reading aloud or listening to one reading aloud may leave this vice unaltered or even encouraged. Perhaps it is in their outside reading of stories and in their study of geography, history, and the like that many school children really learn to read.

The Problem of Meaning in Reading

PAUL McKEE

Paul McKee (1941) continues this discussion of reading comprehension, summarizing the results of related research completed through the midpoint of the last century. He finds of particular concern that problems with understanding seem to become more pronounced as students progress in their educational experiences. As you read this article, note how he builds on the information provided by Thorndike in the previous article. He also provides a list of suggested classroom procedures that teachers might use to help students improve their understanding of text material. From a historical perspective, these teaching suggestions reflect an increased awareness that reading comprehension is a complex thinking process, and for success to take place readers need to take an active role in their understanding of various types of text material. Of particular interest in this article are McKee's observations on student attitudes related to their apparent lack of understanding of their textbooks and teachers' related instructional comments. "It doesn't seem to matter if they don't understand" say the students, and teachers are willing to accept this learning situation in the classroom setting! Despite the fact that these remarks were written in 1941, they still have a disturbingly modern connotation to them.

Some elementary, secondary-school, and college teachers are becoming convinced that the pupils and students in our schools cannot read their textbooks well. Most of these teachers are basing their conclusions upon the poor performances of those relatively few pupils in a class who have difficulty with the mechanics of reading—pupils who are not acquainted with enough printed symbols, who cannot pronounce many words, who are word readers, who read too slowly, who have trouble in getting across the page with what we like to call good eye movements, or who are not able to work out the recognition of strange words.

But even these "reading conscious" teachers do not know half the story! Actually, the reading ability of our pupils and students is much lower than deficiencies in the mere mechanics of reading indicate. It is much lower than most teachers think it is. It is much lower than scores on standardized tests or photographs of eye movements show it to be. These harsh statements are unquestionably true if it is correct to assume that there is no such thing as reading without understanding, that reading is good because the pupil understands clearly and correctly the meaning of the word, phrase, sentence, or paragraph at which he looks, and that reading is poor when the understanding which the pupil achieves is vague or false.

There is not sufficient time here to tell the whole story of what has been done to discover the degree to which pupils and students at all educational levels understand clearly and correctly what they attempt to read in their textbooks. There is not time to give even one example of the meager understandings which a given group of students achieved when looking at a given word, phrase, sentence, or paragraph in one of their textbooks. It must suffice to say that, at all educational levels, pupils and students who made at least average scores on standardized tests in reading and who had little if any difficulty with the mechanics of reading were personally interviewed about the meaning of given selections they had read in their textbooks. In those interviews series of searching and probing questions, pictures, objects, and even actions were used to find out just what understanding a given pupil had achieved for a given word, phrase, sentence, or paragraph in a given selection. The results of the studies show the following facts clearly.

1. The understanding which 80 percent of the pupils in an average class achieve in reading the textbook in any content subject is almost unbelievably vague and incorrect. This condition is at its worst in social studies.

2. The great majority of students are quite able and, willing to recognize, manipulate, and reproduce symbols of meaning without understanding the meaning for which those symbols stand. This activity is called "verbalism."

3. Pupils and students are not particularly disturbed at lack of understanding in reading their textbooks. They are not at all the demanders of meaning which they should be in order to read effectively.

4. The situation grows worse as the educational level advances. The best readers we have are in the first grade; the poorest, in the secondary school and the college. This strange statement has only two meanings: First, our first-grade pupils understand more clearly and correctly the books we have for them to read than high-school and college students understand their textbooks. Second, first-grade pupils insist to a greater degree than do high-school students upon understanding what is meant by this or that statement in the book. Many high-school and college students have told the writer individually that they do not expect to understand much of what the textbooks say or, for that matter, much of what the teacher says in her instructional talking and that it doesn't seem to matter if they do not understand. Those students have learned that apparently there is such a thing as reading without understanding and that we, as teachers, are willing to accept a student's manipulation and reproduction of the language symbols of a meaning as evidence of his possession of that meaning. Those students have also lost most of the attitude of demanding meaning with which they did their first reading at school.

5. Great numbers of students have little if any control of the tools with which they could dig out the meaning of a word, sentence, or paragraph that is a little tough for them. For example, college freshmen, ranging in intelligence from average to distinctly superior, are able to use the context to construct the meaning of only one strange word out of every four strange words they meet in a textbook—when, of course, the needed context is there! Most of them haven't the slightest notion of how to use a picture to construct the meaning of a strange word or phrase. The majority of them know so little about sentence structure that they are unable to sense the relationship between the parts of a sentence.

6. Pupils and students who are able to see the relationship between or among the parts of a sentence are able to understand what that sentence means to a greater degree than are students who do not sense that relationship.

7. For the most part students are not able to see the relationship between or among the sentences in a paragraph. They have great difficulty in sensing whether this or that sentence is a proposition-containing sentence or an explanatory or amplifying sentence. Often when they decide that a given sentence is an amplifying sentence, they don't know which proposition-containing sentence it amplifies!

While the speaker has no panacea for this undesirable reading situation as it exists in our schools, the following suggestions may be helpful.

1. Not long ago reading of the simplest type was defined as the getting of meaning from the printed page. This statement is misleading. No one can get meaning from a printed page for the good reason that there is no meaning on the page. Only the symbols of meaning are there. When observed, a symbol acts merely as a trigger to stimulate the reader to recall the meaning

for which it stands. If the reader does not have the meaning, there is no way by which he can read the symbol. It is at this point that vagueness and misunderstanding in reading begin. Scores of pupils and students simply do not have the meanings or concepts that symbols in their textbooks represent. I know of no way to teach a student how to read those symbols except by helping him to construct the needed concepts before he attempts to read the selection in which they are used. It would seem that in secondary schools and colleges this is the science teacher's task in the teaching of science and the social studies teacher's task in the teaching of social studies. Helping students to construct concepts needed for reading a selection in science or social studies certainly is not the job of the English teacher. He or she has enough to do to make it possible for the student to understand the composition and literature books which it is her responsibility to make clear.

2. We must realize and do something about the fact that reading is an *active* rather than a passive process and a *thinking* process to be done by the mind rather than a mechanical process to be done by the eyes. Even the recalling of the concepts represented by the symbols on the page is active, and often, though not always, it is a conscious, thoughtful procedure. But the recalling of the concepts is just the beginning of what we may call the thinking side of reading. Having recalled the required concepts, the reader must consciously or unconsciously become aware of the relationship that exists between the different concepts in a given sentence. This means that he must be able to sense the relationship that exists between the parts of a sentence. In addition, he must be able to sense, consciously or unconsciously, the relationship that exists between the sentences in a paragraph in order to arrive at the meaning of that paragraph. He must distinguish between the proposition-containing sentences and the amplifying or explanatory sentences. He must sense which explanatory sentence modifies a given proposition-containing sentence. In the meantime the student may have needed to perform the very active and thoughtful job of using the context or a picture, as he read, to construct the meaning of a strange word or phrase.

With these things in mind we should deliberately teach pupils and students how to do what they must do in order to dig out clear and correct understanding of what they read. For example, there should be definite and obvious lessons in such important matters as (1) how to use the context to construct the meaning of a strange word or phrase, (2) how to use a picture to construct the meaning of a strange word or phrase, (3) how to get at the relationship between the parts of a sentence, and (4) how to work out the relationship between the sentences in a paragraph. These lessons should begin at the third-grade level and continue as long as necessary–even through the high school and college if need be. Whether these lessons are taught in a so-called reading period or in a so-called language period is inconsequential. The important thing is that they get taught, preferably by someone who can teach boys and girls that reading is an active, thoughtful process and who can make clear and meaningful the construction of different sentences and paragraphs.

3. We need to do everything we can to keep alive the demand for meaning with which most pupils begin their reading in the first grade. To this end we should take time to help pupils and students to construct concepts that are strange but needed in reading a given selection, and we must teach them to use the tools, mentioned previously, which they need in order to dig out a clear understanding of a sentence or a paragraph. These things must be done if the pupil is to have the continuous experience of reading with adequate understanding—the experience by which he learns to expect to understand when he reads. They must be done if he is to avoid the continuous experience of reading without understanding—the experience by which he learns to expect not to understand.

4. I have been talking about 80 percent of the pupils in your class, who have good control over the mechanics of reading but who do not understand clearly and correctly what they read in their textbooks, and I have tried to suggest a few things that can be done about the matter. I have not been talking about the 10 percent of the pupils in your class who have such meager control over mechanics that they can get little if any reading done. May I add a warning here? Do not expect to improve the ability of that 80 percent of your class—those who do not understand clearly and correctly what they attempt to read—by teaching independent ways of sounding out strange words or by using exercises or machines which are useful in improving eye movements and increasing speed. Teaching ways of sounding out strange words is for pupils who do not have those important tools. Exercises of various types for increasing speed and improving eye movements are distinctly beneficial to those few students who, having established bad habits of eye movement, are able to understand in reading more rapidly than they do understand. And remember, too, this one important point about eye movements. If you have a pupil who reads without regression movements a selection which has in it words and phrases that are a little tough because they represent strange concepts for him, he is a poor reader! He should have the desire and the skill to make those regression movements which are necessary in order to use the surrounding context to attempt to dig out the meaning of those strange words and phrases.

5. One last word: It is about the remedial-reading clinic which you may have in your school. Most of the clinics in our schools and colleges devote themselves too exclusively to the mechanics of reading. They should spend much more time in rendering services to both teachers and students on what I have called the thinking side of reading. They need to mobilize and employ many materials and procedures which are needed in helping pupils and students to understand clearly and correctly what they attempt to read in their textbooks.

Changing the Face of Reading Comprehension Instruction

P. David Pearson

In the following article, P. David Pearson (1985) reviews the contemporary thinking related to reading comprehension. More than ever, there is an emphasis on the realization that effective reading comprehension is the foundation of successful reading and that the classroom teacher must take an active role in the development of successful strategies that will strengthen understanding of text. We see in this article a discussion of the new emphasis on the use of appropriate comprehension strategies that saw their inception in the 1980s and continue to be used today, both in terms of research and of related classroom practices (*see* the Annotated Bibliography in this chapter for current research on reading comprehension). As you read this material, recall McKee's suggestions regarding the role of the classroom teacher as instructional leader in the development of reading comprehension and Pearson's related comments.

There can be no doubt that children's reading comprehension performance concerns educators at all levels today. More than ever before, we are devoting much intellectual and emotional energy to helping students better understand the texts we require them to read in our schools. There are, I think, three reasons why comprehension has achieved this dominant position.

The first reason is that we no longer spend much energy on issues that once dominated the reading field. Reflecting upon the past 15 years in reading education, I am impressed by some significant changes in our concerns about reading instruction.

When I first entered the field, the issues of debate were:

1. What's the best way to teach beginning reading?
2. Should the alphabet be taught as a prerequisite to reading instruction?
3. How can a school build a sound individualized reading program?

Even at that time only a few of my colleagues believed that our energies and efforts should be focused on the comprehension issue. Some even thought that there was little one could do to train comprehension (believing, I suppose, that it was a matter properly left to the fates of intelligence and experience).

But the times have changed. For better or worse, at least if one regards available instructional materials as a barometer of practice, the issue of early reading seems settled, with most commercial programs teaching phonics early and intensively. Also it is hard to find commercial programs that do not teach the alphabet early on, most often in kindergarten readiness programs.

I mean neither to celebrate nor condemn the broad consensus on these issues; rather, I only make the observation that broad consensus frees psychic energy to examine other issues that may have gone unexamined previously.

Regarding individualization, two kinds of conclusions were reached: (1) that progress in reading should be monitored frequently, minutely (note the myriad of specific skills tests at the end of every unit and level in most commercial programs), and individually; (2) that individualized instruction meant offering practice materials for children to complete individually and independently. Unlike the consensus on early phonics and the alphabet, however, I detect serious discontent in the field about our current practices of individualization.

A second reason for the new interest in comprehension comes directly from concerns of practitioners. All too frequently, when meeting with administrators or committees from school districts, I have encountered this scenario. The group expresses the dilemma of their reading program's test results, which goes like this:

> *You know, when we look at our primary grade results we feel good about our program. Our kids are scoring above national norms, which is more than we have a right to expect. Then we look beyond Grade 3 and what we find is a gradual slide in those scores, relative to national norms, all the way into high school.*

This observation is usually followed by the conclusion that:

> *We must be doing a good job of teaching the decoding skills that characterize the primary grades and a mediocre job of teaching the comprehension skills that characterize the intermediate grades. What can we do about it?*

Data from National Assessment should reinforce this concern. The assessment (NAEP 1981) indicates that during the 70s American education made excellent progress for 9-year-olds; however, we did not fare well in helping 13-year-olds or 17-year-olds, particularly in test items requiring inferential and interpretive comprehension.

A third factor promoting comprehension concerns stems from a renaissance in psychology. From 1920 to 1965, psychologists, wedded as they were to their behavioristic models, did not study reading. Reading was generally regarded as too complex a process to examine, given the constraints of the behavioral perspective. But the past decade has witnessed a redirection of perspective among psychologists. Indeed the relatively new field of cognitive psychology considers the reading process to be one of its most precious objects of study, encompassing as it does subprocesses

like attention, perception, encoding, comprehension, memory, information storage, and retrieval.

As a result, psychology has returned to one of its rightful homes—the study of reading. Reading education has benefitted greatly from the return, for new insight into cognition has provided a wealth of ideas and hypotheses worthy of testing in the ultimate laboratory—the classroom.

These three forces (consensus on other matters, heightened concern about comprehension failures, and a new set of intellectual challenges), then, have converged to create an atmosphere in which the psychic energy of the reading field has been unleashed toward the study of comprehension.

The challenge we must meet is the question posed by the school reading committees: "What can we do about it?" Though there may be others, at this time I believe that we have gathered enough research, theory, and practical wisdom to support these six changes.

1. We must accept comprehension for what it is.

2. We must change the kinds of questions we ask about selections children read.

3. We must change our attitude toward and practices of teaching vocabulary.

4. We must change the way we teach comprehension skills.

5. We must begin to develop curricular materials that recognize the fact that comprehension and composition are remarkably similar in process.

6. We must change our conception of the teacher's role in the reading program.

THE TRUTH ABOUT COMPREHENSION

Prior to 1970, our view of the comprehension process was driven by our fixation upon the text as an object of study. Comprehension was viewed as some degree of "approximation" to the text read. And, if we had any notion that readers build mental models as they read, then our standard for what a mental model should look like was the text itself.

For a variety of historical, political, and theoretical reasons too detailed to elucidate here, our views of comprehension and text have changed dramatically. No longer do we regard text as a fixed object that the reader is supposed to "approximate" as closely as possible as s/he reads. Instead we now view text as a sort of blueprint for meaning, a set of tracks or clues that the reader uses as s/he builds a model of what the text means (Collins, Brown, and Larkin, 1980).

In this new view, we recognize that no text is ever fully explicit, no text ever specifies all the relationships among events, motivation of characters, and nuances of tone and style that every author hopes traders will infer as they read. Instead, authors omit from their texts exactly those relationships and nuances they expect (and hope) readers can figure out for themselves. As readers, we would be bored to death if authors chose to specify these matters, saying to ourselves "Well, I knew that!"

In short, this new view suggests that readers play a much more active-constructive role in their own comprehension than our earlier passive-receptive views dictated.

An active-constructive model of comprehension has enormous implications for the role of the classroom teacher in promoting comprehension. A teacher can no longer regard the text as the ultimate criterion for defining what good comprehension is; instead s/he must view the text, along with students' prior knowledge, students' strategies, the task, and the classroom situation, as one facet in the complex array we call comprehension. Now a teacher must know as much about the influence of these other facets (prior knowledge, strategies, task, situation) as s/he knows about the text itself. In fact, these other facets—especially prior knowledge, strategies, and task—form the basis for the remaining five changes outlined in this presentation.

CHANGING QUESTIONS

Durkin (1978–79) and her coworkers, after some 17,997 minutes observing intermediate grade reading lessons, concluded that teachers devote much of their reading class time to asking students questions about stories they have just read. Students, conversely, spend lots of time answering questions, or listening to classmates' answers. Furthermore, these sessions (described by Durkin as assessment rather than teaching) tended to be characterized by relatively low-level, literally-based questions in search of single correct answers.

We have all seen this; probably most of us, myself included, have done it ourselves. I ask a question. I call upon Suzie. She gives an answer other than the one I had in mind. I turn toward Tommy. He gives a second answer, but still not the one I had in mind. My head bobs from student to student until someone finally gives the answer I was looking for. It is a game we play called "Guess what's in my head."

When Durkin (1981) turned from classroom observation to teachers' manuals, she discovered a remarkably similar situation—lots of space devoted to story questions, lots of literal-level questions in search of single correct answers (*and manuals provided correct answers to each comprehension question,* save those that invited almost any and every response, coded as "answers will vary").

Beck and her colleagues (1979) have also examined teachers manual questions. Reading their analysis, one is struck by another facet of the questions in manuals: They represent a random barrage of questions that do not cohere with one another. They do not form a *line of questions* to lead children through the main crises and events of a story so they can build their own coherent representation of its meaning.

The story map. After examining recent research about story comprehension, Beck (1984) suggested that, prior to question generation, teachers need to develop an outline of the important ideas in the story, what Beck has come to call a "story map." A story map specifies the main character's problem in the story and then attempts to solve that problem, leading eventually to a resolution, and perhaps a moral or lesson about life. Beck suggests that, having generated such a map, teachers should develop questions that elicit major components of the story map. Questions that elicit either too general or too specific responses should not be used during initial guided reading discussions. The flow of the story, from inception to resolution, serves as the paramount criterion for question selection or creation.

Translated into practical issues regarding basal reading questions, this analysis suggests that in addition to developing questions that go beyond the literal text, guided reading questions should be limited to eliciting only those details that drive the flow of the story, that is, problems, goals, attempts to solve problems, characters reactions, resolution, and theme (or moral).

Recent research evidence (Beck, Omanson, and McKeown, 1982; Cordon and Pearson, 1983; Singer and Donlan, 1982) validates exactly such a notion. Questions that focus student attention on salient story elements elicit better comprehension and recall of the story in which such questions are embedded as well as better recall of new stories for which no questions are asked. Apparently, the systematic application of such a framework for story comprehension helps students develop their own frameworks for understanding stories; such a framework may well serve as a strategic device for understanding and recalling what is read.

Prereading questions. In addition to guided reading questions, researchers have examined prereading questions intended to build background for story comprehension. Here considerable evidence suggests that it matters a great deal what kind of questions we use: A set for predicting, relating text to prior knowledge, and evaluating predicted outcomes is superior to more literal/factual orientation.

For example, Hansen and Pearson (Hansen, 1981, Hansen and Pearson, 1980, 1983) have done several studies on the effect of story questions, particularly with reference to enhancing children's ability to answer inferential comprehension questions. Two of their findings are relevant to our concerns.

First, simply making sure that guided reading questions (asked either during or after stories) include a lot of inference questions enhances both story specific inferential comprehension and comprehension of new stories. Second, they found that adding a prereading set for invoking relevant prior knowledge and predicting what will happen in a story coupled with discussion of why it is important to do so results in even better inferential comprehension and even helps literal comprehension.

Developing questions to invoke prior knowledge and engage in prediction is not difficult (see Hansen and Hubbard, 1984, for details on this technique). Basically, a teacher must:

1. Read the text.
2. Decide on a few (2–4) key ideas, ideas which usually represent the theme or moral, the main character's basic problem, or a key action, event, or feeling.
3. For each key idea, ask "Have you ever . . . ?" and "What do you think X will do . . . ?"
4. Before reading, spend a few minutes discussing each of the two questions for each key idea.
5. (Optional) After reading, return to the predictions to discuss reasons for differences or similarities between predictions and what actually happened.
6. Somewhere discuss why you are doing all this.

In trying to reconcile the available data on what promotes better understanding of textbook selections with conventional practices, I have derived the following instructional guidelines for asking questions. (For a more complete treatment, see Pearson, 1982.)

1. Ask questions that encourage children to relate the story to prior experiences.
2. Then, try to elicit predictions about what story characters will do in similar circumstances.
3. Ask purpose setting questions that persist as long as possible throughout the reading of a selection.

4. Immediately after reading, return to the purpose.

5. Use a story map to generate guided reading questions.

6. Include follow-up tasks that encourage synthesis of the entire story (retelling, dramatizing, summarizing).

7. Reserve comparison questions (with prior knowledge and other stories) for a second pass through.

8. Reserve author's craft questions (e.g., techniques for persuasion) for a second (even a third) pass.

VOCABULARY INSTRUCTION

Dale Johnson and I have been so concerned about vocabulary instruction that we have written two books devoted exclusively to the topic (Johnson and Pearson, 1978, 1984). Our main concerns in those books are twofold: (1) that people will recognize the primacy of *meaning* vocabulary over *word recognition* vocabulary, and (2) that they will embrace our philosophy of *ownership of a word's meaning* over *facility at defining the word.* Let me explain with an anecdote.

Several years ago a student teacher brought in to my colleague, Robert Schreiner (University of Minnesota), a lesson plan and some student papers from a reading lesson he had taught to some fifth grade students, remarking "Let me tell you about my great vocabulary lesson."

"What did you do?"

Well, first I had them look up the new words in their pocket dictionaries. . . ."

"And then? . . . "

"I knew you'd ask that," he added firmly. "And then I asked them to write the words in sentences."

"Can I see some students' papers?" The first word on the first paper was *exasperated.* The student had written, for a definition, *vexed.* And her accompanying sentence was *He was exasperated.*

At that point, all the student teacher knew was that (1) the child could find the word in the dictionary, (2) she could copy the first available definition, and (3) she recognized that a word ending in -*ed* could serve in the past participle slot in a sentence. He knew nothing about whether the child knew the meaning of the word, or whether the child *owned* the word, to use Beck's (1984) term for knowing a new word in its fullest sense.

The problem illustrated here is similar to the dilemma faced by teachers each time they find a new list of vocabulary for a new reading selection (or when they come to a new chapter in a social studies or science textbook). How much concept development needs to be done *before* children will be able to understand the text at hand and use that new vocabulary when they read different texts?

While we do not have the final answer on these questions, we do have some guidelines derived from recent research on the relationship between knowledge about a topic and comprehension of texts related to that topic. First, there is no question about that relationship: A reader's knowledge about a topic, particularly key vocabulary, is a better predictor of comprehension of a text than is any measure of reading ability or achievement (Johnston and Pearson, 1982; Johnston, 1984).

Second, several studies point to the advantage of a fullblown concept development approach to vocabulary over a more conventional definition and sentence approach. Particularly useful have been semantic mapping and semantic feature analysis approaches (Johnson, Toms-Bronowski, and Pittleman, 1982; Johnson, 1983; Johnson and Pearson, 1984), as well as outer approaches that emphasize semantic elaboration (Beck, Perfetti, and McKeown, 1982; Kameenui, Carnine, and Freschi, 1982). What these more useful approaches have in common is that they emphasize where a word fits in children's semantic repertoire rather than what it means or how it is used in sentences. That's what it means to own a word—to know what it is like and how it differs from other words that a child knows.

To accomplish this goal for vocabulary, we must alter our stance toward vocabulary instruction (for a more complete treatment of these issues, see Johnson, 1983, or Johnson, Toms-Bronowski, and Pittleman, 1982). We must change the questions we ask when we get ready to help a child acquire a new concept. Too often we have asked "What is it that children do not know and how can I get that into their heads?" The better question is "What is it that children *do* know that is enough like the new concepts so that I can use it, as an anchor point?"

We can learn new concepts only in relationship to concepts we already possess. This is a principle that we, as considerate adults, use all the time with our peers when we explain a new phenomenon. We say "Well, it is sort of like X . . . but. . . ." We establish a contact between the new and the known, then we explain how the new concept is different.

We must extend the same courtesy to children. We must refocus our vocabulary efforts on techniques emphasizing semantic elaboration and semantic fit rather than definition and usage. Only then will we achieve the goal of *ownership* we would all like to achieve.

COMPREHENSION SKILL INSTRUCTION

In Durkin's (1978–79) classroom observations, one of her goals was to determine when, how, and how often teachers engaged in direct, explicit instruction for comprehension skills; that is, what did teachers tell students about *how* they should perform the various comprehension tasks assigned on the myriad of worksheets and workbook pages in their reading programs? Of 17,997 minutes, she found precisely 45 minutes devoted to this kind of direct instruction in comprehension (and some 11 minutes of that was on the influence of punctuation).

She found lots of what she labeled mentioning—saying just enough about an assignment so that students understood the formal requirements of the task, but stopping short of demonstrating how to solve the task cognitively or what to look for as clues for generating a solution.

Durkin (1981) conducted a similar analysis of basal manuals, looking for instances of compre-

hension instruction. While the manuals fared somewhat better than the teachers, they still fell woefully short of what we might call substantive instruction. Most of their instructional directives consisted of a single sentence, perhaps something like "Tell the students that the main idea is the most important idea in the paragraph." Rarely was much in the way of modeling, guided practice, or substantive feedback suggested.

Again, Durkin felt that "mentioning" better characterized what the manuals were offering in the way of instructional directives to teachers.

One can argue that the reason both teachers and manuals offer little explicit instruction in how to solve comprehension tasks is that comprehension is such a complex interactive process, influenced by so many situational and individual factors. Until recently we simply have not understood the process well enough to be able to identify and define basic and distinct comprehension skills, let alone determine strategies that teachers could use to help students apply these skills consistently across the range of texts and practice activities they encounter.

Recent researchers, however, have been successful in helping students develop strategies for discovering some regularities across different texts, tasks, and situations.

Questions. Hansen (1981) tried to determine whether she could improve second graders' ability to answer questions that did not have explicit answers in the texts (what we usually call inferential comprehension). She found that giving students several opportunities to respond to inferential guided reading and follow-up questions or employing a prereading strategy that encouraged students to use their own experiences to predict and evaluate story characters' problems and actions both produced reliable increases in the children's ability to answer inferential comprehension questions, at no loss to their performance on literal tasks.

Apparently what happened was that students *either* exposed to lots of questions requiring answers from prior knowledge *or* encouraged to use prior knowledge to predict and evaluate story events learned that it was legitimate to invoke one's prior knowledge in answering questions. Several students actually volunteered that, prior to the training, they did not know that it was "OK" to use "their own words" to answer questions.

In a related study, Hansen and Pearson (1983) combined the two treatments (strategy training and lots of inferential postreading questions) and compared the hybrid to a "business as usual" control group (do whatever the Teachers Manual says) for both good and poor fourth graders. They also trained teachers to administer the treatments instead of having the experimenters do so and stressed the metacognitive dimension (self-awareness of the strategy) in this training. Before each training session, they discussed with students what it was they were doing before each story (using prior knowledge to predict story events) and why.

After 10 weeks of training, few differences emerged among good readers; however, strong and reliable differences surfaced among the poor readers, favoring the hybrid inference training group. In fact, on one measure, the poor experimental students performed as well as the good control students despite a 3-year grade norm difference in average reading test scores. Differences in performance were observed on both literal and inferential measures but were more striking on the inferential measures.

Hansen and Pearson concluded that the training was most effective for precisely those students who typically exhibit frustration on comprehension tasks. The lack of consistent reliable differences among good readers might be attributed to the fact that many good readers often discover such strategies on their own through sheer exposure to various tasks. Poor readers appear to require more and more careful guidance from a teacher.

Teachers who participated in the study expressed great satisfaction with the experimental treatment, stating that their reading group discussions were more lively and interesting. They also expressed some concern in getting used to

the treatment, the variety of responses offered (they had to learn to live with the fact that answers *do* vary), and the difficulty of generating good inference questions.

Inference training. Gordon and Pearson (1983), continuing this general line of inference training research, developed and evaluated an even more explicit technique for helping children become better at drawing inferences. As a first step, they established four subtasks that ought to be completed for every inference task: (1) ask the inference question, (2) answer it, (3) find clues in the text to support the inference, and (4) tell how to get from the clues to the answer (i.e., give a "line of reasoning").

In their 8-week training procedure, they led fourth graders through stages varying along a continuum of responsibility for task completion (Table 1).

In Stage 1, the teacher takes all the responsibility. By Stage 4, the student takes most of the responsibility. In a sense, Stage I represents modeling and Stage 4, independent practice or application; Stages 2 and 3 represent guided practice. Instruction is what happens in those intermediate stages between total teacher responsibility (modeling) and total student responsibility (practice or application). (See Gordon, 1985, for a detailed description of this technique.)

In fact, the whole procedure can be depicted graphically, as in the Figure (from Pearson and Gallagher, 1983, after Campione, 1981). In this model, the assumption is that the completion of any task can be conceptualised as requiring some varying proportion of responsibility from the teacher and the students. The diagonal line from upper left to lower right depicts such varying degrees, ranging from all teacher (i.e., modeling) in the upper left corner to all students in the lower right corner. What ensues between these extremes is guided practice, or the "gradual release of responsibility" from teacher to student.

Question–answer relationships. In another example of the model, Raphael (Raphael and Pearson, in press; Raphael and Wonnacutt, in press) has conducted several studies that focus students'

TABLE 1   Stages of Responsibility in Inference Training Task

	SUBTASKS			
Stages	*Ask question*	*Answer question*	*Find clues*	*Line of reasoning*
1. Modeling	T	T	T	T
2. Guided practice	T	T	S	S
3. Guided practice	T	S	T	S
4. Independent practice	T	S	S	S

After Gordon and Pearson, 1983.

Note: T = Teacher does subtask, S = Student does subtask

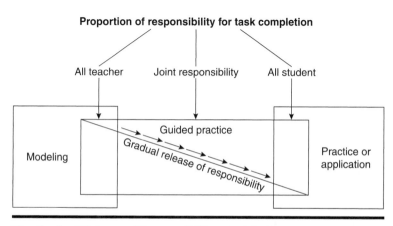

The Gradual Release of Responsibility Model of Instruction

From Pearson and Gallagher, 1983, after Campione, 1981. Printed by permission of P. David Pearson.

attention on how they should vary their strategies for answering questions. Raphael contends that they should vary strategies as a function of the task demands of the question (*Does it look like I should go to the text or to my head for an answer?*) in relationship to the information available (*What does the text say about this?* and *What do I already know about this issue?*).

Using Pearson and Johnson's (1978) trichotomy for classifying question-answer relations (text-explicit, text-implicit, and script-implicit), Raphael has taught fourth, sixth, and eighth graders to discriminate among three response situations, as illustrated in relation to Text 1. Under (a), both the question and the answer come from the same sentence in the text; under (b) the question and answer come from different parts of the text; under (c) the question is motivated by the text but the answer comes from the reader's prior knowledge.

Text: (1) Matthew was afraid Susan would beat him in the tennis match. He broke both of Susan's rackets the night before the match.
- (a) Who was afraid? *Matthew*
- (b) Why did Matthew break both of Susan's rackets? *He was afraid Susan would beat him.*
- (c) Why was Matthew afraid? *Maybe Susan was a better player.*

Raphael and Pearson (in press) and Raphael and Wonnacott (in press) taught the students to label these three strategies *right there, think and search*, and *on my own*, respectively, as they answer the questions. In their work, they have found that students of all ability groups and all grade levels who receive systematic and directed instruction in this technique were better able to comprehend new texts and to monitor their own comprehension. Like students in the Hansen and Pearson (1983) study, one student said, "I never knew I could get answers from my head before."

Raphael's procedure (see Raphael, 1982 or 1984, for complete details) can also be viewed as an application of the model in the figure. Think of the entire procedure as requiring the completion of four tasks (in Table 2), consisting of (1) asking a question, (2) answering it, (3) classifying the Question-Answer relationship, and (4) telling why it deserves that classification.

Notice how Stages 1–4 represent the same sort of logic present in the Gordon and Pearson (1983) work. Raphael, however, has added a Stage 5, one in which students generate their own questions and then apply the other subtasks. I regard this additional step as representing "true ownership" of the strategy because, at this point, it comes under complete student control.

Reciprocal reaching. Palincsar and Brown (1984) have developed a somewhat different application of this model for helping remedial junior high students improve their comprehension of content area materials. Particularly interesting in this work is the interaction between teacher and student in the small group training. Using reciprocal teaching, the teacher meets with a small group (5 to 15 students) and models four tasks for them to perform over each paragraph or segment read from their content area (science and social studies) materials.

1. Summarize the paragraph or segment in a sentence.
2. Ask a good question or two.
3. Clarify hard parts.
4. Predict what the next paragraph or segment will discuss.

Initially the students' role is to concur on the summary and the quality of the questions, to answer the questions, and to help clarify unclear text segments. After a few models by the teacher, the students take over the role of teacher. Whoever plays teacher must generate the summary, ask a few questions, lead a discussion of unclear words or parts, and predict the next subtopic. Whoever is playing student must help revise the summary, answer the questions (or suggest al-

TABLE 2   **Stages of Responsibility in Question-Answer Relationship Task**

	SUBTASKS			
Stages	*Ask question*	*Answer question*	*Assign QAR classification*	*Justify classification*
1. Modeling	T	T	T	T
2. Guided practice	T	T	T	S
3. Guided practice	T	T	S	S
4. Independent practice	T	S	S	S
5. True ownership	S	S	S	S

After Raphael, 1982, 1984.

Note: T = Teacher does subtask, S = Student does subtask

ternative questions), clarify unclear parts, and concur in (or disagree with) the prediction.

After turning over the reins to the students, the teacher:

1. takes a regular turn as "teacher,"
2. provides feedback about the quality of summaries or questions,
3. provides encouragement to students playing "teacher" ("you must feel good about the way you generated that summary!"),
4. keeps the students on track, and
5. encourages each student playing the teacher role to take *one* step beyond their present level of competence (based upon individual diagnosis about where each student is operating).

Additionally, at the end of each 25–30 minute reciprocal teaching period, students receive a completely novel passage for which they must generate a summary or answer several questions independently.

Palincsar and Brown have applied this technique to triads (1 teacher, 2 students), small groups conducted by volunteer remedial reading teachers, and intermediate grade teachers working with regular reading groups. In all cases student gains have been dramatic.

Typically student scores went from less than 40% correct on the daily independent exercises to over 80% correct on questions or summaries. The effects lasted anywhere from 8 weeks to 6 months. And students receiving this training made gains in their social studies and science classwork that moved them, on average, from the 20th to the 60th or 70th percentile.

Referring back to the model in the Figure, reciprocal teaching may provide the clearest and most readily implementable example of gradually releasing task responsibility from teacher to student.

This group of studies provides evidence that comprehension can be taught after all. They also suggest that what is missing in our current milieu (what I like to call our practice-only approach to comprehension) is the critical element of the teacher interacting with groups of students to help them gain more personal control over the instructional environment in which we place them and the tasks we require them to perform in that environment (see Pearson and Leys, in press, for further examples of application of this model).

COMPREHENDING AND COMPOSING

The May 1983 issue of *Language Arts,* the elementary school journal of the National Council of Teachers of English, was devoted to explicating the theoretical and practical interfaces between reading and writing. In reading the issue, one soon discovers that the authors are *not* writing about similarities in phonics for reading and phonics for spelling! Instead, the broad points of similarity are to be found in considering the basic similarity between composing a text and comprehending a text. Several authors, in fact, make the point that readers, at least metaphorically, have to compose their own texts as they read.

Whether this metaphor of a reader as a writer holds up point for point is not really the issue. Truly at issue here is that modern theories of comprehension (as in the first change I suggest) require us as educators to realize that the whole process of comprehension is much more *active, constructive,* and *reader-based* than our older theories suggested. No longer can we think of comprehension as *passive, receptive,* and *test-based.* No longer can we think of meaning as residing "in the text." Instead, we must regard each and every text students read as a blueprint to guide them in building their own model of what the text means. The text sets some broad boundaries on the range of permissible meanings, but it does not specify particular meanings. Particular meanings are negotiations between an author and a reader, with a teacher playing the role of a guide in helping students negotiate a meaning.

To realize the truth of this perspective, all one has to do is to watch a teacher and some students read and discuss a typical preprimer story—a 6-page story of 80 words with 4 to 6 pictures and 20 comprehension questions in the teacher's manual.

The key question is why are there 20 comprehension questions and what are they about? A few, we know, are about the words in the text. A few more, perhaps, are about the pictures. But many are really about students prior knowledge of the scenarios only hinted at by the text and the pictures.

Why are they there? They are there because the people who wrote them realize (most likely intuitively and unconsciously) that a complete understanding of the story could not occur without providing cues to help fill in the gaps left in the combination of text and pictures on the page. To corroborate for yourself that even a novice reader's understanding is richer than the explicit message on the page, ask a student who has just read and discussed one of these "stories" to retell it to you. You'll likely find rich elaborations, indicating that he or she has added much in building a personal model of what the text means.

Tierney and Pearson (1983) have noted the similarity of several subprocesses in composing and comprehending. The writing process, they note, entails planning, composing, and revising. Writers gather information (from their own knowledge or from reading designed to bolster their own knowledge), establish a purpose, and hypothesize an audience when they *plan* their writing. They begin to set pen to paper (or with modern technology to create dots on a cathode ray tube) as they compose. And they can revise the text they have created during and after composing. Tierney and Pearson also note that these subprocesses are not necessarily distinct stages— that one can, for example, revise one's plans or composition, plan one's revisions.

Then they argue that good reading entails exactly the same sort of subprocesses. Good readers will plan their reading (note the kinds of prereading activities described in the earlier section on vocabulary), compose at least a tentative meaning as they read, and constantly revise that meaning in accordance with new information

they gain from the text's blueprint or from new insight from their own store of knowledge.

Also, revision can and does occur when a teacher guides students in a discussion. In fact, the real purpose of a story discussion may be to help students revise their models of what a text means, to help them take new perspectives and align themselves to characters and events in ways they have not yet considered.

The difficulty in separating comprehension and composition can also be seen in certain activities teachers may ask students to do. For example, suppose a teacher gives some fourth graders an assignment in which they are told that a writer was careless in composing a news article and inadvertently included some irrelevant information. The students' task is to edit out that irrelevant information and replace it with better information. Is this an act of composition or comprehension? I cannot tell.

Or suppose a third grade teacher, concerned about figurative language, asks a group of students to replace certain literal expressions with figurative paraphrases (or vice versa). Is this composition or comprehension? I cannot tell.

Or suppose a group of seventh graders rewrites a part of a chapter in their science text to make it more understandable to a group of sixth graders. Is this composition or comprehension? I cannot tell.

Or suppose a teacher, conducting a writing conference with a first grade student, asks that student whether the audience would like to know or needs to know the information contained in a particular paragraph. Is this composition or comprehension? Again, I cannot make the distinction.

Teachers who choose to accept this basic process similarity between comprehension and composition will discover that their role in teaching is not so much to sit in judgment about what is right or wrong in an essay, a story, or an answer to a question, but to act as a sort of tour guide to help students see richness and possibility with different language, different interpretations, different perspectives cued by different questions. (For a more complete treatment of these issues and more specific suggestions on teaching reading and writing together, see *Language Arts*, May 1983, and Indrisano, 1984.)

Were I to make a prediction about the single most important change in language instruction that will take place in the next decade, it would be that we will no longer separate instruction in reading and writing. It is one of the most exciting prospects I can think of.

CHANGING ROLE FOR TEACHERS

Taken together, these first five changes that I am advocating imply a sixth more pervasive change in our prevailing model of the role of the teacher. The model implicit in the practices of the 70s was that of a manager—a person who arranged materials, tests, and the classroom environment so learning could occur. But the critical test of whether learning did occur was left up to the child as s/he interacted with the materials.

Children practiced applying skills: If they learned them, fine; we always had more skills for them to practice; if they did not, fine; we always had more worksheets and duplicating sheets for the same skill. And the most important rule in such a mastery role was that practice makes perfect, leading, of course, to the ironic condition that children spent most of their time working on precisely that subset of skills they performed least well.

Why did we embrace such a model? There were several forces at work. First, the press for accountability and minimal competencies forced us to be accountable for something. And we opted for all the bits and pieces rather than the entire reading process. Second, the notion of mastery learning, presented so elegantly by Bloom (1968) and Carroll (1963), made such a system seem reasonable. Third, our friends in publishing unwittingly aided and abetted the movement by providing seductively attractive materials and management schemes. The fascination with materials became so prevalent that, in a recent survey, Shannon (1983) found that vir-

tually all the administrators and a high proportion of American teachers believe that materials *are* the reading program.

I would like to propose a new model for the late 1980s—a model in which the teacher assumes a more central and active role in providing instruction, a model in which practice is augmented by teacher modeling, guided practice and substantive feedback, a model in which the teacher and the child move along that continuum of task responsibility (the Figure), a model that says just because we want students to end up taking total responsibility for task completion does not mean that we should begin by giving them total responsibility.

In this model, teachers assume new and different roles: They become sharers of secrets, co-conspirators, coaches, and cheerleaders. Because they realize that they are readers and writers who share an interpretive community with their students, they become willing to share the secrets of their own cognitive successes (and failures!) with students.

They often coconspire with their students to see if they can "get to the author" or try to "trick the reader." They act sometimes the way good coaches do; they are there at just the right moment with just the right piece of information or just the right pat on the back. And they act as cheerleaders for their students, encouraging them to take new steps toward independence and focusing on their remarkable strengths rather than their weaknesses.

If we adopt this new view of the teacher, we will be taking the master notions of Bloom and Carroll more seriously than ever, because we will be recognizing an often forgotten feature of mastery learning—that additional teacher assistance was, along with additional time on task, a basic component in the models. We will also be recognizing that true individualization has never meant that instruction is *delivered* individually, only that progress is *monitored* individually, and that what may be best for a given individual is not another worksheet but maybe a live body present to provide the guidance and feedback it will take to bring him or her to an independent level of performance.

As a metaphor for this new model, I would like to replace the metaphor of *teacher as manager* with a metaphor of the *teacher as teacher.* I know the idea is not startlingly fresh, but it does have a nice ring to it.

REFERENCES

Beck, Isabel. "Developing Comprehension: The Impact of the Directed Reading Lesson" In *Learning to Read in American Schools Basal Readers and Content Texts,* edited by Richard C. Anderson, Jean Osborn, and Robert J. Tierney. Hillsdale, N.J.: Lawrence Erlbaum, 1964.

Beck, Isabel L., Margaret G. McKeown, Ellen S. McCaslin, and Ann M. Burkes. *Instructional Dimensions That May Affect Reading Comprehension Examples from Two Commercial Reading Programs.* Pittsburgh, Pa. University of Pittsburgh, Learning Research and Development Center, 1979.

Beck, Isabel L., Richard C. Omanson, and Margaret G. McKeown. "An Instructional Redesign of Reading Lessons: Effects on Comprehension." *Reading Research Quarterly,* vol. 17, no. 4 (1982). pp. 462–81.

Beck, Isabel L., Charles A. Perletti, and Margaret G. McKeown. "The Effects of Long-Term Vocabulary Instruction on Lexical Access and Reading Comprehension" *Journal of Educational Psychology,* vol. 74, no 4 (1982). pp. 506–21.

Bloom, Benjamin S. "Learning for Mastery." *Evaluation Comment,* Vol. 1, no. 2 (1966). pp. 1–12.

Campione, Joseph. "Learning, Academic Achievement, and Instruction" Paper delivered at the second annual conference on Reading Research of the Center for the Study of Reading. New Orleans, La., April 1981.

Carrol, John. "A Model of School Learning" *Teacher's College Record.* vol. 64 (May 1963). pp. 723–33.

Collins, Allan, John S. Brown, and Kathy M. Larkin. "Inferences in Text: Understanding." In *Theoretical Issues in Reading Comprehension,* edited by Rend J. Spiro, Bertram C. Bruce and William F. Brewer Hillsdale, N.J.: Lawrence Erlbaum. 1980.

Durkin, Dolores. "Reading Comprehension Instruction in Few Basal Reading Series." *Reading Research Quarterly,* vol. 16, no. 4 (1981). pp. 515-44.

Durkin, Dolores. "What Classroom Observations Reveal about Reading Comprehension Instruction." *Reading Research Quarterly,* vol. 14, no. 4 (1978–79). pp. 481–533.

Gordon, Christine J. "Modeling Inference Awareness across the Curriculum" *Journal of Reading,* vol. 28 (February 1985). pp. 444–47.

Gordon, Christine, and P. David Pearson. *Effects of Instruction in Metacomprehension and Inferencing on Students' Comprehension Abilities.* Technical Report No. 269 Urbana, Ill.: University of Illinois. 1983.

Hansen, Jane. "The Effects of Inference Training and Practice on Young Children's Comprehension." *Reading Research Quarterly,* vol. 16, no. 3 (1981), pp. 391–417.

Hansen, Jane, and Ruth Hubbard. "Poor Readers Can Draw Inferences." *The Reading Teacher,* vol. 37 (March 1984). pp. 586–89.

Hansen, Jane, and P. David Pearson. *The Effects of Inference Training and Practice on Young Children's Comprehension.* ED 186 839. Arlington, Va. ERIC Document Reproduction Service, 1980.

Hansen, Jane, and P. David Pearson "An Instructional Study Improving the Inferential Comprehension of Fourth Grade Good and Poor Readers." *Journal of Educational Psychology,* vol. 75, no. 6 (1983). pp. 821–29.

Indrisano, Roselmina. *Reading and Writing Revisited.* Occasional Paper No. 18. Columbus, Ohio: Ginn and Company, 1984.

Johnson, Dale D. *Three Sound Strategies for Vocabulary Development.* Occasional Paper No. 3. Columbus. Ohio: Ginn and Company. 1983.

Johnson, Dale D., and P. David Pearson. *Teaching Reading Vocabulary.* New York, NY: Holt, Rinehart, and Winston, 1976.

Johnson, Date D., and P. David Pearson. *Teaching Reading Vocabulary,* 2nd ed. New York, N.Y.: Holt, Rinehart, and Winston. 1984.

Johnson, Dale D., Susan Toms-Bronowski, and Susan D. Pittleman. "Vocabulary Development." *Volta Review,* vol. 84, no. 5 (1982). pp. 11–24.

Johnston, Peter. "Background Knowledge and Reading Comprehension Test Bias" *Reading Research Quarterly,* vol. 19, no. 2 (1984). pp. 219–39.

Johnston, Peter, and P. David Pearson. *Prior Knowledge, Connectivity, and the Assessment of Reading Comprehension.* Technical Report No. 245. Urbana, Ill.: University of Illinois. 1982.

Kameenui, Edward J., Douglas W. Carnine, and Roger Freschi. "Effects of Text Construction and Instructional Procedures for Teaching Word Meanings on Comprehension and Recall." *Reading Research Quarterly,* vol. 17, no. 3 (1982). pp. 367–88.

National Assessment of Educational Progress. *Three National Assessments of Reading: Changes in Performance, 1970–80.* Report No. II-R-01. Denver, Colo.: Education Commission of the States, 1981.

Palincsar, Annemarie S., and Ann L. Brown. "Reciprocal Teaching of Comprehension-Fostering and Comprehension-Monitoring Activities." *Cognition and Instruction,* vol. 1, no. 1 (1984), pp. 117–75.

Pearson, P. David. *Asking Questions about Stories.* Occasional Paper No. 15. Columbus, Ohio: Ginn and Company. 1982.

Pearson, P. David, and Margaret C. Gallagher. "The Instruction of Reading Comprehension." *Contemporary Educational Psychology,* vol. 8, no. 3 (1983). pp. 317-44.

Pearson, P. David, and Dale D. Johnson. *Teaching Reading Comprehension.* New York, N.Y.: Holt. Rinehart, and Winston. 1978.

Pearson, P. David, and Margie Leys "Teaching Comprehension." In *Resource Manual for Comprehension Instruction,* edited by Eric Cooper. New York, N.Y.: The College Board, in press.

Raphael, Taffy E. "Question-Answering Strategies for Children." *The Reading Teacher,* vol. 36 (November 1982). pp. (186–91).

Raphael, Taffy E. "Teaching Learners about Sources of Information for Answering Questions." *Journal of Reading,* vol. 27 (January 1994). pp. 303–11.

Raphael, Taffy E., and P. David Pearson "Increasing Students' Awareness of Sources of Information for Answering Questions." *American Educational Research Journal,* in press.

Raphael, Taffy E., and Clydie A. Wonnacut. "Heightening Fourth-Grade Students' Sensitivity to Sources of Information for Answering Questions." *Reading Research Quarterly,* in press.

Shannon, Patrick. "The Use of Commercial Reading Materials in American Elementary Schools." *Reading Research Quarterly,* vol. 19, no. 4 (1983). pp. 68–87.

Singer, Harry, and Dan Donlan. "Active Comprehension: Problem Solving Schema with Question Generation for Comprehension of Complex Short Stories." *Reading Research Quarterly,* vol. 17, no. 2 (1982). (pp. 166–86).

Tierney, Robert J., and P. David Pearson. "Toward a Composing Model of Reading." *Language Arts,* vol. 60, no. 5 (1983). pp. 568–90.

Comprehension Instruction: Beyond Strategies

Susan Kidd Villaume and Edna Greene Brabham

The final article in this series on reading comprehension (Villaume & Brabham, 2003) discusses recent thinking on this aspect of literacy instruction. The emphasis here is on the continued importance of teaching students how to use appropriate strategies in a variety of reading situations. Not only should these strategies be taught, but readers also need to know their own reasons for selecting and using these different approaches to better understanding. Beyond this basic instruction, readers must be able to evaluate when a specific comprehension strategy is effective for them and when it is not. In the latter case readers should also be able to know and understand when difficulties occur and how to correct them. The classroom teacher is in the best position to model this cognitive process and needs to continually demonstrate what constitutes effective reading comprehension.

In recent months, many teachers on the RTEACHER electronic mailing list (listserv) made comments on the changes they are making in their comprehension instruction. In these online conversations, teachers frequently referenced books such as *Mosaic of Thought* (Keene & Zimmerman, 1997), *Strategies That Work* (Harvey & Goudvis, 2000), and *I Read It, But I Don't Get It* (Tovani, 2000). Listserv members pointed out that these books have challenged them to think about their own reading strategies and to use these understandings as a foundation for revamping their comprehension instruction.

Several listserv discussions focused on ways teachers model and provide guided practice as they help students become aware of and apply strategies used by skillful readers. Listserv members described how they target strategies such as questioning, making connections, visualizing, inferring, summarizing, and synthesizing. We, like many teachers, are delighted when we see how our instruction promotes more strategic and thoughtful reading in our students. However, we share concerns voiced by several listserv members who noted that some students execute the strategies they have been taught in perfunctory rather than thoughtful ways. In this month's column, we wrestle with questions that emerged from conversations about this dilemma and forced us to think beyond strategy instruction. We begin our exploration by examining why we have emphasized strategies in comprehension instruction.

WHY DO WE TEACH COMPREHENSION STRATEGIES?

Our initial response to this question is that we teach comprehension strategies because that is what students need to learn. Research documents that skillful readers are strategic readers; reflections on our own reading processes confirm this finding. Yet, we (and many listserv members) are not satisfied with this response. We know that we must come to deeper understandings of why we read strategically.

As we reflected on our own reading processes, we realized that we do not use comprehension strategies out of a desire to do reading the right way. We are not driven by a "things skillful readers do" checklist. In fact, we noted that these strategies spring forth in flexible, spontaneous, and various ways as we consider information in the text, in light of the knowledge, experiences, attitudes, and beliefs that we bring to it. These reader-text transactions (Rosenblatt, 1978) are the crux of our reading experiences; the strategies we set in motion are merely their manifestations. But what motivates us to create meaning from text in active rather than passive ways?

After much discussion, we concluded that we choose to actively and thoughtfully construct meaning because we experience reading as an act that empowers us. We believe that we have the right and the responsibility as readers to ask our own questions, to make our own connections, to visualize our own images, and to formulate and reformulate our own predictions. Because we view reading in this way and have developed the expertise of skillful readers, we read novels to immerse ourselves in the stories and to gain meaning that is personally significant—not to memorize the names of the characters or the sequence of events. We read informational text to satisfy and stimulate our own curiosities as we discover and learn more about our world—not to regurgitate information. As we read both narrative and expository text, we often find ourselves exploring personal and world issues as we confirm or alter our views in ways that are meaningful to us. In short, we choose to read actively and strategically because to do otherwise means that we must relinquish our rights as readers and submit to the meanings, beliefs, and purposes advocated by others.

With this insight, we realized that we do not want to teach comprehension strategies because it is in vogue or even because it is what the research says to do. We want to teach these strategies because we have a great desire to share with our students the empowering potential of reading experiences. We know that the only way students can tap into this potential is to develop strategies that allow them to become actively and intensely involved in their reading. Through strategic reading, students gain access to the rights, responsibilities, and benefits afforded to skillful readers.

WHY DO SOME STUDENTS APPLY STRATEGIES IN PERFUNCTORY RATHER THAN THOUGHTFUL WAYS?

Having gained greater clarity as to why we teach students comprehension strategies, we began mulling over why some of our students seem to apply the strategies that we teach in obligatory and mechanical rather than responsive and insightful ways. Members of the listserv reminded us that factors such as prior knowledge, automaticity of word recognition, and fluency affect students' abilities to read strategically. However, we agree with several members who suggested that the greatest obstacles to comprehension for many students are their own dispositions toward reading. Dispositions can sabotage the potential of any reading experience if readers enter texts with an unwillingness to participate actively in meaning construction, an aversion to monitoring what makes sense and what does not, a tendency to shut down when the going gets tough, or a mind that is closed to new ideas and perspectives. Existing knowledge and strategies go untapped if readers do not have the motivation to fuel their activation.

Dispositions that interfere with strategic and thoughtful reading are varied. Some students exhibit resistance marked by inattention, a sullen expression, silent apathy, defiant remarks, or distracting and outlandish responses. Other students have dispositions that are more reflective of disenfranchised readers. They seem to have resigned themselves to "doing" school reading assignments. We recognize these students by their lack of personal investment or passion in transactions with text. They obligingly record their predictions in their response logs, litter their

books with sticky notes of their questions and connections, and take their turns sharing these responses during discussion. They compliantly follow the new procedures, but they seem to simply assimilate these new reading "actions" into their old understandings of and attitudes toward reading. We agree with many listserv members who lamented that resistance and disenfranchisement increase as students grow older. We now see the importance of helping students uncover or rediscover the empowering nature of the reading process. Accomplishing this feat is no small challenge.

Several listserv members suggested that teachers can minimize negative attitudes toward reading by allowing students to choose text that is comfortable and interesting. Others focused on helping students develop the skills and strategies that enable them to become actively involved in text. We agree that instruction must be intentionally planned and implemented in ways that begin to dismantle any resistance or disenfranchisement that students may have constructed. However, we will not be successful if we limit our instruction to teaching students the strategies that skillful readers use. We must be concerned with teaching strategies in ways that can transform students' dispositions toward reading.

WHAT KINDS OF COMPREHENSION INSTRUCTION DO WE NEED?

To explore issues regarding effective comprehension instruction, we begin with the notion that instruction needs to have the potential for changing resistant readers into eager readers and disenfranchised readers into active readers. For the past 2 decades, educators have debated the merits of explicit and systematic reading instruction as they participated in what have been called the "reading wars." Several listserv members cautioned that framing discussions of comprehension instruction around the concepts of explicit and systematic instruction could lead to another war. We suggest, however, that developing more in-depth understandings of these concepts may be critical to providing students with the comprehension instruction they need. We cautiously embark on this path as we refine our definitions of explicit and systematic comprehension instruction so that they accommodate our insights about readers' dispositions. Our extended definitions also are enriched by a realization that some forms of instruction proceed from the *outside in* while other forms proceed from the *inside out*.

Our awareness of instructional procedures that move from the outside in and from the inside out emerged from distinctions made by listserv members about their own learning. They described how they work from the outside in as they try out teaching ideas gleaned from professional conversations, workshops, and readings. They also described how they work from the inside out as they reflect on their own reading processes and use these insights to refine their comprehension instruction. Their comments made us realize that effective comprehension instruction must embrace both outside-in and inside-out approaches. On one hand, we must encourage students to work from the outside in as they try out strategies that they are taught. On the other hand, we must invite students to work from the inside out as they uncover their own reading strategies and respond in open-ended ways to their reading. Although the line between outside-in and inside-out approaches is fuzzy, the distinction challenges us to think about explicit and systematic comprehension instruction in more refined ways.

EXPLICIT INSTRUCTION

For us, explicit instruction is simply clear instruction: Students "get" what we are trying to teach. If our goal is to help students become strategic and thoughtful readers, then we must make clear to students what skillful readers do. We concur with many members of the listserv who suggested that modeling is one of the most explicit ways to teach a comprehension strategy such as questioning, making connections, or inferring.

Although modeling is important, it is not enough. Some listserv members highlighted the need for students to read text and practice the modeled strategies under the vigilant tutelage of their teachers. Predictably, some students will have difficulty—difficulties that become visible as teachers listen to their attempts to apply the modeled strategies. We find that a critical piece of explicit instruction is an insightful teacher who is capable of clearing up confusions that emerge as students try out the modeled strategies. We have come to understand that clarity emerges from teachers' abilities to facilitate conversations that reveal and extend students' understandings and that identify and address their misunderstandings. This version of explicit instruction is far removed from the scripted lessons and questioning techniques that are often linked to explicit instruction.

As we sort through what we are learning, we realize that some of our modeling and guided practice is designed to stimulate change from the outside in. For example, when we ask students to focus on the questions that emerge as they read, we impose a strategy based on our knowledge of what the research says about skillful readers. We select the strategy, model it, provide guided practice, and expect students to integrate it with their independent reading. Similarly, listserv members noted the effectiveness of many instructional scaffolds, or frameworks, that are grounded in research describing what skillful readers do. These scaffolds include reciprocal teaching (Palincsar & Brown, 1984), question-answer relationships (Raphael, 1986), questioning the author (Beck, McKeown, Hamilton, & Kucan, 1997), and literature circle roles (Daniels, 1994). Using a scaffold based on someone else's insights on the reading process provides teachers and students with a temporary framework that helps alter teacher-student interaction patterns, promotes personal response, and embeds strategy instruction in text reading (Fielding & Pearson, 1994).

Other types of explicit comprehension instruction described by listserv members reflect procedures that engage students in the reading process from the inside out. For example, one teacher commented on the power of think-alouds to "unpack our brain and show kids *all the things that go on in our heads*" as we read. After modeling this process, teachers then invite students to share what they are thinking but do not ask them to focus on any particular strategy (e.g., questioning) or follow any procedural scaffold (e.g., questioning the author). Although previously taught strategies and familiar scaffolds often influence what students share, teachers encourage students to go beyond the strategies that they have been taught as they reflect on the meanings they have constructed and their own reading process in open-ended ways. One listserv member described how she facilitates conversations about text by inviting students to "stop and jot" whatever they are thinking as they read. Oster (2001) described how think-alouds can be used to help students discover the inner workings of their own active thinking and reading.

Most instructional techniques for teaching comprehension strategies fall along a continuum of more focused, outside-in approaches and more open, inside-out approaches. For example, Tovani (2000) described how she teaches students to mark points in the text that are confusing. This instruction focuses students on the problem-solving nature of the reading process, but it also encourages them to identify and explore many different interferences to comprehension and to think about the many different ways that they can overcome these obstacles. Explicit strategy instruction that works from the outside in helps students refine their visions of reading and sets them thinking in more active ways; explicit strategy instruction that works from the inside out empowers students to go beyond what they are taught and to learn from their own reading experiences. Using this dual instructional path seems important if we want to help students develop the strategies and dispositions that characterize skillful and empowered readers.

SYSTEMATIC INSTRUCTION

Teachers on the listserv helped us understand that the concept of systematic strategy instruction has several dimensions: (a) Comprehension strategies are introduced in a systematic way that is logical, cumulative, and purposeful; (b) a com-

prehensive and interrelated system of strategies unfolds over time; and (c) systematic monitoring of what students can do (and not do) ensures that students receive instruction in what they need—not in what they already know.

Several teachers on the listserv described how they systematically choose one strategy to bring to the instructional foreground. Other teachers model and provide guided practice for a medley of strategies simultaneously. Although both of these instructional approaches may represent a systematic instructional plan, teachers must decide which is more appropriate for their students. Whichever approach is used, we argue that it is important to emphasize to students that a targeted strategy is only part of a complex strategy system activated by skillful readers. For example, if the instructional focus is questioning, we can become stuck in a quagmire of confusion if we try to sort out questioning from predicting, making connections, and inferring. We need to emphasize that strategies do not exist in neat boxes and that the boundaries between them are blurred. Finally, if we are serious about helping our students become empowered readers, we must not spend excessive instructional time focusing on single strategies that students already use in proficient and integrated ways. To do so not only wastes valuable instructional time, but it also undermines opportunities for students to grasp the dynamic nature of building meaning.

If an instructional plan is insufficiently systematic, students may fail to develop the knowledge and strategies of skillful reading, thus remaining unequipped to experience reading as an empowering event. If an instructional plan is excessively systematic, students may never experience the fluid and dynamic nature of the reading process and never glimpse how skillful and empowered readers work freely through a text in ways that are meaningful and significant to them.

A WORD OF CAUTION

Members of the listserv challenged us to think about possible negative effects stemming from an overemphasis on explicit and systematic comprehension instruction. Indeed, their cautions have led us to insights regarding why some of the more skillful readers in our classrooms find that strategy instruction, particularly in large doses, interferes with their reading. These students are not resistant or even disenfranchised readers. They participate in most reading events in active, intense, and empowered ways. A moderate amount of strategy instruction seems to heighten these students' awareness of what they do as they read. However, insistence on prolonged use of imposed strategies and scaffolds seems intrusive and cumbersome as does excessive use of more open-ended think-alouds and reflections. Explicit and systematic strategy instruction should clarify for students what skillful readers do, but it should not constrain them from doing it.

THE ONGOING CHALLENGE

Some teachers attempt to assimilate strategy instruction into prior conceptualizations of reading and comprehension instruction. These teachers borrow instructional agendas and teach them without deep-rooted purposes or understandings. Many listserv members have suggested that the power of strategy instruction will materialize only in the classrooms of teachers who have experienced and are willing to share the active and empowering nature of reading with their students. If we are serious about nurturing active and thoughtful readers, we must also be serious about *being* active and thoughtful teachers who work from both the outside in and the inside out as we continue to develop deeper understandings of our own reading processes and of what constitutes effective comprehension instruction.

We acknowledge that our attempts to grapple with the mystery and complexities of comprehension instruction fall short of the mark; however, we do not intend for the responses that we offer to be definitive. They are only dated entries in our ongoing journey to address what really matters in literacy education. In addition, we do not claim sole authorship for our responses. Our understandings of comprehension are a tapestry of thoughts and ideas woven from the innumerable face-to-face conversations and reader-author conversations that we have had with our colleagues—some whom we know personally and some whom we know only through their written thoughts. We invite you to join us as we continue to weave this tapestry and to move beyond strategies as we think about comprehension instruction that empowers both students and teachers.

REFERENCES

Beck, I. L., McKeown, M. G., Hamilton, R., & Kucan, L. (1997). *Questioning the author: An approach for enchanting student engagement with text.* Newark, DE: International Reading Association.

Daniels, H. (1994). *Literature circles: Voice and choice in the student-centered classroom.* York, ME: Stenhouse.

Fielding, L. G., & Pearson, P. D. (1994). Reading comprehension: What works. *Educational leadership, 51*(5), 62–67.

Harvey, S., & Goudvis, A. (2000). *Strategies that work: Teaching comprehension to enhance understanding.* York, ME: Stenhouse.

Keene, E. O., & Zimmerman, S. (1997). *Mosaic of thought: Teaching comprehension in a reader's workshop.* Portsmouth, NH: Heinemann.

Oster, L (2001). Using the think-aloud for reading instruction. *The Reading Teacher, 55,* 64–69.

Palincsar, A. S., & Brown, A. L (1984). Reciprocal teaching of comprehension-fostering and monitoring activities. *Cognition and Instruction, 1,* 117–175.

Raphael, T. (1986). Teaching question-answer relationships. *The Reading Teacher, 39,* 516–520.

Rosenblatt, L. (1978). *The reader, the test, the poem: The transactional theory of the literary work.* Carbondale, IL: Southern Illinois University Press.

Tovani, C. (2000). *I read it, but I don't get it: Comprehension strategies for adolescent readers.* Portland, ME: Stenhouse.

_____CHAPTER REFERENCES_____

McKee, P. (1941). The problem of meaning in reading. *English Journal, 30,* 219–224.

Mann, H. (1838). *Annual report of the Board of Education, together with the annual report of the Secretary of the Board.* Boston: Dutton and Wentworth.

Pearson, P. D. (1985). Changing the face of reading comprehension instruction. *The Reading Teacher, 38,* 724–738.

Thorndike, E. L. (1917). Reading as reasoning: A study of mistakes in paragraph reading. *Journal of Educational Psychology, 8,* 323–332.

Villaume, S. K., & Brabham, E. G. (2003). Comprehension instruction: Beyond strategies. *The Reading Teacher, 55,* 672–675.

_____ANNOTATED BIBLIOGRAPHY OF RELATED REFERENCES_____

Artley, A. S. (1943). The appraisal of reading comprehension. *The Journal of Educational Psychology, 34,* 55–60.

Discusses the effective assessment of reading comprehension, emphasizing the complexity of this aspect of reading.

Barton, V. F., Lewis, D., & Thompson, T. (2001). *Metacognition effects on reading comprehension.* (ERIC Document Reproduction Service No. ED453 521).

Describes an extensive project for helping students in second, third, fifth grades better comprehend text material and reflect on their reading in a wide variety of literacy techniques.

Coiro, J. (2003). Exploring literacy on the Internet. *The Reading Teacher, 56,* 458–464.

This important article reflects current research and practice in the area of reading comprehension strategies, particularly as they relate to the use of new technology, most notably the Internet.

Crismore, A. (Ed.). (1985). *Landscapes: A state-of-the art assessment of reading comprehension research 1974–1984: Volume 1.* (ERIC Document Reproduction Service No. ED261 350).

Summarizes almost 600 reading comprehension studies completed during a ten-year period.

Durkin, D. (1978–1979). What classroom observations reveal about reading comprehension instruction. *Reading Research Quarterly, 15,* 515–544.

Considered by many to be a classic reference in reading comprehension research. Based on classroom observation, it describes the remarkable lack of effective comprehension instruction in the typical classroom literacy program.

Huey, E. B. (1908). *The psychology and pedagogy of reading.* New York: Macmillan. Reprinted by M.I.T. Press, 1968.

Although this book is considered a classic in the field of literacy education for its discussion of the basic reading process, it also contains an extensive section on reading comprehension. Of particular note is the chapter titled, "The Interpretation of What is Read, and the Nature of Meaning."

Palinscar, A. L., & Brown, A. S. (1984). Reciprocal teaching of comprehension-fostering and monitoring activities. *Cognition and Instruction, 1,* 117–175.

Discusses the use of reciprocal teaching as an important comprehension strategy based on the use of prediction, questioning, seeking clarification when needed, and summarization. *See also* Rosenshine and Meister (1994) for a summary of research in reciprocal teaching.

Pearson, P. D., & Fielding, L. (1991). Comprehension instruction. In R. Barr, M. L. Kamil, P. B. Mosenthal, & P. D. Pearson (Eds.), *Handbook of reading research, Volume 2* (pp. 815–860). New York: Longman.

An extensive review and discussion of the important research on comprehension instruction with particular emphasis on application in the classroom setting.

Pressley, M. (1998). Comprehension strategies instruction. In J. Osborn & F. Lehr (Eds.), *Literacy for all: Issues in teaching and learning* (pp. 113–133). New York: Guilford Press.

Contains an important discussion of the use of strategies in effective reading comprehension.

Pressley, M. (2002). Comprehension strategies instruction: A turn-of-the-century status report. In C. C. Block & M. Pressley (Eds.), *Comprehension instruction: Research-based best practices* (pp. 11–27). New York: Guilford Press.

A continuation of previous work by this author in the area of comprehension strategies (*see* Pressley, 1998). An especially important discussion of appropriate student-related strategies and how they influence effective understanding.

Rosenshine, B., & Meister, C. (1994). Reciprocal teaching: A review of nineteen studies. *Review of Educational Research, 64,* 479–530.
Summarizes the contemporary research on reciprocal teaching, noting its important impact on reading comprehension.

Russell, D. H. (1963). The prerequisite: Knowing how to read critically. *Elementary English, 40,* 579–582.
Written by one of the pioneers in the study of reading comprehension, describes the importance of the ability to read beyond the superficial aspects of a text selection.

Simmons, H. D. (1971). Reading comprehension: The need for a new perspective. *Reading Research Quarterly, 6,* 338–363.
A review of reading comprehension research, noting the need for further study in this area.

Thorndike, E. L. (1917). The psychology of thinking in the case of reading. *Psychological Review, 24,* 220–234.
An early discussion of the relationship between cognition and how this process is represented in the reading process.

Thorndike, E. L. (1917). The understanding of sentences: A study of errors in reading. *Elementary School Journal, 18,* 98–114.
In many respects this reference is a parallel article to the Thorndike material included in this chapter. The primary emphasis in this discussion is on individual sentences as opposed to complete paragraphs.

Thorndike, E. L. (1921). Word knowledge in the elementary school. *Teachers College Record, 22,* 350.

One of the early articles on the importance of vocabulary knowledge, this reference discusses the role of vocabulary as a major aspect of effective reading comprehension.

Tierney, R. J., & Cunningham, J. W. (1980). *Research on teaching reading comprehension.* (Tech. Rep. No. 187). Urbana, IL: University of Illinois, Center For the Study of Reading. (ERIC Document Reproduction Service No. ED195 946).
Reviews the teaching of reading comprehension in terms of two basic questions: 1) In what ways can reading comprehension be improved through effective classroom instruction, and 2) in what ways can research in this area be improved? This reference is of particular importance because of its extensive bibliography.

Tierney, R. J., & Cunningham, J. W. (1984). Research on teaching reading comprehension. In P. D. Pearson (Ed.), *Handbook of reading research* (pp. 609–655). New York: Longman.
An updating of the research on reading comprehension detailed in Tierney and Cunningham (1980).

Tinker, M. (1932). The relation of speed to comprehension in reading. *School and Society, 36,* 158–160.
Representative of a number of research and pedagogical articles concerned with the relationship between reading performance and comprehension accuracy.

Witty, P. (1943). Reading for meaning. *The English Journal, 27,* 221–229.
An important statement on reading comprehension as a critical aspect of an effective classroom reading program. Describes the importance of the teacher in helping students improve reading comprehension.

YOU BECOME INVOLVED

The short selection by Horace Mann (1838) summarizes the contemporary situation in the teaching of reading comprehension.

- What are some of the major problems Mann describes in reading comprehension?
- Based on this selection, how do you believe Horace Mann would define or describe effective reading, especially as this definition relates to the reader's understanding?

Edward Thorndike's article on comprehension is considered by many reading authorities to be one of the most important historical references in the field. Based on your reading of this material, consider the following ideas.

- What are the implications for your teaching of reading comprehension based on the types of responses the author received from the students in his study?

- Many of the responses from the readers reflected factual recall of information as opposed to more general concepts and implications reflective of critical reading. Why do you think this situation was true of Thorndike's students and do you think this situation in reading comprehension has changed dramatically today? If you believe that students today are more aware of facts and details than of general concepts, why do you think this it true? As a teacher how can you change this literacy situation?

McKee's (1941) article is a good summary of almost 50 years of research and practice in reading comprehension.

- Summarize the results of the studies done through the time of publication of this article, particularly as they relate to what the students were understanding in their reading. Has this situation regarding students and their reading comprehension changed much today? If not, why do you think the situation is basically the same?
- What are some of the suggestions McKee makes to help students better understand what they are reading? What are the implications of these ideas, particularly as they relate to the instructional role of the classroom teacher and reading comprehension?

Pearson's article (1985) continues the discussion related to reading comprehension. Evaluate the following implications of this discussion.

- How do the discussions of reading comprehension by McKee and Pearson differ and how are they the same, especially in relation to the role of the classroom teacher in the development of better understanding in their students?
- What does Pearson see as being the role of vocabulary knowledge in the development of effective reading comprehension?
- What is the relationship between writing or composing and reading comprehension?
- What specific suggestions for classroom teachers does Pearson make as to how students can become better at comprehending what they are reading?

Villaume and Brabham's article (2003) reflects current thinking on the teaching of reading comprehension. Consider the following points as you reflect on your reading of this piece.

- In what way has the teaching of reading comprehension changed from the past to today, especially in relation to the role of the classroom teacher?
- What do Villaume and Brabham identify as being some of the reasons students have difficulty understanding the material they are reading?
- How is "explicit instruction" similar to or different from "systematic instruction" in relation to reading comprehension? Can you think of some specific illustrations of each of these teaching methods that you might use in your own comprehension teaching?
- Based on your reading in this chapter, what do you see as being the future developments in this area of literacy instruction?

CHAPTER 5

SPELLING

It's a damn poor mind that can only think of one way to spell a word.
> —Andrew Jackson
> *Writings* (1840)

In any given school, the child's achievement in spelling is to a large extent dependent upon the nature of that school's curriculum.
> —Paul McKee
> *Spelling* (1944)

Two of the most important ways that students learn to spell are through daily reading and writing activities.
> —Gail Tompkins
> *Literacy for the 21st Century* (2003)

The ability to spell correctly has long been considered by society to be one of the most important characteristics of an educated person. In fact, spelling success is viewed today by many parents and teachers as being the single most important aspect of effective writing (Turbill, 2000). Despite the acknowledged importance of the role of spelling in the language arts program, there has historically been much controversy and disagreement as to the most effective methods of teaching this subject. For many teachers, learning to spell "was separate from both learning to read and developing new vocabulary" (Asselin, 2001, p. 1). The spelling curriculum in many classrooms was often based on rote memorization of a carefully determined list of words selected either by the teacher or taken from a spelling textbook. Mastery was measured through traditional paper and pencil tests with little opportunity to show understanding of the spelling words through writing activities or other language experiences. The success of this approach to spelling was often of limited value as students learned to spell the words correctly for their tests but unfortunately were unable to use them appropriately in other language applications, especially in their writing activities.

Educators have been aware of the many problems associated with the teaching of spelling. From almost the beginning of literacy instruction, various approaches and methods have been suggested to help students become good spellers. For instance, rather than the use of a predetermined set of spelling words, such as those found in a spelling textbook, words are selected by the student based on personal interest or current reading activities. Related issues such as the use of "embedded or contextualized" spelling, or the timing of students' learning to spell specific words as they find a need for these terms in their individual reading and writing activities, have historical roots as well (Graves, 1983; Read, 1971).

AS YOU READ

The selections that follow show the historical development of thinking related to the many difficult issues associated with spelling instruction. Note how many of the current concerns about spelling have been of interest to educators for many years. Also observe how various solutions to the problems associated with spelling in the past are still being considered in the modern classroom.

An Experiment in Teaching Spelling

Martha J. Fulton

The first article, by Fulton (1914), is one of the earliest related to spelling instruction. This description of a simple study of several different methods is mentioned by many subsequent literacy authors and has had important implications for the teaching of this subject. As you read this short article, observe the different approaches used to teach spelling and consider the conclusions of this classroom research.

Aside from the teaching of Reading, perhaps, no other study in the curriculum of school education leads to more discussion than the subject of spelling.

Many tests of spelling ability of school children have been made in the past few years with results varying as widely as the prejudices of the experimenters; in one instance the test seems to show absolutely no benefit from the years of spelling-book "grind;" in another the spelling drill shows appreciable results. The chief difficulty lies in the interpretation of the results, a difficulty which would disappear if the tests were of methods rather than mere results. . . .

To determine the exact benefit, if any, arising from persistent drill in the spelling words the following experiment was made with a 4–B Grade in a public school where the children in attendance are of average ability.

One hundred words were taught in two weeks (ten school days), ten each day, using this procedure:

I. *Write word upon the board.*

This presents to the child an opportunity to visualize the given word, or, expressed differently, to enable the child to form a visual image of the word before him. The basis for this lies in the fact that a large percent of children learn best by the process of "seeing."

II. *Explain the meaning of the word.*

Many words are entirely lost to the child for the want of a thorough understanding. When the meaning of a word is clear in the mind of a child, the successive appearances of that word make a far greater impression than if it is unknown. This is aided by the next step:

III. *Children use the word in a sentence.*

Knowledge becomes useful when one possess the ability to apply it. A child takes a greater amount of interest in words that he can use freely, taking his own vocabulary as a means of supporting the new word.

IV. *The children write word ten times and while writing say each letter aloud.*

Most individuals can learn more readily and retain longer the words gained by writing and talking at the same time. The letters are made to implant a mental word picture in the minds of the children, through the ears for those with "audible" memories, and from the lips and fingers for those with "mobile memories."

V. *Emphasize by intonation of voice or by colored chalk on blackboard the difficult parts of the word.*

A thing is better remembered when it reaches the mind with greater intensity than ordinarily. If the "hard" part of the word for instance, "yg" in "hygiene," stands out prominently and is memorized thereby the other parts tend to go along with it.

At the end of ten days drill a test in the one hundred words was given with the results shown in column I, Table I.

Following this a group of one hundred words, of similar difficulty were given the children during ten school days with no directions except to "study the lesson." The children were "heard" in their spelling each day and the next lesson assigned, but no effort was made to teach the spelling. A test of these words at the end of ten days produced the results shown in Column III.

Three weeks after the test of the first group of words (no mention of them had been made in the meanwhile) another test was made to see what percent of the words had been retained. The results are shown in column II. A test of the second group three weeks later produced the results shown in column IV.

Table II shows the number of children who fell below, remained stationary or increased their averages after the three weeks interval. The few cases of increase are due probably to the children having accidentally seen the words in reading or otherwise and thus become familiar with them. It will be seen that not only was there a 25% loss in spelling ability when the drill was stopped, but the ability to retain over a long period of time was affected in 25% of the children.

TABLE I

NUMBER OF PUPILS	I SPELLING WITH DRILL	II THREE WEEKS LATER	III SPELLING WITHOUT DRILL	IV THREE WEEKS LATER
1	100	100	78	64
2	100	98	74	68
3	100	100	94	94
4	100	100	86	84
5	100	98	86	80
6	100	100	54	40
7	100	100	72	60
8	100	100	86	80
9	100	98	90	92
10	100	98	72	68

TABLE I *continued*

NUMBER OF PUPILS	I SPELLING WITH DRILL	II THREE WEEKS LATER	III SPELLING WITHOUT DRILL	IV THREE WEEKS LATER
11	100	98	80	80
12	100	98	84	86
13	98	100	82	74
14	98	98	78	70
15	100	100	88	72
16	94	100	74	70
17	98	96	72	72
18	98	94	92	92
19	98	90	64	60
20	98	92	46	40
21	98	90	70	68
22	98	88	44	40
23	96	100	70	66
24	96	94	58	50
25	96	96	64	60
26	94	88	68	68
27	94	96	58	50
28	90	90	54	50
Average	98	96	73	68
Average deviation	1.9	3.4	11.2	11.8

TABLE II

Summarized from columns I and II of Table I:

	With drill	Below in the second	14 or	50%
		Same in both	10 or	36%
		Above in the second	4 or	14%
			28	100%

Summarized from columns III and IV of Table I:

	Without drill	Below in the second	21 or	75%
		Same in both	5 or	17%
		Above in the second	2 or	8%
			28	100%

Daily Results, All Pupils
With drill   99%
Without drill   78%

CONCLUSIONS

The results of this experiment may be summarized in the following statements:

I. Spelling drill is necessary in any class where the children vary in ability.

II. The best results are obtained by presenting the words in as many ways as possible.
  1. Spelling orally
  2. Visualization of words.
  3. The combination of writing and talking
  4. The correlation of word with its meaning, to fix a permanent impression

III. Constant drill

IV. Awaking of interest
  By presenting devices which will appeal to children of various stages of intellectuality

V. Actual supervision
  Methods of study should be given to the children and continually supervised by the teacher.

Method in Teaching Spelling[1]

John C. Almack and E. H. Staffelbach

The second article, by Almack and Staffelbach (1933), reflects almost thirty years of research and discussion among educators relative to the teaching of spelling. Observe as you read this article the number of issues that are mentioned that have a surprising "modern" connotation to them. For instance, the suggestion on the first page as to "children learn to spell 'incidentally,' that is without specific instruction," is a theme which will reappear again in future debates about the effective teaching of spelling skills. Other issues such as oral and written spelling activities, specific assessment procedures in spelling, and group and individual instruction are also addressed in this article.

THE VALUE OF METHOD

As soon as a suitable body of words has been selected, spelling efficiency becomes, to a great degree, dependent on the method of teaching and study. Hilderbrant (6)[2] says that there are probably no "born spellers" and that persons who spell well do so because they have adequately directed their word experiences or their word experiences have been well directed by a teacher. Their attention has been called early in life to the correct arrangement of letters in words, and they have had adequate practice in using these words in practical written discourse.

The view has been advanced now and then, however, that children learn to spell "incidentally," that is, without specific instruction in the subject. To illustrate, a pupil who is taught to read and who, in learning to read, also learns to spell has learned spelling "incidentally." Evidence favoring "incidental" teaching of spelling rests on comparisons of results obtained under *poor* direct teaching and *good* incidental teaching in connection with reading and composition. It is not surprising that poor direct teaching does not yield good results. However, when incidental teaching is matched against good direct teaching, the results are uniformly favorable to the latter.

Thompson estimates this gain at double the gain "to be expected as a function of general maturity and incidental learning" (18:71).

The problem in teaching spelling is not to choose between *no method* and the *best method* but rather to choose the *best method* from the many methods offered. The term itself ("method") is derived from the Latin *methodus,* which comes from the Greek *methodos.* In the Greek word, *met* means "after" and *hodos* "away"; thus "method" indicates a general or an established way or order of doing anything. True method or *best* method has its basis in science; that is, it has been *proved* best. A person who is very skillful is sometimes said to be scientific and may be called "an expert." The value of method in spelling is the value of expert method in any other aspect of life. It gets the best results in the quickest possible time and in the most agreeable and beneficial way.

Poor progress in spelling may result from lack of study technique on the part of pupils. Gilbert (4) examined the eye-movements of a group of sixty-seven children made up of good spellers and poor spellers. Among the poor spellers he found many fixations, long and irregular pauses, and lack of systematic procedure. These pupils studied by small sections, going over and over the same ground, seeing many minute and unrelated details, but failing to grasp the word as a whole. In contrast, the good spellers studied each word as a unit or as a whole made up of related parts. The typical record of a good speller showed a relatively small number of fixations in orderly arrangement with few regressions. The pauses were short, and the unit grasped was broad.

The value of method in spelling was also demonstrated by Fulton (2). Her experimental group followed systematic method; her control group was given no study directions. The difference in method was the sole difference in the two groups. In the final test the experimental group spelled correctly an average of 98 percent of the words; the control group, 73 percent. In a retention test given three weeks later the experimental

group averaged 96 percent; the control group, 68 percent. Every pupil in the experimental group did better than any pupil in the control group.

THE BASIS OF METHOD IN SPELLING

The science of biology (or of its derivative, psychology) supplies the basis of spelling method. Children learn to spell by seeing the letters of a given word or by hearing their sounds and by writing and speaking the letters in the order in which they are seen and heard. Seeing and hearing are forms of "impression"; writing and speaking are forms of "expression." These two form the bases for four kinds of images: (1) the sight of a word, (2) the sound of a word, (3) the way it "feels" when written, and (4) the way it "feels" when spoken (17: 109).

Studies have been made to determine the share which sight, hearing, speech, and writing have in developing the ability to spell. Almost without exception, these studies show that the motor presentations which occur through the activity of the hand and the vocal organs are of great importance and that *the eye is far more important than the ear.* Gates and Chase (3) found that deaf children were superior in spelling to normal children of the same reading age. They considered this superiority a result of the more careful visual study of word forms.

Kellner, as cited by Burnham (1: 480), distinguished between the spelling of those words which are written as they are pronounced and the spelling of non-phonetic words. He considered the ear the supreme judge in spelling phonetic words; there the rule is, "Write as you speak." For non-phonetic words that vary in form from their sounds, the eye should be chiefly active, and the rule is, "Write according to the custom."

For thirty years the leading authorities in spelling have maintained that the muscle sense of the hands and the speech organs should go along with sight and hearing. These sense perceptions play the significant part in the comprehension, the retention, and the reproduction of words. Oral spelling may be rejected altogether in favor of exercises in writing words. This point is well made by Burnham (1). It is in the writing of words that the real test of ability comes. Forming motor images by writing produces fewer errors than are produced when visual imagery alone is used. Writing is *better than seeing.*

Smedley (15) says that the aim in teaching spelling should be to render so well known the most frequently used words that they will flow automatically from the point of a pen (or from the keys of a typewriter), requiring but little thought for their formation. He stresses the fact that the spelling of words is rendered automatic by writing them. The first acquaintance with a word may be through hearing and seeing, but the teaching for final retention should be through audio-visual-hand-motor memory.

In class study new words should be seen, heard, pronounced, and written. One type of association reinforces the other. Since writing involves both visual and kinaesthetic sensations, it is more effective than seeing, hearing, or speaking alone. It also has the advantage of being the form in which spelling functions in life. Doubtless there are children who do not need to do more than to write many words in order to master their spelling; yet the more complete method of presentation is better for most children and makes for retention in all (6: 381).

GENERAL METHOD OF TEACHING SPELLING

Two statements have already been made about spelling method (1) that the best method is scientific and (2) that psychology is the basis of method. These statements are perfectly consistent because psychology is a branch of science. Scientific method has two main divisions. The first of these starts with a *problem,* goes next to facts, and from facts to a generalization which describes the facts and solves the problem. The proof of the generalization is tested by trying it out. One in possession of the proper, tested generalization can control results. His teaching is certain; it cannot fail. The second division of scientific method starts with an *objective,* goes to a plan or program

consisting of a number of activities in definite order and of definite time duration, and ends with results. This division is called applied science. It is that part of scientific method in which the controlling generalization is tried out. It is to this division that spelling method properly belongs. Its controlling principles are those which arise from the science of psychology.

Three stages in the process of applied science may be observed: *planning, doing,* and *evaluating.* In the planning stage the teacher and the pupils select their objective and justify it (motivation). They next make an estimate of the situation, which includes an inventory of their own knowledge and skill, and indicate a standard which they expect to attain. Then they proceed to lay out a time schedule, adopt a technique, demonstrate that they can use the approved technique, and are thus ready to begin their task.

In the doing stage each pupil puts into effect the procedure which has been planned. At the end of the time period the results are measured and compared with a standard. If the results are not satisfactory, one of two things may be done: (1) The process may be continued until the goal is reached. (2) A diagnosis may be made and the process altered entirely or in part.

In the evaluating stage the final results are compared with the accepted standard. The process is also examined critically, and suggestions for its improvement are made. Effort is made to find the difficulties of pupils and to understand why the difficulties exist. Methods for overcoming future difficulties are devised. Additional work toward the objective may be required by going over the process or parts of it, by adding to the materials to be taught, or by modifying the process and attacking the objective in a new way.

Most of the emphasis in teaching method is rightly put on the doing stage. The work should be systematic and may in general, when applied to spelling, follow directions such as these:

First, the attention of the children is called to the whole word on the board or in the book. The word is pronounced by the teacher and, if quite unusual or unfamiliar, by the children. The word is used in a sentence or defined. The teacher writes the word on the board in syllables. . . . The children are told to look away from the word and try to see it as it looks on the board. The word is spelled orally by individuals or by the class under controlled conditions. In either case oral spelling is preceded by a clear and accurate pronunciation of the word. Finally, the word is written several times [19: 71].

The plan described in the Eighteenth Yearbook of the National Society for the Study of Education (7) has been widely used. It begins with a pretest on Monday over the list prescribed for the week. On Tuesday the pupils study the words which they missed the previous day, the teacher directing their activity as necessary. Wednesday is devoted to retesting and to review and drill. Special attention is given on Thursday to individual difficulties. The unit is completed on Friday with a retest, usually in the form of timed sentences.

This system is methodical. Pupils are not called on to give unnecessary time to words which they already know, and the teacher is given opportunity to direct study and to discover special difficulties. The method also has its disadvantages. Nearly all the emphasis is put on spelling as such; that is, in getting the right letters in the right order. Little stress is placed on pronunciation or use. The plan is also somewhat over-formal. Every day has its assigned task; every week a unit must be completed. This plan assumes that the units are of equal difficulty and demand the same time distribution week in and week out. It assumes uniform effort and response on the part of the pupils week after week. There is little or no chance for a teacher to introduce desirable variations in order to increase interest and to develop initiative. It is an inflexible plan, not in accord with modern theories of child freedom and self-activated instruction. It puts too much emphasis on group testing and not enough on individual learning.

The writers are not disposed to question the value of testing before teaching. Experiments have been made to determine whether it is more effective to test first and then study or to study first and then test. Without exception, these experiments show the superiority of the test-study plan. Kilzer (9) supplies typical proof. In a study of one thousand pupils in thirty-four schools in eight states, he found the test-study method significantly better than the study-test method. The number of misspellings were appreciably fewer in the test-study plan—about seventeen less on a hundred words.

Senour (14) also shows that satisfactory results can be obtained with the test-study method. His subjects were 694 pupils in Grades III–VIII. While the children did not attain complete mastery, their scores were close to perfect. At the end of one month they retained 94 percent of the words; at the end of four months, 92 percent.

Kingsley (10) furnishes definite support for the test-study method. As the result of two years' experience he says, "Fifty-five per cent of the pupils missed no words; 25 per cent missed one word; 10 per cent missed two words; 5 per cent missed three words; 1 per cent missed four words; and 1 per cent missed five words." He concludes that "to ask these pupils to spend a fifteen-minute study period on the lesson, before testing, would be to waste nearly 95 percent of the time and, in some cases, actually to reduce the spelling ability. For a class of 30, figured as a business manager keeps time, 425 minutes of the aggregate 450 made no return" (10: 128).

The subject of spelling method has been well summarized by Zyve (21). She recommends teacher-directed study, the use of both lists and sentences in presenting words, visual aids, teacher-directed review, and a time allotment of fifteen minutes daily for new words. She considers indispensable a variety of approaches—visual, auditory, motor. Her final plan continues the formal organization of materials on daily and weekly bases.

Excellent criteria for judging spelling method have been set up by Zirbes (20). She declares:

Any spelling method which does not meet the following requirements does not qualify for wide use: (a) The method must reach the individual poor spellers and raise the quality of their spelling markedly by every test. (b) The method must be practical and economical of time and labor. . . . (c) The method must take into account the necessity for later recall of words with definite review or relearning. . . . (d) The method must appeal to the responsibility of the pupil, enlist his best efforts, and develop his spelling conscience [20: 784–85].

GROUP METHOD VERSUS INDIVIDUAL METHOD

The question has often been raised whether it is more effective to teach several individuals simultaneously (the group method) or to teach individuals independently of each other. The group method doubtless represents common practice, while the growing tendency is toward the independent plan. It does not follow that either method should be followed exclusively; common sense inclines to the view that each has a place. The question really is: Which method should predominate and what is the proper place of each?

A clear description of the group method has been published by Keener (8: 31–32), a summary of which follows.

1. The teacher writes the word to be studied on the board. She pronounces the word distinctly, sounding each syllable. The meaning is next explained, and the word is used in a sentence. The teacher next spells it orally, noting the division into syllables.
2. The word is next spelled with the pupils in concert, and attention is called to difficult parts. The word is then erased from the blackboard, and the pupils write it on paper. The teacher then spells the word orally, and the pupils check their spelling.
3. After all the words have been studied in this way, the pupils are tested. Each pupil keeps a list of the words that he missed. The study of these words is directed for each pupil independently. At the end of the week the pupils are tested over all the words they have been taught during the week.

Keener likewise gives the characteristics of the individual method (8: 32). A summary of his description is as follows:

1. The pupils are first tested on twenty words. Each pupil keeps a list of the words that he missed, and these words become his individual study lesson for the week.
2. Each pupil is trained to study his own lesson by (*a*) pronouncing the words in a whisper, (*b*) learning the meaning, (*c*) using the words in sentences, (*d*) spelling the words in a whisper, (*e*) checking his spelling against the correct forms of the words, (*f*) writing the words on paper, and (*g*) repeating the process until sure of the spelling of each word.
3. As a final step, the pupils are tested individually over their lists, and a second list of words missed is kept. These they proceed to study as before, together with words missed in other subjects.

As a result of an experiment to determine which method is the better, Mr. Keener found individual instruction slightly superior "when all grades were combined." This superiority existed even when "teachers were more skilled in using the group method" (8: 35). When one teacher taught first one method and then the other, she was more successful with the individual plan. The testimony of the teachers was markedly in favor of the individual method. The author advises this method, particularly for Grades IV–VIII.

Keener's findings failed to substantiate the earlier study of Pearson (13). The latter conducted four experiments in Grades IV, V, and VI "to compare the effectiveness of a series of recitations of the customary or independent type with a series of the class-study type" (13: 50). In three experiments he found the class method to be superior. In his fourth experiment he allowed fifteen minutes a day for class study and twenty-five minutes a day for individual study. Despite the larger time allowance for the individual plan, he found "that the class study method was about as efficient as the independent-study method" (13: 66).

The writers of this article make no attempt to reconcile or to explain these differences. Learning is individual, and the best method has been found when conditions are set up in which each pupil has the most favorable opportunities to learn what he does not know and should know. The time factor should necessarily be considered, and the matter of retention or permanence should not be overlooked.

Time may often be conserved by teaching the class as a unit, but in the last analysis each pupil should know how to work effectively when working alone. A system which integrates the two plans and takes the best of both seems most promising. In any event the teacher should be free to vary the method from day to day as the pupils' needs demand and to vary at will the relative emphasis put on each plan. Common needs may be met economically by class teaching; individual needs may be best served when the pupils work independently of each other under the direction of the teacher.

SPECIFIC ILLUSTRATIONS
OF SPELLING PRACTICES

Approved procedures may be further illustrated by referring to specific practices. Mearns (12) reports on a method in which improvement was significant and in which wide distribution disappeared and there were no "poor spellers." The main steps in his plan included (1) selection of a tested, socially useful list of words, arranged in the order of grade difficulty; (2) dictation of a small portion of the list as an inventory test; (3) a pupil check on errors from the teacher's oral spelling; (4) pupil recording of individual errors; (5) pupil study of misspelled words only; and (6) teacher dictation to test retention, followed by the repetition of the third, fourth, and fifth steps.

The class method used at Amsterdam, New York, has been described by Springsteed (16). The teachers employ the test-study plan. The words are first dictated. Each pupil then checks his own work against the list which has been put on the blackboard. He draws a line through every word which he has misspelled and then writes out the correct form. The meanings of the words are next taught. The pupils then study their own lists. The individual plan as used in the same school system is also described. The pupil pronounces the first word on his personal list and acquaints himself fully with its meaning. He then spells it orally, checks his spelling against the correct form, and repeats the word four or five times until he is sure that he knows it. His next act is to write the word, repeating this act until it becomes automatic. The teacher gives special help to pupils having difficulty.

The work of Miss Martin (11) may be cited as a final example of modern practice. She made assignments over an extended period of time and required the careful use of uniform record books. One day a week was set aside for review and trial lessons. Most of the stress was put on teaching rather than on testing, and the problems of each child were considered individually. Class and individual records were charted and kept in view. The children were encouraged to surpass their own past records. Interest was kept up by varying the kinds of activities.

A difference of opinion exists as to the wisdom of calling the attention of the pupils to difficult parts of words. Miss Springsteed opposes the practice because "the type of error made by pupils varies to such an extent that common study to avoid certain errors is unwarranted" (16: 294). Guiler (5) recommends analysis of difficulties in order that the teacher may know where to focus attention. The practice is in the direction of marking the difficult parts, but the value of this procedure has not been proved experimentally. Probably the procedure is of minor importance, occasionally effective and at times of no value. The teacher must decide whether or not to use it as she thinks best in a particular situation.

This discussion may be brought to a close by saying again that systematic method in teaching spelling adds greatly to results. The method has been well formulated. It makes appeal to sight and to hearing and requires directed expression in speaking and writing. Pretesting is essential in order that no time may be lost in the study of what the pupils already know. Common needs should be cared for by teaching in groups, but the greatest economy comes from teaching in terms of individual needs and through independent activity.

NOTES

1. This is the first of a series of three articles dealing with the teaching of spelling which are to appear in the *Elementary School Journal.*

2. The numbers in parentheses refer to the bibliography appearing at the end of this article. In case of quotations, page references are also given.

BIBLIOGRAPHY

1. Burnham, William H. "The Hygiene and Psychology of Spelling," *Pedagogical Seminary,* XIII (December, 1906), 474–501.

2. Fulton, Martha J. "An Experiment in Teaching Spelling," *Pedagogical Seminary,* XXI (June, 1914), 287–89.

3. Gates, Arthur I., and Chase, Esther Hemke. "Methods and Theories of Learning to Spell Tested by Studies of Deaf Children," *Journal of Educational Psychology,* XVII (May, 1926), 289–300.

4. Gilbert, L. C. "Experimental Investigation of a Flash-Card Method of Teaching Spelling," *Elementary School Journal,* XXXII (January, 1932), 336–51.

5. Guiler, Walter Scribner. "Improving Ability in Spelling," *Elementary School Journal,* XXX (April, 1930), 594–603.

6. Hilderbrant, Edith L. "The Psychological Analysis of Spelling," *Pedagogical Seminary,* XXX (December, 1923), 371–81.

7. Horn, Ernest. "Principles of Method in Teaching Spelling as Derived from Scientific Investigation," *Fourth Report on the Committee on Economy of Time in Education,* pp. 52–77. Eighteenth Yearbook of the National Society for the Study of Education, Part II. Bloomington, IL: Public School Publishing Co., 1919.

8. Keener, E. E. "Comparison of the Group and Individual Methods of Teaching Spelling," *Journal of Educational Method,* VI (September, 1926), 31–35.

9. Kilzer L. R. "The Test-Study Method versus the Study-Test Method in Teaching Spelling," *School Review* XXXIV (September, 1926), 31–35.

10. Kingsley, John H. "The Test-Study Method versus the Study-Test Method in Teaching Spelling," *Elementary School Journal,* XXIV (October, 1923), 126–28.

11. Martin, Getrude E. "The Teaching of Spelling," *Elementary School Journal,* XXI (November, 1920), 201–7.

12. Mearns, Hughes. "A Report of a Specific Spelling Situation," *Teachers College Record,* XXVI (November, 1924), 220–29.

13. Pearson, Henry Carr. "Experimental Studies in the Teaching of Spelling," *Teachers College Record,* XIII (January, 1912), 37–66.

14. Senour, A. C. "An Investigation of the Effectiveness of the Test-Teach-Test Method of Instruction in Spelling," *Elementary School Journal,* XXX (May, 1930), 700–706.

15. Smedley, Fred Warren. *Report of the Department of Child-Study and Pedagogic Investigation, 1900–1901,* p. 63. Child-Study Report No. 3. Chicago: Chicago Public Schools, 1902. Quoted in William H. Burnham (1: 485).

16. Springsteed, Clara B. "How One City Improved the Teaching of Spelling," *Journal of Educational Method,* IV (March, 1925), 290–95.

17. Sudweeks, Joseph. "Practical Helps in Teaching Spelling: Summary of Helpful Principles and Methods," *Journal of Educational Research,* XVI (September, 1927), 106–18.

18. Thompson, Robert S. *The Effectiveness of Modern Spelling Instruction.* Teachers College Contributions to Education, No. 436. New York: Teachers College, Columbia University, 1930.

19. Tidyman, Willard F. *The Teaching of Spelling.* Yonkers-on-Hudson, New York: World Book Co., 1919.

20. Zirbes, Laura. "An Experimental Evaluation of Method in Spelling," *Elementary School Journal,* XIX (June, 1919), 778–98.

21. Zyve, Claire Turner. *An Experimental Study of Spelling Methods.* Teachers College Contributions to Education, No. 466. New York: Teachers College, Columbia University, 1931.

Invention, Convention, and Intervention: Invented Spelling and the Teacher's Role

Lawrence R. Sipe

Sipe's article (2001) describes "developmental, temporary, constructed, or invented spelling." In this approach to spelling instruction, students are encouraged to spell words phonetically on beginning drafts. Revision and further editing of these early drafts is part of the writing process, so that finished manuscripts reflect correct spelling. This is one of the most controversial areas in spelling today. Sipe also discusses the use of invented spelling, in relation to the role of the classroom teacher. Note in particular the theory and the recommended procedures for optimal use of invented spelling in the typical classroom language arts program.

The following two vignettes of first-grade children and their writing are used to indicate subtle confusions and tensions that seem to be present in both teachers' and children's ideas about early attempts to spell. All names are pseudonyms.

Kelly is in first grade and is receiving individual help in reading. She's doing very well, and her reading teacher thinks that she is probably functioning in the average range of her fellow classmates, but Kelly's classroom teacher disagrees. She shows the reading teacher Kelly's classroom journal, and the two teachers confer. It seems Kelly is able to spell many words on her own when she writes with her reading teacher, but the same words are not spelled conventionally in her journal. The reading teacher decides to talk to Kelly about this. The next time Kelly comes to her lesson, she places her classroom journal and her writing folder side by side. "Kelly," she says. "you spelled all these words correctly when you were with me, but look at your journal—you spelled them any which way in here. Why?" Kelly shrugs her shoulders. "My teacher gives me a break—she just wants me to come close."

Fred chews thoughtfully on his pencil as he tries to encode the word *down*. For the past 30 minutes, he has been deeply engaged in writing the sentence "Bats hang upside down" following a group lesson about bats. The process has been full of signs of metacognition, as he thinks aloud, rereads his message, evaluates it, and changes it when it doesn't match what he has in mind. He's justifiably proud of his effort, and beckons to his teacher, reading the sentence to her. She praises his efforts, and asks him if he could write one more thing about bats. He immediately thinks of writing, "Bats sleep in the daytime," while the teacher moves on to another child. He copies *bats* from his previous sentence. Then, while saying "bats sleep" to himself, he writes a *B* and a *T*, followed by a series of scribbles and letter-like shapes, ending with a backwards *N*, a lowercase *n*, and a *Y*. This is done very quickly, with no sounding out or apparent subvocalization. He calls his teacher again, and the following exchange occurs:

FRED: Mrs. Myron, I'm done. "Bats hang upside down."

TEACHER: What else did you write? You have two things. What does the other thing say?

F: This one? Bats hang up—I mean Bats . . . sleep . . . in . . . the . . . day . . . time (pointing to the words and the scribbles in the second sentence).

T: Good. You wrote two things down.

Then something very interesting happens:

FRED: I didn't get this right, did I? (pointing to the second sentence)
TEACHER: What didn't you get right?
F: Words.
T: Did you get some of it right?
F: Yeah.
T: Well, you just need to get as many right as you can. You don't need to spell all of these words yet. When you do, then you'll get'em all right, but right now I just want you to get as many right as you can. Good for you. You did a good job.

What is happening in these two situations?

Kelly had mistakenly concluded that her classroom teacher's expectations were not the same as those of her reading teacher; "coming close" was good enough, even when she knew how to spell the word. Fred was demonstrating a form of mature metacognitive self-evaluation. He knew that what he had written was nonsense; he wasn't satisfied with it, and in his own way he let the teacher know. Fred was self-aware to the point of being able to realistically evaluate his writing, isolating the sentence in which he had merely pretended to write.

In this article, I argue that we need to look closely at children's emerging capacities as writers, focusing especially on the issue of invented (or temporary) spelling, and its use and misuse in classroom practice. In order to understand the current situation, we need to examine the history of the concept of invented spelling and its theoretical underpinnings in the general context of the paradigm of emergent literacy. We need to deal with perceived tensions between the honoring of children's approximations and our desire to assist them in making the transition to conventional literacy. In the second part of the article, I describe in detail several teacher interventions that both honor children's attempts and actively assist

them in their journey to becoming more mature readers and writers.

THE CONCEPT OF INVENTED SPELLING

The idea that children achieve mastery of the conventional forms of literacy through gradual and successive approximations is one of the most important concepts in the emergent literacy model. Invented spelling is an elegant example of this approximation (DeFord, 1980). Discussions of invented spelling often begin with the seminal work of Charles Read (1971), who examined preschool children who constructed their own spellings of words before they received formal instruction. Longitudinal case studies of children's writing (Bissex, 1980) found that spelling progressed from scribbles to letter-like shapes to sequences of letters. When the alphabetic principle was grasped, children often encoded words by their initial consonants, followed by ending sounds. Medial sounds were the last to be heard and encoded. The whole process seemed to be like a camera lens coming very slowly into focus, as the spellings gradually came closer to conventional forms. Such research showed that, contrary to the behaviorist view that incorrect spellings contributed to confusion and the formation of bad habits, children's attempts at writing were evidence of the active process of meaning making that had sustained them when they had learned spoken language (Temple, Nathan, & Burris, 1982). Parents had responded to their meaning when they had asked for "wa-wa;' ignoring the incorrect pronunciation; in a similar way, researchers argue that children's incorrect spellings should be seen in a developmental light as well. Just as children had eventually learned correct syntax and articulation of oral language, they would gradually self-construct the generative rules which would lead them into more mature and conventional uses of written language.

From this perspective, spelling errors made during the process of writing were not viewed as impediments to learning, but as opportunities for the observant teacher to notice how children were making sense of sound-letter relationships. They provided a window on the process children were engaged in, and they could be analyzed: A child's spelling of *monster* as "MSTR" tells us about the sophistication of that child's understanding of the way words work (Henderson, 1980). In a parallel way, children's miscues in reading were valued as indications of their attempts at using visual, semantic, and syntactic information and integrating this information to make meaning. The miscues could be analyzed to gain insight on children's internal theories of reading (Goodman, 1969).

Accentuating the positive qualities of children's attempts at meaning making and communication, whether in reading or writing, is another of the major legacies of the paradigm shift from a readiness model to an emergent model of literacy. Researchers and teachers let children show what they could do and what they did know rather than what they had not yet mastered. Clark's (1988) research indicated that children's writing and the ability to spell regularly are developed by invented spelling. Closely connected to this positive emphasis was the idea that children are empowered by our acceptance of their invented spelling. They are able to write purposefully and with communicative intent from the very beginning of school, and even before. They can say, "I can do this myself. I am a writer" (Hansen, 1987).

Finally, by engaging in the process of invented spelling, children discover for themselves more about the relationships between sounds and letters. They practice applying the alphabetic principle and gain in phonemic awareness (Gentry, 1981, 1987). One first-grade teacher called the invented spelling her children did during writing her "applied phonics program." Invented spelling thus assists in the development of reading, and is one powerful component of reciprocal gains afforded by the connections between reading and writing. Writing slows down the whole process of dealing with text, so that children can see relationships between sounds and words more clearly (Clay, 1991a). It is possible that, at least for some children, writing may be an easier "way into" literacy than reading. In reading, the message is not known, but in writing the writer already knows the message. In reading, the task involves going from letters and letter sequences to sounds, whereas in writing the process is reversed: going from sounds (which are already known and automatic) to letters. In this way, writing can be viewed as an easier task than reading, because it proceeds from the known to the unknown, rather than from what is unknown to what is known (Chomsky, 1971, 1979).

WHERE IS THE TEACHER?

The theoretical and descriptive research, therefore, has been quite rich in describing what is happening cognitively as children learn to spell. What is still lacking is an equally rich articulation of *what adults do* that assists children's development. As Cazden (1992) wrote, "We now know much about the active child, but we still have much to learn about the active teacher" (p. 15). The stage was set for the careful *descriptive* research about children's invented spellings to be interpreted in a *prescriptive* way. The way it was falsely interpreted was "hands off." The message received (though not necessarily the message given) was this: Children will learn to spell in their own good time, and teacher interventions of any kind are suspect. Perhaps the most critical voice in questioning an "anything goes" approach to invented spelling was that of Marie Clay: "[C]hildren use what they know to solve their new problems, and that, young though they are, they form hypotheses about what might work in print. I have a sense that many teachers are directing children to produce writing nonsense and children are obliging them, as they typically do" (1991b, p. 268).

In the last two decades, educators have rediscovered a theoretical voice that provides a way of conceptualizing the teacher as an active participant in the classroom without ignoring the child as the constructor of his or her own meaning. Vygotsky's (1978, 1986) theories came as a welcome antidote to the hands-off approach. Although Vygotsky felt that peers could also assist, he did not argue that interaction with peers was the *primary* way in which learning occurred. Whereas a Piagetian model places perhaps greater emphasis on social interaction of peers (Kamii & Randazzo, 1985), for Vygotsky interactions between the learner and an "expert other" are crucial, and his concept of "mediation" provides a way of conceptualizing a strong role for the teacher in assisting the child in that "zone of proximal development" between what was already grasped firmly and what was unknown. He argued that what children can do with assistance today, they can do independently tomorrow; he described learning in such a way as to emphasize its dynamic process rather than its products.

Yet, for many teachers, the hands-off message remains. We seem to have created inaccurate metaphors, which limit our understanding of the learning process. Newkirk (1991) wrote,

> *We are trapped by organic metaphors that suggest that the child's "unfolding" will be hindered if the teacher has objectives for that unfolding. We use misleading metaphors of property—"ownership"—that invariably imply that the teacher is an outsider in the learning process. (p. 69)*

When we use organic metaphors, we are trapped into thinking that children's rate of growth is predetermined, as if any attempt to assist were an intrusion and a dangerous action, like forcibly opening the petals of a flower bud, and thereby ruining the flower. Power, empowerment, and "ownership" are falsely conceived as a zero-sum game, where if the teacher exerts more influence, the children will necessarily exert less (e.g., Garan, 1994). Even the use of the common metaphor of "construction" implies the same thing: The teacher stands on the sidelines and observes while the real activity, the real construction of meaning, is accomplished by children alone. Perhaps we need to think more of the "co-construction" of meaning, so that the partnership among children, their peers, *and* adults is emphasized.

The dichotomies we have set up are subtly false, as well: process versus product; children's invention versus teachers' imposition of convention; student ownership versus teacher intervention; risk-taking versus passive reception; transaction versus transmission. The realities of the classroom are much more subtle, fluid, and dynamic than this, and should not be dichotomized in this way. The sensitive teacher will sometimes find it appropriate to emphasize products and conventions. According to Newkirk (1991),

> *If we stress child-centeredness and the lack of teacher direction, the almost divine right of the child to choose from a wide array of options the teacher helps place before him or her, then we may appear more permissive than we are. We are often trapped into a rhetoric of freedom that makes it difficult to acknowledge our own influence in the process classroom. By stressing process over product (as if they can be separated), we fail to demonstrate that we expect a high quality of writing from students—and usually get it. (p.70)*

An active role for the teacher is suggested by Calkins (1986), Cazden (1992), Routman (1993), Schickedanz (1990), and Weaver (1990) who feared that the constructivist theory of literacy learning has been translated into laissez-faire classrooms, and who argued for both active students and active teachers. It may be that some children (particularly children whose culture does not match the school's "culture of power") will fare best when teachers are explicit in their directions and in their teaching, without harming children's independence and sense of self-worth (Delpit, 1988; Ladson-Billings, 1994).

SOME EXAMPLES OF HELPFUL TEACHER INTERVENTION

It is important to recognize that teachers' activities during the drafting stage of writing, when children are first getting down ideas, must not inhibit children's willingness and desire to write. How can we help children make the transition to more conventional forms of spelling? This is of particular concern for children who don't seem to be taking on the tasks of reading and writing. If the answer is not simply more time and more immersion in purposeful and meaningful literacy activities, then how can the teacher help? What does instruction look like when both the child and the teacher are active participants? What does scaffolding look like?

HEARING SOUNDS IN WORDS

One of the techniques used in the writing portion of the Reading Recovery lesson (Clay, 1993) provides an elegant example of scaffolding in a one-to-one situation. It can also be adapted for classroom use during conferences. During the lesson, the child generates her or his own sentence or story, which is composed on the bottom portion of a double page. The top portion is the "practice page," for trying out words of which the child is unsure. After having read the book *Mrs. Wishy-Washy* (Cowley, 1999), for example, Kenny decides to write his own story about it. He generates the sentence, "She got them all clean." He confidently writes *She* and then rehearses the sentence again. "*Got* has a *g*," he says, "but I know it has some more letters." The teacher says, "Let's make a box for it." She quickly draws a rectangle on the practice page, and draws partitions within it so that it has three compartments, corresponding to the three sounds in *got*.

This is a technique adapted from the Russian psychologist Elkonin (Clay, 1979), who developed it in order to assist children in hearing the sounds in words. The teacher places three round markers or pennies under each of the compartments. As Kenny says *got* slowly, he pushes the markers up into the boxes.

The teacher has taught him to synchronize the pushing with his articulation of the sounds. He knows that he has to "stretch out" the word so that he is saying the last sound just as he comes to the final box. As Kenny says the /t/, his

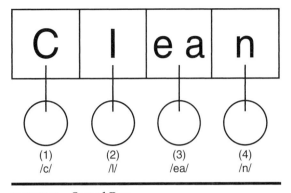

FIGURE 1   Sound Box

finger pushes the third marker into the box above it. "I heard the *g* here," he says, pointing to the first box, and he writes it there.

He then moves the markers down below the boxes, and pushes them up again, saying the word slowly. This time, he says, "I hear a *t* here," pointing to the third box, and writes it as well. The third time, he hears the medial vowel, and writes *o* in the middle box. He's then ready to add the word to his story. For the word *them,* he pauses, and the teacher says, "It starts like a word you know." Kenny thinks for a minute and says "*the*—it starts like *the.*" He writes *th,* and the teacher says, "It has an *e* like *the,* too." After saying the word slowly, Kenny hears the final sound and writes the *m.* He's able to write *all* independently, but needs another sound box for *clean.* The same procedure is employed as for *got:* The teacher draws a rectangle with four boxes (corresponding to the four phonemes in *clean*).

Kenny pushes up the markers, saying the word slowly. He says "k" for the first sound, and the teacher praises him. saying, "Yes, it could be a *k;* is there anything else it could be?" He writes *c,* then *l,* saying, "I heard an *l,* too." Pushing up again, he hears the long *e,* and the teacher tells him that it is spelled the same way as *eat,* a word she knows he can write. He is able to hear the *n* by himself. Kenny has made some links to words he already knows, and the similarity between *k* and *c* has been made clearer to him. He has learned that the way words sound is not necessarily the way they look—it sounds like there is only an *e* in *clean*, but it turns out that there are two letters; this has been linked with another word he knows, *eat*. Kenny has contributed a great deal to the task, and the teacher has assisted him with the parts that are difficult; she has "scaffolded" the task. At the end of the process, the words are spelled conventionally, *but that was not the purpose of the task:* The purpose was to help him hear sounds in words. In a sense, we might say that it has helped to prepare him for invented spelling.

Most children may not need this kind of help; but without it, independent writing time would be a frustrating and defeating activity for Kenny. He now has a tool that can help him to write. For the teacher to say, "Write it like it sounds, and I'll be able to read it" is not useful for Kenny, because that is precisely what he is unable to do. Children who know this procedure have been observed pushing up with their fingers as they say words slowly, and then being able to write a tricky word. When children have been introduced to the technique, the teacher can employ it quickly while circulating during independent writing time. For children who are already good at invented spelling, the technique can stretch their capacities and help them make links to what they already know. A further refinement of the technique (used with more advanced children) is to make boxes corresponding to the number of letters (rather than sounds) in the word. Children who are ready for this can consider what *looks right* as well as what *sounds right*.

If Kenny were writing a multisyllable word, he would be taught to clap the syllables. The purpose is not to tell how many parts the word has, but rather to assist him in segmenting the parts of the word so that it can be more easily written. If a child is trying to write the word *yesterday*, for example, it is easier to hear the sounds (and represent them in writing) in three smaller segments. Classroom teachers have found this simple technique to be greatly effective in helping children to hear sounds in words and record them.

HAVE-A-GO

A variety of activities can be used to support students in identifying and correcting mispelled words with guidance from the teacher or peers. An additional activity that also involves attention to syllabication, teacher scaffolding, and sounding out syllables is the use of a Have-a-Go chart (Bolton & Snowball, 1993). When the student is interested in working on words within his text, he gets the Have-a-Go chart (see Figure 2). The chart is divided into four columns. The student begins with the left column, writing the word or words that he or she has identified as incorrect and would like assistance in spelling. In the second column, "Have-a-Go," he or she attempts to spell the word correctly with assistance from the teacher or a peer. As demonstrated in the previous examples, the teacher can scaffold understanding with a variety of instructional techniques, including the use of clapping syllables or "stretching" the word. The student then writes a revision of the word. If this is incorrect, the teacher either refers the student to a dictionary or writes the word for the student. In the final column, the student rewrites the word after finding out the correct spelling. Students should be encouraged to recall the correct spelling when writing in the last column in order to commit the spelling to memory.

INTERACTIVE WRITING

Interactive writing (Pinnell & McCarrier, 1993) is a technique of group composition intended for use with emergent writers. It is both similar to and different from the traditional language experience approach. Like the language experience approach, it is done with a group of children and their teacher, the children deciding as a group on the message they wish to write. Like language experience, interactive writing places a high value on using children's own words to ensure

Word from text	Have-a-Go	Correct spelling	Copied spelling
Brids	Birds		Birds
Luch	Lnch	Lunch	Lunch

FIGURE 2   Have-A-Go Chart

that the message relates to their own experience and use of oral language. Another similarity is that the message is written on a large piece of paper with lettering of a size that can easily be seen by the children. In interactive writing, however, the children are more involved in the actual writing of the message. The children contribute what they know about spelling and letter formation, and the teacher scaffolds their attempts by supplying spellings and other items of knowledge they lack. Thus the pen is shared between the teacher and the children, and the children do most of the recording of the text. Interactive writing is done for a wide range of purposes. Like traditional language experience, it demonstrates that what we say can be written down and then read, making clear the vital links between reading, writing, listening, and speaking. Unlike language experience, it not only models conventional reading and writing behavior, but also scaffolds children's participation in the process. By actively involving the children, interactive writing helps them feel that they are "members of the literacy club," through structuring an environment for taking risks. Children draw upon their fund of literacy knowledge and have the experience of integrating and using that knowledge for a real and functional purpose.

Interactive writing does not occur in isolation. It is set in the context of a holistic early literacy framework (Glasbrenner, 1989), which includes several other literacy activities: reading aloud, both collaborative and independent familiar rereading, shared reading, various activities done as text extensions, and independent writing. In order to explain interactive

writing more fully, I will present a summary of an interactive writing session conducted by a Kindergarten teacher.

The children have been working for several days on activities related to *The Three Billy Goats Gruff* (Galdone, 1981). They have heard the story read several times by the teacher and have also written a list of characters and words to describe the setting. These words have been written on chart paper and posted on the wall.

To begin the interactive writing lesson, the teacher reads the book aloud again. The children frequently chime in with words and phrases they remember. Then the teacher is ready to begin the interactive writing itself, which is done on a horizontally ruled piece of chart paper on an easel that is low enough for the children to use. The teacher sits on a low chair beside it. She connects what the children are going to do with what they have already done by saying that the class has written about the characters and the setting, but they now need to "tell our story." The children decide to write the sentence, "The three billy goats gruff were hungry." What follows is not a transcript, but is a fairly detailed record of the interactions.

1. The teacher asks what word should be written first. The task is writing *the,* and a child comes up to the chart to write it.
2. A child writes *the,* but the *e* is backwards. The teacher points this out, saying it's all right to make a mistake—we just fix it with correction tape. The child writes *e.*
3. The children remember the entire sentence again, in order to locate the next word that needs to be written—*three.*

4. Children call out various letters. One spells *three* correctly. The teacher acknowledges this.

5. A child [not the one who spelled *three* correctly] comes to the easel and writes the numeral 3. Another child helps to make a "three-finger space" at the teacher's request.

6. The children reread what has been written so far: *The 3.*

7. When they get to the next word, *billy,* several children call out *b.*

8. The teacher asks a child to come write "her" *b* (because this letter begins her name). Another child helps by making a space after 3.

9. The teacher encourages children to say the word *billy* slowly. Several children say *l.*

10. The teacher says there are two *l's* "and an *i* in here that you can't hear so well." (She's already put in the *i* herself because she knows that most children in the group are not at the stage where they use medial vowels in their writing.)

11. For the long-*e* sound at the end of *billy,* the teacher asks, "Who remembers when we talked about this sound?" Some children say *e,* but the teacher reminds them that it sounds like the sound at the end of *Suzy,* one of the children's names. Children say *y.*

12. Suzy writes the *y.*

13. This child also rereads what is written so far: *The 3 billy.*

14. The children proceed similarly for the word *goats.* The teacher assists with a prompt for the final *s* by saying, "What do I need to make it more than one?"

15. The teacher says, "Now we want to write *gruff.*" Several children call out letters.

16. A child comes to write. The teacher says, "We have a problem—there's not enough room [at the right side of the page]. So where do we go?" The child shows where to start a new line and writes the *g.*

17. Children are prompted to say the word slowly. Several call out different letters. The same child who wrote *g* also writes *r.*

18. The teacher says, "Then there's a *u* (writing it). And then finish it."

19. Children call out *f.*

20. The teacher says, "It's Frank's *f,* and mine, (the teacher's first name begins with *F*). A child writes two *f's,* as the teacher says that there are two *f's.*

21. The children proceed similarly for the words *were* and *hungry.*

22. The teacher prompts for a period, and a child writes it.

23. The child who wrote the period reads the whole sentence, pointing to the words.

24. The teacher calls on a few more children to come up and read the sentence. One child makes a matching mistake, realizes it, and goes back to the beginning of the sentence to reread.

25. When she is finished, the teacher says, "I like the way you went back [to make it match]. When you say *hungry,* where do you get to?" Children say, "the end," and one child points to *hungry* in the sentence.

This interactive writing lesson lasted 13 minutes and 30 seconds. All of the children were involved in writing and reading the sentence. The children had done interactive writing many times before; they frequently anticipated what question the teacher would ask next. A number of children had a clearly developed sense of the initial and final letters in words: They could hear the sounds in these positions, and represent them with letters. Medial vowels and internal nasals (*billy; hungry*) were much more difficult, as research suggests (Read, 1971). The teacher dealt with some variants (for example the final *y* having the long-*e* sound) as the opportunity arose. One word (*the*) was written fluently without any analysis. The teacher accepted a child's decision to write the numeral 3 instead of the word. One structural feature was dealt with (*s* to indicate plurals in *goats*). Conventions of writing (left to right; top to bottom; spacing; punctuation) were modeled by both the teacher and the children. After rehearsing the sentence, the children were able to remember the text they had decided upon, and rereading the sentence kept this fresh in their minds. Some children were clearly more able than others, but the teacher was able to find ways for everyone to be actively involved and to feel successful. The completed sentence was the first part of the retelling of a story that the children had heard and discussed several times before, and thus was heavily contextualized. The teacher later added a few more sentences to complete the short summary of the story in several more interactive writing lessons.

LINKING THE KNOWN TO THE NEW

A third teacher intervention for spelling is one that can be done with the whole class, small groups, or individuals. This technique draws from a variety of sources, including the word sort method (Zutell, 1996), schema theory (Anderson, 1984), Goswami's research on onset and rime (1986), other research on phonemic awareness, and the work of Clay (1979, 1991a, 1991b). The phrase "known to new" is Clay's. The basic idea is that learning anything new is a matter of linking this new knowledge in some way with what is already known. This theoretical principle of all learning is naturally applied by many children without help from the teacher. Mike, for example, was trying to write the word *like,* and had already written an *l.* He knew how to spell his own name; and he looked up at the top of his paper at his name as he vocalized "like—Mike." Then he was able to complete the spelling of *like* because he had made a link between a known word and the new word he was working on.

It may be that many (or most) children grasp this powerful principle of linking the known to the new. Whenever children "overgeneralize" a spelling pattern, they are making use of this principle. However, some children need to be explicitly taught the ways and means of linking new spellings with words they already know how to spell. The level of teacher scaffolding varies with what the child needs. Here is one possible sequence of increasing support, based on Brad's desire to write *bright:*

1. "Do you know a word that starts like (rhymes with, is like) *bright*?" Brad may need no more than this to make a link and proceed.

2. It Brad cannot think of a word that is like the word he wants to write, the teacher may suggest a word, asking, "Do you know how to write *light*?" If this is a known word, this may be enough of a scaffold to get the child started.

3. Often, children can read a word which they cannot write conventionally. The teacher may write a word, for example, *light,* and say, "I'm writing a word you know that will help you with *bright."* If Brad can read *light,* he may be able to use that knowledge to spell *bright.*

All of these examples show joint problem-solving situations where the child becomes a co-constructor of meaning along with an "expert other." The creativity and independence of children who participate in such activities is not hampered, but rather is enhanced by the teacher's active involvement and scaffolding.

ACTIVE TEACHING AND ACTIVE LEARNING

In the last two decades, educators have made enormous strides in theory and classroom practice related to writing. No one would want to return to the days of delaying writing until children could spell conventionally. Writing without being overly concerned with conventions that may impede the flow of thoughts is one of the most powerful literacy activities for children (Adams, 1990). It has made it possible for children to engage in writing meaningful, communicative text far earlier than we ever dreamed. It honors children as active participants in their own construction of literacy in a way that enables the development of phonemic awareness and fosters independence and control.

But an active child does not imply an inactive teacher. Teachers should be more than just close observers of children, as important as that is. Active intervention by the teacher and judicious use of direct, explicit instruction can help children along the literacy road (Spiegel, 1992). For some children, this is critical; simply waiting for them to bloom will not help (Clay, 1991a).

Though our intentions were good, the dichotomies we have created—invention versus convention; process versus product; meaning versus surface features; even independence versus dependence—have probably made the transition to conventional literacy harder, not easier, for children. The metaphors we use—"ownership"; "growing"; "unfolding"—have become traps rather than heuristic guides. In an essay entitled "The Enemy Is Orthodoxy," Graves (1984) pointed out that age and extensive use produce rigid ways of interpreting and implementing even the most robust theories. He argued that the writing process approach was being applied in inflexible ways, and that teachers needed to be aware of this natural tendency. In the same way, perhaps, we need to reexamine the orthodoxies that have grown up around the concept of invented spelling and the way it is applied in the classroom. In another book on writing, Graves (1994) stated that "when first-grade children learn to spell, they need much more teaching than I've demonstrated in the past" (p. xvi). We need to grapple long and hard with the concept of "development," and consider how learning (and teaching) may enhance and encourage development. We need to recognize that active teaching and active learning go hand in hand. Kelly and Fred, the two children whose stories began this article, deserve that clearer vision.

REFERENCES

Adams, M. (1990). *Beginning to read: Thinking and learning about print.* Cambridge, MA: MIT Press.

Anderson, R. (1984). Role of the reader's schema in comprehension, learning and memory. In R. Anderson, J. Osburn, & R. Tierney (Eds.), *Learning to read in American schools: Basal readers and content texts* (pp. 243–257). Hillsdale. NJ: Erlbaum.

Bissex, G. (1980). *Gnys at wrk: A child learns to write and read.* Cambridge, MA: Harvard University Press.

Bolton, F., & Snowball, D. (1993). *Ideas for spelling.* Portsmouth, NH: Heinemann.

Calkins, L. (1986). *The art of teaching writing.* Portsmouth, NH: Heinemann.

Cazden, C. (1992). *Whole language plus: Essays on literacy in the United States and New Zealand.* New York: Teachers College Press.

Chomsky, C. (1971). Write first, read later. *Childhood Education, 47,* 296–299.

Chomsky, C. (1979). Approaching reading through invented spelling. In L. Resnick & P. Weaver (Eds.). *Theory and practice of early reading* (Vol. 2, pp. 43–65). Hillsdale. NJ: Erlbaum.

Clark, L. K. (1988). Invented versus traditional spelling in first graders' writings: Effects on learning to spell and read. *Research in the Teaching of English, 22,* 281–309.

Clay, M. M. (1979). *The early detection of reading difficulties: A diagnostic survey with recovery procedures.* Auckland, New Zealand: Heinemann.

Clay, M. (1991a). *Becoming literate: The construction of inner control.* Portsmouth, NH: Heinemann.

Clay, M. (1991b). Developmental learning puzzles me. *Australian Journal of Reading, 14,* 263–275.

Clay, M. (1993). *Reading Recovery: A guidebook for teachers in training.* Portsmouth, NH: Heinemann.

DeFord, D. (1980). Young children and their writing. *Theory Into Practice, 19,* 157–162.

Delpit, L. (1988). The silenced dialogue: Power and pedagogy in educating other people's children. *Harvard Educational Review, 58,* 280–298.

Garan, E. (1994). Who's in control? Is there enough "empowerment" to go around?" *Language Arts, 73,* 192–199.

Gentry, J. R. (1981). Learning to spell developmentally. *The Reading Teacher, 34,* 378–381.

Gentry, J. R. (1987). *Spel . . . is a four-letter word.* New York: Scholastic.

Glasbrenner, C. C. (1989). Elements of a literacy lesson. In G. S. Pinnell & A. McCarrier (Eds.), *Literacy matters, 13* (p. 306). Columbus, OH: The Martha L. King Language and Literacy Center, The Ohio State University.

Goodman, K. S. (1969). Analysis of oral miscues: Applied psycholinguistics. In F. Smith (Ed.), *Psycholinguistics and reading* (pp. 158–176). New York: Holt, Rinehart & Winston.

Goswami, U. (1986). Children's use of analogy in learning to read: A developmental study. *Journal of Experimental Psychology, 42,* 413–424.

Graves, D. (1984). The enemy is orthodoxy. In *A researcher learns to write: selected articles and monographs* (pp. 184–193). Exeter, NH: Heinemann.

Graves, D. (1994). *A fresh look at writing.* Portsmouth, NH: Heinemann.

Hansen, J. (1987). *When writers read.* Portsmouth, NH: Heinemann.

Henderson, E. H. (1980). *Developmental and cognitive aspects of learning to spell: A reflection of word knowledge.* Newark, DE: International Reading Association.

Kamii, C., & Randazzo, M. (1985). Social interaction and invented spelling. *Language Arts, 62,* 124–133.

Ladson-Billings, G. (1994). *The dreamkeepers: Successful teachers of African American children.* San Francisco: Jossey-Bass.

Newkirk, T. (1991). The middle class and the problem of pleasure. In N. Atwell (Ed.), *Workshop 3 by and for teachers: The politics of process* (pp. 63–72). Portsmouth. NH: Heinemann.

Pinnell. G. S., & McCarrier, A. (1993). Interactive writing: A transition tool for assisting children in learning to read and write. In E. Hiebert & B. Taylor (Eds.), *Getting reading right from the start: Effective early literacy interventions* (pp. 149–170). Needham Heights, MA: Allyn & Bacon.

Read, C. (1971). Pre-school children's knowledge of English phonology. *Harvard Educational Review, 41,* 1–34.

Routman, R. (1993). The uses and abuses of invented spelling. *Instructor, 102,* 36–39.

Schickedanz, J. A. (1990). Developmental spelling: What's the teacher's role? *Orbit, 21,* 10–12.

Spiegel, D. L. (1992). Blending whole language and systematic direct instruction. *The Reading Teacher, 46,* 38—44.

Temple, C., Nathan, R., & Burris, N. (1982). *The beginnings of early writing.* Boston: Allyn & Bacon.

Vygotsky, L. (1978). *Mind in society.* Cambridge, MA: Harvard University Press.

Vvgotsky, L. (1986). *Thought and language.* Cambridge, MA: MIT Press.

Weaver, C. (1990). *Understanding whole language: From principles to practice.* Portsmouth, NH: Heinemann.

Zutell, J. (1996). The directed spelling thinking activity (DSTA): Providing an effective balance in word study instruction. *The Reading Teacher, 50,* 98–109.

CHILDREN'S BOOKS CITED

Galdone, Paul. (1981). *The three billy goats gruff.* New York: Houghton Mifflin.

Knowley, Joy. (1999). *Mrs. Wishy-Washy.* New York: Philomel.

Teaching Words That Students Misspell: Spelling Instruction and Young Children's Writing

Diane Beckham-Hungler and Cheri Williams

The final article on spelling, by Beckham-Hungler and Williams (2003), addresses a number of the fundamental issues in the effective teaching of this aspect of language arts. Of particular interest here is the question of teaching those words that students find of interest and importance in their personal writing activities.

We have a keen interest in how children learn to spell, how word knowledge transfers to writing, and how teachers can best support children as they learn to spell and develop as writers. We share the concerns of teachers who struggle with the role of spelling instruction in the language arts program. Moreover, we know that parents see spelling as extremely important in their children's literacy education (Chandler & The Mapleton Teacher-Research Group, 1999); indeed, generally speaking, our society values correct spelling above all writing conventions (Turbill, 2000).

For several years, we have investigated the role of spelling instruction in young children's writing. The focus of our research has been the ubiquitous spelling list and the widely held assumption that children learn to spell through its weekly use. We knew from our experiences as elementary school teachers that students often perform well on weekly tests yet transfer little of this word knowledge to their writing. Other educators have expressed the same concern (Chandler & The Mapleton Teacher–Research Group, 2000; Gill & Scharer, 1996; Laminack & Wood, 1996; Wright, 2000). What *is* the role of spelling lists and explicit instruction in learning to spell? What impact do they have on young children's writing? We designed a series of studies to address these questions.

The spelling lists we used in our first study (Rymer & Williams, 2000) were created by district personnel; the words were chosen from spelling and vocabulary lists in the district's basal reading series. The classroom teacher, Rebecca, spent approximately 20 minutes each day explicitly teaching and then testing the children on those words. The children subsequently did well on their posttests. But, when we systematically examined the children's journals, we found that they rarely used these spelling words in their writing, and when they did, they misspelled these words 50% of the time, despite having spelled them correctly on the weekly tests. The study caused us to question the impact of prepackaged spelling programs on young children's writing development.

We decided to examine the impact of a spelling program that was based on words students misspelled in their own writing. We reasoned that this was a productive place to choose words for spelling instruction, since the students had already demonstrated a need for those words in their self-selected writing. We wanted

to know if, after explicit instruction, the students would reuse these words in their journals, and if so, whether the words would be spelled correctly the second time around. Diane is a second-grade teacher, and we conducted our study in her classroom. We share the results of that second investigation in this article.

THE CLASSROOM CONTEXT

Our studies are grounded in the belief that learning to spell is a psycholinguistic process that involves developing an understanding of the basic principles of English orthography and the interrelationships between phonology and morphology in our writing system (Hodges, 1982; Perfetti, 1997). Children develop this understanding as they engage in meaningful reading and writing activities (Temple, Nathan, & Burris, 1982; Templeton, 1991) and as they actively investigate the regularities, variations, and derivational relationships among words (Zutell, 1978). Memorization is only a small part of the process (Beers & Beers, 1977; Wilde, 1992). To be good spellers, children must also learn and be able to apply a wide range of strategies for spelling unknown words as they write (Dudley-Marling, 1997). We also believe that spelling knowledge supports children's reading and writing development (Gill, 1992; Richgels, 1995; Sulzby, 1985; Zutell & Rasinski, 1989).

Diane is an experienced elementary school teacher with a graduate degree in literacy education and Reading Recovery® training. For the past eight years, she has been a Title I language arts teacher in an urban school district where over half of the student population qualifies for the free or reduced lunch program. The year of our study, Diane was the Title I language arts teacher for the second grade. For two hours each morning, the nine lowest-achieving second grade children received language arts instruction in Diane's "replacement" classroom; that is, her Title I program replaced language arts instruction in the children's regular classroom. The small class size provided opportunities for Diane to provide explicit one-on-one and small group instruction.

Language Arts Block

Diane began the language arts block with 15 minutes of sustained silent reading (SSR). She made mental notes about the children's book selections and then she read, too, demonstrating the value she placed on reading. Journal writing, also 15 minutes, typically followed SSR. Occasionally Diane assigned topics, but the majority of the time the children wrote on topics of their choosing to create a meaningful message. At the beginning of the school year, students frequently asked Diane how to spell specific words. Her response was to "spell the words the way they sound," "listen for the sounds you can hear," or "spell it the best you can." She also encouraged the students to use scrap paper and "write the word to see how it looks," a modification of Routman's (1991) "Have-a-Go" sheets. While the children wrote in their journals, Diane also wrote in her journal, demonstrating that she, too, was a writer. Diane's journal consisted primarily of her observations of the children's writing behaviors and her reflections on the children's progress and her own instruction.

After journal writing, Diane called the students together for group time, a 15-minute session that typically included a read-aloud, shared reading, journal sharing, mini-lesson on spelling, or an interactive writing lesson (Button, Johnson, & Furgerson, 1996; McCarrier, Pinnell, & Fountas, 2000). To create the message for interactive writing, Diane pulled two or three names out of a jar and these students shared "news" with their classmates. Then, Diane and the children "shared the pen" (Pinnell & McCarrier, 1994) to construct their message on chart paper. Early on, Diane did most of the writing, but as the year progressed, the students took increased responsibility for the task. In fact, as the students became more proficient writers, Diane modified the technique and gave each child a pen and pad of paper. The students wrote on their individual pads as Diane wrote on the chart. In March, Diane modified the technique again, giving her students primary responsibility for the task. Each morning, she chose one student to write a message on the message board. During group time, Diane and the children read the message, then proofread and discussed needed changes and corrections. Diane knew that proofreading plays an important role in the learning-to-spell process (Turbill, 2000).

After group time, Diane divided the students into two flexible groups for guided reading (Fountas & Pinnell, 1996) and independent work. The guided reading lessons were typically 30 minutes each and focused on specific strategies for solving unknown words, fluent reading, and comprehension monitoring. Guided reading typically ended with word study (Joseph, 2000; Pinnell & Fountas, 1998; Snowball & Bolton, 1999). Diane taught specific strategies for studying the patterns in words. The foremost strategy was, "Notice the way a word looks and listen to the way it sounds." Diane taught the children to notice distinct features of the words they studied and to look for similarities and differences among them. She talked about the meanings of words, using homophones, synonyms, and antonyms to discuss the relationships among English words. They made comparisons to previously studied words, particularly their spelling words. Diane asked the students questions like, "What do you notice about this word?" "Is this word like any other word you already know?" "Is there a part of this word that's unique?" "What's tricky about this word?"

Word study consisted primarily of game-like activities that helped the children internalize these strategies. These games often involved building words with magnetic letters or writing with markers on dry erase boards. A favorite game was "Change the Letter." Diane started with a familiar word, like *cat*, and then said, "Change one letter to make it say, *hat . . . hit*," and so on. Diane also had the children write lists of rhyming words, and she engaged them in several activities using common onsets and rimes (Rasinski & Padak, 2001). Sometimes

Diane dictated words orally and asked the children to categorize each word by vowel sound (e.g., short ă or long ā). The children made word stairs, using the last letter of a word to start the next word on the stair (Pinnell & Fountas, 1998). These activities were powerful tools for helping the children discover how words work in English orthography. Students frequently did these activities in their word study notebooks, which provided a record of their work. Diane often used spelling words for the word study activities, focusing the children's attention on the orthographic-phonographic patterns being taught in the weekly spelling lesson.

The two-hour language arts block concluded with 15 minutes of direct phonics instruction as mandated by the school district. Diane was required to use a systematic phonics program that involved children standing at the chalkboard, writing words the teacher dictated, and then marking the words short or long vowels and any consonant blends. For example, Diane would say, "Write and mark the word *bag*." Students would repeat what Diane said, then turn around and write the word, then mark the short ă vowel. Diane varied the lessons by asking the students to make a list of rhyming words or by dictating a sentence that incorporated the required phonics words and the weekly spelling words. Occasionally they played "basketball phonics," where two teams competed as students wrote and marked phonics and spelling words on the chalk board. Because of the nature of Diane's spelling instruction, the students were ahead of the phonics program, and they found the lessons easy.

SPELLING INSTRUCTION

Diane's approach to literacy instruction provided numerous opportunities each day for the children to read and write conventionally spelled words (Hughes & Searle, 1997; Smith, 1982; Temple et al., 1982), and spelling instruction was interspersed throughout the morning's activities. But, Diane also had a regular routine for introducing the weekly spelling words, teaching the specific concept(s) to be learned that week, and engaging the children in focused spelling activities. Every Monday, Diane gave the students a pretest of 12 spelling words. After the pretest, Diane displayed the spelling words on individual cards in a large pocket chart and engaged the children in a discussion of what the words had in common. Her instruction focused on a particular concept, often a specific phoneme and the way it was spelled to each word. For example, one list featuring the short ĕ included the words *next, said, anyway, friend, been, and already*. Diane explained that, "All of these words have the /ɛ/ sound, but it's spelled six different ways." Not all the lessons emphasized vowel sounds. One, for example, was a lesson on diagraphs, and Diane explained that, "All of these words have diagraphs, two consonants that work together to make one unique sound." Diane's instruction emphasized "how words work," and she focused on both the auditory ("listen to the way it sounds") and the visual features ("notice the way it looks") of the words on each spelling list.

Throughout the week, Diane used various games and activities to help the children understand the nature of the letter–sound relationships and to learn to spell the words. For example, she used a variety of word sorts (Bear, Invernizzi, Templeton, & Johnston, 1996, Fresch & Wheaton, 1997; Fresch, 2000; Zutell, 1996) and the "look, say, cover, write, check" activity (Pinnell & Fountas, 1998). The children often used magnetic letters to practice building the words. They quizzed each other and had spelling bees. Diane also assigned spelling homework. She added an important element by discussing with students the strategies they were using to learn the weekly spelling words. By verbalizing these strategies, students were encouraged to examine and reflect on their learning.

This was the instructional context for our study. The children participated in a wide range of meaningful reading and writing activities during the language arts block, including a systematic spelling program based on words they had misspelled in their own writing.

Creating the Spelling Lists

There were 9 students in Diane's language arts replacement class and 8 parents gave consent for their child to participate in our study (5 boys and 3 girls). On October 4, we began recording words that these 8 students misspelled in their journals, adding each word to an alphabetized list. If more than one child misspelled a word, we put a tally mark (/) beside that word; each time the word was misspelled, we added another mark. We continued to document misspelled words in this way through the end of April.

In late December, we met to review the alphabetized list of misspelled words and to create weekly spelling lists for January. Our goal was to develop spelling lists with a central theme (e.g., short ĕ sound, VCE pattern, consonant clusters), so that Diane's weekly spelling instruction could focus on the particular orthographic-phonographic relationship that characterized each list of words. In theory, we knew it would be best to generate individual spelling lists for each child, but doing so would have prevented Diane from focusing her instruction on a particular orthographic-phonographic pattern that would be reflected in the words the children were learning to spell each week.

We created four lists in that first meeting, using the words the children had misspelled in their journals from October through December. One list, for example, highlighted the long ē sound and included seven spellings of this phoneme (eagle, week, cookies, believe, turkey, scary, machine). Every month we met to create spelling lists for the following month's lessons. Four principles guided our work. We wanted to (1) use the most frequently misspelled words (i.e., those with the most tally marks), (2) have at least two examples (words) for each orthographic-phonographic pattern included in a list (e.g., puppy, gravy, scary), (3) avoid selecting words that would have little utility for the children's writing (e.g., gremlin), and (4) avoid lists where words are so similar that students can predict consistent elements (hate, rate, mate, late, state) (Fresch, 2000).

We found it difficult to follow these guidelines. For example, the children frequently misspelled the word *because,* so we wanted to include it on our short ŭ list. At that point in time, there were no other words on our alphabetized list that included the *au* spelling for the short ŭ sound. Nevertheless, we added the word because frequent misspellings was our first guiding principle. A similar situation occurred with *Halloween.*

This word would not have high utility for the children's writing (principle #3), but we had few words on our alphabetized list that included the *ee* spelling of the long ē sound. We decided to include it giving us two examples of the *ee* pattern, in keeping with principle #2.

So challenging was our task that during our second meeting, we considered adding words to the spelling lists that the children had not misspelled in their journals, that is, words that we would generate, or words from spelling books or other instructional resources. Doing so would have allowed us to include more examples of the orthographic-phonographic patterns on each list. In the end, we returned to our original premise that using misspelled words would make spelling instruction more meaningful and relevant to the children and to their writing endeavors.

Over the course of the study, we generated 18 spelling lists, typically of 12 words each. In all, there were 204 different spelling words, and approximately one half of these were high-frequency words (Fry, Kress, & Fountoukidis, 2000). We used 8 words twice, either for the purpose of review, or because the words fit into two orthographic-phonographic patterns (e.g., the word *like* fit both the VCE "rule follower" pattern and the long ī sound). The lists included multiple spellings of all the short and long vowel sounds, consonant diagraphs, two- and three-letter consonant clusters, r-controlled vowel sounds, contractions, rule followers (e.g., *dream, least*), rule breakers (e.g., *believe, steak*), and silent letters.

We explained the theme of each week's spelling lesson to the children's parents by writing a short explanation at the top of the list that went home with the students every Monday afternoon. For example, "This week's lesson includes four spellings of the *au* sound, as in the word *raw*." These four spellings were then underlined in the words on the list. Diane began to use these lists for spelling instruction on January 3 and continued to use them through the last week of May.

GATHERING AND ANALYZING CHILDREN'S RESPONSES

Our data collection and analysis procedures were similar to those we used in our first study. We kept a notebook for each student that contained photocopies of pretests, posttests, and weekly journal entries. We created a list for each student, "Words Spelled Correctly on Pretests," to record the words that each child spelled correctly on the Monday pretests. On Friday, we compared each student's posttest to his or her pretest to determine the words the child had presumably learned through explicit spelling instruction. We coded all words that were spelled correctly on the posttest that had not been spelled correctly on the pretest as "Words Learned" and recorded these words on a separate sheet for each child.

On Friday afternoons, we examined the children's journal entries for that week to determine whether the children were re-using their spelling words—the "words learned"—in their journals, and, if so, whether the words were spelled correctly this time around. To code these data, we created two additional lists for each child: "Words Learned & Spelled Correctly in Journal," and "Words Learned but Misspelled in Journal." We used these data collection and analysis procedures from January through May. The goal of our analysis was to determine whether using children's misspelled words for spelling instruction, instead of prepackaged spelling lists, would prove beneficial to the children's writing.

From Misspellings to Respellings

One of the first things we noticed as we analyzed our data was that the children did well on their pretests (Wilde, 1992). They spelled correctly on the pretests many of the words they had misspelled in their journals, on average 47%. Of the 204 spelling words, Karla spelled 136 correctly on her pretests (67%), and even at the low end, Aaron spelled 58 words correctly (28%). We were surprised by this because we had taken precautions to avoid it. In our original study, Rebecca's first graders did well on their pretests; in fact, half of her students knew more spelling words than they had to learn. We attributed this to the prepackaged spelling program Rebecca was required to use, which could not take into account the children's prior knowledge of words. In the current study, however, we had intentionally guarded against this problem by choosing words for spelling instruction that Diane's second graders had misspelled in their writing. Why, then, did the children perform so well on their pretests?

Perhaps the children knew how to spell these words but had misspelled them in their journals due weren't much better at predicting the words students would need for their journal writing than the prepackaged lists we used in our original study. We know, of course, that in the children's lives, both in and out of school, these "words learned" certainly will have high utility for them.

Use of Spelling Patterns in Journals

Finally—and the best news of all—as we searched the children's journals for "words learned," we were impressed by the number of words the children spelled correctly that contained the same orthographic-phonographic patterns as in the weekly spelling words. For example, on April 3, Diane talked about the word *attack*, focusing on the *ack* rime. The next day, Tyler wrote the word *wacky* in his journal, using the *ack* rime as well as the *y* spelling for the long ē sound, which Diane had taught on January 18. A few days later, both Denise and Karla wrote the word *snacks* in their journals. After Diane taught the *ay* spelling for the long ā sound, Daniel wrote the word *pray*, and Denise wrote *gray*. After Diane taught the *ow* spelling for the long ō sound, Austin wrote the word *slow* and Aaron wrote *snowed.*

We decided to examine the children's journals a second time and search for words that contained the orthographic-phonographic patterns Diane had taught. We only counted a word if it appeared in a child's journal after Diane had taught the pattern. We coded these as "other words," and, for each child, we counted the number of different "other words" as well as the number of repetitions. The children generated an average of 88 "other words" in their journals; Karla had a total of 135 at the high end and even at the low end Aaron generated 52 different examples.

During her word study activities, Diane had purposefully discussed how new words could be generated by analogy to words already known (Goswami, 1988). It is possible that a considerable number of the "other words" the children spelled correctly in their journals were influenced by Diane's direct instruction on common orthographic-phonographic patterns. We celebrated this finding! The children were trying new words by transferring what they had learned, pointing to the effectiveness of Diane's spelling and word study programs.

The findings of our study indicated that the children did well on their pretests and on their posttests. Although the children reused relatively few of their "words learned" in their journals, when they did, the words were typically spelled correctly. Further, the children correctly spelled many "other words" in their journals, perhaps generalizing to new and different words the orthographic-phonographic patterns they had learned through spelling instruction and systematic word study.

LIMITATIONS AND POSSIBILITIES OF SPELLING LISTS

This is our second study on spelling instruction and young children's writing. Results of our first study indicated that the prepackaged spelling program had little impact on the children's daily journal writing. We initiated this second study to investigate whether thoughtfully developed spelling lists, created by knowledgeable teachers within the context of the immediate classroom, might have greater impact on young children's self-selected writing. Our results lead us to believe that spelling lists of any kind—whether thoughtfully developed by classroom teachers (as in this study) or prepared by curriculum specialists outside the classroom (as in our first study)—are limited in their ability to take into account children's prior knowledge of words or to anticipate the specific words that will be of greatest use to children in their self-selected writing.

Nevertheless, the spelling lists we generated proved useful for in-depth word study instruction. Each list was created around a central concept to be learned (e.g., various spellings of the short ĭ sound). Diane introduced and explicitly taught this concept during the time allotted for spelling instruction. Then she reviewed and reinforced the concept as part of her word study program, using spelling words as examples during her games and activities. It is this in-depth word study program that appears to have been the primary contributing factor to the increased transfer of "words learned" to the children's journals and to the "other words" they wrote.

We spent a good deal of time each month creating these lists. When the study was over, we wondered if our results would have been similar if we had used spelling lists from one of the professional resources we consulted—lists that are organized around particular orthographic-phonographic patterns. But Diane's observations indicated that one of the reasons the children were so motivated to learn the spelling words was because they realized (eventually) that the spelling lists were words they had misspelled in their writing. In fact, students would occasionally tell Diane, "I know where you got that word—it was in my story last week!" In the end, we were glad we used the students' misspelled words. We felt it made the spelling program more relevant to the children.

We do know that all of the children made progress in their spelling development during the academic year, as evidenced by the conventional spellings in their journals and other academic writing, and on more formalized assessments. In September, Diane administered the *Elementary Qualitative Spelling Inventory* (Bear et al., 1996, p. 38), and all of the children scored in various phases of the Letter Name stage. In June, Diane re-administered this assessment. All of the students had progressed to at least the Within Word Pattern stage; they were representing long vowels, spelling short vowels correctly, and beginning to internalize spelling rules. Two students, Brian and Karla, scored in the early phase of the Syllable Juncture stage. They were beginning to use double consonants and common prefixes and suffixes.

While we do not believe that children move rigidly through developmental stages of spelling (Goswami & Bryant, 1990; Treiman & Cassar, 1997), we do believe these kinds of assessments can help document young children's developing word knowledge and provide important information for further instruction. Clearly, Diane's language arts "replacement" program, which included a range of meaningful reading and writing activities, as well as formal spelling instruction and word study, supported this growth and development.

The results of this second study give us pause. We have been focusing our studies on spelling lists and testing, but now we are wondering about the specific role of word study instruction on young children's writing development. How does a systematic word study program influence young children's independent writing? How often do children transfer example words from word study games and activities to their journals? Are the words spelled correctly? How often do children generate words in their spontaneous writing using the orthographic-phonographic patterns taught during word study instruction? Can a systematic word study program effectively replace traditional spelling instruction and weekly testing? We are currently addressing these questions in two related projects designed specifically to investigate the nature of word study instruction and its impact on young children's self selected writing.

AUTHORS' NOTE_____

The authors would like to thank Sandy Lingo for a careful reading and helpful suggestions on an earlier version of this manuscript.

REFERENCES_____

Bear, D., Invernizzi, M., Templeton, S., & Johnston, F. (1996). *Words their way: Word study for phonics, vocabulary, and spelling instruction.* Upper Saddle River, NJ: Prentice-Hall.

Beers, C., & Beers, J. (1977). Three assumptions about learning to spell. *Elementary School Journal, 19,* 238–242.

Button, K., Johnson, M., & Furgerson, P. (1996). Interactive writing in a primary classroom. *The Reading Teacher, 49,* 446–454.

Chandler, K., & The Mapleton Teacher-Research Group. (1999). *Spelling inquiry: How one elementary school caught the mnemonic plague.* York, ME: Stenhouse.

Chandler, K., & The Mapleton Teacher-Research Group. (2000). Squaring up to spelling: A teacher-research group surveys parents. *Language Arts, 77,* 224–231.

Dudley-Marling, C. (1997). *Living with uncertainty: The messy reality of classroom practice.* Portsmouth, NH: Heinemann.

Fountas, I. C., & Pinnell, G. S. (1996). *Guided reading: Good first teaching for all children.* Portsmouth, NH: Heinemann.

Fresch, M. J. (2000). What we learned from Josh: Sorting out word sorting. *Language Arts, 77,* 232–240.

Fresch, M. J., & Wheaton, A. (1997). Sort, search, and discover: Spelling in the child-centered classroom. *The Reading Teacher, 51,* 20–31.

Fry, E., Kress, J., & Fountoukidis, D. L., (2000). *The reading teacher's book of lists* (4th ed.). Englewood Cliffs, NJ: Prentice-Hall.

Gill, T. (1992). The relationship between word recognition and spelling. In S. Templeton & D. Bear (Eds.), *Development of orthographic knowledge and the foundations of literacy: A memorial Festschrift for Edmund H. Henderson* (pp. 79–104). Hillsdale, NJ: Erlbaum.

Gill, C. H., & Scharer, P. (1996). "Why do they get it on Friday and misspell it on Monday?" Teachers inquiring about their students as spellers. *Language Arts, 73,* 89–96.

Goswami, U. C. (1988). Children's use of analogy in learning to spell. *British Journal of Developmental Psychology, 6,* 21–33.

Goswami, U. C., & Bryant, P. (1990). *Phonological skills and learning to read.* Hillsdale, NJ: Erlbaum.

Hodges, R. E. (1982). Research update on the development of spelling. *Language Arts, 59,* 284–290.

Hughes, M., & Searle, D. (1997). *The violent "e" and other tricky sounds: Learning to spell from kindergarten through grade 6.* York, ME: Stenhouse.

Joseph, L. M. (2000). Developing first graders' phonemic awareness, word identification and spelling: A comparison of two contemporary phonic instructional approaches. *Reading Research and Instruction, 39,* 160–169.

Laminack, L., & Wood, K. (1996). *Spelling in use: Looking closely at spelling in whole language classrooms.* Urbana, IL: National Council of Teachers of English.

McCarrier, A., Pinnell, G. S., & Fountas, I. (2000). *Interactive writing: How language and literacy come together, K–2.* Portsmouth, NH: Heinemann.

Perfetti, C. (1997). The psycholinguistics of spelling and reading. In C. Perfetti, L. Rieben, & M. Fayol (Eds.), *Learning to spell: Research, theory, and practice across languages* (pp. 21–38). Mahwah, NJ: Erlbaurn.

Pinnell, G. S., & Fountas, I. C. (1998). *Word matters: Teaching phonics and spelling in the reading/writing classroom.* Portsmouth, NH: Heinemann.

Pinnell, G. S., & McCarrier, A. (1994). Interactive writing: A transition tool for assisting children in learning to read and write. In E. Heibert & B. Taylor (Eds.), *Getting reading right from the start: Effective early literacy interventions* (pp. 149–170). Needham Heights, MA: Allyn & Bacon.

Rasinski, T., & Padak, N. (2001). *From phonics to fluency. Effective teaching of decoding and reading fluency in the elementary school.* New York: Addison-Wesley.

Richgels, D. (1995). Invented spelling ability and printed word learning in kindergarten. *Reading Research Quarterly, 30*(1), 96–109.

Routman, R. (1991). *Invitations: Changing as teachers and learners K–12.* Portsmouth, NH: Heinemann.

Rymer, R., & Williams, C. (2000)."Wasn't that a spelling word?: Spelling instruction and young children's writing." *Language Arts, 77,* 241–249.

Smith, F. (1982). *Writing and the writer.* New York: Holt, Rinehart & Winston.

Snowball, D., & Bolton, F. (1999). *Spelling K–8: Planning and teaching.* York, ME: Stenhouse.

Sulzby, E. (1985). Kindergarteners as writers and readers. In M. Farr (Ed.), *Advances in writing research* (pp. 127–199). Norwood, NJ: Ablex

Temple, C. A., Nathan, R. G., & Burris, N. A. (1982). *The beginnings of spelling.* Boston: Allyn & Bacon.

Templeton, S. (1991). Teaching and learning the English spelling system: Reconceptualizing method and purpose. *The Elementary School Journal, 92,* 185–201.

Treiman, R., & Cassar, M. (1997). Spelling acquisition in English. In C. Perfetti, L. Rieben, & M. Fayol (Eds.), *Learning to spell: Research, theory, and practice across languages* (pp. 61–80). Mahwah, NJ: Erlbaum.

Turbill, J. (2000). Developing a spelling conscience. *Language Arts, 77,* 209–217.

Wilde, S. (1992). *You kan red this!: Spelling and punctuation for whole language classrooms. K–6* Portsmouth, NH: Heinemann.

Wright, K. (2000). Weekly spelling meetings: Improving spelling instruction through classroom-based inquiry. *Language Arts, 77,* (218–223).

Zutell, J. (1978). Some psycholinguistic perspectives on children's spelling. *Language Arts, 55,* 844–850.

Zutell, J. (1996). The directed spelling teaching activity (DSTA): Providing an effective balance in word study instruction. *The Reading Teacher, 50,* 98–108.

Zutell, J., & Rasinski, T. (1989). Reading and spelling connections in third- and fifth-grade students. *Reading Psychology, 10,* 137–155.

_____CHAPTER REFERENCES_____

Almack, J. C., & Staffelbach, E. H. (1933). Method in teaching spelling. *Elementary School Journal, 34,* 175–185.

Asselin, M. (2001). Supporting students' spelling development. *Emergent Librarian, 29,* 1–3.

Beckham-Hungler, D., & Williams, C. (2003). Teaching words that students misspell: Spelling instruction and young children's writing. *Language Arts, 80,* 299–309.

Fulton, M. J. (1914). An experiment in teaching spelling. *The Pedagogical Seminary, 21,* 287–289.

Graves, D. H. (1983). *Writing: Teachers and students at work.* Portsmouth, NH: Heinemann.

Read, C. (1971). Pre-school children's knowledge of English phonology. *Harvard Educational Review, 41,* 1–34.

Sipe, L. R. (2001). Invention, convention, and intervention: Invented spelling and the teacher's role. *The Reading Teacher, 55,* 264–273.

Turbill, J. (2000). Developing a spelling conscience. *Language Arts, 77,* 209–217.

_____ANNOTATED BIBLIOGRAPHY OF RELATED REFERENCES_____

Ayres, L. P. (1915). *Measurement of ability in spelling.* New York: Russell Sage Foundation.

One of the earliest books on various approaches to the assessment of spelling, describing both formal and informal tests.

Chancellor, W. E. (1910). Spelling. *Journal of Education, 71,* 488.

Describes the early thinking on the effective teaching of spelling in the language arts classroom.

Gates, A. I. (1922). *Psychology of reading and spelling. Contributions to Education, No. 129.* New York: Teachers College, Columbia University.

Written by one of the pioneers in literacy education, an extended discussion of the relationship between effective reading and spelling instruction.

Hanna, P. R., & Moore, J. T. (1953). Spelling: From spoken word to written symbol. *The Elementary School Journal, 53,* 329–337.

Discusses the problems that develop in spelling between spoken and written English. It suggests ways in which the classroom teacher can help students make the transition from oral language to the written symbol.

Hilderbrant, E. L. (1923). The psychological analysis of spelling. *The Pedagogical Seminary, 30,* 371–381.

Details problems and success students have in spelling based on individual interviews. It is a particularly interesting discussion, providing student comments about their strategies and thinking processes related to the spelling of new and unknown words.

Hodges, R. E. (1964). A short history of spelling reforms in the United States. *Phi Delta Kappan, 45,* 330–332.

Describes various attempts through history to reform traditional English spelling of words and how for the most part they have failed.

Horn, T. D. (1969). Spelling. (ERIC Reproduction Service No. ED 029897)

A survey of spelling research and practices from the thirteenth century to the publication date of this paper. Contains an extensive bibliography of related articles on different aspects of spelling instruction.

Miller, H. M. (2002). Spelling: From invention to strategies. *Voices from the Middle, 9,* 33–37.

Describes how students make critical decisions about spelling choices as they write, noting especially the responsibilities of the writer in making these choices.

Sudweeks, J. (1927). Practical helps in teaching spelling: Summary of helpful principles. *Journal of Educational Research, 16,* 106–118.

A review of the most important research, with references to sixty articles, done in the area of spelling instruction through the publication date. It includes a listing of fifty spelling principles based on this review of relevant research on the topic.

_____YOU BECOME INVOLVED_____

The reading material in this chapter deals with many of the important issues related to spelling instruction. The first article by Fulton (1914) written over ninety years ago addresses many of the same issues in spelling that teachers face today in their instruction.

- Fulton describes a four-step process of spelling instruction. What do you think are the positives and the negatives of this approach to spelling? Are there some aspects of this view of spelling instruction that might have some application in your classroom teaching today?
- What are your feelings about the five summary statements related to spelling instruction?

The second article by Almack and Staffelbach (1933) discusses a number of recurring issues and problems related to spelling instruction.

- In the second paragraph of this article, the authors discuss the fact that some educators believe "that children learn to spell 'incidentally,' that is, without specific instruction in the subject." Based on your teaching experience and the material you have read in this chapter, what is your feeling about this view of spelling instruction?
- Almack and Staffelbach review what they call "spelling method" in their article. Summarize what they believe is the value of spelling method. Do you feel these conclusions are relevant for your current teaching of spelling?
- What are the similarities and the differences between "group method versus individual method" in the teaching of spelling words?

Many current concepts of spelling instruction are presented by Sipe (2001) in his article. Of particular note is the extended discussion of invented spelling. Consider the following points based on your reading of this article.

- Briefly consider the major concepts of invented spelling. How do these ideas differ from those of more traditional views of spelling instruction? What are the implications of invented spelling for both reading and writing activities?

- What should be the instructional role of the classroom teacher in the implementation of invented spelling in the literacy program?
- Do you think there may be problems with parents in the implementation of invented spelling in your classroom as opposed to the use of more traditional methods of spelling? If so, what might you do to inform them of your views on an invented spelling program?

The final article, by Beckham-Hungler and Williams (2003), discusses recent views of spelling instruction.

- The authors discuss the "language arts block" of related instructional activities. Briefly consider what learning experiences take place in this block and how they are organized. What implications do you see from this discussion for your own literacy teaching in general and for spelling instruction specifically?
- Based on your reading of this article, how do you think words should be selected for spelling instruction, for either individual or group learning? Should there be words selected for the entire class or should spelling lists be developed based on each student's interests, personal reading, and educational needs?
- What is the relationship between reading and spelling as described in this article? How can each of these aspects of literacy be taught so that they enhance each other?
- In your own teaching of spelling, what are some of the major issues you face in your instruction? How has your approach to instruction in spelling been changed by reading the material in this chapter?

CHAPTER 6

CONTENT AREA READING

Every teacher a teacher of reading.

> —Report of the National Committee on Reading, National Society
> for the Study of Education (1925)

. . . the greatest opportunity for progress in teaching reading during the next decade lies in the intelligent attack on the reading problems that arise in the content fields.

> —Committee on Reading of the National Society for the Study of Education (1948)

Students read and write all through the day as they learn science, social studies, and other content areas.

> —Gail Tompkins
> *Reading and Writing for the 21st Century* (2003)

The concept that reading is much more than a skill to be learned separately from its actual use in learning is hardly new. Neither is the realization by educators that literacy must be a total school effort. The ultimate goal of a successful reading curriculum needs to be much more than teaching students the mechanics of how to read effectively. It must also include the abilities needed to use this literacy knowledge in a wide variety of applications and experiences as well. The old adage that "students spend their first few years in school learning to read and the remainder of their education reading to learn" is very true. Although it is readily apparent that reading should be a part of all instruction, in reality, this is not the result in many teaching situations.

As the educational curriculum has become more segmented according to discipline, there has been a tendency by content area teachers to place less emphasis on appropriate related instruction in literacy skills. As noted by Stewart and O'Brien (1989) the reasons for this negative feeling about "content area reading " include the following.

Many teachers feel inadequate to contend with the reading problems they face in their classrooms.

Many believe that literacy activities would infringe on subject matter time.

Many deny the need for content area literacy techniques in their particular discipline area. (pp. 397–398)

AS YOU READ

As you read the articles in this chapter, note that many of the issues facing content teachers of the past still seem relevant for their contemporary counterparts. Examples of these issues include content organization that includes reading, specific literacy skills and their importance, and the role of the content teacher.

The Relation between Study and Reading

WILLIAM S. GRAY

The first article on content reading is by the noted reading authority William S. Gray (1919). It is considered by a number of subsequent reading authorities (Summers, 1963; Courtney, 1980; Moore et al., 1983) to be one of the earliest discussions, if not the first, of the importance of reading in relation to subject matter instruction. The term *study* that Gray uses in this article can also be read as meaning content instruction in a more modern sense. Observe in the early part of this article the list of specific reading skills the author recommends for effective subject matter reading instruction. At the end of this piece, Gray lists three important goals for content instruction, with particular emphasis being given to reading comprehension.

Supervised study periods have been organized because pupils need help and direction in the preparation of their lessons. The extent to which a pupil needs help is determined largely by the character of his reading and study habits. The pupil who studies carefully as he reads and who selects appropriate methods of work usually progresses rapidly and requires little or no help from teachers. On the other hand, the pupil who uses poor methods of study and who reads carelessly usually progresses slowly and requires frequent assistance. It is therefore a matter of first importance that pupils be trained to study effectively as they read. It is the purpose of this paper to discuss the uses which are made of reading during study periods and to outline types of instruction which pupils should receive to develop economical and appropriate methods of study.

In order to secure a list of the uses made of reading during study periods the teachers of the high school of the University of Chicago were asked to name the various ways in which reading is used in the preparation of assignments. Twenty-nine statements were submitted in response to this request, and they appear in the following list. Attention is specially directed to the starred statements.

The Uses of Reading Ability in Preparing High-School Assignments

1. To stimulate interest in and appreciation for a given field of study.
2. To acquire more effective modes of expression.
*3. To interpret and remember for the purpose of reproducing what is read.
*4. To determine the main outline of a story or article.
5. To enlarge one's vocabulary.
*6. To determine central ideas or fundamental principles.
7. To comprehend clearly and visualize described details.
*8. To determine and organize the principal points and the supporting details in a topic, article, or book.
9. To acquire more effective modes of thinking or reasoning.
10. To extend one's general range of information thru quantitative reading of materials directly related to a given subject.
11. To master sentence structure, grammatical relationships, word forms, idioms, etc.
12. To obtain definite information for the purpose of making specific reports or of asking intelligent questions.
*13. To analyze the argument of an address or article into its essential parts.
14. To increase one's rate of reading.
15. To fund collateral and illustrative materials in regard to problems or topics under discussion.
*16. To follow directions with accuracy and reasonable speed.
17. To determine the relative importance of different facts.
18. To increase one's information in regard to specific topics.
*19. To draw valid conclusions from data or statements.
*20. To find facts or materials which will aid in the solution of a problem or in answering questions.
21. To review the material of earlier readings for information needed in the discussion of present problems.
22. To appreciate the significance of each word used in a concisely exprest statement or principle.
*23. To gain a clear comprehension of the essential conditions of a problem which is to be solved.
24. To interpret and remember for the purpose of reproducing in another language.
25. To discover new problems in regard to a topic under discussion.
26. To determine whether statements are based on fact, opinion, inference, or supposition.
*27. To determine the validity of statements or inferences.
28. To discover the full significance of fundamental laws or conditions by correctly interpreting descriptions of their applications.
29. To gain the meaning of words peculiar to a subject or to master the particular meanings they have in the subject.

Each of these statements describes a familiar use of reading. Altho they are not all mutually exclusive, they are sufficiently different in character to indicate clearly that numerous and varied uses are made of reading in school work. One cannot escape the impression as he studies the list that high-school pupils are confronted with a complex problem, if all of the purposes of assignments are realized during study periods.

In order to determine the relative importance of the different uses of reading in the various subjects, the list was submitted to two hundred and fifty teachers representing all departments of typical high schools. The teachers were askt to check the five uses of reading which were most important in preparing assignments in their departments. The replies were recorded by departments and the results exprest in terms of the percentages of teachers mentioning each use. The results are represented graphically for the departments of English, science, mathematics, history, modern languages, and for all departments combined. Each vertical column represents a use which is made of reading. The uses are arranged from left to right in the order in which they appear on the printed list. The heights of the columns represent the percentages of teachers mentioning the different uses of reading.

English	1	2	3	4	5
Science	6	18	1	12	20
Mathematics	23	20	19	22	7
History	6	8	3	10	1
Modern Language	5	11	24	1	3

The accompanying diagrams show the five most important uses of reading in each subject as indicated by the teachers who cooperated. When one compares the ways in which reading is used in the the different departments he is imprest with the fact that different departments use reading for widely different purposes. This fact is illustrated in a very striking way in the modern-language departments, where some of the most important uses of reading have little or no value in other departments.

Since reading is used for a large number of purposes in the preparation of high-school assignments, a significant question is brought pointedly to our attention. Are the same reading habits and attitudes employed in connection with all the uses of reading, or is each use of reading characterized by its own set of appropriate habits? An examination of adult reading habits reveals some interesting and relevant facts. When one reads the morning newspaper to determine what the important events are which have transpired recently, interesting sets of habits are employed. The eyes take in the large headlines and the column headings almost instantly, and certain columns are selected as the most interesting. The eyes run down a column, catching rapidly items of information here and there. After a short period attention shifts to another column, and the skimming process continues. In two or three minutes an effective

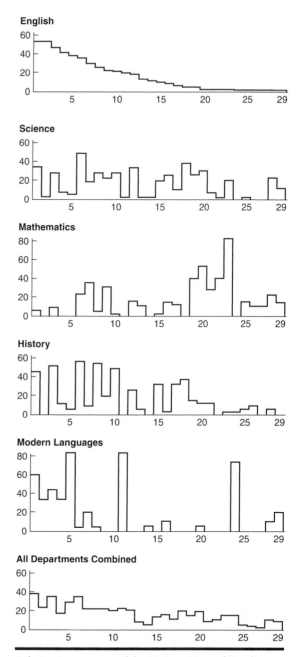

Relative Importance of the Various Uses of Reading

reader has secured a large number of important news items. Again, one reads a popular novel rapidly for pleasure, dwelling upon those parts which appeal to his interest. On the other hand, an article in the *Atlantic Monthly,* dealing with some modern social problem, requires more deliberate reading. One may read slowly in such cases, pausing on each sentence or line. Often each statement is carefully considered, and a judgment is reacht with regard to its validity. The significant fact which attaches to the foregoing discussion is that the various types of reading can be carried on most effectively thru the use of different sets of habits.

A comparison of reading for the purpose of remembering and reproducing with reading for the purpose of drawing valid conclusions reveals distinct differences in both the attitude of the reader and the habits of study which are employed. When a pupil reads for the purpose of remembering and reproducing what he reads, he sets about his task with a determination to remember what he reads. He reads the selection rapidly the first time to see what it is about and to select the main points. He reads it a second time to select and organize the details which belong appropriately to each main point. He then closes his book and recalls as much as he can. It is probable that he will then skim thru the selection to verify his outline of the essential points and supporting details. Some time later in the day or before the next recitation period he will again recall the facts which he wishes to present and will check his memory of the content by skimming thru the selection.

A pupil who reads for the purpose of drawing valid conclusions begins reading to discover evidence bearing on either side of a problem. The first reading is done carefully to determine the facts as they are presented. The reader then makes a summary of the evidence and draws a tentative conclusion. The second reading considers each point carefully to determine its validity and the weight it should be given. As the reading continues the facts which point to a positive conclusion are markt +, and those which point to a negative conclusion are markt –. These markt passages are finally reviewed, and a definite conclusion is reacht.

The foregoing discussion has emphasized the fact that the procedure in reading differs in the two cases. Any number of comparisons could be made in which equally markt differences would be apparent. Enough has been said, however, to show that a large variety of reading habits are employed as one studies. The specific habits which are used during a given study period depend on the purpose of the assignment which has been made.

These facts suggest a second important question. Should children be trained more definitely than they are at present in the establishment of reading habits which are appropriate for the various purposes of study? Recent tests of the study habits of college Freshmen show clearly that even the brighter pupils pass thru the elementary and high schools without acquiring effective habits of study. Tests and observations of high-school classes show clearly that a large majority of the pupils cannot read and study effectively. Teachers in the upper grades of elementary schools and in high schools admit frankly that instruction in the most important habits of reading and study is unorganized for the most part and very poorly done. The teachers of one of the best-organized elementary schools of Illinois recently stated that they were failing to give adequate instruction along these lines because they did not know how to train pupils effectively.

Accumulated evidence justifies the statement that most boys and girls go thru the elementary and high schools without acquiring effective habits of study. Instead of developing effective habits which render pupils progressively independent of assistance during study periods, they are too frequently left more and more dependent on the teacher for assistance as the study problems change from a simple to a more difficult level. This situation cannot be remedied wholly in supervised study periods. It is one of the fundamental problems of instruction and must be attackt intelligently and systematically in every grade, beginning with the earliest. In the remaining sections of this report a constructive program of instruction for developing effective habits of reading and study will be discust briefly.

The basic training in effective habits of reading and study should be given in the elementary school. Instead of devoting all the reading time to training in oral expression, much of the time should be given to training pupils in the art of independent, effective silent study. Frances Jenkins in her book entitled *Reading in the Primary Grades* recommends that training of this type be started in the first and second grades. Two types of study problems are discust in detail, namely, finding the heart of the story and separating a selection into its main sections. As much training should be given along these lines as may be necessary to quicken the thought of the pupil, to broaden his understanding of a selection, and to deepen his appreciation. Instead of merely hearing reading lessons day after day, teachers of the lower grades should devote a large amount of time and attention to the development of a thoughtful reading attitude. This is prerequisite to effective expression and to the development of ability to study independently and intelligently.

By the beginning of the fourth grade pupils should be able to read fluently untechnical paragraphs in Carpenter's *Geographical Readers*. When they have reacht this point in their development they are ready for specific instruction in the methods of silent reading and study. Altho instruction should be given in all phases of silent reading during the fourth, fifth, and sixth grades, the present discussion is limited to the methods of developing effective study habits as one reads. In the organization of instruction of this type three principles of organization should be observed: (1) Pupils should be trained definitely in specific habits of study. (2) Regular periods should be utilized for such instruction. (3) Instruction should proceed systematically from simple to more difficult study problems. By the end of the sixth grade the more important study habits should have been develop. The following illustrations describe some of the essential characteristics of instruction of the type which is recommended.

1. Pupils should be trained to get the central idea of what is being read. Both understanding and appreciation depend on finding the central theme. In the fourth grade short passages may be chosen as the basis for this work. Pupils should be instructed concerning the most effective methods of procedure. The important part should be markt. If two or three different sentences contain possible central themes, the pupils should mark them and then study their value and importance. The central ideas chosen by different pupils should be discust in class. Reasons should be presented for the final choice, and each pupil should recognize why his selection was approved or rejected. There should be sufficient training of this type to develop the attitude on the part of the pupils of searching for the author's main point. The training should be continued in the fifth grade thru the use of more difficult passages and longer selections. In the sixth grade the pupils should be able to attack relatively difficult passages and should be able to find the central theme of long selections or books. Twenty minutes of silent study to find the central idea of a selection fifteen or twenty pages in length provides excellent training in developing habits of effective silent study.

2. Definite training should be provided in finding a series of large important points. In the fourth grade the pupils may mark the passages in the selection which include the important points, or the teacher may write them on the board as they are suggested. After the entire series has been indicated the passages should be re-read to determine whether or not all of the essential points have been included. Instruction should be continued along this line in the fifth grade by requiring the pupil to select the points independently, to express them concisely, to place them in the form of an organization, and to include some of the supporting details. In the sixth grade pupils should be trained to organize effectively the material which they read and to develop considerable skill in working out refined organizations as to both form and content.

3. Pupils should be trained to determine the validity of statements. In the fourth grade the teacher must lead largely in this work. Selections should be chosen in which the writer's experiences or statements differ from the experiences of the class. By means of skilful questions the teachers can provoke discussion with regard to such points. In this connection pupils should realize that experiences may differ, and that two people may give entirely different accounts of the same event. In the fifth grade conflicting statements by different authors may be studied. In this connection pupils should learn that the author's qualification to write on a given topic determines to a large extent the amount of confidence which can be placed in his statements. In the sixth grade pupils should be taught the use of source-books in various fields and should be given frequent opportunity to check the validity of questionable statements thru the use of reliable sources of information.

We must depend for leadership in this work on the superintendents, supervisors, and principals of the country.

I am confident that our leaders will give this problem the consideration, stimulus, and impetus which it merits.

The Relation of Reading to Content Subjects and Other School Activities[1]

BESSIE GOODYKUNTZ ET AL.

The second article, by Goodykuntz et al. (1925), is taken from the *Twenty-Fourth Yearbook of the National Society For the Study of Education*. It continues the earlier discussion of Gray, noting especially the importance of the role of relating reading in the content areas to real-life experiences both within and beyond the classroom.

The importance of developing effective reading habits in content subjects. It is a strange though undoubted fact that pupils are often said to be "satisfactory" in reading who yet fail in certain informational subjects, such as geography and history. This condition was revealed in the study of school failures in the Cleveland Survey. The proportion of failures in reading generally is small as compared with those in other subjects. The reason is apparent. The reading done in the so-called "reading period" has been largely narrative. Yet studies[2] have demonstrated that the pupil who reads narrative material quite well may read very poorly when the passages tell the conditions of an arithmetic problem[3] or give directions to be followed in the study of grammar. Such situations indicate that there must be a broader conception of the variety of skills and habits to be developed before pupils can be said to read adequately.

Partial solution of the problem of training pupils to read effectively lies in the cultivation of appropriate reading habits in every school subject and activity. Just as spelling and language habits must be emphasized in every subject, so essential reading habits must be cultivated in the study of literature, arithmetic, history, geography, and other content subjects. Each subject, in addition to the general habits employed in reading, requires specific skills peculiar to its purposes and subject matter.

Purpose of this chapter. It is the purpose, therefore, of this chapter to show the relationship which exists between the objectives set forth in Chapter I and the various activities of the school that involve reading. This includes three steps:

1. *Calling attention to the situations arising in the regular work of the school which give occasion for learning through reading.* This is of particular importance in the primary grades, where reading is built largely upon the experiences of the pupils and upon meanings already established. All grades, however, neglect to use many situations which afford good opportunity for reading. Pupils would learn to follow the printed directions in the texts if the teachers didn't read them first. Pupils should learn to read recipes as well as to follow them. New games to be played, dresses to be cut out, radios to be built, all require reading. In these and similar situations reading should function in school as it does in life outside of school.

2. *Showing how the reading which pupils do in the study of various school subjects contributes to the development of interests and abilities.* The study of every subject requires the use not only of the essential reading habits but also of additional specific skills. These skills depend both upon the nature of the subject matter and upon the purposes for which it is read. For example, pupils comprehend geography problems and arithmetic problems by means of very different reading habits. Furthermore, geography material is read differently when one is vicariously enjoying life in the tropics than when getting ready for an examination.

Perhaps the most important of the purposes for which pupils read is that of extending experience in various fields of interest. The classroom can contribute to this purpose only as it stimulates pupils to read extensively and with enjoyment. Such reading has been designated in this report as "recreatory reading." It has as its immediate objectives vicarious experience, informational background, appreciation, enjoyment. It has as its ultimate objectives the development of permanent interests and of habits of reading which will provide for the use of leisure time. This reading, while not requiring intensive work and reflection, should nevertheless be guided. Pupils should have the impetus which comes from an interesting purpose in reading. They need not be held accountable for all they read, but there should be some sort of check which is in line with the purpose of their reading. They may prepare a dramatization of some episode, may read or tell to the class a distinctive bit of information. Some teachers may find it necessary to give "extra credit" for extensive reading in order to foster it. In all events, such reading should be judged not alone for quantity but also, and more especially, for worth-whileness and quality.

In addition to this extensive reading, every subject requires intensive reading. Provision must be made for the understanding of simple terms which have a technical use. Again, problems must be solved, and the solution may require a search for data involving the reading and re-reading of material in order to select main ideas. Material must be organized; it must be associated with experience, and definite steps taken to remember it. Such reading is referred to in this report as "work-type reading."

While work-type reading is usually the sort thought of as study, both types are used in the study of a subject, and no lesson or series of lessons is apt to use one exclusively. Whenever reading is not merely cursory, but is done for a conscious purpose, it is study. The reason for thus labeling reading as "recreatory" or "work-type" reading is to call the attention of teachers to the place of each in the study of a subject. When teachers have failed to differentiate between materials appropriate for recreatory reading and for work-type reading, they have frequently used literary materials to give pupils training in skills necessary only to work-type material, such as finding answers to questions, selecting main points, outlining. The result is that, instead of finding enjoyment in reading, pupils dislike to read and will not engage in such activities independently. In view of these facts, many recent reading books have furnished, in addition to literary material, information from various fields, encyclopedia references, and tests. The guidance given in the reading of these various types of subject matter is usually very suggestive as to methods of study. The difficulty is, however, that these methods are not applied by the pupils when the actual study of a subject is at hand. Consequently, the skills are never used habitually.

3. *Suggesting by means of illustrative lessons how pupils may develop habits of work.* Teachers should use these lessons merely as illustrations and in turn make their own daily assignments reading situations. The chief purpose of these lessons is to show the importance of assignments which require pupils to read actively and to react in very positive ways. The conduct of the class conferences which follow, the way in which pupils attack the work, the distribution of time, the adaptation of work to individual abilities and other details of procedure are all important aspects to be considered by the teacher when she makes an assignment. . . .

NOTES_____

1. The following persons contributed suggestive materials for this chapter of the report: Bessie Goodykuntz, Alice Brennan, Minnie Kinker, Charmian Johnson, Alice Phelps, Irene Conway, Aileen Stowell, Elizabeth Whitcomb, Sue Snow, Florence Hawkins, Flora Nettleman, Betsy Jane Welling, Isabel Smith, Harriet Hinman, June Mapes, Rosemary Featherstone, Myrtle Best, Vilma Rottenstein, Ilo Hatfield, Morrison Van Cleave, Carl Cotter, John Dambach.

2. Charles H. Judd and Guy T. Buswell, *Silent Reading: A Study of Various Types.* Supplementary Educational Monographs, No. 23. Chicago: Department of Education, University of Chicago, 1922.

3. Estaline Wilson, "Specific teaching of silent reading." *Elementary School Journal,* 22 (1921), 140–146. Chicago: Department of Education, University of Chicago.

What Research Has to Say about Reading in the Content Areas

Leo C. Fay

The third article, by Leo Fay (1964), is included here because of its extensive coverage of the writing and research done on the subject of content reading. Of importance here is the discussion of the specific content areas and their unique requirements in literacy instruction.

At one time nearly everyone assumed that reading was a generalized ability that once learned could be easily transferred and used in any situation that required it. It remained for Judd and Buswell (9), writing in 1922, to point the way toward the consideration of reading as it relates to the various subject areas. During the last 30 years enough opinion has been expressed and research conducted to lead the Committee on Reading of the National Society for the Study of Education (15) to observe that in their judgment "the greatest opportunity for progress in teaching reading during the next decade lies in an intelligent attack on the reading problems that arise in the content fields." This statement of the Committee on Reading can rightfully be considered a challenge to thoughtful teachers who recognize the host of problems related to successful reading in the various subject areas. Fortunately, research findings are now available to give definite help to classroom teachers.

STRONG GENERAL READING ABILITY IS NEEDED

A number (1, 3, 5, 11, 20) of experimental studies, as well as studies of the relationship between general reading ability and achievement in the various content areas, attest to the importance of a strong basic reading program. Fundamental skills involved in reading must be learned before those skills can be expected to function in content reading. Lee's study (11) indicated, for example, that before a child in grades four, five, and six could hope to have a chance for success in his content subjects, as they are usually organized and taught, he should have a basic reading ability of at least fourth grade level. *The basic conclusion to be drawn from all these studies is that one of the first steps involved in improving reading in literature or science or history is to build as good a foundation as possible in the basic habits, skills, and abilities in reading.* Nor is such a program appropriate for the elementary grades alone for a number of experiments have demonstrated the importance of continuing the teaching of basic reading skills throughout the secondary years as well.

SPECIFIC SKILLS FOR EACH AREA

The second major conclusion to be drawn from the research is that specific skills and patterns of skills are related to successful achievement in the various subject areas. A number of investigators (4, 8, 10, 17, 18) have clearly shown that the nature of reading in one area may differ radically from that in another. So much so in fact, that ability to read well the material of one subject may

not be a good predictor of ability to read in other subjects. These studies which have involved pupils in all grades from third through twelfth lead to the following conclusions of major importance to classroom teachers.

1. At all grade levels above the second, specific instruction should be given for reading in the different content areas. As the child progresses through school and the curriculum content becomes more specialized this need increases.

2. Instruction is most effective when directly related to the work being carried on in the content field in which improvement is desired. Ideally, as topics are studied in science or history or any other area, the problems of reading the appropriate materials would be dealt with. It can not be assumed that merely because the teacher gives an assignment that the children will be able to handle it automatically.

3. Instruction should be concerned with the comprehension abilities specifically related to success in each area. The importance of well defined purposes is emphasized again and again in the related research. Having a well understood reason for reading a selection is one of the best guides a reader has for the efficient reading of a passage. In addition, however, there are unique comprehension problems in the various areas for which special attention is needed.

4. The body of basic ideas and the way of organizing these ideas should be developed. Knowledge in any field is certainly more than the mere collection of information. Egypt, for example, is more than the Nile, Cairo, The Suez, and the pyramids. These facts are all interrelated to such an extent that real understanding can be based only upon the further knowledge of how these facts fit together. There is some evidence that summary textbooks may foster neglect of these abilities. Much more extensive reading and other contacts (audio-visual aids, field trips, etc.) are also highly important.

5. Word meanings are a major block to successful content reading. Since words are the vehicles for expressing ideas, understanding will invariably suffer if pupils are seriously limited in the specific and technical vocabulary of an area. It is quite revealing at any educational level to ask pupils to define some of the basic terms for the project or topic being studied. It appears that terminology is so much a part of the teacher's background that he is often guilty of assuming that word meanings are obvious and consequently neglects to check them. Studies in arithmetic, social studies, science, and literature all show that power in word meanings is significantly related to successful achievement.

6. Materials are a source of difficulty for the following reasons:

Fact and concept load are often unduly heavy.

Format variations from area to area lead to confusion.

Materials in the content areas are often uninteresting and unappealing to children.

The readability of content materials is often significantly harder than general reading texts.

Authors of content books often assume greater background than children actually possess.

In each area a need exists for carefully fitting materials to children. To do this successfully will call for an understanding of the materials as well as the reading ability and the background of the children. Materials represent an area in which, although much progress has been made, much further work is needed to make more effective use of the better materials now being produced.

7. Individual differences cast a shadow over the entire area of content reading. Researchers have pointed out the importance of differentiated use of materials by means of which problems of differences in basic reading ability may be met. In addition the unit approach to content teaching, which is quite common in the elementary schools, makes possible adjusting to the differing interest patterns of children.

8. A final conclusion to be drawn from the research is that improvement of pupils' reading can best be achieved where the teacher actively attempts to increase his own professional effectiveness through experimentation. Reading research and reviews of research may stimulate a teacher's thinking; however, improvement in reading will take more than thinking about it. Improvement proves to be the result of action on the part of both pupils and teachers.

DIRECTION AND ACTION IN THE VARIOUS SUBJECT AREAS—ARITHMETIC

A number of carefully controlled studies of reading as related to success in arithmetic have been reported in the literature. Two of these rather emphatically reveal the importance of giving special attention to reading skills as they are related to the work being done in arithmetic. Lessenger (12), working with a group of elementary school children, gave special reading instruction for a semester. The range of gain for the semester's work was from one and a half to two years' growth in arithmetic computation. Stright (19) conducted a controlled experiment with high school freshmen with similar results. The control group had algebra five days a week, the experimental group had four days of algebra and spent the fifth day on reading and study skills. The gain of the experimental group over the control group in algebra achievement was significant at the two per cent level of significance. A number of classroom experiments conducted under the author's direction have been able to show gains averaging well over a year in a semester's time by working directly with the reading skills involved in arithmetic. Research indicates that the reading problems to be found in arithmetic are:

1. *Vocabulary.* A twofold problem exists in relation to vocabulary. Arithmetic possesses a technical vocabulary which must be mastered. Secondly, the vocabulary of arithmetic textbooks is not so carefully controlled as that in basic readers, with the result that children are faced with a greater proportion of strange words.

2. *Abbreviations, symbols and form.* In testing a large group of sixth grade pupils the author found that a change in the symbols and form of a given problem often resulted in a significant change in the difficulty of the problem. For example, changing the conventional multiplication problem

$$\begin{array}{r} 213 \\ \times\ 65 \end{array}$$ to: 213 times 65 = ?

resulted in well over a ten percent drop in the group's efficiency in solving the problem. Children should encounter problems in many different forms and should be masters of the symbols and abbreviations used to express the problems in various ways.

3. *Problem solving.* Much could be said of the inadequacy of many arithmetic materials in regard to their problem solving exercises. It is rather difficult for a child to be a clever problem solver when the problems are completely outside the realm of his experiences, or are so briefly stated that it is difficult to visualize them. Positively stated, experimentation has indicated the importance of problem situations that are of significance to children and of problems that are completely enough stated for children to have a chance to understand them.

4. *Adjusting to individual differences.* A search of the literature reveals a minimum of serious consideration being given to this fundamental problem. Classroom experimentation reveals that grouping is just as necessary for arithmetic instruction as for reading.

SOCIAL STUDIES

Studies, of which those by Shores (17) and by Rudolph (16) are typical, present convincing evidence of the need for providing reading instruction in social studies classes if pupils are to be helped to master more adequately the content of the social studies. That this is a desirable goal is evidenced by the findings that the social studies are typically rated as their most disliked subject by upper elementary and high school youth. Research points to some of the reasons for this dissatisfaction as well as ways in which work in the field may be improved. Findings related to reading are:

1. *Complexity of ideas.* Analyses of social studies materials reveal that the social studies are staggering under an almost unbearable load of difficult concepts. A number of factors combine to make the concept load a major block to successful learning. Concepts are presented at too fast a pace, and in an unrelated and sketchy way to children who lack the richness of experience to make sense out of them. Extensive reading, which is an excellent means of adding meaning and substance to concepts may add to the problem unless a sensible restriction is made in the number of topics to be studied. Experimentation reveals that limiting the number of topics and considering them more thoroughly results in greater total achievement.

2. *Vocabulary.* The social studies vocabulary problem is as great as that in any area. The names of people, places, and events fill the pages of social studies texts. Not only are there many names and terms but, as if to add insult to injury, a large proportion are derived from other languages and cultures which, in turn, add to the problem of pronouncing and learning them. It simply is not safe to assume that words are known without testing the assumption. Vocabulary study is a definite part of effective social studies instruction.

3. *Reading-study skills.* Each of the social studies makes use of rather unique types of materials that call for skill in a variety of reading-study techniques. Much of the success in the experimental studies was related to special work in map reading, reading of charts, graphs and tables, use of reference books, indices, dictionaries, skill in locating, organizing and using information. Such skills can be approached diagnostically with individualized remedial work given where appropriate.

4. *Comprehension skills.* Especially important in social studies are the abilities to skim, to evaluate, and to interpret what is read. The need for these skills arises especially in those situations where reading goes beyond a single text and where it is necessary for students to locate information, reconcile differences of opinion, and make judgments of what they read.

SCIENCE

Classroom experimentation such as that conducted by Pierce (14) reveals that achievement in science can be increased significantly by working with the reading and study skills used with science materials and content. As with social studies, the experimenters found that special instruction should center in vocabulary, symbols, abbreviations, study skills and comprehension skills. Particularly important among the comprehension skills are the ability to note detail, to follow directions, and to relate relevant items.

A final conclusion to be drawn from what research has to say about reading in the content areas is that any classroom teacher can achieve better results in content achievement if he will help his students sharpen their use of the tools of learning—their reading and study skills.

REFERENCES

1. Artley, A. S. "A Study of Certain Relationships Existing Between General Reading Comprehension and Reading Comprehension in the Specific Subject-Matter Areas." *Journal of Educational Research,* XXXVII, February, 1944, pp. 464–473.
2. Bond, Guy L. and Eva Bond Wagner. *Teaching the Child to Read,* New York: Macmillan and Co., 1950.
3. Dolch, E. W. "Fact Burdens and Reading Difficulties," *Elementary English Review,* 16: 135–138, May, 1939.
4. Fay, Leo C. "The Relationship Between Specific Reading Skills and Selected Areas of Sixth Grade Achievement." *Journal of Educational Research,* 43: 541–7, March, 1950.
5. Finck, Edgar M. "The Relation of Ability in Reading to Success in Other Subjects." *Elementary School Journal,* XXXVI, December, 1935, pp. 260–267.
6. Gray, William S. *Improving Reading in All Curriculum Areas,* Chicago: Supplementary Educational Monograph, Number 76, University of Chicago Press, 1951.
7. Gray, William S. *Improving Reading in the Content Fields,* Chicago: Supplementary Educational Monograph, Number 62, University of Chicago Press, 1947.
8. Hansen, Carl W. "Factors Associated with Superior and Inferior Achievement in Problem Solving in Sixth Grade Achievement." Unpublished doctor's thesis. Minneapolis: Graduate School, University of Minnesota, 1943.
9. Judd, C. and Guy T. Buswell. *Silent Reading: A Study of Various Types,* Chicago: Supplementary Educational Monograph, Number 23, University of Chicago Press, 1922.
10. Koenker, Robert. "The Characteristic Differences Between Excellent and Poor Achievers in Sixth Grade Division." Unpublished doctor's dissertation, Minneapolis: Graduate School, University of Minnesota, 1941.
11. Lee, Doris Mae. *The Importance of Reading for Achieving in Grades Four, Five, and Six,* Teachers College Contributions to Education. No. 556. New York: Teachers College, Columbia University, 1933, 64 pp.
12. Lessenger, W. E. "Reading Difficulties in Arithmetical Computations." *Journal of Educational Research,* 11: 287–291, April, 1925.
13. Phipps, William R. "An Experimental Study in Developing Historical Reading Ability with Sixth-Grade Pupils Through the Development of an Active History Vocabulary." *Journal of Experimental Education,* 7, September, 1938.
14. Pierce, Cecilia A. "Problems in Reading in Intermediate Grade Science." Unpublished master's study, Minneapolis: University of Minnesota, 1951.
15. *Reading in the High School and College.* Forty-seventh Yearbook of the National Society for the Study of Education, Part II, Chicago: University of Chicago Press, 1948.
16. Rudolph, Kathleen Brady. *The Effect of Reading Instruction on Achievement in Eighth-grade Social Studies.* Contributions to Education, Number 945: New York, Teachers College, Columbia University, 1949, pp. vi † 79.
17. Shores, J. Harlan. "Skills Related to the Ability to Read History and Science." *Journal of Educational Research,* XXXVI, April, 1943, pp. 584–593.
18. Stevens, B. A. "Problem Solving is Arithmetic," *Journal of Educational Research,* XXV, April–May, 1952, pp. 253–260.
19. Stright, Isaac L. "The Relation of Reading Comprehension and Efficient Methods of Study to Skill in

Solving Algebraic Problems." *The Mathematics Teacher,* 31: 368–372, December, 1938.

20. Swenson, Esther J. "A Study of the Relationships Among Various Types of Reading Scores on General

and Science Materials." *Journal of Educational Research,* XXXVI, October, 1942, pp. 81–90.

Content Literacy: A Definition and Implications

Michael C. McKenna and Richard D. Robinson

The article by McKenna and Robinson (1990) is a discussion of the term *content literacy* and how it is different from *content knowledge.* As you read this material, consider how an understanding of content knowledge by the teacher has particular importance in decisions made concerning the teaching of reading in various content areas.

In the past century, the word *literacy* has undergone numerous changes in the broad array of concepts it has denoted (e.g., see Purves, 1984; Stedman & Kaestle, 1987; Venezky, 1990). Some changes, such as the generalization of the term to denote mere knowledgeability of a specific subject (as in *computer literacy, cultural literacy,* etc.), have been unfortunate and continue to make consistent usage difficult. Other changes, such as a multidimensional conceptualization of literacy (Guthrie & Kirsch, 1984; Taylor, 1989) and the necessity that it embrace both situational demands (Guthrie, 1983; Mikulecky, 1990) and cultural considerations (Kazemek, 1988; Levine, 1982) have reflected a growing appreciation for the complexity of literacy processes.

One especially important advance in our understanding has been the recognition that both reading and writing are constructive processes in which information is organized and accommodated into memory structures (see Squire, 1983). Accordingly, the writing-to-learn movement has stressed that writing, like reading, is a means of clarifying, refining, and extending one's internalization of content (Myers, 1984). Writing as well as reading therefore becomes a tool for acquiring content. These realizations together suggest the following further expansion of the concept of literacy.

Content literacy can be defined as the ability to use reading and writing for the acquisition of new content in a given discipline. Such ability includes three principal cognitive components: general literacy skills, content-specific literacy skills (such as map reading in the social studies), and prior knowledge of content.

This definition has significant implications for content area teachers—implications that may add to the arguments used to encourage these educators to view matters of literacy with an open mind.

• *Content literacy is not the same as content knowledge.* Content literacy represents skills needed to acquire knowledge of content; the terms are in no way synonymous, as popular usage might suggest. Nor is content literacy a prerequisite of content knowledge, for it is certainly possible to acquire knowledge of content without recourse to reading or writing. On the other hand, content knowledge is a prerequisite of content literacy. In a cyclical pattern, the more prior knowledge one possesses, the more such knowledge will facilitate reading and writing as activities leading to the integration of still more knowledge, and so forth.

• *Teaching content automatically makes students more content literate.* Whether they know it or not, content area teachers enhance the ability of their students to read and write about content simply by teaching it. There is an irony in this notion, for even those teachers refusing to embrace the ideas of "reading in the content areas" and "writing to learn" have nevertheless improved their students' ability to read and write within their disciplines whenever their instruction has been successful. This is because enhanced knowledge enhances any subsequent reading and writing germane to that knowledge. What is unfortunate is that many teachers, by providing high-quality direct instruction, set the stage for even greater levels of content acquisition— through reading and writing—but never realize this potential with appropriate assignments.

• *Content literacy is content specific.* To be literate in, say, mathematics is not to know mathematics per se but to be able to read and write about the subject as effective means of knowing still more about it. While the general ability to read and write obviously bears on one's success in this process, prior knowledge of the specific topics involved is a vital variable of content literacy. Thus, an individual who is highly literate in math may have a far lower level of literacy in history or economics. This circumstance is largely the result of differences in prior knowledge and is true even though the individual brings the same general literacy skills to all reading and writing tasks.

• *In content literacy, reading and writing are complementary tasks.* While reading and writing can serve well enough as alternative means of enhancing content learning, the greatest gains can be expected when the two are used in tandem. When printed materials are assigned to be read and when written responses are also required, students are placed in the position first of constructing an internal representation of the content they encounter in print and next of refining that representation through such processes as synthesis, evaluation, and summarization.

• *Content literacy is germane to all subject areas, not just those relying heavily on printed materials.* Teachers of subjects such as art, music, physical education, and other fields tending to involve little use of prose materials have frequently objected that content area reading coursework, now compulsory for teachers in at least 36 U.S. states (Farrell & Cirrincione, 1986), does not apply to their instructional situations. Certain states have in fact excluded such groups from these course requirements. The notion of content literacy, however, suggests that students' understanding of the content presented in all subjects could be substantially enhanced through appropriate writing assignments or through supplemental reading.

While the primary presentation may comprise lecture and demonstration rather than reading, and while the principal domain involved may be psychomotor rather than cognitive, content acquisition nevertheless invariably includes an understanding of key concepts and their interrelationships. Such understanding can always be fostered through literacy activities.

• *Content literacy does not require content area teachers to instruct students in the mechanics of writing.* A longstanding misinterpretation has hampered the effort to encourage content area reading techniques. It is that such techniques call for subject matter specialists to teach the minutiae of decoding, requiring them in consequence to master a new and very different curriculum and, worse, to take class time away from subject matter instruction. This false notion has lingered tenaciously despite widespread efforts to overcome it. It is therefore important in elaborating the idea of content literacy, which embraces writing as well as reading, to make clear that it includes no responsibility for developing the mechanical skills of writing.

As Myers puts it, "Writing to learn is not learning to write" (1984, p. 7). It is true that mechanical aberrations severe enough to distort meaning may require a teacher's attention, especially in disciplines like mathematics, where precise usage is an absolute necessity (Orr, 1987). However, the focus of such follow-up should be meaning, not mechanics.

• *Content literacy is relative to the tasks expected of students.* The literacy requirements of a classroom, like those of a workplace or of an entire culture, readily define who is literate and who is not (Guthrie, 1983; Mikulecky, 1990; Wedman & Robinson, in press). In an effort to reduce or eliminate the "illiterate" subpopulation in their classes, teachers all too frequently resort to slashing literacy requirements. Reading assignments may be circumvented or minimized while writing may never be seriously considered. Although students consequently meet the literacy demands of the instructional setting—so that all are technically literate—the opportunity to enhance content learning through reading and writing is in effect waived. Students at even a rudimentary level of general literacy are equipped to advance their understanding through literacy activities, provided that reading materials are commensurate with ability (or steps are taken to facilitate comprehension of more difficult material) and writing assignments are within the range of student sophistication.

• *Content literacy has the potential to maximize content acquisition.* While reading content materials may introduce new ideas into a student's knowledge base and while writing about content may help the student to organize and store that information more effectively, it can be argued that similar results can be accomplished without resort to reading or writing. Instructors may indeed spoon feed new content in carefully organized curricular designs using direct oral instruction. This argument has been strong enough to permit the aliterate environments, mentioned earlier, that have been deliberately established by some teachers.

There are, however, at least four persuasive reasons for not depending exclusively on direct instruction. One is the fact that the products of literacy activities will never precisely match those of oral instruction. They therefore serve to complement such instruction and broaden student perspectives. Another is the individualized extension made possible through such activities as a natural follow-up to direct instruction. Students are in a position to pursue content on their own, following in some measure their personal predilections, needs, and interests.

A further reason is that present models of direct instruction incorporate practice phases that follow up the presentation of content for the purpose of reinforcing it (e.g., Rosenshine, 1986). Such practice could certainly incorporate literacy activities, which seem ideally suited to these models. Finally, students who have been afforded opportunities to become content literate will be better able to use content literacy as a means of extending their knowledge of a discipline even after they have completed a given course.

REFERENCES

Farrell, R. T., & Cirrincione, J. M. (1986). The introductory developmental reading course for content area teachers: A state of the art survey. *Journal of Reading, 29,* 717–723.

Guthrie, J. T. (1983). Equilibrium of literacy. *Journal of Reading, 26,* 668–670.

Guthrie, J. T., & Kirsch, I. S. (1984). The emergent perspective on literacy. *Phi Delta Kappan, 66,* 351–355.

Kazemek, F. E. (1988). Necessary changes: Professional involvement in adult literacy programs. *Harvard Educational Review, 58,* 484–487.

Levine, K. (1982). Functional literacy: Found illusions and false economies. *Harvard Educational Review, 52,* 249–266.

Mikulecky, L. (1990). Literacy for what purpose? In R. L. Venezky, D. A Wagner, & B. S. Ciliberti

(Eds.), *Toward defining literacy* (pp. 24–34). Newark, DE: International Reading Association.

Myers, J. W. (1984). *Writing to learn across the curriculum.* Bloomington, IN: Phi Delta Kappa.

Orr, E. W. (1987). *Twice as less: Black English and the performance of Black students in mathematics and science.* New York: Norton.

Purves, A. C. (1984). The potential and real achievement of U.S. students in school reading. *American Journal of Education, 93,* 82–106.

Rosenshine, B. V. (1986). Synthesis of research on explicit teaching. *Educational Leadership, 43,* 60–69.

Squire, J. R. (1983). Composing and comprehending: Two sides of the same basic process. *Language Arts, 60,* 581–589.

Stedman, L. C., & Kaestle, C. F. (1987). Literacy and reading performance in the United States, from 1880 to the present. *Reading Research Quarterly, 22,* 8–46.

Taylor, D. (1989). Toward a unified theory of literacy learning and instructional practices. *Phi Delta Kappan, 71,* 184–193.

Wedman, J., & Robinson, R. D. (in press). Workplace literacy: A perspective. *Adult Literacy and Basic Education.*

Verezky, R. L. (1990). Definitions of literacy. In R. L. Venezky, D. A. Wagner, & B. S. Ciliberti (Eds.), *Toward defining literacy* (pp. 2–16). Newark, DE: International Reading Association.

Reading, Writing, and Understanding

Vicki A. Jacobs

The final article by Jacobs (2002) reflects recent thinking on the role of literacy in content instruction. Note how some of the issues discussed here are very similar to those mentioned by Gray almost eighty-five years earlier. Why do you think there remain so many unresolved problems related to reading in the content areas?

Why hasn't the concept of secondary reading—also known as "reading and writing across the curriculum" and "content-area reading and writing"—become better rooted in our schools? One reason is an understandable reluctance among secondary school teachers to think of themselves as reading or writing teachers.

Secondary school teachers rightfully consider themselves first and foremost teachers of such content areas as science, history, and mathematics. When we ask them to integrate reading and writing in their instruction, it sounds as if we are asking them to teach additional content. As a result, we get such reactions as, "That's not my job," "I don't have time," or "Why doesn't the reading teacher do it?" (Jacobs & Wade, 1981). For subject teachers to implement principles and practices of secondary reading and writing, they must first recognize reading and writing as meaning-making processes that can support their instructional goals, particularly those related to understanding content.

Certainly, most teachers would agree that a central purpose of their instruction is to help students understand something significant about their content area. What do we really mean when we say that we want our students to understand? Understanding is more than "doing" or "knowing": Students may do multiplication problems or know historical facts without understanding much about them. Understanding is a problem-solving process that involves making meaning of content. Teaching for understanding, in part, involves choosing topics into which students can find their own points of entry; directly telling students the goals for their understanding; and developing assessments that allow students to demonstrate their understanding (Perkins & Blythe, 1994). The principles and practices of secondary reading and writing provide means by which students can move from understanding goals to demonstrating understanding.

READING-TO-LEARN AS A MEANS OF UNDERSTANDING

The difference between primary and secondary school reading is the difference between learning to read and using reading to learn (Chall, 1983). Through about the 3rd grade, students learn to read. They become familiar with the roles that literacy can play in various contexts, the value of reading, and the enjoyment that reading can provide. They build their vocabulary, acquire conceptual knowledge, learn about letter-sound relationships and the relationship between oral and written language, and practice the skills necessary to become automatic and fluent readers who can tackle the more specialized and technical texts of secondary reading (Chall, 1983; Chall & Jacobs, 1996; Jacobs, 2000).

At about the 4th grade, students begin using these early reading skills to learn. Reading-to-learn is a matter of meaning-making, problem-solving, and understanding.

The process through which students come to understand something from a text is called *comprehension*. In order for students to focus on comprehension, the teacher must present a text as a mystery—a dilemma or problem to be solved. Comprehension is a three-stage process in which teachers engage students in problem-solving activities that serve as scaffolds (Bruner, 1975)—between reader and text, and from one stage of the comprehension process to the next.

Stage 1: Prereading

Frequently, a struggling secondary reader will come to class and say, "I read last night's homework, but I don't remember anything about it (let alone understand it)!" How successfully students remember or understand text depends, in part, on how explicitly teachers have prepared them to read it for clearly defined purposes.

During prereading, teachers help students activate and organize the "given"—the background knowledge and experience they will use to solve the mystery of the text. The "given" includes students' cultural and language-based contexts, their biases (for example, from previous successes or failures with learning about the subject), and the relevant factual and conceptual knowledge that they have gained from daily experience and formal study. When teachers know what students bring to their trading, they can purposefully choose strategies that serve as effective scaffolds between the "given" and the "new" of the text—clarifying unfamiliar vocabulary and concepts, helping students anticipate the text, and helping them make personal connections with it—thus promoting their interest, engagement, and motivation (Jacobs, 1999).

Prereading activities can include brainstorms, graphic organizers of students' background knowledge (using concept maps, clusters, or webs), or cloze exercises (during which students attempt to replace important vocabulary or concepts that the teacher has deleted from the text in order to draw attention to those points). In addition, the teacher or students may develop questions, through directed writing or interactive discussions, such as. "What do I already know and what do I need to know before reading?" or "What do I think this passage will be about, given the headings, graphs, or pictures?" (Jacobs, 1999, p. 4; 2000, p. 38). Such prereading activities not only prepare students to understand text but also help build their vocabulary and study skills.

Stage 2: Guided Reading

During guided reading, teachers provide students with the structured means to integrate the background knowledge that they bring to the text with the "new" knowledge provided by the text.

During guided reading, students probe the text beyond its literal meaning for deeper understanding. They revise their preliminary questions or predictions; search for tentative answers; gather, organize, analyze, and synthesize evidence; and begin to make generalizations or assertions about their new understanding that they want to investigate further (Jacobs, 1999; Scala, 2001).

Common guided reading activities include directed writing (such as response journals or study guides) and collaborative problem-solving activities that engage students in searching beyond the text's literal meaning. For example, teachers might take the factual questions that texts usually provide at the end of a chapter and transform them into questions that ask how or why the facts are important or how information that students have to locate in the text informs the problem that the students are trying to address through their reading (Jacobs, 2000). As in prereading, such guided reading activities not only enhance comprehension but also promote vocabulary and study skills.

The ability to self-monitor often distinguishes effective from poor readers in the secondary years. Thus, guided reading activities might also ask students to reflect on the reading process itself: to keep a process log of how their background knowledge and experience influences their understanding of the text, where they get lost in their reading and the possible reasons why, and what questions they have for the author or the text to clarify their growing understanding. Teachers can then use these reflections to decide whether they need to be more explicit about the particular reading strategies that students should use to understand their texts.

Stage 3: Postreading

During postreading, teachers provide students with opportunities to step back and test the validity of their tentative understanding of the text. For example, students might "believe" and "doubt" one another's assertions in light of evidence from the text or outside the text (Jacobs,

2000). By doing so, students help their peers revise and strengthen their arguments, and also reflect on and improve their own.

Reading Comprehension and Understanding

The stages of instruction in reading comprehension—prereading, guided reading, and postreading—essentially describe how students can move from understanding their goal to demonstrating their understanding. This insight can help teachers view these strategies as a means to accomplish the content-based goal of understanding, rather than simply as add-on activities.

WRITING-TO-LEARN AS A MEANS OF UNDERSTANDING

Purposes of Writing in Secondary School

We most frequently use writing in secondary schools in two ways. More often, we use writing as a means to evaluate students' mastery of content or of the written form. Less often, we use writing as a means to engage students in learning (Applebee, 1981).

For learning, the act of writing provides a chronology of our thoughts, which we can then label, objectify, modify, or build on; and it engages us in becoming invested in our ideas and learning. Writing-to-learn forms and extends thinking and thus deepens understanding (Fulwiler, 1983; Knoblauch & Brannon, 1983). Like reading-to-learn, it is a meaning-making process.

The Pedagogy of Writing-To-Learn

Research about the most effective ways to improve composition has found positive effects for such strategies as literary models, prewriting, sentence combining, and scales (also called rubrics). The strategy most solidly supported by research to improve composition is a process called *inquiry* (Hillocks, 1986).

Inquiry treats writing as a problem-solving activity in which students come to understand something that they want to say before they begin drafting. In an inquiry-based classroom, teachers guide students through the development of assertions and arguments about these assertions. They choose instructional strategies to help students 1) find and state specific, relevant details from personal experience; 2) analyze and generalize about the text or pose assertions about it; and 3) test the validity of their generalizations, arguments, or assertions by predicting and countering potential opposing arguments (Hillocks, 1986). The inquiry process is a way to discover something worth writing about.

Strategies that accomplish the purposes of composition-based inquiry engage students in developing their thinking in preparation for drafting (also called prewriting). These writing-to-learn strategies can include freewriting, focused freewriting, narrative writing, response writing (for example, response logs, starters, or dialectic notebooks), loop writing (writing on an idea from different perspectives), and dialogue writing (for example, with an author or a char-

acter) (Bard College Institute for Writing and Thinking, n.d.; Elbow & Belanoff, 1989). Not surprisingly, writing-to-learn activities are also known as "writing-to-read" strategies—means by which students can engage with text in order to understand it.

THE RELATIONSHIPS AMONG READING, WRITING, AND UNDERSTANDING

Figure 1 illustrates how reading, writing, and understanding are related. The cognitive processes involved in the stages of comprehension (prereading, guided reading, and postreading) are virtually the same as the cognitive processes involved in the three inquiry stages that promote effective composition. Both reading-to-learn and writing-to-learn are meaning-making activities that result in understanding—a central goal of content-based instruction. They both help students proceed from understanding goals to demonstrating understanding. As a result, if we have engaged our students well in reading-to-learn, then we will have also prepared them to

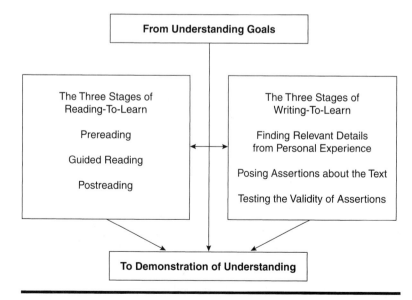

FIGURE 1   The Interrelation among Reading, Writing, and Understanding

draft well. As a bonus, we can also use writing-to-learn strategies to engage students in the prereading, guided reading, and postreading process.

STAFF DEVELOPMENT

Most inservice programs on reading and writing across the curriculum offer teachers a variety of strategies for integrating reading or writing into their content-based instruction. But such programs rarely ask teachers to examine their own instructional goals and then to consider how well various reading and writing strategies actually support those goals.

If teachers decide that their goals for students' learning include understanding, then professional development programs should give them time to think about what they mean by "understanding" and how they engage students in the process of understanding. Teachers might consider the following questions: What strategies do they use to engage students in the process of making their own meaning? What strategies do they use to prepare and guide students in problem-solving—allowing students to integrate the "given" of what they bring to a text and the "new" that the text pro-

vides? What means do teachers provide for students to test assertions of their understanding before they have to demonstrate their understanding? How explicitly do they share with students the purposes of any given activity in light of their instructional goals? And how faithfully do the reading and writing strategies that they use serve their goals?

Only after teachers have examined whether teaching for understanding suits their instructional goals and after they have defined their role in facilitating understanding can they consider how the principles and practices of reading-to-learn and writing-to-learn might support their instruction.

Teachers might begin by discussing what they are already doing with reading and writing and their reasons for doing so in light of their purposes for students' learning. Frequently, teachers will discover that they are already making good use of strategies characteristic of reading- and writing-to-learn. The framework suggested here can help teachers integrate reading-to-learn and writing-to-learn strategies into content-area instruction more systematically to support their students' development of understanding.

REFERENCES

Applebee, A. N. (1981). *Writing in the secondary school: English and the content areas.* (NCTE Research Report No. 21). Urbana, IL: National Council of Teachers of English.

Bard College Institute for Writing and Thinking Web site. (n.d.). [Online]. Available: www.writingandthinking.org

Bruner, J. S. (1975). *The relevance of education.* New York: W. W. Norton.

Chall, J. S. (1983). *Stages of reading development.* New York: McGraw-Hill.

Chall, J., & Jacobs, V. A. (1996). The reading, writing, and language connection. In J. Shimron (Ed.), *Education and literacy* (pp. 33–48). Creskill, NJ: Hampton Press.

Elbow, P., & Belanoff, P. (1989). *Sharing and responding.* New York: Oxford University Press.

Fulwiler, T. (1983). Why we teach writing in the first place. In P. L. Stock (Ed.), *forum: Essays on theory*

and practice in the teaching of writing (pp. 273–286). Montclair, NJ: Boynton/Cook.

Hillocks, G., Jr. (1986). *Research on written composition: New directions for teaching.* Urbana, IL: ERIC Clearinghouse on Reading and Communication Skills and the National Conference on Research in English.

Jacobs, V. A. (1999). What secondary teachers can do to teach reading: A three-step strategy for helping students delve deeper into texts. *Harvard Education Letter, 15*(4), 4–5.

Jacobs, V. A. (2000). Using reading to learn: The matter of understanding. *Perspectives: The International Dyslexia Association, 26*(4), 38–40.

Jacobs, V. A., & Wade, S. (1981). Teaching trading in secondary content areas. *Momentum, 12*(4), 8–10.

Knoblauch, C. A., & Brannon, L. (1983). Writing as learning through the curriculum. *College English, 43*(5),465–474.

Perkins, D., & Blythe, T. (1994). Putting understanding up front. *Educational leadership, 51*(5), 11–13.

Scala, M. C. (2001). *Working together. Reading and writing in inclusive classrooms.* Newark, DE: International Reading Association.

CHAPTER REFERENCES

Courtney, L. (1980). *Content area reading in retrospect.* Paper presented at the annual meeting of the International Reading Association, St Louis, MO.

Fay, L. C. (1964). What research has to say about reading in the content areas. *The Reading Teacher, 8,* 68–72; 112.

Goodykuntz, B. et al. (1925). The relationship of reading to content subjects and other school activities. In G. W. Whipple (Ed.), *The Twenty-Fourth Yearbook of the National Society For the Study of Education* (pp. 97–140). Bloomington, IN: Public School Publishing Company.

Gray, W. S. (1919). The relations between study and reading. *National Educational Association, Addresses and Proceedings of the Fifty-Seventh Annual Meeting* (pp. 580–586). Milwaukee, WI: National Educational Association.

Jacobs, V. (2002). Reading, writing, and understanding. *Educational Leadership, 60,* 58–61.

McKenna, M. C., & Robinson, R. D. (1990). Content literacy: A definition and implications. *Journal of Reading, 34,* 184–186.

Moore, D W., Readence, J. E., & Rickleman, R. J. (1983). An historical exploration of content area reading instruction. *Reading Research Quarterly, 18,* 419–438.

Stewart, R. A., & O'Brien, D. G. (1989). Resistance to content area reading: A focus on preservice teachers. *Journal of Reading, 32,* 396–401.

ANNOTATED BIBLIOGRAPHY OF RELATED REFERENCES

Alvermann, D. E., & Moore, D. W. (1991). Secondary school reading. In R. Barr, M. L. Kamil, P. Mosenthal, & P. D. Pearson. *Handbook of Reading Research, Volume 2* (pp. 951–983). New York: Longman.

This complete reference covers the research relevant to content area reading and is an excellent beginning for those interested in the historical development of this aspect of literacy education.

Artley, A. S. (1959). Critical reading in the content areas. *Elementary English, 36,* 122–130.

The author defines critical reading as being "the process of judging with severity the ideas expressed by the author," showing important factors that predispose a reader to do critical reading.

Ayer, A. M. (1926). *Some difficulties in elementary school history* (Teachers College Contributions to Education, No. 212). New York: Columbia University, Teachers College.

One of the first studies of potential problems of students reading in various types of content material, especially those related to comprehension.

Barry, A. L. (2002). Reading strategies teachers say they use. *Journal of Adolescent & Adult Literacy, 46,* 132–141.

Discusses the results of a recent survey of content teachers regarding what they believe and what they are actually doing in the teaching of literacy skills in content classrooms.

Courtney, L. (1980). *Content area reading in retrospect.* Paper presented at the annual meeting of the International Reading Association, St Louis, MO.

An extensive review of the important research and writing in the field of content reading instruction through the publication date. Of particular note here is the discussion of the historical roots of reading instruction and how it relates to various content areas.

Cunningham, P. M., & Cunningham, J. W. (1987). Content area reading-writing lessons. *The Reading Teacher, 40,* 506–512.

Develops several lessons that integrate reading and writing activities in various content areas.

Fay, L. (1966, 1969, 1975). *Reading in the content fields.* Newark, DE: International Reading Association.

These three annotated bibliographies provide a detailed listing of the important references in the field of content reading.

Gray, W. S. (Ed.). (1947). *Improving reading in content fields. (Supplementary Educational Monographs, No. 62).* Chicago: University of Chicago Press.

Gray, W. S. (Ed.). (1952). *Improving reading in all curriculum areas (Supplementary Educational Monographs No. 76).* Chicago: University of Chicago Press.

These two monographs discuss the importance of reading in various content areas, from both theoretical and practical viewpoints, giving specific classroom applications of each.

Herber, H. L. (1970). *Reading in content areas.* Englewood Cliffs, NJ: Prentice Hall.

Considered to be one of the important early references related to the training of teachers in the area of content reading.

McCallister, J. M. (1936). *Remedial and corrective instruction in reading.* New York: Appleton-Century.

An often-referenced, early textbook containing an extensive discussion of reading in the content areas with particular emphasis on classroom applications of various types of literacy techniques.

Moje, E. B. et al. (2000). Reinventing adolescent literacy for new times: Perennial and millennial issues. *Journal of Adolescent & Adult Literacy, 43,* 400–410.

A summary article noting the important literacy issues that face adolescents and the roles content teachers must assume in effectively dealing with these language needs.

Moore, D. W., Readence, J. E., & Rickleman, R. J. (1983). An historical exploration of content area reading instruction. *Reading Research Quarterly, 18,* 419–438.

A historical discussion of the beginning and development of various aspects of reading in the content areas. The extensive bibliography included in this discussion is a valuable one.

O'Brien, D. G., & Stewart, R. A. (1990). Preservice teachers' perspectives on why every teacher is not a teacher of reading: A qualitative analysis. *Journal of Reading Behavior, 22,* 101–129.

Examines the inherent reluctance of preservice teachers to include literacy activities in their content area instruction. Suggests specific modifications to preservice content reading courses to change these beliefs prior to student teaching.

Vacca, R. T. (2002). From efficient decoders to strategic readers. *Educational Leadership, 60,* 6–11.

Describes the importance of the use of content reading as an important tool for addressing various problems of adolescents.

_____ YOU BECOME INVOLVED _____

Reading in the content areas is currently a controversial area in literacy. The articles in this chapter were selected to provide a historical view of this aspect of reading instruction.

Gray (1919), in this very early article, notes the importance of reading and study. Consider the following points as you reflect back on this discussion of reading as it relates to study.

- Gray lists twenty-nine reasons why literacy instruction is directly related to what he recommends for high school assignments, but these could easily be directed to content reading at all levels. How relevant do you feel these ideas are for today's teachers? What would you add to or discard from his list?
- What does he identify as being some problems for students reading in the content areas? Are

these similar to or different from those facing students today?
- Do literacy problems differ between content areas or are there similarities and differences across disciplines?
- What three recommendations does Gray make at the end of his article relative to effective content instruction? Do you believe these suggestions are as relevant today as they were when he made them in 1919?

Goodykuntz et al. (1925) expands on the work of Gray by noting the importance of relating reading as a subject area to other academic areas and to a student's life beyond the classroom.

- In what specific ways can the classroom teacher make literacy activities a relevant aspect of a student's reading in various disciplines as well as outside the classroom? Are the suggestions in this article relevant for today's students and their modern literacy experiences?

- In what ways can both the reading teacher and the content area teacher help students see literacy as a vital aspect of their learning in school activities and beyond the classroom setting?

Leo Fay's article, though written in 1964, still has much to say about the value of literacy instruction, especially to the content area specialist.

- Note Fay's suggestions for literacy instruction that extend across academic disciplines and are relevant to all instructional areas. Of the eight he identifies at the beginning of this article, which do you believe are particularly relevant to today's content teacher?
- In your own teaching of the academic disciplines, how might you incorporate his literacy ideas into your teaching? What are some of the problems that may limit the teaching of reading in various content areas?

McKenna and Robinson (1990) describe the term content literacy, noting how this concept differs from simply knowing more about individual content areas.

- In what ways does content literacy differ from content knowledge? How do teachers often confuse these two terms in their teaching of literacy skills in the content areas?
- How can the concept of content literacy be developed in various disciplines? What are some possible problems in encouraging students to become content literate as opposed to simply knowledgeable in the content areas?
- In what ways might you specifically develop content literacy in your own classroom instruction?

Jacobs (2002) discusses recent thinking about the role of reading in various content areas. Note the following as you reflect on this article.

- In what ways has reading in the content areas changed, or in some cases stayed the same, between the writing of Gray and Jacobs? What are some of the persistent issues related to reading in the content areas?
- Based on your reading in this chapter, how might you better incorporate various reading activities into your content reading?

CHAPTER 7

VOCABULARY INSTRUCTION

"When I use a word," Humpty Dumpty said, in rather a scornful tone, "it means just what I choose it to mean—neither more nor less." "The question is," said Alice "whether you can make words mean so many different things." "The question is," said Humpty Dumpty "which is to be master—that's all."

—Lewis Carroll
Through the Looking Glass (1871)

Since one of man's most important activities is the communication of ideas, it follows that one of his most important forms of knowledge is knowledge of words.

—David Russell
Children Learn to Read (1949)

Knowing the meanings of the words decoded improves overall comprehension, and hence there is plenty of motivation to make certain that young readers know the meanings of at least the most frequently encountered words in English.

—Cathy Collins Block & Michael Pressley
Comprehension Instruction: Research-Based Practices (2002)

The need for effective readers to know a large number of words is obvious. Less clear is the role of the school and the teacher in the development of vocabulary knowledge. For instance, the issue of whether students benefit more from having specific instruction on a limited number of words or from learning indirectly through wide reading is an unresolved dilemma. Perhaps the answer in this situation is really a combination of both methods of learning. What format for vocabulary learning should teachers consider? Should words be introduced prior to reading a selection (specific instruction) or is it more helpful to discuss vocabulary as it is actually encountered in the reading (incidental learning)? What is the best use of the dictionary in learning new terms and should there be specific instruction in its use? These are only typical of the questions teachers have considered in their planning for vocabulary teaching.

Historically a related issue in the area of vocabulary has been the number of actual words a person needs to know to be successful in various literacy activities. What constitutes a total number of vocabulary words a person should know and understand to be successful is even today an unanswered question. Closely related is the interest of researchers in determining a basic list of commonly used words that would be of value as a foundation for effective reading. While lists of this type have been developed, most prominently by Dolch (1936; 1939) and more recently by Johnson (1971), Otto and Stallard (1975), Dreyer et al. (1985), and Venetis (1999), these compilations of words have proven to be less than effective in classroom literacy instruction. Simply memorizing isolated words from a list did not ensure that students understood the meanings of these vocabulary terms.

AS YOU READ

As you read these articles on the development of vocabulary knowledge, notice how many of the basic issues have been debated and discussed almost from the beginning of interest in this subject. Of particular importance are concerns about the learning of a basic number of words and specific teaching strategies that seem to work best for classroom teachers.

A Vocabulary Test

Professor E. A. Kirkpatrick

The first article on vocabulary, by Kirkpatrick (1907), though written almost a hundred years ago has a surprisingly modern view of this aspect of reading instruction. Discussed here are issues such as estimates of the total number of words known by the typical adult and student as well as the inherent value of teaching selected vocabulary word lists. These two themes have become dominant issues in the study of vocabulary. Note especially the discussion of how estimates of the number of words known by an individual are determined.

I

Of all the inventions of the human race nothing compares in importance, as regards mental development, with language. In the development of each person also, nothing exercises a greater influence in molding and developing thought and feeling than his language environment. The vocabulary of a person represents in a condensed and symbolic form all that he has experienced and imagined. The breadth of his mental experience is indicated by the number of words that have for him a meaning, while the accuracy of his thinking is shown by the constancy and exactness of meaning with which he uses words. The study of vocabularies ought therefore to be an important branch of psychological investigation.

Studies have been made of the number of words used by great writers, and by children a few years old. The latter studies have shown that a child may not use words that are perfectly familiar to him for months merely because he has no occasion to use them, *e.g.*, words frequently uttered in the summer or when in the country may never be used in the city or in the winter. Adults are familiar with many words that they have rarely, perhaps never, used. The difficulties in the way of counting accurately the number of words *used* by an adult or even by a child over three years of age are almost insurmountable.

When we attempt to estimate the number of words that *have a meaning* for an individual the difficulties are less although the number of words is much greater. The writer long ago estimated the number of words in his own vocabulary by going carefully through an unabridged dictionary and counting the number of familiar words on every tenth page (see *Science,* 0. S., Vol. XVIII, pp. 107–108). Since then he has often had his students estimate the number of concepts that they possessed by counting the number of words that had for them a fairly definite meaning, on a few pages of the dictionary, and then calculating from the proportion of familiar words the total number of words they knew.

When a student began, say on page 2, and counted all the words in boldface type and the number of these known on every fiftieth page, and then did the same beginning with page 20, the results were so nearly the same as to convince me that the method was fairly accurate. Some preliminary tests were then made that showed that a hundred words taken by chance from various parts of the dictionary might serve as a fairly accurate measure of the size of one's understanding vocabulary. The words used in the final test consisted of fifty words taken from the first four words on every fiftieth page of Webster's academic dictionary and fifty words from the first of other pages leaving out different forms of the same root word (*e.g.*, photograph, photographer). This was done with the thought that older persons might be able to infer better

the meaning of unfamiliar words than younger persons. The results were negative and the author now considers that the best list of words is obtained from Webster's academic dictionary (which contains about 28,000 words on 645 pages), by taking the first, second, or last word, or any other definite word on every sixth page. For general purposes and for all ages this is probably better than to take a hundred words from an unabridged dictionary which contains so many various and obsolete forms of the same words, along with rare words, and technical terms not found in the smaller dictionary. Estimates based on words from the academic dictionary give less than half as many words in the vocabulary as those based on data from the unabridged, but they are more representative of fundamentally different concepts.

The method of using the test was to place the printed list before the subjects and ask them to mark the words that they knew with a plus (+) sign, those that they did not know with a minus (–) sign, and doubtful ones with a question mark (?). The tests which numbered about two thousand were made chiefly upon pupils from the fourth grade up through the high school and university, although a few were made upon younger children. Control tests showed that if the same test was given orally, there was some difference in the words marked as known and unknown. This difference was of course very great in the second and third grades, where a few tests were made, and became less with age, yet it usually amounted even in the case of adults to from one to three percent. In a few individuals the difference was quite marked.

The reason for this is that some words are more often heard than others, while others are more often seen, hence in one case the auditory stimulus arouses familiar associations while in the other case the visual stimulus is more effective. In general the auditory stimulus is more effective for children, but, as they read more, the visual stimulus becomes more effective and later many words are seen that are rarely or never heard; hence for such words the visual stimulus is the most effective and sometimes the only stimulus which will produce the reaction of familiarity. The test is more accurate if both forms of stimuli are used, *i.e.,* the words pronounced as the pupils look at them.

There is another cause of difference and also of inaccuracy. In the auditory test unfamiliar words are often mistaken for familiar ones having a similar sound, *e.g.,* barque for bark, baron for barren, and in the visual test similarity of appearance plays a similar part. A striking case of this form of error was made by a third grade boy who marked the word amaranth as known. I said to him, 'You don't know that word, do you?' He said, 'Yes,' in a tone that implied surprise that I should question it. I then said, 'What is the word?' He replied, 'Arithmetic.' Another boy for similar reasons, partly visual and partly auditory, marked 'eschar' as known and when questioned called it 'sister.'

On the other hand, young children often do not mark words that are perfectly familiar to them, because the sounds and forms without any other stimuli of suggesting words or circumstances are not sufficient to immediately arouse the sense of familiarity. One second grade boy who marked only eighteen words in the test, when questioned, showed by synonyms or definitions, or illustrations, that he knew the meaning of thirty of the words.

Individual habits of thinking or judging is probably the largest factor in tending to make the marking of words an unreliable index of the actual mental furniture of the subject of the test. Some mark as known every word that arouses the feeling of familiarity, while others mark as known only those for which they are confident they can give a correct definition. The differences in this respect are, however, most shown in the doubtful marks while the plus mark usually means the arousal of a specific idea by the word form. This idea may be vague or distinct, narrow or broad, general or detailed, correct or incorrect, but it is the idea usually aroused by the word.

Upon defining a list of words to a class of normal students after they had marked them, it was found that the errors in marking words as known and unknown usually cancelled each other, so that the number finally reported as known and unknown was for most members of the class about the same as when they were first marked.

Instruction as to what shall be the standard for deciding whether a word is known such as "Count as known all words that you would not, as to their meaning, need to look up in a dictionary if you saw them in a sentence," helps to render the marking more uniform. Another and more accurate method of bringing about uniformity of standard is to ask the pupils to define or put in sentences some of the words, then to mark the rest according as they think themselves able or unable to indicate their meaning.

If students are asked to define a certain proportion of the words as accurately as possible, giving all meanings where there are more than one, depth and accuracy as well as breadth of knowledge may be tested. In college classes where twenty of the hundred words were defined, 114 out of 246 students were found to have defined the same proportion of words that they marked as known and only seventeen showed a difference of as much as three words of the twenty from the corresponding proportion of the hundred words marked. The overestimations slightly exceeded the under estimations.

The author is convinced that one hundred words selected as has been described and marked with care gives sufficient basis for an approximate estimate of the size of the understanding vocabulary of college and high school students, and of the higher grades of the grammar school. In the author's own classes where students were ranged in three grades according to the number of words marked as known in one list of words, other lists of words similarly selected resulted in 60 percent to 80 percent of them being again in the same grade, while none were changed from the lowest to the highest grade.

Using Webster's Academic Dictionary as a basis it appears from averaging about two thousand papers that the size of vocabularies are likely to approximate the following:

Grade	II	4,480
Grade	III	6,620
Grade	IV	7,020
Grade	V	7,860
Grade	VI	8,700
Grade	VII	10,660
Grade	VIII	12,000
Grade	IX	13,400

High School

Freshmen	15,640
Sophomore	16,020
Junior	17,600
Senior	18,720

The average for normal school students is 19,000 and for college students 20,120. The colleges represented in this test were Bryn Mawr, Smith, Columbia, Brown University and Pratt Institute, while the grades and high schools were mostly in Massachusetts cities.

There seems to be no constant difference between the sexes. On only a part of the papers was age given, but there is reason to believe that vocabularies increase up to thirty. In Pratt Institute where students varied greatly in age, those above twenty-five knew from five to ten per cent more words than those in the same classes who were below twenty years of age. It is not likely that the growth of vocabulary is great after thirty; when deeper specialized and executive activities have taken the place of general advancement into new fields of knowledge and many words once known are forgotten.

One important factor in the growth of vocabularies was investigated by accompanying the list of words with a request to write names of papers and magazines frequently read and of books read since the beginning of the year. It was found that in general those who named the most books and magazines had the larger vocabularies, regardless of their grade.

The individual differences in size of vocabulary were very great, some ninth grade children falling to the rank of second grade children while some third or fourth grade children ranked with the average of those in the ninth grade or high school.

Sometimes a very small vocabulary was accounted for by the fact that the child was of foreign parentage and did not hear English at home, but the mere fact of being of foreign parentage was no assurance that the vocabulary would be small.

II

The relation of size of vocabulary to school standing was considered, but owing to the scarcity of data and uncertainty as to its reliability (only a small proportion of the papers were accompanied by the class records or teacher's estimate of ability), no conclusive results were reached. In the grades there was no clear proof of relationship though in one room, where there was reason to think the teacher's estimate had been carefully made, the grading corresponded almost exactly to the size of the vocabularies. In one normal class nearly all of those who had been named by the faculty as belonging to the lower third of the class had small vocabularies. In another class there seemed to be little or no relation between size of vocabulary and estimates of teaching ability. In two colleges, one for women, the other for men, the marks given to the women in English and to men in all subjects were secured for the freshman class and compared with the number of words known. The average number of words known by the men who in general ranked in the various subjects above the average of their class was 5 per cent greater than for those ranking below the average; while the women who ranked highest in English, averaged nearly 4 per cent better in vocabularies than those who ranked lowest in English.

In the case of individuals there was often a wide divergence between the marks and the size of the vocabulary. In some instances exceptionally poor definitions indicated a difference in the standard used in marking words as known, but not always. This divergence is not, however, greater than between marks in different subjects, *e.g.*, students have honor marks in some subjects and fail to pass in others.

Is size of vocabulary any indication of attainment or ability? An affirmative answer to this cannot readily be proved by experiment, because we have no reliable standard of ability and attainment by which the value of the vocabulary test may be determined. It is well known, however, that persons who do well in one subject often do poorly in others and that success in life after school bears little relation to success in school. It has recently been shown by Dr. Thorndike that entrance examinations bear little relation to college marks.

From the side of experimental psychology, no accurate measure of intellectual ability has been established in spite of many persistent and painstaking researches. The various tests used are found to be special in their character. There are also indications that what are good tests at one age or stage of development may have no significance at another stage. Sensory and motor tests are probably valuable indications of mental ability in young children, memory and imagination tests in older children and reasoning tests in youths.

The function of the nervous system is to respond in an appropriate way to the various phases of the stimulating environment. The most common phase of environment to which human beings respond is the word environment, first to auditory words by movements, then to auditory and visual words by images and concepts. The number of words that are known by any person depends upon two factors, the variety in his word environment, auditory and visual, and his own readiness to respond to the various elements of this environment. It is perfectly natural therefore that children who are surrounded by intellectual people or who read a great deal should have large vocabularies and yet that the size of individual vocabularies should vary with their readiness to respond to this word environment. The accuracy of response or quality of knowledge can be judged not by the number of words but by the accuracy of definitions or use of words.

The question naturally arises whether size of vocabulary and ability to define and use words is not a sufficiently accurate measure of the intellectual ability of youths to justify the use of vocabulary tests in examinations for entrance to college. College work is supposed to be general in its character, demanding general ability, of which the vocabulary test ought to give an indication. Of course if students should devote their time to a special study of the dictionary, the test would become special and valueless, since size of vocabulary would not then be an accompaniment and indication of experiences and intellectual advances, but of special study of modes of defining words in terms of other word symbols.

III

A study of the kind of definitions given by persons of different ages is an interesting indication of the sources of word knowledge and of the modes of thought at different ages.

The first words are of course obtained from direct association with acts and objects and this continues to be a source of vocabulary growth. A large proportion of words, however, come indirectly from experience through the medium of words that have already become familiar. These new words are sometimes received as equivalents of other words, because of synonyms and definitions or of special descriptions. The greater part of them, however, gain their significance from their association with familiar words in various situations, just as the original words were gained from association with various real situations.

These truths may be illustrated by the definitions of gourd given by college students. 'A drinking cup made from the gourd vine.' 'A vegetable which grows in the ground having a hard shell and many seeds.' 'A vessel for holding water or other liquid.' 'A receptacle for carrying water about, usually of skin.' 'A water bottle made from a pumpkin or squash.' 'Vessel sometimes made by scooping out, for example, making a vessel by scooping out a pumpkin.' Evidently most of these definitions represent ideas gained from sentences in which the word, 'gourd' is used, though those who speak of them as pumpkins or as a 'summer squash,' may have seen the real thing without the discriminating eye of the gardener or botanist. The idea that it is a vessel of some kind evidently predominates and this idea is sufficient for interpreting most sentences in which the word occurs.

It is interesting to notice the various forms of the subordinate idea of the object itself as the various persons picture it under the stimulus of the context. 'A shell of certain nuts, fruits and vegetables, or of the cocoanut, squash, cucumber, etc.' 'In many countries it is used as a receptacle for food and drink.' 'A fruit on a tree whose shell is used for carrying water.' 'The dry fruit of some sort of tropical tree.' 'It is hard and round, and some are the size of an apple and rattle when you shake them.' 'A species of dried melon.' 'An old style wooden drinking vessel.' 'A hollow piece of cane.' 'A fruit characterized by the fibrous outer shell similar to the cocoanut.' Few of the writers of the above had a sufficiently correct idea of the article to be able to identify it if it were shown them. They react satisfactorily (to themselves) to the book situation though they would be laughed at by the gardener and botanist. It is an interesting fact that in a prominent college for women the word 'decemvirate,' which only readers of Roman history would be likely to encounter, was correctly defined by most of the young ladies, while some could give no definition for gourd, and many others gave such definitions as have been quoted. This is a striking illustration of the difference between the word environment of scholastic halls and that of the industries and the literature of to-day.

The following definitions of gourd are inexplicable until one realizes that one word form has been mistaken for another. 'To spur on' (goad); 'To plunge a weapon into some one, to make a jagged wound' (gored); 'An animal' (goat?); 'A greedy person' (gourmand); 'A chasm or piece of land that is very much lower than the surrounding land' (gorge).

The definitions thus far quoted are by college students, and though most of them are exceptional rather than characteristic of the definitions of college students, they are surprising as well as amusing.

One English teacher was so astonished at the 'depth of ignorance' displayed by the definitions of his freshman class in English that he had all the papers looked over by his assistants, who all agreed that the results were 'shocking.' They, however, saw no relation between the definitions and the scholarship of individual pupils. (As has already been stated the figures show that those ranking high in scholarship knew on an average about 5 percent more words than those ranking low in scholarship.)

Character of the definitions changed greatly with age. Descriptions which are so common in the high school and college papers are rarely or never given by children in the kindergarten and primary grades. The same is true of definitions by synonyms and inclusions under larger terms. The younger children nearly always define by mention of some specific incident, *e.g.*, 'A *chair* is to sit on'; 'Baby stands up by a *chair*'; 'A *bee* goes around a piazza and makes a noise.' What anything can do, or what can be done to it, or with it, is of most importance, in early knowledge of all things, hence we find the definitions of children expressing action and use more than anything else. Reference to personal experience of self and friends is also common. These facts are of great significance to pedagogy, strongly endorsing the change now being made from the old descriptive 'object lesson' to the better forms of nature study in which use is made the center of interest.

A Basic Sight Vocabulary

E. W. DOLCH

The second article, by Edward Dolch (1936), describes the background and the development of his famous list of 220 sight words. This group of service words represents sixty-five percent of all the words in the reading material of primary grades and sixty percent of those encountered by students in the intermediate grades (Bond & Tinker, 1967, p. 286). Despite the fact that this word list was developed a number of years ago, the Dolch Basic Sight Vocabulary remained useful even with more modern text material (Johns, 1976).

Teachers of all grades, from Grade II on, find pupils who have very small or no sight vocabularies. The teachers wish to remedy this condition by drilling on the sight words that will be of most value to these children in their reading. But which are those sight words? The vocabulary of a particular primer will not do because the child's reading is now chiefly in books other than the basal series with which he started and also because the vocabularies of most primers contain many words that, though needed at the primer stage, are later not of general usefulness. No standard word list will do because all such lists contain five hundred words or more, too many to be given drill as a sight vocabulary.

In view of these facts, it may well be assumed that the most essential of the words that are basic to children's reading, and therefore needed as a sight vocabulary, will surely be included in *all* the best lists of words used by children. A comparison of those lists was therefore the logical means of securing a basic sight vocabulary. The first list considered was naturally the vocabulary published by the Child Study Committee of the International Kindergarten Union,[1] which is a summary of many studies in this field. This list contains 2,596 words, which are the most frequent of 7,000 different words found to be known to children before entering Grade I. It was found that, if the words of a frequency of 100 or more

(inflected forms being combined) were chosen from this list, a total of 510 words was secured, which is about the number of words on the other two lists which were used. The second list was the first five hundred of the Gates list,[2] which is too well known to need description and which has been used as a basis for many studies in reading vocabulary. The third list was that compiled by Wheeler and Howell,[3] consisting of the 453 words most frequently found in ten primers and ten first readers published between 1922 and 1929. This list represents as well as does anything available the actual reading materials common in Grade I and therefore the vocabulary upon which, presumably, all later grade reading is built. Each of these three lists is compiled on a dictionary basis (that is, regularly inflected forms of a single root are combined), and a comparison of the three lists could easily be made. From this comparison the list was secured.

This list may well be called "basic" because it includes the "tool" words that are used in all writing, no matter what the subject. Conjunctions join clauses regardless of what the clauses are about; prepositions introduce phrases of every kind; pronouns stand for any and all persons and things; adverbs modify every kind of verb; and adjectives modify every kind of noun. Verbs denote action or being of every sort of subject, and the auxiliaries, practically all of which

A Basic Sight Vocabulary of 220 Words, Comprising All Words, Except Nouns, Common to the Word List of International Kindergarten Union, the Gates List, and the Wheeler-Howell List

Conjunctions	*its	much	blue	three	found	put
and	me	never	both	two	gave	ran
as	my	no	brown	warm	get	read
because	*myself	not	*clean	white	give	ride
but	our	now	cold	yellow	go	run
if	she	off	*eight		*goes	said
or	that	once	every	**Verbs**	going	saw
	their	only	*five	am	got	say
Prepositions	them	out	four	are	grow	see
about	these	so	full	ask	had	shall
after	they	soon	funny	ate	has	show
at	this	then	good	be	have	sing
by	*those	there	green	been	help	sit
down	us	today	hot	bring	hold	sleep
for	we	*together	kind	buy	*hurt	*start
from	what	too	*light	call	is	stop
in	*which	up	little	came	jump	take
into	who	very	long	can	keep	tell
of	you	*well	many	carry	know	thank
on	your	when	new	come	laugh	think
over		where	old	could	let	*try
to	**Adverbs**	why	one	cut	like	*use
under	again	yes	*own	did	live	walk
*upon	*always		pretty	do	look	want
with	around	**Adjectives**	red	does	made	was
	away	a	right	*done	make	*wash
Pronouns	*before	all	round	don't	may	went
he	far	an	*seven	draw	must	were
her	fast	any	*six	drink	open	will
him	first	*best	small	eat	*pick	wish
his	here	*better	some	fall	play	work
I	how	big	ten	find	please	would
it	just	black	the	fly	pull	*write

*The twenty-seven words marked with asterisks were included in only two of the lists.

are included in this list, are used with all the verbs of the language.

This list is not perfect, since no list secured from frequency counts can be flawless. The chances of use that enter into frequency counts cause some unimportant words to secure higher frequencies than some more important words. For instance, "jump" cannot be considered a word of wide usefulness, yet on these vocabulary lists it ranked with words like "do" or "make." Perhaps the most unexplainable case is the word "cut." Word-counting will always give some such cases. Word-counting is also certain to leave out of a list some words of importance which should be included but which did not happen to be used often enough in the sampling of material counted.

If the criterion of appearance on all three lists had been rigidly adhered to, the twenty-seven words marked with asterisks would have been cut from the list. This elimination would have been unfortunate, since these words appear in the first 510 of the International Kindergarten Union list and in the first 500 of the Gates list. Many of these words obviously belong with others on the basic list. "Which" belongs with "who" and "that," "done" and "goes" belong with "did" and "go," "start" belongs with "stop," and "write" with "read." The numbers under ten belong with the other numbers listed. For this reason these twenty-seven words are included in the basic list; they add a few that do not belong but more that seem as important as others on the list.

It is to be especially noted that this basic sight vocabulary includes no nouns. Nouns cannot be of universal use because each noun is tied to special subject matter. If new subject matter is used, new nouns must be used. Unfortunately, teachers have spent a great deal of energy in teaching the nouns in primers as sight words, and then, as the later books take up new materials, new nouns must be used and not those that have been learned. Perhaps one reason that many children in the intermediate grades do not know by sight the words on this basic list is that the emphasis on sight teaching has been on nouns instead of on these "tool" words. Some few nouns, such as "thing" or "man," do recur a great deal, but in the case of most nouns the rule applies that they are "local" to a particular activity or interest. The nouns common to the three lists are mainly local to young children's interests and to first-grade activities. They are in no sense basic to all elementary-school reading. That the reader may see this fact for himself, the list of nouns is given.

It is not claimed that the basic list of 220 words includes all the words that the elementary-school pupil should know by sight; the claim is only that he should at least know these. Consequently, when a child in any grade is found lacking in sight vocabulary, he should be tested to see which of these words he does know and should then be trained to recognize instantly by sight the words that he does not know. For this purpose

95 Nouns Common to the Three Word Lists But Not Recommended for a Basic Sight Vocabulary

apple	farmer	party
baby	father	picture
back	feet	pig
ball	fire	rabbit
bear	fish	rain
bed	floor	ring
bell	flower	robin
bird	game	Santa Claus
birthday	garden	school
boat	girl	seed
box	goodbye	sheep
boy	grass	shoe
bread	ground	sister
brother	hand	snow
cake	head	song
car	hill	squirrel
cat	home	stock
chair	horse	street
chicken	house	sun
children	kitty	table
Christmas	leg	thing
coat	letter	time
corn	man	top
cow	men	toy
day	milk	tree
dog	money	watch
doll	morning	water
door	mother	way
duck	name	wind
egg	nest	window
eye	night	wood
farm	paper	

small cards with the words printed in primer type on both sides are most convenient. The cards can be flashed before the pupil by the teacher or by another pupil, any unknown word named for the subject by the tester (who sees the word on the reverse of the card), and the pack gone over again and again until all 220 words are known with certainty. A daily record of words known can be used to show the learner a curve that indicates how he is improving. When the pupil recognizes these 220 words instantly and easily, he will have a "capital" of word knowledge with which he can attack any reading matter and, with guessing from context and perhaps some help from sounding, get something out of it. If his sounding is weak, training in that skill will com-

plete the remedial process, and the pupil will be able to do the learning from books that school work demands.

NOTES

1. Child Study Committee of the International Kindergarten Union, *A Study of the Vocabulary of Children before Entering the First Grade.* Washington: International Kindergarten Union (1201 Sixteenth Street, N.W.), 1928.
2. Arthur I. Gates, *A Reading Vocabulary for the Primary Grades.* New York: Teachers College, Columbia University, 1926.

3. H. E. Wheeler and Emma A. Howell, "A First-Grade Vocabulary Study," *Elementary School Journal,* XXXI (September, 1930), 52–60.

Incidental vs. Instructional Approaches to Increasing Reading Vocabulary

William E. Nagy and Patricia A. Herman

Nagy and Herman (1985) address one of the most important issues in the development of vocabulary: the most effective method of instruction. Should teachers follow specific avenues of instruction? Or is it better for students to learn new vocabulary through incidental learning, such as from wide reading? This article presents evidence that supports each of these views of vocabulary instruction.

Our concern is with the effectiveness of different approaches to vocabulary, relative to two major, related educational goals: Increasing the overall size of students' reading vocabulary and increasing students' ability to comprehend text. Educators and basal publishers rightly recognize the importance of vocabulary knowledge in reading and, therefore, include some form of vocabulary instruction in most current reading programs. Our thesis, however, is that explicit vocabulary instruction, even at its best, is not very effective at producing substantial gains in overall vocabulary size or in reading comprehension. Major progress towards these goals can

only be attained by increasing incidental vocabulary teaming.

In the first section of this article we consider the size of the task: that is, the number of words students would have to learn to make any substantial gains in overall vocabulary size. We feel that the size of the task is almost universally underestimated, or else simply not taken into account. Teaching the meanings of individual words may be effective for a specific reading lesson but it cannot result in any substantial increase in overall vocabulary size.

In the short run, incidental learning looks ineffective compared to almost any other instructional approach to vocabulary growth. But when the size of the task is accurately assessed, it is seen that the bulk of children's vocabulary growth necessarily comes through incidental learning. We will argue that regular and sustained reading can lead to substantial gains in vocabulary size.

In the second section we will consider the nature of the task: that is, the type of word knowledge that is necessary to facilitate reading comprehension. Evidence from a number of studies[1] shows that reliable gains in reading comprehension can be produced through instruction of words from a given passage only if the instruction provides multiple encounters that supply a variety of information about the instructed words. Since vocabulary instruction can supply multiple, rich encounters for only a small number of words (or a small number of encounters for a slightly larger number of words), students must have additional opportunities to encounter large numbers of words repeatedly.

THE SIZE OF THE TASK

What would count as a reasonable yardstick for measuring the size of the task? That is, how can we decide how many words would be "a lot" to learn, and how many words would be "far too few?" One such measure is the number of words children are actually learning. According to our estimates,[2] the reading vocabulary of the average child grows at a rate of 3,000 words per year between grades three and 12.

Another possible measure of the size of the task is in terms of individual differences. According to figures reported by M. K. Smith[3] for grades four through 12, there is about a 6,000-word gap in vocabulary size between a child at the 25th percentile in vocabulary and a child at the 50th percentile. While Smith's figures for absolute vocabulary size are probably inflated, it still appears that bringing a low-vocabulary student up to the median would involve a gain of 4,000–5,000 words or more—not to mention

keeping up with the yearly 3,000-word vocabulary growth of the average student.

Another measure of the size of the task is the number of unknown words a student encounters in reading. Unfortunately, there is little information available on the number of unfamiliar words students find in-text. However, additional analyses of data reported in part by Anderson and Freebody[4] indicate that reading 25 minutes per school day an average student in the fifth grade would encounter tens of thousands of different words a year which he or she did not know, even by a lenient criterion of word knowledge. For a student with a smaller-than-average vocabulary, the number of unfamiliar words would be even higher.

Implications of the Size of the Task

No matter how one measures the task, then, it is extremely large. Most children encounter new words by the tens of thousands per year, and learn thousands of them. Given this yardstick, what is the role of vocabulary instruction in children's vocabulary growth? Surveys of classrooms[5] reveal that very little explicit vocabulary instruction occurs. The number of words covered in such instruction is, at best, a few hundred a year. Thus, it is evident that most children must be acquiring the vast bulk of their vocabulary knowledge apart from instruction specifically devoted to vocabulary learning. It also follows that children who acquire a larger-than-average vocabulary—who may be learning 1,000 words per year more than the average student—are not doing so simply through better vocabulary lessons.

Should one take this as an indication of the sorry state of current vocabulary instruction in our schools and call for more time spent teaching words? There is room for improvement in the area of vocabulary instruction, but the size of the task is such that just teaching more words cannot be seen as the answer. With very few exceptions,[6] even extremely ambitious vocabulary programs do not cover more than a few hundred words per year.[7] While there are good reasons for teaching children the meanings of individual words, it is important to recognize the limitations of such instruction. Teaching children specific words will not, in itself, contribute substantially to their overall vocabulary size. Even an ambitious and systematic approach to vocabulary will not cover enough words to bring a low-vocabulary student up to average.

Promoting Large-Scale Vocabulary Growth

Given the size of the task, it is clear that teaching individual word meanings cannot, in itself, produce large-scale vocabulary growth in school children, or make up for the deficiencies of students with inadequate vocabularies. However, this fact should not lead to a fatalistic or *laissez-faire* attitude about vocabulary. On the contrary, the size of average annual vocabulary growth shows that most children are capable of learning new words rapidly and effectively. Therefore, it is very important to determine *where* and *how* children are learning so many words, and to determine how maximum use can be made of all these avenues of vocabulary acquisition. It is also important to find out why some children fail to utilize them effectively.

Learning Word Meanings from Context

If only a few hundred of the 3,000 words the average child learns in a year are learned in instruction specifically aimed at vocabulary, where are all the other words learned? A number of sources are possible: The speech of parents and peers, classroom lectures and discussions, school reading, free reading, and television. Speech of parents and peers may well be the most significant source of vocabulary for many children, but this factor is the least under the teacher's control. We want to focus on the possible contribution to vocabulary growth of a factor that is, to large extent, under the teacher's control: Reading.

Many believe that incidental learning of words from context while reading is, or at least can be, the major mode of vocabulary growth

once children have really begun to read. This is our position also. It is not, however, held universally. There are a number of grounds on which one can question the effectiveness of learning from written context as an avenue of vocabulary growth.

For the most part, arguments for learning from context have been largely "default" arguments.[8] That is, learning from context is assumed to be effective because nobody can figure out where else children could be learning all those words.

Even if one accepts the "default" argument for learning from context, this does not establish that learning from *written* context is an effective means of vocabulary acquisition; much of the incidental word learning that makes up the bulk of children's vocabulary growth might be from *oral* context.

Learning word meanings from *oral* context is obviously a major mode of vocabulary acquisition, especially in the preschool years. Many, if not most, of the thousands of words that children learn before they enter school are learned without any explicit definition or explanation. However, there is good reason to believe that written context will not be as helpful as oral context in illuminating the meanings of unfamiliar words. When a child learns a word from oral context, there is also a rich extralinguistic context—in the easiest case, the object named might be physically present. There are also clues from intonation and gesture that can make the context richer. In addition, the speaker will usually have some sensibility to gaps in the listener's knowledge, and the listener can always ask questions if something isn't understood. Written context will, therefore, usually not be as rich or helpful as oral context in providing information about the meanings of new words.

Some studies have, in fact, found written context ineffective at providing information about the meanings of new words.[9] Written contexts usually supply only limited information about the meaning of unfamiliar words, and are sometimes even misleading.[10] Also, experimental studies have generally found inferring meanings from context to be less effective than more intensive or explicit forms of instruction.[11]

Such results pose a problem for those who would like to believe that inferring meanings from written context is an effective means of learning new words. We believe that the discrepancy can be resolved by specifying more precisely how incidental learning of word meanings from written context takes place.

Two recent studies[12] have attempted to assess the volume of incidental word learning from context under as natural conditions as possible. Subjects were asked to read silently, without any information about the nature of the experiment. Texts were taken from school materials at the grade level of the subjects and represented narratives and expositions. Word knowledge was assessed after reading (in one study, a week later) without the text present. Target words were real words, selected by teachers as being the most difficult words in the text.

In most learning-from-context experiments, prior knowledge of the target words is controlled for by using either nonsense words or real words for which it can be demonstrated or assumed that subjects have no prior knowledge. In the two studies by Nagy et al., on the other hand, it was assumed that subjects would have at least partial prior knowledge of some of the target words. Degree of prior knowledge was controlled for statistically through pre-testing and control groups.

A basic presupposition of these studies was that learning word meanings from context proceeds in small increments. Any single encounter with a word in context is likely to provide only a small gain in knowledge of that word.[13] If one starts with words about which nothing is known, a single encounter in context is not likely to produce a measurable degree of word knowledge, especially if the test of word knowledge used requires a fairly complete knowledge of the meanings of the words tested. This, it is argued, accounts for the failure of some experiments to find a significant amount of learning from context.

Using real words from grade-level text insures that for any given subject, there will be target words at various points along a continuum

of word knowledge. Even a single encounter with the word in context should move most of these words a little bit higher on the scale of knowledge. For any given criterion of word knowledge, it is likely that some words not previously known to that criterion will be known to that criterion after reading.

The results of the studies by Nagy et al., indicate that reading grade-level texts does produce a small but statistically reliable increase in word knowledge. This effect was found in all grades tested (three, five, seven, and eight). While different texts produced differing amounts of learning from context, there was no indication that the younger or less-able readers were not able to learn new word meanings through reading.

The absolute amount of learning found was small; the chance of learning a word to any given criterion from one exposure in-text is somewhat around one in twenty. This low figure shows why learning from natural context appears ineffective compared to any other type of instruction on word meanings.

However, learning from context must be evaluated in terms of its long-term effectiveness. The long-term effectiveness of learning from written context depends on how many unfamiliar words are encountered over a period of time. If students were to spend 25 minutes a day reading at a rate of 200 words per minute for 200 days out of a year, they would read a million words of text annually. According to our estimates, in this amount of reading children will encounter between 15,000 and 30,000 unfamiliar words. If one in twenty of these words are learned, the yearly gain in vocabulary will be between 750 and 1,500 words.

Such a gain is substantial, considering the proportion of yearly vocabulary growth that is covered and the fact that it would be extremely difficult, if not impossible, for any word-by-word approach to vocabulary instruction to cover the same number of words in the same amount of time. The amount of reading required—25 minutes per school day—may involve more reading than many students actually do, but could hardly be called excessive.

Incidental learning of word meanings from written context may, therefore, account for a large proportion of the annual vocabulary growth of those students who do read regularly. A period of sustained and silent reading could lead to substantial yearly gains in vocabulary, probably much larger than could be achieved by spending the same amount of time on instruction specifically devoted to vocabulary.

Given the size of the task—the number of words children should be learning in a year—an effective approach to vocabulary development has to take advantage of all avenues of word learning. Since the bulk of children's vocabulary growth occurs incidentally, that is, outside of situations specifically devoted to word learning, the most important goal of vocabulary instruction should be to increase the amount of incidental word learning by students. There are two complementary approaches to increasing incidental word learning: First, increasing children's *ability* to profit from potential word-learning situations outside of vocabulary instruction, and, second, increasing children's *opportunities* to learn.

There are a number of ways in which children's ability to learn words independently might be increased. Reasonable arguments can be made for teaching affixes, for the use of context clues, and for finding ways of increasing children's motivation to learn new words. All of these are undoubtedly of some value, but we are not aware of any published research demonstrating a successful method for making students into better independent word learners. However, it is clear how children's opportunity to learn words independently can be increased: By increasing the amount of time they spend reading. Incidental learning of words during reading may be the easiest means of promoting large-scale vocabulary growth.

THE NATURE OF THE TASK

So far, we have presented evidence that the size of the vocabulary-learning task is larger than is often recognized. The large number of words to be learned shows the limitations of any form of vocabulary instruction taking words one at a time, and shows the need for maximizing students' abilities and opportunities for learning words on their own. Now we want to consider the *nature* of the task: What kind of word knowledge one hopes to produce in students and how different labels of word knowledge affect comprehension.

Vocabulary Knowledge and Reading Comprehension

Educators and researchers have long known that a strong correlational relationship exists between vocabulary knowledge and reading comprehension: Children who know more words understand text better.[14]

This relationship is the motivation for what is done in vocabulary instruction. There are, of course, other reasons for teaching words—increasing students' speaking and writing vocabularies, improving scores on standardized tests, or teaching specific concepts in content areas. Much of the time, however, words are taught to enable students to understand what they read. Even if the words are taught for another purpose—for example, for use in writing—the instruction would be suspect if it did not also enable students to understand sentences containing the instructed words. An appropriate measure of the effectiveness of most vocabulary instruction, then, is its effectiveness in increasing comprehension.

The strong correlational relationship between vocabulary knowledge and reading comprehension would seem to imply that teaching words should automatically increase reading comprehension. This is not the case, however, as surveys of attempts to increase reading comprehension through vocabulary instruction[15] reveal that approaches to vocabulary instruction differ widely in their ability to increase the comprehension of texts containing the instructed words. Stahl and Fairbanks report that "methods which provided only definitional information about each to-be-learned word did not produce a significant effect on comprehension, nor did the methods which gave only one or two exposures to meaningful information about each word.[16] Pearson and Gallagher found that studies which were successful in increasing passage comprehension through pre-teaching vocabulary were the exception rather than the rule.[17] The exceptional studies were those in which the vocabulary instruction was richer than a simple definitional approach.

It appears that the following are attributes which can make vocabulary instruction effective at increasing reading comprehension: Multiple exposures to words, exposure to words in meaningful contexts, rich or varied information about each word, establishment of ties between instructed words and students' own experience and prior knowledge, and an active role by students in the word-learning process.

The Difficulty of Producing Overall Gains in Reading Comprehension through Vocabulary Instruction

Some types of vocabulary instruction have been shown to increase reading comprehension for passages containing the instructed words, although much of current practice does not seem to fall into this category of instruction. But can vocabulary instruction produce overall gains in comprehension for passages which have not specifically been targeted for instruction?

Stahl and Fairbanks found that vocabulary instruction did, in fact, produce significant, although small, gains in general reading comprehension.[18] We find it surprising, not that the gain is small, but that it occurs at all. The number of words in print is so great that even an extensive program of vocabulary instruction is unlikely to cover much more than a minute percentage of the words in a text selected at random. Stahl and Fairbanks hypothesize that the general increase in reading comprehension produced by vocabulary instruction may be the result, not of the words specifically covered in the instruction, but

in increased incidental learning that the instruction may also produce.[19]

It is highly unlikely that teaching individual word meanings could ever produce more than a very slight increase in general reading comprehension. Overall improvement in reading comprehension requires improvement in skills and strategies. In fact, explicit training in comprehension strategies has generally produced measurable gains in comprehension.[20]

Reading and Reading Comprehension

Although hard experimental evidence is not at hand, one can make a well-reasoned argument that reading itself can be an effective way of increasing reading comprehension. First, as we have already argued, wide reading seems to be an effective way of producing truly large-scale vocabulary growth. There is also reason to believe that the type of word knowledge gained through wide reading would be the type that is effective at facilitating comprehension. Wide reading will lead to multiple encounters with words in a variety of meaningful contexts. To the extent that the rest of the text is comprehensible, these encounters will help the reader establish ties between the new word and prior knowledge. Pearson and Gallagher, in reviewing the effects of pre-teaching vocabulary on passage comprehension, conclude that "knowledge acquired gradually over time in whatever manner appears more helpful to comprehension than knowledge acquired in a school-like context for the purpose of aiding specific passage comprehension."[21] This description certainly fits the type of knowledge gained through wide reading.

Increased vocabulary knowledge is not the only benefit of wide reading that might increase comprehension. There is also the increase in general knowledge. Crafton found that reading one article on a topic strongly improved comprehension of a second article on the same topic.[22] In addition, practice in reading would lead to improvement or automatization of a wide range of reading skills that contribute to comprehension.

Improving reading comprehension is certainly an important instructional goal. However, vocabulary instruction as such is of limited usefulness in this regard. Teaching the meanings of individual words appears to be an efficient means of increasing comprehension only with specific passages and with a relatively small number of words. To produce general gains in comprehension, the most profitable use of instructional time would appear to be a focus on comprehension skills and strategies. Reading itself should also increase comprehension through the accumulation of background knowledge and practice in various reading subskills.

In Defense of "Superficial" Vocabulary Instruction

It has been argued[23] that the benefits of even definitional methods of vocabulary instruction have been underestimated in the following sense: We have shown so far that the level of word knowledge required to improve reading comprehension can only be gained by multiple exposures to a word which provide a variety of information about that word. Learning definitions alone does not produce this level of word knowledge and, therefore, does not enhance reading comprehension. However, just as we have already argued in the case of learning from written context, one should not underestimate the value of any meaningful encounter with a word even if the information gained from that one encounter is relatively small.

A single encounter with a word in a definitional approach to vocabulary will not produce very deep word knowledge; but it is very likely to provide more information than a reader's initial encounter with that word in context, which, in fact, is likely to be rather uninformative, and, at worst, possibly misleading.[24] This initial definitional encounter may provide a good foundation for learning from additional exposures to the word in context.[25]

This line of reasoning is plausible enough. If demonstrated to be valid, such definitional en-

counters might provide grounds for the use of less-intensive methods as one component of a comprehensive approach to vocabulary, even though these methods by themselves cannot reliably increase reading comprehension. Less-intensive methods would allow a larger number of words to be covered. However, the value of such methods depends on later multiple exposures to the instructed words in meaningful context. Therefore, such an approach to vocabulary would still require a large volume of reading to produce the kind of word knowledge that is actually the proper goal of vocabulary instruction.

CONCLUSION

The purpose of this article has been to make a case for the importance of incidental vocabulary learning. We do not want to overstate our case and imply that no words should be explicitly taught. But reports of new effective methods of vocabulary instruction seldom contain any warnings about their limitations. We feel that methods of vocabulary instruction can be effectively developed and implemented only if their limitations as well as their strengths are clearly understood. The major limitation of any approach to vocabulary development which takes words one at a time is that it can only cover a small fraction of the words that students should be learning.

The ultimate test of a comprehensive approach to vocabulary must be whether it results in large and long-term gains in reading vocabulary and reading comprehension. Success in these terms cannot be attained without increasing students' incidental word learning. It is important to determine what types of vocabulary instruction can effectively increase students' ability to learn independently. Attention must be given to affixes, context clues, awareness of words and their meanings, and motivation to learn them. But any attempt to increase incidental learning substantially must include an increase in the opportunity to learn new words, and this will occur primarily through regular, sustained reading.

NOTES

1. Pearson, P. and M. Gallagher. "The Instruction of Reading Comprehension," in *Contemporary Educational Psychology, 8,* 317–334, 1984. Also, S. Stahl and M. Fairbanks, "The Effects of Vocabulary Instruction: A Model-Based Meta-Analysis" unpublished manuscript, Western Illinois University, 1984.

2. Nagy, W., P. Herman and R. Anderson. "Grade and Reading Ability Effects on Learning Words From Context," paper presented at the National Reading Conference, St. Petersburg, Florida, December 1984.

3. Smith, M. K. "Measurement of the Size of General English Vocabulary Through the Elementary Grades and High School," in *General Psychological Monographs, 24,* 311–345, 1941.

4. Anderson, R. and P. Freebody. "Reading Comprehension and The Assessment and Acquisition of Word Knowledge," in B. Hutson, ed., *Advances in Reading/Language Research,* 231–256, Greenwich, Connecticut: JAI Press, 1983.

5. Durkin, D. "What Classroom Observations Reveal About Reading Comprehension Instruction," in *Reading Research Quarterly, 14,* 481–533. 1979. Also, N. Roser and C. Juel, "Effects of Vocabulary Instruction on Reading Comprehension," in J. Niles and L. Hams, eds., *New Inquiries in Reading Research and Instruction,* Rochester, New York: National Reading Conference, 1982.

6. Draper, A. and G. Moeller. "We Think With Words (Therefore, To Improve Thinking, Teach Vocabulary), in *Phi Delta Kappan, 52,* 482–484, 1971.

7. Beck, L., C. Perfetti and M. McKeown. "The Effects of Long-Term Vocabulary Instruction on Lexical Access and Reading Comprehension," in *Journal of Educational Psychology, 74,* 506–521, 1982.

8. Jenkins, J., and R. Dixon. "Vocabulary Learning," in *Contemporary Educational Psychology, 8,* 237–260, 1983.

9. Sachs, H. "The Reading Method of Acquiring Vocabulary," in *Journal of Educational Research, 36,* 457–464, 1943. Also, R. Baldwin and E. Schatz. "Are Context Clues Effective With Low-Frequency Words in Naturally Occurring Prose?", paper presented at the National Reading Conference, St. Petersburg, Florida, December 1984.

10. Beck, I., M. McKeown and E. McCaslin. "All Contexts Are Not Created Equal," in *Elementary School Journal, 83,* 177–181, 1983. Also, L. Deighton, *Vocabulary Development in the Classroom,* New York: Bureau of Publications, Teacher's College, Columbia University, 1959.

11. Margosein, C., E. Pascarella and S. Pflaum. "The Effects of Instruction Using Semantic Mapping on Vocabulary and Comprehension," paper presented at the annual meeting of the American Educational Research Association, New York, April 1982. See also, M. Pressley, J. Levin and H. Delaney, "The Mnemonic Keyboard Method," in *Review of Educational Research, 52,* 61–91, 1982.

12. Nagy, et al. *op. cit.,* see Footnote 2.

13. Deighton, *op. cit.,* see Footnote 11.

14. Anderson, R. and P. Freebody. "Vocabulary Knowledge," in J. Guthrie, ed., *Comprehension and Teaching: Research Reviews,* 77–117, Newark, Delaware: International Reading Association, 1981. Also, F. Davis, "Fundamental Factors of Comprehension in Reading," in *Psychometrika, 9,* 185–197, 1944, and "Research in Comprehension in Reading," in *Reading Research Quarterly, 3,* 499–545, 1968. And, L. Thurstone, "A Note on a Reanalysis of Davis' Reading Tests," in *Psychometrika, 11,* 185–188, 1946.

15. Pearson, et al., *op. cit.,* see Footnote 1.

16. Stahl, et al., *op. cit.,* see Footnote 1.

17. Pearson, et al., *op. cit.,* see Footnote 1.

18. Stahl, et al., *op. cit.,* see Footnote 1.

19. *Ibid.*

20. Pearson, et al., *op. cit.,* see Footnote 1.

21. *Ibid.*

22. Crafton, L. "The Reading Process as a Transactional Learning Experience," unpublished doctoral dissertation, Indiana University: also cited in Pearson, et al., see Footnote 1.

23. Personal communication between authors and Isabel Beck, November 30, 1984.

24. Beck, et al., *op. cit.,* see Footnote 10. Also, Baldwin, et al., *op. cit.,* see Footnote 9.

25. Jenkins, J. R., M. L. Stein and K. Wysocki. "Learning Vocabulary Through Reading," in *American Educational Research Journal, 21,* 767–787, 1984.

REFERENCES

J. Jenkins, D. Pany and J. Schreck, *Vocabulary and Reading Comprehension: Instructional Effects.* Tech Rep No. 100, Urbana: University of Illinois Center for the Study of Reading, 1978.

W. Nagy and R. Anderson. "The Number of Words in Printed School English," in *Reading Research Quarterly, 19,* 304–330, 1984.

W. Nagy, P. Herman and R. Anderson. "Learning Words From Context," in *Reading Research Quarterly,* in press.

Vocabulary Development: Teaching vs. Testing

ALLEEN PACE NILSEN AND DON L. F. NILSEN

Nilsen and Nilsen (2003) place the teaching of vocabulary skills in the context of today's increased emphasis on the results of standardized literacy assessment procedures. They emphasize the fact that good classroom instruction in vocabulary is different from those practices often associated with success on standardized tests. Their discussion of these issues represents recent thinking of literacy educators concerning effective vocabulary instruction.

For several reasons vocabulary items have garnered a disproportionate amount of space on the high-stakes tests that are currently popular throughout American education. Contributing factors are that test makers find it easy to question the meanings of words, and such questions can be machine-scored at little cost compared to the expensive individualized scoring demanded for writing samples. Also, unlike the questions about literature, vocabulary items do not force test makers to choose between being inclusive and focusing on the "literary canon." And while there is little agreement on the value of teaching formal grammar to students, virtually everyone agrees that understanding the meanings of words is crucial to reading, listening, writing, and speaking.

Such conditions mean that vocabulary skills are likely to remain a part of standardized tests, and because of the truth in the old adage that "What gets tested, gets taught," vocabulary instruction is likely to receive increased attention in America's classrooms. But, unfortunately, as Jim Burke points out in *The English Teacher's Companion* (Boynton/Cook Heinemann, 1999), there are few references to teaching vocabulary in the professional books that English teachers read, nor do many preservice programs offer actual practice or advice on how to incorporate vocabulary instruction into the English curriculum. The result has been that the first serious thinking many teachers have done about vocabulary instruction has been as a direct response to the standardized tests on which they and their students are being judged.

With no training in how to teach vocabulary skills, many teachers transfer to their classrooms the same techniques that they see test makers using. For example, last spring we had a controversy in one of our local high schools, where each Monday a teacher would pass out an alphabetized list of words, which students were to "look up" and learn for a Friday quiz. These bright students in an affluent neighborhood divided up the research part of the assignment and posted their findings on a Web site for everyone's use. When the teacher found out, she accused the students of cheating and asked the principal to devise "appropriate punishment." Parents, the local school board, and the press got involved. Once it was understood that the students had cooperated only on finding the definitions and that the quizzes had been given in class with students being individually responsible for their own answers, the idea of punishing the students received little support.

Based on their own experiences, people realized that sitting alone and copying out a single definition from a dictionary was not a very effective way to learn new words. It would have been better for the students to work in groups and to come up with several meanings instead of one. Language is a social phenomenon, which means that students need to interact with other speakers and hear pronunciations and intonations, as well as words used in more variety than brief dictionary entries can capture.

We offer this chart to encourage thinking about the ways that standardized testing techniques differ from good teaching and learning practices. Space precludes our developing each of these points, but we will try to illustrate a few of the less obvious ideas.

THE VALUE OF RIGHT ANSWERS

The fact that test makers seek a healthy portion of wrong answers, while teachers want everyone to succeed, naturally influences the kinds of tasks assigned to students. A common testing technique, for example, is to give four reasonable sounding sentences, all using the word being tested. Students are asked to select the one sentence out of the four that is correct. Since all the sentences are made to sound acceptable, this is a "good" testing technique in

CHARACTERISTICS OF STANDARDIZED, MACHINE-SCORED TESTING	CHARACTERISTICS OF GOOD CLASSROOM TEACHING AND LEARNING
Students work silently.	Students and teachers engage in lots of talk.
Students work individually.	Students work in small and large groups, as well as individually, so that they have more opportunities for hearing and speaking the words.
Words are tested for single meanings.	Students learn multiple meanings, along with linguistic principles about the way words acquire extended and metaphorical meanings. This gives students predictive abilities to figure out new usages and new meanings.
Students spend only a few seconds focusing on any particular word.	Students engage in various activities including puzzles, discussions, artwork, creative writing, drama, extensive reading, and the making of individual notebooks because their minds need time to absorb new meanings, while their tongues learn new pronunciations.
The focus is on obscure words.	The focus is on words students are likely to meet in everyday life. While using the old to teach the new, teachers start with basic words and move into increasingly complex terms.
Clear-cut answers and an easy-to-grade format are important.	Teachers encourage conjecturing and intelligent guessing because with the meanings and the histories of many words there are no "right" or "wrong" answers.
Words are tested in random or alphabetical order.	Words are taught in gestalts so that related meanings reinforce each other. Students work with both similarities and differences among lexical extensions and metaphors.
The premium is on getting a wide range of scores.	The premium is on success for all students.

that it truly discriminates. However, it is counterproductive to learning because three-fourths of the student's time is spent looking at wrong or inappropriate usages, which, as students read and reread them, begin to sound more and more acceptable.

A better kind of exercise is to present sentences requiring students to think—not about faulty usages, but about correct ones. For example, if you are teaching the word *amble,* you can list these related words and then ask students to ponder the following sentences and choose the correct word to go in each blank. Notice how these sentences are unlike sentences that would be devised by a test maker because they give purposeful clues to help students succeed.

ambulances	ambulatory
perambulators	somnambulant

1. By remembering that *insomnia* relates to sleeping, I can figure out that someone who walks while sleeping is a _____.
2. What American mothers call *strollers,* British mothers call _____, or *prams,* for short.
3. The first _____ were stretchers and medical kits carried onto battlefields where their name meant something like *walking treatment.*
4. In nursing homes, the cost of care is less for _____ patients because they can walk to the bathroom and the dining room.

Each of these sentences reinforces the connection between *amble* and *walk,* while also introducing and clarifying meanings of related words. The sentences are forthright in sharing basic information about the words, while at the same time providing raw material for a teacher to use in a minilesson. In such a lesson, teachers can lead students to think about how the *preamble to the Constitution* walks in front, and about the efficiency of the term *ambulance chaser* for describing those lawyers who are overly enthusiastic in pursuing potential clients. *Ambulatory* also has a meaning in formal, legal language, where it is used to describe the fact that wills can be

"moved" or changed up until the time the writer dies or is declared incompetent.

THE VALUE OF CONJECTURING AND INTELLIGENT GUESSING

Once students begin relating words to other words, they will probably begin to see relationships beyond the ones the teacher brings to class. For example, in one of our class discussions, a student added the word *ramble* to our list of *amble* words. When we embarked on a dictionary search, we found *amble* defined as "a leisurely walk," while *ramble* was defined as "an aimless walk." *Ramble* has been in the language since 1620, while *amble* dates back to the 1300s. One dictionary said that *ramble* was "perhaps" related to the Middle English *romblen* meaning "to roam."

Students were surprised that, even by looking in several dictionaries, they could not find a definitive answer about whether *ramble* descended from *amble.* However, in what we call intelligent guessing based on such criteria as phonological (sound) similarities, orthographical (spelling) similarities, semantic (meaning) similarities, and historical connections between the users of both words, most of us in the class agreed that the pronunciation of *ramble* may well have been influenced by its similar meaning to *amble,* a word that had already been in English for 300 years. We also agreed that similarities in meaning and pronunciation probably made it easier for speakers to learn and remember the new word.

These kinds of research problems make dictionary work interesting, but we are quick to caution students that tracing the histories of words and their connections will not "prove" the meaning of any particular word as it is used today. However, knowing earlier meanings of words can provide some wonderful insights. For example, when a seventh-grade boy told us that *managers* are supposed to be men because "it says *man* right in the word," we were happy to lead the class on a search for words that have come into English from the Latin *manus,* meaning hand. We were probably more surprised than were the students at how many direct connections we found. The most surprising was the word *emancipate*, which means something like "being freed from the hands of someone else." Clearer examples include the way that *manuals* are referred to as *handbooks*; a *manuscript* is prepared by hand as opposed to being printed; to *manacle* a prisoner is to *handcuff* him or her; a *manicurist* takes care of people's *hands*, and the *manual alphabet* allows deaf people to communicate through finger spelling. After hearing these examples, the class was more willing to believe that *manual training*, the *manual arts*, and *manual labor* all relate to people—either male or female—developing skills with their hands, and that a *manager* is someone who *handles* the affairs of a business.

The students were also interested to learn how words change meanings based on different conditions. In the 1500s, when the term *manufacture* came into the language, it meant *made by hand* as opposed to something grown or made by nature. But then came the industrial revolution and the kinds of technology that today make us think of something *manufactured* as being machine-made rather than hand-made.

A PROCESS APPROACH
TO VOCABULARY INSTRUCTION

What this last example shows is that words do not exist in isolation. They belong to speakers in a culture and their meanings change along with changes in the culture. Because of the mass media and the Global Village in which we live, the English language is changing faster today than at any other time. It is therefore important for us to teach students processes of language change so that they have a head start in figuring out the meanings of words they've never seen before and that are too new to be in dictionaries. For example, in the last Presidential election, conflicts over the ballot-counting in Florida, with all the references to *butterfly ballots, hanging chads, dimpled chads,* and *pregnant chads,* required people to understand metaphorical processing.

The September 11 terrorist attacks with the subsequent arguments about the "true" meaning of *jihad,* whether Osama bin Laden has the authority to issue a *fatwa,* and the nature of the *madrasahs* (Koranic schools) and the *Taliban* and *al-Qaeda* training camps required people to think about how words get transferred from one language to another and how different users of the same words may be thinking of quite different meanings. *TIME* magazine (October 15, 2001) devoted a double-page photo to the message "THE SITE: That's the name preferred by those who work the ruins, not '*ground zero.*'" Only people who know that *ground zero* was coined to refer to the center point of a nuclear explosion can understand the difference in connotations.

Clipping and blending was responsible for the word *humint* (from *human intelligence*) that appeared in news stories about deficiencies in today's CIA. The anthrax scare brought another clipped and blended word into the language: *hazmats* to refer to specialists in hazardous materials.

While most of us will agree that it is important for students to develop inquiring minds and the skills needed to unravel new words, teachers whose main goal is to improve their students' performance on standardized tests will not want to make room for this kind of time consuming questioning and exploring. They know that test makers are more likely to ask about old words rather than new ones because new words may not be "settled" enough to support the kinds of clear-cut answers that can be machine-scored.

In reality, the chances of a class studying, much less remembering, words appearing on specific tests is slim because test makers have thousands of complex, low frequency words from which to choose. They are required to select words so obscure that each test will produce a wide array of scores. Trying to outwit the test makers can actually damage student learning because teaching words in alphabetical or random order, as they are given on most tests, means they have few semantic, phonological, or orthographical relationships.

People who prepare word-study materials know that the human mind has to make connections in order to remember things, so they exert themselves to devise memory hooks. For example, the Princeton Review's *Illustrated Word Smart: A Visual Vocabulary Builder* series (Random House, 1999 and 2001) is clearly test-driven as shown by the cover statements, "Includes the 'SAT HIT PARADE'—Important words to know for the test," and "Includes key words you need to know for the SAT and other standardized tests."

The creators try to draw relationships by organizing their words into general categories, but other than an occasional cross-reference, they teach each word separately through a full-page cartoon-style drawing, three or four lines of explanatory type, and a word or phrase designed to serve as a "memory device." The problem with the "memory devices" is that they are based on puns, which rely on coincidental similarities rather than on meaning related connections. For example, they tie *palpable* in with the *pulp* of an orange, *tangible* with a *tangerine,* and *tentative* with a *tent to live.* On the page devoted to *quarantine,* the "memory device" is the phrase *GUARANTEED Time Alone.* In the small print explanation, they do say that *quarantine* comes from the Latin word *quarant* meaning *forty,* but the big print "memory device" leaves the impression that *quarantine* somehow relates to *guarantee,* which it doesn't.

If the authors hadn't been in such a rush to move on to the next word that might be on a test, they could have provided a more honest memory device based on humankind's long time fascination with the word *forty.* Throughout history people have used *forty* to represent any surprisingly big number. Noah's ark was rained on for *forty days and forty nights,* Moses and the Jews wandered in the desert for *forty years,* and in the *New Testament,* Christ stayed alone for *forty days* as he prepared for the Crucifixion. *Ali Baba and the Forty Thieves* is a famous Middle Eastern story, while modern speakers refer to naps as *catching forty winks.*

In the 1600s, when the word *quarantine* came into use to name the forty days that ships suspected of carrying diseases were required to stay in a harbor so as not to infect people on land, scientists did not know the details of how particular diseases were spread. This means the number must have been based on the popular conception of *forty* as a general representation of a long time. As often happens with number words, the numerical concept became less important than the name so that today the number of days infectious people are *quarantined* or isolated depends on their condition. This disappearance of the literal interpretation of a name taken from a number is similar to how people no longer expect to pay $6.00 to stay at a Motel-6, nor do they expect all *7-Eleven* stores to be open only from *7:00 A.M.* to *11:00 P.M.* or to pay only *ten cents* for whatever they buy at a *dime store.*

THE VALUE OF LANGUAGE GESTALTS

The point we are thing to make is that the true stories of words are as interesting to students and have wider applicability than artificially created mnemonic devices. And because true stories are set in the real world, they provide natural transitions to related words. For example, after teaching students about *quarantine,* it's only a small step to teach about Latin *quartus,* meaning *four,* from which English gets such words as *quart, quarter, quarterly, quadruped, quadruplet,* and *quadrangle* or *quad.* In football, the *quarterback* is identified from his position on the field, but because he calls the plays and directs the offense, the word has come to be used metaphorically to describe someone directing or *quarterbacking* a situation.

When we *quarter* an apple or buy a *hindquarter* of beef, we expect to get approximately one-fourth, but when we talk about the *quarters* of a town we mean the sections of a town, as with the *Latin Quarter* in New York and the *French Quarter* in New Orleans. These sections may or may not be four in number.

The *quarters* on a ship are the sections reserved for living, which again may or may not be one-fourth of the ship. The same is true for the *soldier's quarters* on a military base. In contrast to *living quarters, headquarters* are the central place from which something is run as with a *headquarters office building* or a *headquarters hotel.*

As you talk with students about the various English applications of *quartus,* you can ask them to think of words in various semantic areas. For example, with MONEY banks usually pay interest on a *quarterly* basis and a *quarter* is one-fourth of a dollar or twenty-five cents. In TEAM SPORTS, football games and some basketball games are divided into *quarters.* With TIME, a *quarter* of an hour is fifteen minutes while a quarter of a year is three months. With SPACE or AMOUNT, McDonald's sells *Quarter-Pounders,* while cloth stores sell *fat quarters* (cut in 18" squares instead of 9" strips) for making quilt blocks. We also have *full, half,* and *quarter* moons.

Going into such detail with a single word probably doesn't seem very efficient, but the point is that students are not learning just one word, they are learning about language processes and how meanings change and grow. English has a finite number of letters and sounds, which speakers must use to communicate about a nonfinite world; the result is that the most basic and the best known of the words in any language get adapted for use in many different ways. English and reading teachers frequently tell students to "use the context" to figure out a word's meaning. However, this is easier said than done because rather than telling readers what a word means, context clues serve primarily to screen out meanings that won't fit. The reader is then left to come up with a meaning that makes sense in a particular context. Students are at a disadvantage if they don't know several meanings of a word or if they mistakenly think words have only one meaning.

When we teach words that fit into gestalts, we are tapping into the collective unconscious because it is the words that have been in the language the longest and that name the most basic concepts that have the most extended and metaphorical meanings. These include words naming body parts, animals, plants, weather, astronomical and geological formations, numbers, food, clothing, work, and birth and death.

By starting with basic concepts and then moving outwards, teachers are following the educational principle of moving from the old to the new—from the known to the unknown. When students can relate words to the real world, they are better able to understand some of the things about English that on the surface appear chaotic. For example, English has several words for basic numbers because traders who went to different countries had to learn "foreign" number words to keep from being cheated. This left English with *uni, primus, mono, solo, once, only, first,* and *single,* all with the basic meaning of *one,* and *bi, duo, duet, second, twice,* and *twin,* all with the basic meaning of *two.* And if we think of the concept of *halves* being related to the *two* parts that make a whole, we can add to the list of two words *ambi-, amphi-, half, hemi, semi,* and *demi.* Because these terms are not interchangeable but are still related, it makes sense to study them as gestalts rather than as individual words. Students need to know what the words have in common as well as how they are different.

Analogy questions often appear on vocabulary and academic aptitude tests because rather than measuring knowledge of individual words, they test students' abilities to see patterns and to make connections. The chances of teaching students the exact analogies that will appear as test items are even less likely than out-guessing test makers on particular words. Nevertheless, it makes sense to work with analogies as part of teaching language gestalts because they help students focus on particular features and patterns. Walking students through the creation of such simple metaphors as "*Elbows* are to arms as, *knees* are to legs," and "*Fingers* are to people as *talons* are to birds," will help them learn to look for both similarities and differences. Older or more sophisticated students can go on to work with analogies that tie English and Latinate names together as in "*Pedestals* are to *feet* as *capitals* are to *heads,*" "*Pulmonary* is to *lungs* as *cardio* is to *heart,*" and "*Cerebral* is to *brains* as *cordial* is to *heart.*"

As students grow in their sophistication, they can also begin to think about the sources of metaphors. For example, they might compare *nostril* and *nose* to *window* and *eye* because *nostril* comes from *nose hole* while *window* comes from *wind eye,* that is, a hole or an eye left in houses for ventilation. They also might compare the way human *chests* or *trunks* hold the treasures of our bodies in a similar way to how people keep valuables in *treasure chests* and in the *trunks* of their cars. Once students begin to look for the metaphorical sources of everyday words, they can compare the sources of the phrases on the left to those on the right:

A headline in a newspaper	A footnote in a book
A vein of ore	An arterial highway
A nose for news	Sniffing out the facts
Capital punishment	The capital on a column
A faucet nozzle	The nose cone on an airplane
The facing on a building	*Prima facie* evidence
A digital society	Doing things by numbers
Corporal punishment	The Marine Corps
A skeleton outline	A barebones approach
A cordial greeting	A hearty hello

IN CONCLUSION

We are suggesting that test makers and teachers have understandable reasons for using different techniques. And in what might seem like a contradiction, but really isn't, we also believe that students will fare better both in their intellectual growth and in their performances on standardized tests if their classroom time is spent in the kinds of activities listed in the chart and illustrated in the photos as appropriate to teaching and learning rather than to testing. Test makers, whose goals are different, prepare discrete bits of material for intense work over short periods of time. In contrast, we as teachers work with students on a continuing basis, which means we are the ones to guide students in conjecturing, interacting, and molding new information to fit with what they already know.

In today's world, one of the best things we can do for students is to provide them with knowledge about linguistic processes. We can accomplish this by providing guided practice in figuring out how new words come into a language and how old words acquire new meanings. If we do this right, students' life-long interest in words, as well as higher scores on standardized tests, will come as *serendipity*—a wonderful word that Horace Walpole playfully coined in 1754 from what he said was an old Persian fairy tale, "The Three Princes of Serendip." *Serendib* is the former name of Ceylon, where the heroes of the tale were the fortunate recipients of unsought and unexpected blessings.

CHAPTER REFERENCES

Bond, G. L., & Tinker, M. A. (1967). *Reading difficulties: Their diagnosis and correction.* New York: Appleton-Century-Crofts.

Dolch, E. W. (1936). A basic sight vocabulary. *The Elementary School Journal, 36,* 456–460.

Dolch, E. W. (1939). *A manual for remedial reading.* Champaign, IL: Garrard Press.

Dreyer, L. G. et al. (1985). Sight words for the computer age: An essential word list. *The Reading Teacher, 39,* 12–13.

Johns, J. L. (1976). Some comparisons between the Dolch Sight Vocabulary and the Word List for the 1970's. *Reading World, 15,* 144–150.

Johnson, D. D. (1971). The Dolch list reexamined. *The Reading Teacher, 24,* 449–457.

Kirkpatrick, E. A. (1907). A vocabulary test. *Popular Science Monthly, 70,* 157–164.

Nagy, W. E., & Herman, P. A. (1985). Incidental vs. instructional approaches to increasing reading vocabulary. *Educational Perspectives, 23,* 16–21.

Nilsen, A. P., & Nilsen, D. L. F. (2003). Vocabulary development: Teaching vs. testing. *English Journal, 92,* 31–37.

Otto, W., & Stallard, C. (1975). One hundred essential sight words. (ERIC document Reproduction Center No. ED 116 156).

Ventis, A. (1999). Teaching vocabulary: Within the context of literature and reading or through isolated word lists. (ERIC document Reproduction Center No. ED 427 312).

_____**ANNOTATED BIBLIOGRAPHY OF RELATED REFERENCES**_____

Babbitt, E. H. (1907). A vocabulary test. *Popular Science Monthly, 70,* 378.

One of the earliest references to the measurement of vocabulary knowledge.

Beck, I. L., McKeown, M. G., & Kucan, L. (2002). *Bringing words to life: Robust vocabulary instruction. Solving problems in the teaching of literacy.* New York: Guilford Publications.

An extensive discussion of the latest research and thinking in the area of vocabulary development. Particular emphasis is given to the role of the classroom teacher in the effective development of vocabulary knowledge in students.

Chall, J. S. (1983). Vocabularies for reading: How large? What kind? (ERIC Document Reproduction Service No. ED235 460).

This study discusses the importance of vocabulary knowledge as the foundation of effective reading comprehension.

Dickinson, D. (1920). The importance of vocabulary in reading. *The Elementary School Journal. 20,* 537–546.

A discussion of the role of the classroom teacher in vocabulary instruction, showing the importance of a student's background and prior education in determining the level of vocabulary knowledge.

Gates, A. I., Bond, G. L., & Russell, D. H. (1938). Relative meaning and pronunciation difficulties of the Thorndike 20,000 words. *Journal of Educational Research, 32,* 161–167.

Written by three of the leading pioneers in the field of literacy education, discusses the value of the use of the Thorndike vocabulary list in the classroom reading program.

Lorge, I., & Chall, J. (1963). Estimating the size of vocabularies of children and adults: An analysis of methodological issues. *The Journal of Experimental Education, 32,* 147–158.

An important article detailing research in the estimation of the vocabulary knowledge of both children and adults. Of particular note is the discussion of some of the problems that must be addressed in this type of literacy research.

Stahl, S. et al. (1991). Defining the role of prior knowledge and vocabulary in reading comprehension: The retiring of number 41. *Journal of Reading Behavior, 23,* 487–508.

Details the relationship between prior knowledge and vocabulary understanding, and their importance to effective literacy comprehension.

Thorndike, E. L. (1931). *A teacher's wordbook of 10,000 words.* New York: Teachers College, Columbia University.

Thorndike, E. L. (1938). *The teacher's wordbook of 30,000 words.* New York: Teachers College, Columbia University.

These two references represent some of the first attempts to identify a list of vocabulary words that would be appropriate for use in the classroom setting. The work of other literacy researchers, particularly Dolch's *Basic Sight Vocabulary of 220 Words,* were a result of Thorndike's initial efforts in this area.

YOU BECOME INVOLVED

This chapter on the various issues related to the teaching of vocabulary begins with an article by Kirkpatrick (1907). Based on what you have read, consider the following questions.

- How did the author determine the approximate number of words a student might know? How effective do you think these procedures were and do you believe they would work with today's students?
- What were some of the problems described in this article related to how students learned new vocabulary words? Do you think these problems still exist for students today?

Edward Dolch's work (1936) with vocabulary is best represented today by the famous 220 Sight Vocabulary Word List.

- Describe how this sight word vocabulary list was developed.
- Do you think the first 220 words on this list should be changed to reflect today's reading? What words would you add or delete?
- Why are most of the words included in this sight vocabulary so difficult to teach in isolation? What are some better ways for students to learn this vocabulary list?
- Do you believe the Dolch list is still relevant for teaching today's students?

Nagy and Herman (1985) address the problems connected with the development and use of the most effective methods of vocabulary instruction.

- Based on your reading of this article, what do you think are some of the most effective classroom approaches to the teaching of vocabulary? What are some of the inherent problems commonly associated with the teaching of vocabulary words?
- What is the role of context in the learning of vocabulary words? Why do many teachers tend to ignore context and use less effective vocabulary instruction methods such as teaching new words in isolation using lists of terms?
- Based on what you have read, what would be some effective vocabulary teaching strategies to use in your classroom?

The final article by Nilsen and Nilsen (2003) in this chapter on vocabulary instruction reflects the latest developments in this aspect of literacy learning.

- What is the role of standardized testing in the current teaching of vocabulary? Do you believe these developments have had a positive or negative effect on students' learning of new vocabulary?
- Summarize the information presented in this chapter on vocabulary development and consider how you might implement these ideas in your classroom literacy program.

CHAPTER 8

REMEDIATION OF
READING DIFFICULTIES

*The [reading and writing] activities of the school life will naturally create a
need for making certain records of what is done, and a need for reading these
records [by the teacher].*

—Edmund Huey
The Psychology and Pedagogy of Reading (1908)

*This study shows clearly that a large proportion of children who are considered
"unteachable" may learn to read when adequate diagnostic and remedial steps
are taken.*

—Helen M. Robinson
Why Pupils Fail in Reading (1946)

*Teachers must decide whether to focus on what is wrong in order to "fix"
things, or they must use what is right as a springboard to delve into deeper
learning [in reading].*

—Margaret Taylor Stewart
The Reading Teacher (2003)

Students who experience difficulties in learning to read have always been of concern to educators. Because reading is the primary foundation for success, not only in education but in many other of life's activities as well, the early identification and remediation of literacy problems is of the utmost importance. After fifty years of experience with problem readers, Harris (1980) noted certain basic principles of successful reading remediation that became widely accepted by literacy professionals. In summary, they included the following:

- The vital importance of beginning at an appropriate level of instruction and teaching in small steps that ensure initial success
- The development of a positive rapport between teacher and each pupil
- The need for flexibility in choosing both method and materials, based on the reader's feelings as well as abilities
- The use of materials that combine appropriate review and repetition.

- The need for keeping lines of communication open with the child's classroom teacher and parents.
- The importance of celebrating the child's successes and arranging for praise and support from other significant adults and peers. (pp. 9–10)

The readings in this chapter reflect almost one hundred years of research and study in the remediation of reading difficulties. The authors represented here build on previous knowledge of the reading process and its often inherent difficulties, adding their insight and wisdom to prior beliefs and practices.

AS YOU READ

As you read these articles, note the common themes that appear from the beginning of work in this area. For instance, the significance of the classroom teacher in the early identification and remediation of reading difficulties has long been considered of primary concern. In addition, the idea that there is only one cause of most reading problems has frequently been questioned by these authors.

Remedial Cases in Reading:
Their Diagnosis and Treatment

WILLIAM S. GRAY

William S. Gray (1922), in a perceptive article on the diagnosis and treatment of reading disabilities, emphasizes the fact that most literacy problems are the result of a multitude of causes. This fundamental belief stood in opposition to those of many others, both at the time of Gray's article and in subsequent years, who believed that reading disabilities were the result of a single cause, often related to reading method or material. Of particular interest here are Gray's suggestions as to how teachers can best correct reading problems.

SUMMARY OF CAUSES

Difficulties in practically all phases of reading are due to a wide variety of causes. Those which were of most significance in the cases reported in this chapter may be summarized briefly as follows: (1) low native intelligence, inadequate language habits, and lack of general experience; (2) little or no interest in reading, a careless, indifferent attitude toward school work, and ineffective attention and application; (3) inadequate attention to the content, difficul-

ties in the mechanics of reading, ineffective rates of reading, an inadequate meaning vocabulary, failure to think independently about the content, and inability to picture unfamiliar situations; (4) poor home environment, distracting social influences, and inadequate parental supervision; and (5) inadequate or inappropriate reading materials and poor instruction. The list is a relatively long one and includes many of the causes mentioned in earlier chapters. It is apparent that the teacher who attempts to determine the causes of failure in an individual case must canvass various possible explanations systematically before reaching final conclusions and planning remedial instruction.

Conclusions Concerning Remedial Instruction

The following specific suggestions concerning remedial instruction are based on the study of cases reported in this chapter. (1) Individual instruction is preferable. (2) The confidence and co-operation of the pupil must be secured. (3) Keen interest must be aroused in reading through the use of material directly related to the pupil's interests. (4) The first selections must be simple enough to enable the pupil to read with a fair degree of success. (5) Specific problems should be assigned to direct his attention to the important points. (6) These problems should increase in difficulty as his power of interpretation develops. (7) The problems which are assigned must vary in order to include all important phases of interpretation. (8) In connection with training in interpretation, he must be given exercises to promote rapid and accurate recognition of individual words and words in groups. (9) Drill exercises to increase his span of recognition and to establish regular eye-movements should also be given. (10) Exercises must be included to assist the pupil in reading rapidly as well as thoughtfully. (11) As soon as the pupil has made some progress in accurate interpretation and in the mechanics of reading, he should be assigned types of exercises which require independent thinking. (12) He should also be encouraged to read as much as possible out-

side of class in order to secure a large amount of practice in reading which is necessary in establishing fluent habits. (13) Remedial instruction should not be discontinued until pupils have substituted good habits for poor ones in all phases of reading and can read content subjects rapidly, intelligently, and independently.

Remedial instruction for pupils who are weak in most phases of reading must be both comprehensive and specific. A well-balanced program should be adopted which provides adequate training in each phase in which weakness is discovered. As a rule, training should be carried on simultaneously along all lines, although major emphasis may be placed at any time on a given phase in which serious difficulty is encountered. As training continues, the most important need of a pupil may change and the emphasis in instruction must be shifted. For example, a pupil who is weak in all phases of reading may need first of all exercises which direct his attention to the content in order to aid him in both interpretation and recognition. As he overcomes his difficulties in the interpretation of simple passages, it may be necessary to emphasize in turn each of the following: the interpretation of passages of a problematic type, increasing his rate of silent reading, or developing independence in the recognition of polysyllabic words. The remedial teacher must study the pupil's needs continuously, and must supplement a well-balanced program of reading instruction with specific emphasis from time to time on particular phases of reading which require immediate attention.

Teacher Analysis of Reading Disabilities

EMMETT ALBERT BETTS

Emmett Betts (1934) sees the role of the classroom teacher as critical in the identification and remediation of reading difficulties. He wrote during a period of literacy history in which there was an increased interest in the development and use of various types of special teacher, including those in reading education. It is Betts's belief that the major responsibility for the identification and correction of reading problems belongs to the classroom teacher.

Watch your *p's* and *q's*!" Such has been the stern admonition of teachers in the past. The *symptoms* of certain reading disabilities were recognized but the *causes* remained unidentified. In the time that has elapsed since the country school master coerced his pupils into minding their *p's* and *q's*, many conflicting hypotheses and theories have been formulated to explain these phenomena of reading. Unfortunately, the weird and sometimes far-fetched explanations have left the classroom teacher without enlightenment and without a solution to her age-old problem.

The problems of cancer and common cold have not yet been solved, but they are yielding to persistent research workers. A diversity of laboratory technicians has been at work on such fundamental problems. In like manner, contributions to the solutions of many of our educational problems have been and will continue to be made by workers in fields other than education and psychology. Engineers, opthalmologists, pediatricians, anatomists, bio-chemists, and others have made heavy inroads on the problems of the pedagogue. An intelligent educational leadership should integrate and apply the findings.

In the Shaker Heights Reading Clinic, we have been investigating the preventative and remedial aspects of reading. The program is twofold: first, the clinical identification of the child who may encounter difficulty with reading; second, the clinical analysis of reading disabilities. In order to make the analyses, diagnostic instruments were developed, which could be used for kindergarten or upper grade children. Remedial materials, where needed, are being constructed to parallel the analyses.

Four fundamental policies were followed for the development of the techniques: First, the materials should be administered and the responses given practicable interpretation by the classroom teacher. Without intelligent understanding of the problem by the classroom teacher, the results possible of attainment will be greatly reduced in effectiveness. Second, a serious reading disability can not be analyzed by tests used for the so-called "diagnosis" of the reading abilities of *normal* children. It is unfortunate that any group reading test designed for normal classroom situations should ever have been designated as "diagnostic." Third, the tests should possess a high degree of validity and reliability. In brief, the size of type and the leading in the tests should approximate that used in the books with which the child is confronted in his daily reading. Otherwise, difficulties are analyzed for situations which are quite different from the real ones. This is especially significant when viewed in the light of visual defects which often characterize the non-reader or the retarded reader. Another aspect of validity is that of using characters, such as letters, phrases, and sounds which the child actually encounters during the initial learning-to-read period. Fourth, the teacher should be provided with techniques and devices which provide unrefined indices to the actual visual, auditory, or psychological handicaps of the preschool child or the disabled learner.

In summary, a program has been evolved to permit the *teacher* analysis of reading disabilities. Too often the school administrator or the parent has held the teacher responsible for the reading achievement of a child who has not been physiologically ready to read. As a result much wrong has been done to both teacher and child. Too frequently have educators overlooked the fact that social pressure in the average community creates a situation where the normal child would read if it were in his power to do so. Educators, not parents, are primarily responsible for the early emphasis on reading.

At least six major factors contribute to reading success: namely, maturation, vision, hearing, kinaesthetic imagery, language, and emotional reactions. Although the factor of maturation has gone by default in the past, most progressive thinkers are giving it due consideration in curriculum construction. The implications are manifold. In this respect, our whole primary and secondary curriculum needs to be subjected to critical surveillance, for we have been taking years of the learners' time to teach and to maintain skills which should probably be introduced later and thereby taught in a much shorter unit of time.

The factor of maturation—or better still, immaturity—might help to explain why more boys than girls are found to have reading disabilities. The late Baldwin of Iowa and Todd of Brush Foundation in Cleveland have found that adolescent girls were in advance of adolescent boys for certain anatomical maturations. When measures are sufficiently refined, it is quite probable that we may find kindergarten girls in advance of the same aged boys for those physiological maturations which govern readiness to read. Already many leading doctors and educators maintain that a child should not be *required* to read until he is about nine years of age. By the same token some children might be ready to read before six years of age. It is a truism to state that no pedagogue can teach a child to read before he is ready.

The concept of maturation in relation to reading embraces physiological readiness in the larger sense. Hence, general intelligence should be measured as an incidental factor, for a test of general intelligence can be of no final value when the specific maturation levels directly related to reading are in question. We have, therefore, constructed tests which provide indices to *specific reading maturities*.

Six tests, involving visual functions, have been constructed in order to secure an index to this phase of maturity for kindergarten and first grade children and to analyze pedagogically the reading disabilities of upper grade pupils. The first three use the technique of identifying unlike word, phonetic element, phrase, and sentence forms and do not require a knowledge of reading. The fifth test is one for visual analysis of words; the sixth, for letter recognition. Five auditory tests have proved to be valuable for prognosis on kindergarten level and for analysis of disabilities on other grade levels: auditory span, auditory-visual span, phonic power, auditory discrimination, and auditory acuity.

The second factor, vision, has not been sufficiently emphasized by either doctors or educators. Maturity, as well as identifiable defects, has been discussed by investigators of physiological optics. It is probably not amiss to say at this point that all teachers of reading should be familiar with available information on eye hygiene. "There is not yet sufficient research on the effect of intensive reading during the early years of the child upon the development of the eyes, but educators should at least be sensitive to the possible damage. Considerable research has been done with regard to certain environmental factors, such as lighting. Sight meters are now available for the convenient measurement of light intensity on the desks in the classroom. A survey of the lighting conditions under which the children in some parts of classrooms work has seldom failed to reveal highly unhygienic conditions.

In the past, schools have been able to detect only a few of the most serious eye defects. Simple and convenient tests were not available for the teacher or school physician to analyze binocular (two-eyed) vision at reading distance (approximately 13 to 16 inches). The usual procedure has been to have the pupil stand 20 feet from a Snellen chart and interpret what he saw with each eye independently. Unfortunately, this procedure will detect fewer than 50 percent of the cases with visual disabilities at reading distance, for normal children read with two eyes and most of the school reading is done at the near point (approximately 13 to 16 inches).

In co-operation with the medical department, tests have been developed for the detection of visual defects by the classroom teacher. Tests of the following functions have proved to be of inestimable value: Visual superimposition (fusion of two images into one), visual acuity (keenness of vision), eye muscle imbalance (horizontal and vertical), stereopsis (depth perception), hyperopia (far-sightedness), myopia (near sightedness), astigmatism, and eye regressions. All of these tests can be made with an inexpensive telebinocular (a modification of the stereoscope). With the exception of the tests for hyperopia, myopia, and astigmatism, binocular (two-eyed) vision is necessary to pass them. A knowledge of optics is not required by the classroom teacher; she needs only to follow the simple directions and if the child cannot pass the tests, he should be referred to the family eye doctor for a competent examination.

It is imperative that a teacher should not "drive" a child into reading until she has made an attempt to analyze or define the problem. Our records show that almost 90 per cent of the severe reading cases should have medical attention before receiving pedagogical help. In such instances, tutoring aggravates the problem and many times an apparent gain in reading achievement is due to maturation rather than to the pedagogical methods used.

The need for these particular tests was determined by a careful examination of doctor's reports of cases referred by our clinic. A typical example of a beginning pupil is that of a six year old who could make no progress in reading until he was fitted with glasses. The teacher found the difficulty with the aid of the above enumerated tests. The doctors report came back as follows: "Norman's vision was just 1/3 normal in each eye. He has a mixed astigmatism, being both near-sighted and far-sighted in each eye. With the proper glasses, we were able to obtain better than normal vision. I believe that you will find that this will make a marked difference in the quality of his school work." Needless to say, considerable improvement was noted by the teacher within four weeks time. Norman is now one of the best readers in his class.

The more difficult cases are those which are permitted to carry their reading disability beyond first or second grade. Norman's case is of one type: several other types have been identified by means of these procedures. Typical visual characteristics of a child who has reversal difficulties (i. e. reads "saw" for "was," "lap" for

"pal," "bone" for "done," etc.) are an eye-muscle imbalance coupled with near-sighted or far-sighted astigmatism. For such cases, not more reading but glasses and eye training exercises often given at home under the direction of the doctor, have been necessary before giving pedagogical help. In all cases where visual handicaps have existed, the doctors have been most co-operative with the school and the home. This constant supervision by the doctor and the teacher is vital to such a program, especially for pupils who should not be required to read for a period of a semester or more.

Auditory imagery as a re-enforcement to visual imagery is a third important factor in reading. The five tests used in our clinic are designed for the analysis of the pupils' memory span, ability to discriminate between and fuse sounds, and keenness of hearing. It is a well established fact that a test of acuity does not provide an adequate index to the child's auditory capacities and abilities. Phonic power (or the ability to fuse sounds into words), auditory discrimination (the ability to discriminate between sounds), and auditory span (ability to repeat correctly a succession of sounds) contribute directly to reading ability in the primary grades. The educational implications of the foregoing statement are given in the *Twenty-fourth Yearbook* of the National Society for Study of Education (p. 87). The authors declare that children respond differently to phonetic training, some requiring very little, if any formal training to gain independence in word recognition, while others, even after considerable teaching, are still helpless.

Both in spelling and in reading, kinaesthetic imagery—the fourth factor—is recognized as a desirable reinforcement to auditory and visual imagery. It is difficult to isolate certain phases of the kinaesthetic imagery problem from auditory imagery. For example, the test of auditory discrimination also provides an index to the child's ability to pronounce words correctly. Although the data are not complete, manuscript writing is probably less confusing to first grade children than cursive writing because the characters involved are more nearly alike. A thorough investigation of the possibilities of postponing handwriting, especially for immature children, until after the first grade would be a worthy enterprise.

The fifth factor—language—is a well-known item contributing to certain reading difficulties. We have encountered a few cases where the writing of Hebrew proved to be an interference factor. Problems of articulation and enunciation arise oftentimes when another language is spoken in the home.

Undesirable emotional reactions—the sixth factor—are usually correlates of reading disabilities, but the relationship is more nearly symptomatic than causal. Too few cases can be analyzed on this basis to make it a significant factor in identifying the causes of the reading disabilities which affect about 10% of our school population. We have found many of these emotional disturbances to be normal reactions to a situation which the child cannot understand. The stressing of phonics for a child who can not respond to high frequency sounds creates a situation which he cannot define. In like manner, a pupil's efforts are fruitless if he has a visual defect. Difficulties on a perceptual level are also beyond self-help.

Specific tests of eyedness and handedness are given as a matter of routine. Hand preference has proved to be specialized; therefore, we require the child to use the right hand for writing only when there is sufficient evidence from the tests which involve the items in question. Ocular dominance is of minor significance.

Our research efforts are now being directed toward the study of the relation between monocular regressions and reading reversals. *No one theory can be expected to account for all types of reading disabilities.*

Diagnosis and Correction of Reading Problems as a Problem-Solving Process

James D. Riley and Jon Shapiro

Riley and Shapiro (1989) present a model for reading remediation in the form of a problem-solving process. They suggest that this view of reading disability enables the classroom teacher to better understand the complex process of reading and select the most appropriate remedial strategies and related instructional needs of problem readers. It is interesting to note how their work builds on the writing of others who have preceded them in the field of reading remediation.

I've studied the texts and attended conferences. I've learned how to use formal and informal tests, and I think I have a basic understanding of the reading process. I mustn't overemphasize data-aware strategies to the detriment of concept strategies. . . . But is that all there is to diagnosing and remediating kids who have problems reading? Give a test, spot their weaknesses, write an IEP, find a program, and then have them complete the exercises? That seems awfully mechanical. Do I have to stick to the original prescription? What do I do when the prescription doesn't work? Do I change the diagnosis, or do I change the technique? There must be more to it than that!

In spite of the voluminous professional literature discussing the diagnosis and remediation of reading problems, the process of diagnosis and remediation remains elusive. The confusion exemplified in the above passage from a classroom teacher's observations is understandable.

Perhaps this elusiveness stems from the very complexity of reading. One early description compared the study of the reading process to the study of the human mind (Huey 1908). The process of diagnosing and correcting reading difficulties involves consideration of aspects of reading itself, as well as the contexts in which reading takes place. It is no wonder that diagnosis can be confusing and that we tend to rely on formulae or mechanical approaches to diagnosis.

This article presents a framework for diagnosis and correction of reading difficulty. The framework is based on the problem-solving process. It sees diagnosis as a dynamic, everchanging, yet manageable process. Just as readers become proficient when they monitor their own reading strategies, so teachers become proficient when they monitor their own diagnostic and teaching strategies.

First, we briefly describe problem solving in order to illuminate diagnosis as a problem-solving process. Then we examine the parallels between problem solving and diagnosis and correction of reading problems. Finally, we apply the problem-solving process to a case example.

COMPONENTS OF PROBLEM SOLVING

Consider this variation of a well-known problem in problem-solving literature:

> *Three sheriff's deputies and three prison trustees are returning from a road detail. The trustees will not try to escape, but they could be tempted to overpower the deputies in order to get their weapons. To reach the prison, they must cross a river using a small boat with room for only two. At no time can there be more trustees than deputies. Describe, step by step, how all the trustees and deputies make it across the river.*

When a variation of this problem was presented to subjects in an experiment (Thomas 1974), it was reported that subjects' responses

consisted of units of moves that attempted to meet the conditions of the problem (Catania 1979; Wessells 1982; Woolfolk 1987). If you were attempting to solve this problem, chances are that you would do what some of our students did. Several drew pictures of a river with symbolic representations of deputies and trustees (see Figure 1). Others used verbal sequences to solve the problem: First, one deputy and one trustee cross, then two deputies, then two trustees, and so on.

No matter which method was used to attempt a solution, the problem-solving process for these students consisted of the same basic components. They included (1) identifying the problem, (2) understanding the conditions of the problem, (3) hypothesizing and applying possible solutions, (4) testing the solutions, and (5) recycling the hypothesized solutions.

In the problem presented, one has to *identify the problem*—how to move the deputies and trustees back to the prison. The key *conditions* are twofold: (1) the boat can hold two persons only, and (2) at no time can trustees outnumber deputies. In the initial attempts to *hypothesize alternative solutions,* most of the students tried a quick approach. Some at first tried to move all the trustees or all the deputies but discovered that the deputies soon were outnumbered. Others tried to move one deputy and one trustee at a time and soon discovered that the deputies would be outnumbered on either side, depending on whether a deputy or a trustee made the return trip.

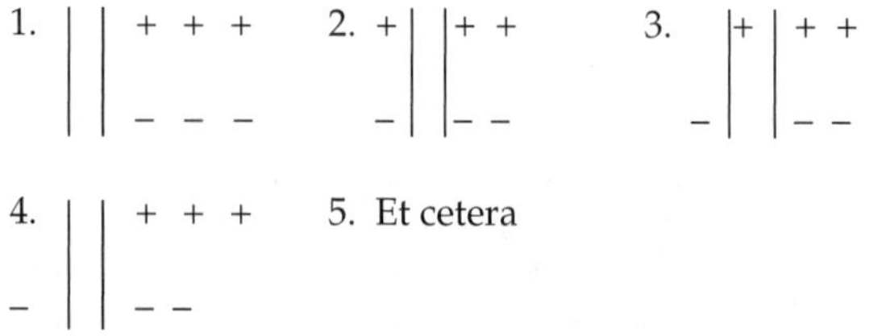

FIGURE 1   **Sample Graphic Attempt to Solve the Problem**

As they *tested their solutions,* they found that they had to use a variety of travel combinations in order to solve the problem. They had to *recycle* their tentative hypothesis (Figure 2).

What are some of the other features of problem solving that will bear on our later discussion of reading diagnosis as problem solving? Consider Skinner's famous luggage dilemma (Skinner 1966). Essentially, the problem is that you must pick up a friend's luggage at the airport, and all you have is a matching ticket stub. Unfortunately, the bags move by too quickly on the conveyor belt for you to read the tags. Skinner suggests a partial solution to this problem. Mark each bag checked—luggage you determine is not your friend's—with a piece of chalk. In that way you can "discriminate" already-tested solutions from those not attempted. As before, you must first *identify the problem*—in this instance, to get your friend's suitcase, which you have never seen. You also must *understand the conditions,* which are twofold: (1) the conveyor belt never stops, and (2) the suitcases must be removed one at a time. To test hypothesized solutions efficiently, you must devise some way of discriminating between those *hypothesized solutions* already attempted and those not yet attempted.

In this problem there is minimal *recycling* if a chalk marker becomes an added element; continuous and rather inefficient recycling or re-thinking of potential solutions would, however, be necessary if the suitcases were not marked. Thus two additional features of problem solving are reflected in the suitcase problem. These are the (1) efficient discrimination between appropriate and inappropriate solutions, and (2) willingness to add new elements (chalk marker) to the problem-solving process (Skinner 1966).

PARALLELS BETWEEN COMPONENTS OF PROBLEM SOLVING AND THE DIAGNOSTIC PROCESS

There are direct parallels between the problem-solving process and diagnosis and correction of reading problems. Consider the parallels reflected in Figure 3.

Identifying the problem in problem solving is similar to the *recognition of a reading problem.* Understanding the conditions of a problem is parallel to *understanding processing deficiencies* of a student who has problems in reading. As the problem solver hypothesizes possible solutions, so does a teacher *hypothesize remedial strategies* to correct those processing deficiencies. The remedial strategies are hypothesized on the basis of what the teacher knows about the reading process. Furthermore, the strategies are designed and tested as to whether or not they improve the recognized processing deficiencies. Ideally, the strategies are *revised* and *recycled* if they do not successfully address processing deficiencies.

APPLYING DIAGNOSIS AND CORRECTION AS A PROBLEM-SOLVING PROCESS

In order to better understand the diagnosis and correction of reading problems as a problem-solving process, we apply this process to a specific case. Imagine yourself as a classroom teacher of third graders. A new student enters your classroom from another school district. You

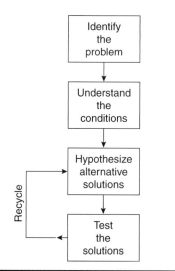

FIGURE 2   Components of Problem Solving

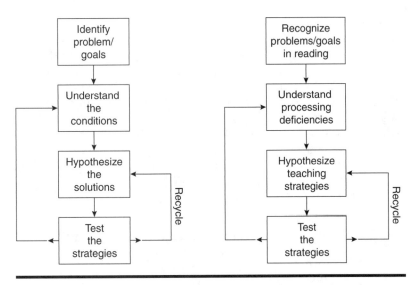

FIGURE 3   Parallels between Problem Solving and Diagnosis and Correction as a Problem-Solving Process

have virtually no data on her except that she has "some problems in reading"—a quotation from her mother. What do you do?

Recognizing the Problem

First, you would need to recognize the existence and specific nature of the reading problem. Is the mother's opinion enough? What does it mean? "Some problems in reading" could mean almost anything. Her mother could be, unintentionally, either exaggerating the problem or soft pedaling it. The mother simply is communicating, in a general way, her impressions of the previous reading history of her child.

Even though you have no data, you must begin instruction immediately. The chances are that you might temporarily place her in the bottom reading group to see how she functioned with the lowest-level material available in your class. You probably would suspend judgment about her reading ability. Changing locations and reading programs can be disruptive and even traumatic. Such changes may create a tem-porary reading problem. The different format, stories, scope, and sequence may make a new student appear less proficient than the individual really is.

In addition, you would begin to observe her performance in the reading group to see whether she has identifiable problems in reading. But what would you observe? The effectiveness of casual observation of a child's performance in a reading group is not clear. For all the above reasons, it may be very easy to misjudge her reading ability.

Understanding Processing Deficiencies

You also may choose to test her to continue or refute the initial hypothesis—that she has "some problems in reading." What test or method of assessment would you choose? In our discussions with numerous classroom teachers and reading teachers, we found that methods of assessment in similar situations ranged from the use of word lists, such as the Dolch Basic Words, to the complete and involved use of informal reading inventories, as well as variations of miscue inventories.

With all the teachers with whom we discussed these issues, the methods of examining deficiencies in reading power seemed to have been predetermined on the basis of unspoken beliefs about the pupil's reading powers, rather than on the basis of how readers process print. Although teacher beliefs are an important part of instruction, we believe that these beliefs must accommodate and reflect a broad view of the reading process. With all the research that has accumulated, correction of reading problems can no longer rest on folklore.

To enhance the effectiveness of their teaching, teachers must *first understand the student's processing deficiencies.* This understanding is reflected in the following six questions that could be asked about an individual's reading processing of text:

1. Is there reading behavior that indicates difficulty in processing the data on the printed page?
2. Is there reading behavior that indicates difficulty in linking previous knowledge and experience to information in the passage?
3. Does the student understand what reading is—the functions of reading—that reading is a sense-making process?
4. Does the student then know when the processing efforts are ineffective or effective?
5. To what degree has the student had an opportunity to read connected print?
6. To what degree can the student adjust his or her processing efforts to fit the demands of the material, individual purposes, and the environment in which reading takes place?

We apply these questions to our case, and the answers help us to hypothesize effective teaching strategies.

Hypothesizing Teaching Strategies

The answers to the six questions are determined primarily by observation and test interpretation. To see how the identification of hypothesized

strategies works, consider the answers to the above questions as they evolved for our case.

1. *Difficulty in processing data?* Student performs well on test of isolated phonics skills but "has a pattern of reading miscues in context."
2. *Difficulty in processing concepts?* Student can answer questions related to a passage when the questions are passage independent (Who rode Midnight the horse? Answer: A cowboy).
3. *Reading as a sense-making process?* Student's self-corrections in oral reading don't make sense. Impulsively supplies several answers to detail questions, none of which is related to the story.
4. *Student recognizes own ineffective processing strategies?* Student becomes visibly frustrated *before* her responses are evaluated by the teacher; says repeatedly, "I don't understand this."
5. *Student reads connected print at any level?* The parent says there are books at home, but the student cannot remember the name or characters of a single story.
6. *Student adjusts processing strategies to fit the text?* Little information; however, student shows evidence of lack of fluency even in first grade stories.

The responses to these questions are part of the framework for hypothesizing the most effective teaching strategies. If the questions are considered part of a framework, specific teaching strategies or combinations of teaching strategies can be identified as an approach for this child. This framework illustrates how such strategies evolve (Figure 4). It is apparent that questions one and two, concerning the processing of data and concepts, are focal aspects of the reading process. Questions three and four relate to the student's ability to self-monitor the effectiveness of individual processing strategies. Questions five and six refer to the presence or absence of the ability to vary processing strategies for a variety of materials and situations.

To hypothesize the teaching strategies, it is useful to summarize the needs of this student

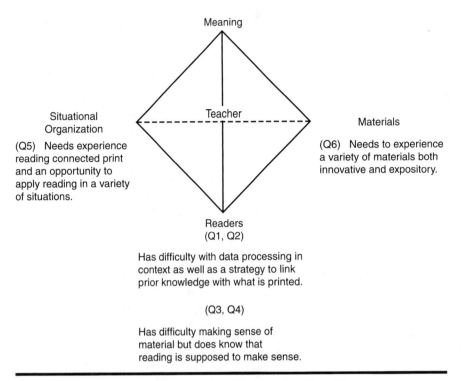

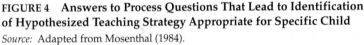

Meaning

Situational
Organization

Teacher

Materials

(Q5) Needs experience
reading connected print
and an opportunity to
apply reading in a variety
of situations.

(Q6) Needs to experience
a variety of materials both
innovative and expository.

Readers
(Q1, Q2)

Has difficulty with data processing in
context as well as a strategy to link
prior knowledge with what is printed.

(Q3, Q4)

Has difficulty making sense of
material but does know that
reading is supposed to make sense.

**FIGURE 4   Answers to Process Questions That Lead to Identification
of Hypothesized Teaching Strategy Appropriate for Specific Child**
Source: Adapted from Mosenthal (1984).

according to the responses to questions and according to the information we have *at this time.* The student needs teaching strategies that particularly do the following:

1. Focus on data processing (decoding) in context
2. Help the student link what is known to what is in the text being read
3. Emphasize comprehension as the end product of *each* lesson
4. Include connected print as the basic reading material
5. Include a variety of material and guidance in adjusting to the demands of the material

As one examines the problem-solving framework for hypothesizing appropriate teaching strategies, it quickly becomes apparent that this process is far different from the more common pattern of testing and teaching to eliminate a *specific* skill weakness. This structure is intended to integrate all aspects of the reading process into an attempt to correct the deficiencies that prevent the problem reader from engaging in reading as a meaningful, or meaning-getting, activity.

Testing the Teaching Strategies

Of course, the hypothesized teaching strategies, although based on responses to the questions posed, need to be tested. As outlined in our earlier discussion of the Skinner problem, there are two additional features of problem solving. One of these is the ability to discriminate between appropriate and inappropriate solutions. In diagnosis and correction, we must distinguish between effective and ineffective strategies. In the Skinner suitcase problem, the new element of chalk was added to aid in discriminating between the suitcases that had been examined and those that had not been examined. Without the chalk one would have been reduced to continuously examining suitcases at random. Without systematic discrimination between effective and ineffective strategies, one must simply try various approaches at random.

In our case, what discriminates effective teaching strategies and the ongoing responses to the diagnostic questions are what are known as *diagnostic process discriminators.* Two questions are asked continuously throughout the instructional process: Has the teaching strategy improved the reader's ability to process the data? Has the teaching strategy improved the reader's ability to engage in concept processing?

Continual modification of instruction may occur, depending on the answers to these questions. It is, however, entirely possible to improve on one or the other of these abilities without improving the overall reading ability of the student. We are all too familiar with the problem reader who improves in ability to pronounce words in isolation but who cannot decode them in connected print. Likewise, we all know the reader who improves in the ability to answer correctly passage-independent questions but, when pinned down, cannot relate details of the story because of limited vocabulary and decoding skills.

The second measure of the success of remediation is the student's ability to understand what is read—that is, the *product discriminator.* Ultimately it is the student's enlarged capacity to think about and enjoy what he or she reads that determines the effectiveness of teaching strategies.

The other feature is the ability and willingness to add new elements. Although process and product discriminators represent the "chalk" of the instructional program, we also have to be open to including new components. These may range from adoption of existing techniques to changing the situation in which instruction occurs or changing the materials.

It was stated earlier that teachers can become more proficient when they monitor their own diagnostic and remediation strategies. By carefully identifying the existence of a reading problem, understanding processing deficiencies, hypothesizing appropriate teaching strategies, and by continually adjusting and refining the hypotheses and strategies, teachers will maximize the effectiveness of their diagnostic and corrective activities. By considering diagnosis and correction as a problem-solving exercise, the effectiveness of remedial programs as well as on-the-spot classroom correction of reading instruction can be greatly enhanced.

REFERENCES

Catania, A. C. 1979. *Learning.* Englewood Cliffs, New Jersey: Prentice-Hall.

Huey, E. 1908. *The psychology and pedagogy of reading.* New York: Macmillan.

Mosenthal, P. 1984. Decoding comprehension research from a classroom perspective. In *Promoting reading comprehension,* edited by J. Flood. Newark, Delaware: International Reading Association.

Skinner, B. F. 1966. An operant analysis of problem solving. In *Problem solving,* edited by B. L. Kleinmuntz. New York: John Wiley and Sons.

Thomas, J. C., Jr. 1974. An analysis of behavior in the hobbits-orcs problem. *Cognitive Psychology* 6:257–69.

Wessells, M. G. 1982. *Cognitive psychology.* New York: Harper and Row.

Woolfolk, A. E. 1987. *Educational psychology.* Englewood Cliffs, New Jersey: Prentice-Hall.

Helping Struggling Readers

NANCY PROTHEROE

Recent thinking on the remediation of reading problems is reflected in the article by Protheroe (2003). Discussed here is the position that responsibility for helping those students with reading difficulties is not the sole duty of each individual teacher but is one that is school wide.

Teachers in the primary grades are charged with the enormous responsibility of teaching children to read. Given children's varied range of abilities and experiences, teaching this essential skill to such a diverse group of learners can be a daunting task.

But the challenge is not confined to the primary grades. Teachers in grades through high school continue to deal with students' reading problems, even after they have received high-quality reading instruction in the early grades. The bottom line is that schools and teachers at all grade levels must be prepared to help struggling readers.

IDENTIFYING EFFECTIVE READERS

While noting that reading is a complex process, Burns *et al.* (1999) identify three main accomplishments that characterize good readers:

- They use the alphabetic system of English to identify printed words.
- They use background knowledge and strategies to obtain meaning from print.
- They read fluently.

We also know what good reading looks like in older students. They have mastered enough of the basic skills embedded in reading so that their energies can be focused on the meaning instead of the decoding of words. They are also strategic learners. For example, when they don't understand a portion of the text, they will take corrective action, such as rereading the text or referring to a previous section. (Pressley *et al.* 1995).

IDENTIFYING STRUGGLING READERS

To help students become good readers, teachers must first understand the continuum of literacy development so that they can provide effective, age-appropriate reading instruction as well as identify students who are struggling. . . . They need to be alert to these specific warning signs of reading problems:

- A labored approach to sounding out unknown words;
- Repeated misidentification of known words;
- Reading that is hesitant and includes many stops, starts, and mispronunciations; and
- Poor comprehension (Lyon 1997).

Poor performance on written work is often another sign of a reading difficulty that has not yet been diagnosed or addressed. Poorly organized paragraphs, lack of a sequential train of thought, many spelling and punctuation errors, and limited vocabulary may all signal a student whose literacy skills are lagging.

PROVIDING EFFECTIVE READING INSTRUCTION

While many young children learn to read almost naturally, research tells us that others need explicit, focused instruction on skills such as phonemic awareness to be able to effectively make the move to reading. Therefore, teachers and principals should look for a balanced program for beginning readers that provides:

- Both direct instruction in sound-symbol relationships and exposure to interesting reading materials;
- A focus on the relationships between letters and sounds and the process of obtaining meaning from print;
- Materials that students can read to themselves easily and more difficult texts that they can learn to read with the teacher's help; and
- Frequent and intensive opportunities for students to read both aloud and to themselves (U.S. Department of Education 2000).

But even with excellent instruction, some students will still experience problems with reading. Providing support for struggling readers in content-area classes after the primary grades is an important part of an effective reading program and serves several purposes:

- Students receive more opportunities for support than if responsibility was limited to reading teachers or other specialists.
- Assistance is embedded in content instruction, providing students with meaningful opportunities to learn, apply, and practice reading skills.
- Students are less likely to be left to struggle with grade-level material they cannot understand.

Content-area teachers at the middle-grade levels should also consider themselves teachers of reading and weave instructional strategies designed to help struggling readers into everyday instruction. Students need to be taught strategies that can help them retain, comprehend, and apply the material they are reading. These should include:

- Using background knowledge;
- Stopping periodically to summarize what has been read and how it connects with what has been read previously; and

- Monitoring their own understanding of the text (Learning First Alliance 1998; Rose 2000).

TARGETING SUPPORT

Even with high-quality reading instruction in the early grades, some students will need additional help. Many interventions are available, varying in nature, duration, and focus. The following are some common characteristics of successful approaches:

- Students receive individualized or small-group instruction.
- Students are taught to read using meaningful texts to which they can relate.
- There is opportunity for repeated reading of passages.
- Books are used that contain predictable vocabulary and sentence structures.

Principals should consider the following criteria when designing or selecting a reading intervention program:

- The intervention must match the student's level of reading, because each stage of growth requires a special focus.
- It must be intensive enough to close the ever-widening gap between poor readers and their grade-level peers as quickly as possible.
- It should be grounded in research.
- For very poor readers, the instruction must be designed to develop students' phonological skills. Their inability to correctly identify speech sounds typically acts as a barrier to developing other reading-related skills.
- Text reading fluency should be the target for instruction for less impaired readers who *can* decipher words through sounds. Vocabulary development should be targeted through direct instruction as well as through providing opportunities for and encouraging extensive reading (Moats 2001).

DEVELOPING AN ACTION PLAN

Teaching reading must be considered a school-wide responsibility. It takes careful planning to develop an approach that is integrated across the grades. You should begin by focusing on questions such as these:

- Is our approach to teaching reading in the early grades balanced and research-based?
- Has it been effectively communicated to all staff so that what is intended is actually what is taught?
- Do we have a comprehensive and ongoing approach to identifying struggling readers and their specific problems that ensures that no student will be overlooked for so long that he or she has little chance of catching up?
- Do we have a system developed for intervening and providing intensive support for struggling readers that uses a variety of approaches and that provides more reading instruction and time for these students?

By providing high-quality, research-based reading instruction, schools can reduce the number of struggling readers and better target limited resources to those students who need them most.

REFERENCES

Allington, Richard L. *What Really Matters for Struggling Readers: Designing Research-based Programs.* New York: Longman, 2001.

Burns, M. Susan; Griffin, Peg; and Snow, Catherine E. (eds.). *Starting Out Right: A Guide to Promoting Children's Reading Success.* Washington. D.C.: National Academy Press, 1999.

Green, Marguerite. "A Rapid Retrieval of Information: Reading Aloud with a Purpose." *Journal of Adolescent and Adult Literacy* (December/January 1997–1998): 306–307.

Learning First Alliance. *Every Child Reading: An Action Plan of the Learning First Alliance.* Washington, D.C.: Author, 1998.

Learning First Alliance. 2000. *Every Child Reading: A Professional Development Guide.* Washington. D.C.: Author, 2000. Online: www.learningfirst.org/readingguide.pdf

Lyon, Reid. Statement made before the Committee on Education and the Workforce. United States House of Representatives, Washington. D.C., July 10, 1997.

Moats, Louisa C. "When Older Students Can't Read." *Educational Leadership* (March 2001): 36–40.

Pressley, Michael, *et al.* "The Comprehension Instruction that Students Need: Instruction Fostering Constructively Responsive Reading." *Learning Research Disabilities Research and Practice* (Fall 1995): 215–224.

Pressley, Michael, *et al.* The Nature of Effective First-Grade Literacy Instruction. Albany, N.Y.: State University of New York at Albany, 1998. Online: http://cela.albany.edu/1stgradelit/literacy.html

Rose, Adrienne. "Literacy Strategies at the Secondary Level." *Leadership* (November–December 2000): 12–16.

Snow, Catherine E.; Burns, M. Susan; and Griffin, Peg (eds.) *Preventing Reading Difficulties in Young Children.* Washington, D.C.: National Academy Press, 1998.

Steinberg, Adrian. "Reading Problems: Is Quick Recovery Possible?" *Harvard Education Letter* (September/October 1989).

U.S. Department of Education, National Institute for Literacy. *Reading: Know What Works.* Washington, D.C.: Author, 2000.

WestEd. "Reading for Understanding: A Modern Urban Success Story." *R&D Alert* (Summer 1999).

CHAPTER REFERENCES

Betts, E. A. (1934). Teacher analysis of reading disability. *The Elementary English Review, 11*, 99–102.

Gray, W. S. (1922). Remedial cases in reading: Their diagnosis and treatment. In W. S. Gray (Ed.), *Re-*

medial cases in reading: Their diagnosis and remediation (Supplementary Educational Monographs, No. 22) (pp. 185–187). Chicago: University of Chicago Press.

Harris, A. J. (1980, May). What is new in remedial reading. Paper presented at the Annual Meeting of the International Reading Association (ERIC Document Reproduction Service, ED186 886).

Kirdel, C. E. et al. (1996). *Teachers and mentors: Profiles of distinguished twentieth-century professor of education.* (ERIC Document Reproduction Service, ED393 362).

Moore, D. W. (1986). Laura Zirbes and progressive reading instruction. *Elementary School Journal, 86,* 663–672.

Protheroe, N. (2003). Helping struggling readers. *Principal, 82,* 44–47.

Riley, J. D. & Shapiro, J. (1989). Diagnosis and correction of reading problems as a problem-solving process. *Clearing House, 62,* 250–255.

Yeaman, A. R. (1985). *Visual education in the 1920s: A qualitative analysis.* (ERIC Document Reproduction Service, ED271 091).

ANNOTATED BIBLIOGRAPHY OF RELATED REFERENCES

Allington, R. L. et al. (1986). What is remedial reading? A descriptive study. *Reading Research and Instruction, 26,* 15–30.

An extended discussion of the purposes and goals of remedial reading, noting the strengths and weaknesses of the traditional views of this approach to the correction of reading problems.

Betts, E. A. (1936). *The prevention and correction of reading disabilities.* Evanston, IL: Row, Peterson.

An important reference in the development of the reading clinic and the development and training of classroom teachers in the diagnosis and remediation of reading disabilities.

Clay, M. (1985). *The early detection of reading difficulties* (3rd ed.). Portsmouth, NH: Heinemann.

Examines various informal diagnostic procedures (running records, reading recovery teaching procedures) that teachers can use in their classrooms with students who are having literacy difficulties.

Gates, A. (1927). *The improvement of reading: A program of diagnostic and remedial methods.* New York: Macmillan.

One of the first discussions of the role of a specific program of remediation for various types of reading disability.

Harris, A. J. (1968). Five decades of remedial reading. In J. A. Figurel (Ed.). *Forging ahead in reading* (pp. 25–33). Newark, DE: International Reading Association.

Harris, A. J. (1977). Ten years of progress in remedial reading. *The Reading Teacher, 31,* 29–35.

Harris, A. J. (1980). What is new in remedial reading. Paper presented at the Annual Meeting of the In-

ternational Reading Association (ERIC Document Reproduction Service, ED186 886).

These pieces by Harris provide a comprehensive review of almost eighty years of research and classroom practices in the area of reading remediation.

Monroe, M. (1933). Helping children who cannot read. *Progressive Education, 10,* 456–460.

A discussion of the role of the classroom teacher in the treatment of reading disabilities.

Robinson, H. M. (1946). *Why pupils fail in reading: A study of causes and remedial treatment.* Chicago: University of Chicago Press.

Considered a landmark in the history of the diagnosis and remediation of reading difficulties. It is one of the first studies to treat reading disabilities as being the result of multiple causes.

Uhl, W. L. (1916). The use of the results of reading tests as a basis for remedial work. *Elementary School Journal, 17,* 266–275.

This early article by one of the pioneers in the study of reading difficulties discusses the role of formal assessment in the remediation of reading difficulties.

Valtin, R., & Naegele, I. M. (2001). Correcting reading and spelling difficulties: A balanced model for remedial education. *The Reading Teacher, 55,* 36–45.

Develops a cognitive model for the remediation of literacy difficulties, noting that acquisition of reading, spelling, and writing skills result from a sequence of characteristic strategies.

Zirbes, L. (1918). Diagnostic measures as a basis for procedure. *Elementary School Journal, 18,* 505–522.

An early discussion of the value of using more than one assessment procedure in the diagnosis of reading problems.

_____YOU BECOME INVOLVED_____

As you read this material related to the diagnosis and remediation of literacy problems, note the number of similar themes that are discussed from the beginning of the previous century. Topics such as the role of the teacher, causes of literacy problems, and suggestions for specific remedial procedures seem to follow a common thread. What are the implications of these discussions for your current work with literacy problems of different types?

The first article by Gray (1922) sets the foundation for the diagnosis and remediation of reading problems.

- Gray identifies a number of causes of reading difficulty. How do you think these problems have changed and how many are still prevalent today?
- What does he recommend as general guidelines for remediation of reading difficulties? How relevant do you think his suggestions are for today's literacy teacher?
- Based on Gray's comments, what do you think should be the role of the classroom teacher in the remediation of reading problems?

Betts (1934) emphasizes the importance of the classroom teacher in the diagnosis and remediation of reading difficulties. Consider the following based on this article:

- What four fundamental remediation techniques does the author discuss? Why do you think these are important in the diagnosis and remediation of reading problems of various types?

- What specific suggestions does Betts make regarding the role of the classroom teacher in helping the student experiencing reading problems?
- How have diagnosis and remediation techniques changed in the area of literacy instruction since this article was written?

Riley and Shapiro (1989) discuss a model for teachers to consider as they work with the struggling reader.

- Briefly describe the remediation model illustrated in this article. What do you believe are the strengths and the weaknesses of this concept?
- How might you implement these ideas in your classroom as you both assess and remediate those students who are having reading problems?

Protheroe's article (2003) reflects recent thinking on the assessment and remediation of reading problems in the classroom setting.

- Based on your reading in this chapter, how do you think the views of the remediation of reading difficulties have changed? How have the views of such issues as the use of standardized tests and various remediation techniques changed over time?
- What do you believe is the role of the classroom teacher in relation to students with reading difficulties?

CHAPTER 9

TECHNOLOGY AND LITERACY INSTRUCTION

[Reading machines] have no control over those factors which ultimately make for good comprehension, i.e., intelligence, experience, and vocabulary.

—Irving H. Anderson
Teachers College Journal (1941)

In every study that has been attempted to evaluate the use of machines, it has been found that they are no more effective in increasing speed of reading than are less complicated but sound classroom [reading] procedures.

—Guy Bond & Miles Tinker
Reading Difficulties: Their Diagnosis and Correction (1967)

Technology profoundly affects the learning and teaching of literacy, as well as the nature of literacy itself.

—William H. Teal et al.
Exploring Literacy on the Internet (2002)

The use of various types of technology in the teaching of reading has long been a part of literacy instruction. In the late nineteenth and early twentieth centuries, studies on eye movements and their relationship to reading were much in evidence (Dearborn, 1906; Dodge, 1906; Huey, 1908). This interest in the technology of eye movement measurement and its relationship to effective reading has continued through most of the history of the teaching of reading (Tinker, 1936; Anderson, 1941; McConkie, 1976) and remains active in recent research in this area (Rayner, 1997; Marrs & Patrick, 2002). Other forms of technology combined with reading have included programmed reading systems of various types (Townsend, 1964) and speed reading machines (Berger, 1970; Palmatier, 1971). These applications of technology to reading instruction met with various levels of success and generally have disappeared from current application to literacy instruction today.

Perhaps the most evident use of technology and reading today is the current emphasis on the use of the computer. It is clearly an understatement to say that literacy instruction has been affected and changed in many significant and fundamental ways by the computer. In a position statement on the Integration of Technology and Literacy in the Curriculum (2001), the International Reading Association stated that students today had the right to have the following.

- Teachers who are skilled in the effective use of information and communication technology
- A literacy curriculum that integrates the new literacies of information and communication technology into instructional programs
- Instruction that develops the critical literacies essential to effective information use
- Assessment practices in literacy that include reading on the Internet and writing using word processing software
- Opportunities to learn safe and responsible use of information and communication technologies
- Equal access to information and communication technology

AS YOU READ

In the following articles notice how the current use of technology and reading today has been affected by the research and practices of the past. Observe how some of the current issues in the use of the new technologies have in reality been of interest and concern in the past as well.

Guidelines for Computers and Reading

DOROTHY S. STRICKLAND, JOAN T. FEELEY, AND SHELLEY B. WEPNER

The first reading in this chapter (Strickland, et al., 1987) is a listing of guidelines for the evaluation and selection of computers that are to be used in various ways for reading instruction. This particular excerpt was included here because of its completeness and ease of application to various types of computers. Note the emphasis placed here on the importance of all aspects of the reading process, especially comprehension. Because of its application to the other articles in this section it was placed first and is not in chronological order with the remaining material.

1. Computer instruction in reading should focus on meaning and stress reading comprehension.
   a. Learners should have opportunities to work with whole, meaningful texts. Programs that offer learners a chance to process large chunks of related text, rather than bits and pieces of unrelated language fragments, allow students to use and extend what they know about reading comprehension.

b. Learners should have opportunities to work with word-recognition programs that stress the use of word meanings in conjunction with phonics and structural analysis. Care must be taken to make sure that, when programs feature the study of individual words and phrases, they are offered within a contextual framework that helps them make sense to the learner. Assessment programs for teachers should also be provided in meaningful context.

c. Learners should have opportunities to apply the skills being taught in some meaningful way. Programs that deny the learner an opportunity to make use of what is being "taught" are merely assessment tools and do little to further the learner's growth.

d. Learners should have opportunities to work with computer materials that use content and language that are within the range of their conceptual development. Tasks should be challenging but not frustrating. Student interests, previous experiences, and purpose play a role in determining whether or not a computer task is comprehensible and worthwhile.

2. Computer instruction in reading should foster active involvement and stimulate thinking.

a. Learners should have opportunities to discuss the purpose of the computer task or program as well as its nature. They should be aware not only of what they are supposed to do but also of why doing it is important.

b. Learners should have opportunities to make decisions that control or influence the computer task. Programs that build in opportunities for students to make choices and test predictions help them learn to think and act on their own rather than merely react to someone else's thinking.

c. Learners should have opportunities to monitor their own learning. Tasks that

offer students opportunities to self-check and correct their own errors support the development of independent learners.

3. Computer instruction in reading should support and extend students' knowledge of text structures.

a. Learners should have opportunities to encounter a wide variety of text structures upon which to apply and refine their comprehension skill. A variety of narrative and expository structures should be provided. Commercially prepared teacher-authored and student-authored materials also should be included. Reading instruction can take place through all kinds of computer-based materials, not merely those designated specifically for that purpose.

b. Learners should have opportunities to experiment with text in creative ways to suit their purposes. When students reorganize a story or an informational piece on the computer, they are employing and strengthening what they know about the structure of texts.

4. Computer instruction in reading should make use of content from a wide range of subject areas.

a. Learners should have opportunities to use the computer as a means of applying reading strategies to all areas of the curriculum. Programs related to science, social studies, and math require the use of strategies for reading comprehension. Unless students are being helped to use what they know about reading comprehension under these circumstances, they are not progressing as competent readers.

b. Learners should have opportunities to use the computer in conjunction with other modes of instruction. The computer should not operate as a separate and isolated means of learning. Its use should be integrated with that of books and other learning materials. Students need to think of the computer as one additional means of sharing and retrieving information and practicing skills in interesting and meaningful ways.

5. Computer instruction in reading should link reading to writing.

   a. Learners should have opportunities to create text with the computer for sharing and use by others. When students enter information into the computer for someone else to retrieve and use, they must compose with the reader in mind. This frequently involves making explicit use of what they know about what makes a text comprehensible. For example, decisions might be made about how much information to give, what to stress, whether or not to use topic headings, whether or not the ideas are clearly stated, whether or not spelling, punctuation, and other writing conventions are accurately applied, and so on. Revision and proofreading strategies such as these clearly involve the combined application of reading and writing skills.

   b. Learners should have opportunities to use the computer as an information-retrieval system. Classroom data bases, where several students input information on a particular topic, are excellent opportunities for students to collect, organize, and store information for others to retrieve, reorganize, and use. The information collected may be lists of items or short passages on various topics. In either case students are acting as readers and writers as they peruse information to make decisions about what to collect and store. Later, they search and sample the stored information to make decisions about what to retrieve and how to use or report it in some written fashion.

Programed Materials

ARTHUR I. GATES

Today's use of technology and reading was preceded by the development of various types of programmed materials. Gates wrote the following article in 1967. This was during the early stages of what was to become a technology revolution in the teaching of reading. Even at this early stage, Gates cautions against an overemphasis on the delivery system rather than the programs actually being taught using various forms of technology. Despite the historical methods, such as the extensive use of movies, and so on, much of what he says has application to today's advanced technology systems in the area of literacy education.

A number of eminent psychologists believe that learning can be greatly facilitated by reducing each activity or skill to a series of very minute steps. The teaching can then be programed in a sequence of units so detailed and fully controlled by a machine, scrambled book, or other pencil-and-paper device as to ensure learning the right and avoid learning the wrong response. Such a program may be largely or entirely self-teaching. These persons contend that a major fault of current teaching is that it proceeds by steps so large and imprecise that a learner can go astray at almost any point. Even the shrewdest teacher has difficulty in detecting these little slips. The history of remedial reading and certain earlier forms of practice materials bear out this contention. Some of the best remedial reading instruction represents in part an effort to proceed by this small-unit, check-up-every-step procedure. Very detailed work-type organizations, one of them composed of a thousand pages of material, were developed a third of a century ago for teaching reading to very young children and to children who had been deaf or otherwise disabled since birth. These were programed materials. Although by modern standards they were crude, poorly controlled, and inadequate in many ways, they worked very well.

Many other possibilities for improving reading instruction are now at hand. We have barely made a beginning in exploring ways of using sound motion pictures and television to demonstrate in slow motion effective methods of tackling unfamiliar words or methods of rapid reading and skimming and other skills. These devices can also make the unique artistry of master teachers available in every classroom. Effectively used, first-class programed materials and other aids will not replace the teacher. A physician or surgeon is not made less important or less helpful by giving him more and better tools with which to work. On the contrary, better equipment increases his insight, effectiveness, and prestige. The same should be true of the teacher.

At this point, however, a word of caution is in order. The next few years will witness a flood of new programed materials, teaching machines, canned television and sound-motion picture sequences, "skill-builder" booklets, phonic systems, workbooks, and other materials and gadgets. Many of these may be inexpertly conceived and hastily prepared. Sales campaigns of unprecedented vigor and volume may be launched. The panicky spirit of the times may feed the urge toward hasty changes. Under these circumstances, the classroom teacher should be calm and cautious. He should realize that a novice, untrained in the field of reading, is as un-

likely to make a good program in reading as a hack songster is to compose a fine opera. Indeed, for precisely the reason that programed material requires that the best general pattern of reading abilities be reduced to very minute and rigorously controlled steps, the highest degree of expertness is necessary. Teachers, however, should not be overawed by mechanical or psychological mysteries. Programed materials are, after all, merely materials similar in nature to printed workbooks. Teachers should study and judge them with care and confidence.

The heart of the teaching machine is the program which it presents. The teaching machine is merely a device, exactly as a sound motion picture projector is a mechanism for presenting material. The teaching machine program may be good or bad, exactly as a motion picture program may be. This new type of teaching machine should not be confused, however, with certain other mechanical devices which have been developed as teaching aids. Each should be appraised in terms of certain principles. For example, machines which expose a line of print in parts, such as three or four phrases, one after another, are recommended to increase the rate of reading. While such a machine may have value for demonstration purposes, it does not really teach the pupil to read as he should read in a normal situation, and it forces him to learn adjustments that do not exist when he sits down to read a book by himself. A book will not conveniently flash the phrases one after another as the mechanical apparatus does. A pupil may learn to read "thought units" when the machine forces them on him, but he may read a book in quite another way. Another popular pacing machine requires that the teacher or pupil place a book under the metal covering, turn on the motor, and then try to keep reading the lines as a metal shutter moves down the page covering line after line. This calls for a less artificial departure from the natural situation than some other gadgets, but the same effect can be obtained with less distraction without the machine. All the pupil needs is a piece of cardboard which he himself moves down the page at a pace to suit his ability. He can force the pace as he desires; he can make it faster or slower or skip back and repeat a line as needed. Every such device—mechanical or other—should be appraised in terms of the extent to which it introduces artificial factors, distorts the natural process, or lacks proper flexibility and adaptability to the reader's needs.

Computers in Reading: A Review of Applications and Implications

Barbara J. Thompson

Thompson (1980), in an early article on the use of computers and the teaching of reading, addresses a number of fundamental issues related to this application of technology. Even though this article was written almost twenty-five years ago, consider how many of her concerns are still relevant.

Computer development and technical advancements have been burgeoning during the last 20 years. Since 1963, with O. K. Moore's usage of the "Talking Typewriter," machines have begun to play an important role in the educational process of our increasingly technological society. Barriers which impede the use of computers are being eliminated. Improvements in efficiency and quality and refinements in design coupled with decreased costs make computer technology more and more accessible.

Reading development and instruction is an area of priority at all educational levels. However, the impact of computers on educational practices in teaching reading has been minimal. Although numerous examples of computer usage can be cited, possibilities and capabilities far outweigh existing practices.

Whenever computers in education are mentioned, educators usually make an association to an automated concept of programmed instruction. This behavioristic model served as the initial application of the computer to the learning process. However, this sequential, reinforced, step-by-step process *does not guarantee* success, as there are no panaceas in education. Computer usage in education should not be equated with this single mode of learning. Computers are a multimedia resource. According to Banet (1978), "Computer-assisted instruction will be to all computer applications in education what programmed textbooks and workbooks are to the total universe of applications of PAPER in education!"

Current implementation of computer usage in education has fostered a variety of labels. Two distinctions identify system types: the user—student or teacher—and the objectives of the instructional program. Adaptable to multiple instructional roles, the computer can serve as text, test, or tutor. Also, the great variety of input/output modalities—speech synthesizers, teletypewriters, television-like screens, touch-sensitive screens, beams of light pens, color graphics, mobile units—can support diverse student needs and interests. Other advantageous features include: immediate feedback; self-pacing; self-selection; non-threatening, challenging, motivating multi-language capabilities; and impartiality (for, as Atkinson and

Fletcher [1972] have noted, boys and girls are equally successful).

COMPUTER-ASSISTED INSTRUCTION

Using the computer to teach reading was instigated with the work of Richard Atkinson and his associates at Stanford, funded by IBM and the Carnegie Foundation. CAI, computer-assisted instruction, is not a separate and different approach to teaching reading, such as phonics or linguistics: CAI can serve as an interface for reading development with any approach. Both comprehensive developmental programs and programs that focus on specific skills are available. Computers in reading are capable of:

1. containing programs based on different theories of reading;
2. supporting a variety of reading content, such as word recognition, vocabulary development, and comprehension;
3. being used with different types of learners—gifted, average, remedial, or handicapped;
4. being accessed under a variety of conditions—group or individual; in the home, library, or school; at any time; and
5. facilitating achievement of a variety of educational goals and purposes.

With the student as the primary user, modes of CAI include drill-and-practice, tutorial, problem-solving, and games and simulations. These systems are not mutually exclusive. Maeger (1972) has described the diversity of CAI programs, including the use by deaf children in Washington, D.C., by retarded readers in New York City, and by illiterate prison inmates.

Drill-and-Practice

The most extensively implemented form of CAI in school systems is the drill-and-practice mode. The Chicago Public School System, whose project has been supported through Title I, has been one of the largest users of this mode. The drill-and-practice mode is designed to integrate and supplement classroom curriculum, providing practice for needed skill development. When tasks require drill and practice, it seems hardly innovative just to automate it. However, emotional fear and embarrassment often accompany classroom drill, and different students require various amounts of time for skill development, which can be alleviated through CAI. With CAI, motivation and enjoyment are increased, active involvement is demanded, and teacher time can be more effectively utilized.

Another feature of drill-and-practice CAI is flexibility of sequencing. Steps or skills within a program can be accelerated, repeated, or skipped through branchings (usually dependent on the correctness of a student response). PLATO and the Stanford Project are examples of this type of program.

Many systems offer additional special features. The PLATO system, for example, has an on-line dictionary. When the student is working and becomes unsure of a word, the word "term" is typed along with the unknown word. The definition and picture are subsequently supplied by the computer. Another aspect of this system includes branchings to receive special help and explore references or resources.

Drill-and-practice devices sometimes face the criticism of "dehumanization." However, personal interaction with *any* form of drill is not guaranteed. Also, the high-interest involvement the child has with the device seems significant.

Tutorial

Direct, programmed instruction is usually referred to as the tutorial mode of CAI. Interactive systems currently allow more "flow," where the student does not get trapped into a particular sequence or become locked into an author's predetermined plan. In this medium, students can request more information or reviews, solicit a quiz, or ask for additional examples. Rather than replacing a teacher, the computer can enhance instruction by providing an alternate mode when the traditional delivery system has been unsuccessful; provide a variety of content offerings which are not dependent on teacher training; or extend the current curriculum. For example, through tutorial CAI, a fourth grader can learn Spanish, even though an individual Spanish tutor is not available; explore word origins and word histories; or pursue an interest in reading mythology without reliance on teacher offerings. Also, with multi-language capabilities, computerized instruction for a bilingual reader can be more appropriate.

Problem-Solving, Games, and Simulations

The problem-solving capabilities of the computer can be utilized whenever the student is required to process certain types of information. Students can freely manipulate symbols and words. Children can even create their own personal stories or programs on some computers, similar to the language experience approach. The ability to edit and update makes on-line composing motivating. Students can arrange generated words to form sentences, or read a story part and add an ending or predict an outcome. Also, entering only corrections or changes and having a completely corrected copy is expedient. Reference files can also be built and accessed by the student as needed for continuous study.

Computer games and simulations can be used to reinforce skills or practice decision-making. Mass storage and file handling capabilities of the systems could allow the computer to generate games and activities based on data from an individual student's data base. There are, for example, word games to teach specific vocabulary, hangman type word games (beat the dictionary), anagrams, and activities developed from an individual's personal word bank or sight vocabulary. Student text files can always be scanned to keep sight vocabulary lists up-to-date.

COMPUTER-MANAGED INSTRUCTION

In computer-managed instruction (CMI), the teacher uses the computer as a tool to assist in diagnostic, prescriptive, and evaluative tasks. Teachers have access to current group and individual achievement profiles, diagnostic reports, and grouping recommendations.

Skills management or system approaches, such as the Wisconsin Design for Reading Skill Development, with prescriptions, specific objectives, and criterion-referenced tests, are readily adaptable to CMI.

In reading diagnosis, usually based on tests built into a computer program, the computer yields reading levels and areas of skill deficiency. A computer printout suggests corresponding activities in many CMI programs. The Fountain Valley Teacher Support System (Richard Zweig Associates) and Croft Inservice Reading Program (Croft Educational Services) are among the most well-known examples.

In the near future, CMI could serve as an asset in the mandated educational plans for learners—both gifted and handicapped. Individualized programs appropriate for each learner could be readily accessed and updated.

With the growing public concern over accountability in teaching reading skills, computer-managed instruction (CMI) could offer some possible solutions to the problem in the future. Using CMI to monitor reading progress creates an awareness of student abilities and progress; methods and materials can be examined along with the time element and cost to derive a cost-effective program. CMI can allow a matching of teacher method to students' differing individual needs. Computer modeling can be done to attempt to bring econometrics to a school system.

COMPUTER-BASED RESOURCE UNITS

Computer-based resource units may be in the form of a library, activity and idea file, or suggestions or guides generated by the computer for the teacher to use in planning instruction covering any topic. In addition, in the near future, the computer could contain lists of available and supplemental materials or resources for an entire school system. Computer generated book listings corresponding to interests, grade levels, and availability are beginning to be used successfully. Computer storage for titles of books and articles is an integral part of most large library systems. In the near future, the possibility exists to have entire periodicals available rather than only titles.

OTHER COMPUTER APPLICATIONS

Current computer applications for developmental reading have taken place within community colleges and the armed forces. Programs are being developed to meet the inservice needs of teachers, for training teachers to teach reading in the content areas, to aid teachers in reading diagnosis (simulating situations), for teacher training in reading to facilitate mainstreaming, and in competency-based teacher education programs in reading. Again, adaptations for differentiated needs, flexible time usage, and non-threatening atmosphere are important aspects for the computer as a medium for disseminating information.

Telephone dialogue interaction is providing instruction to more learners. The computer is being used much like a traveling classroom. The college student can enroll in developmental reading courses, and the student teacher can have greater access to reading courses.

The computer is put into service preparing cloze text. The computer will delete every nth word, omit high-frequency words or words from a pre-programmed list, or insert blanks and retain initial letters of deleted words to use in reading-comprehension exercises.

Utilizing the computer to scan textual passages has resulted in generated word lists, such as the *American Heritage Word List*. Also, the computer is used to tally word frequencies, sentence lengths, and word lengths, and will print out the readability of a textual passage according to multiple readability formulas.

In teacher-training, the computer simulated diagnosis and simulated educational situations provide valid practice for prospective teachers.

RESEARCH

Research has indicated that the computer seems to be an effective medium for delivery of in-

structional services (Kearsley, 1976). Unfortunately, many current research projects exploring computer-based education have been minimal, superficial, have yielded inconclusive results, or have been inadequately funded. Also, educational software developed by computer programmers who are not educators has created difficulties due to lack of awareness of educational techniques.

Possibilities for the use of the computer in reading research appear unlimited. Data banks can accumulate information on learners' abilities, progressions, diagnostic results, and successes and failures. Such data banks could provide insights into types of learners; allow for correlations of abilities and successes; and offer modes of presentation for skill attainment.

A continual concern has been to define the variables and interactions of reading comprehension. Models of information processing and examinations of the algorithm of what the computer must do in order to comprehend meanings may provide future insights. Furthermore, the computer could be used to form models to test cognitive theories. If desired, the computer could match teacher techniques and approaches of reading instruction to the individual's most effective learning modality.

Other research possibilities deserving exploration are attitudinal changes toward reading through the use of the computer and the Hawthorne Effect. Longitudinal studies are also needed to yield more conclusive and substantial results.

Cost-effectiveness of computer usage is directly related to the computer's instructional application in a specific setting, rather than on equipment and software costs. Outcomes must definitely be considered. Instructional techniques that may work in one setting may not work in other situations.

Whereas schools and other institutions have been relatively impervious to technological change for instruction, in reading research some extensive computer application has occurred. Use of statistical packages, computer banks to work with larger samples and increase data analysis and handling, and computer searches of research literature are examples. In the near future, in computer searches of the literature, the potential exists to have any article at your fingertips in minutes rather than just title/author lists of related research.

Ellis (1974) stated: ". . . thinking about the computer and its role in instruction does not mean thinking about the computer. It means thinking about instruction." Future reading research needs to be examined in this context.

The advent of the computer in education has led to numerous cautions and criticisms. However, criticisms can only serve to make refinements, encourage re-thinking, and reformulate usages.

CONCLUSION

Revolutionary innovations embodied in computer usage have generated a lot of discussions, yet despite the wide possibilities for application, implementation is still somewhat limited. The computer in reading cannot be viewed as a reading panacea, a magic step to success, or even suggestive of universal application. However, it can respond effectively to the learner and his or her needs, inasmuch as the computer is manipulable and not manipulative.

Initial applications of CAI were based on the Skinnerian paradigm. Yet, technological potentials with interactive systems promote the tradition of Dewey and Progressive education through curriculum choices. While the potential is great—instant access to any book in the Library of Congress, any course, any teacher resource file—availability does not insure usage. Reduced hardware costs with adequate purchasing funds do not promise purchase priority. The computer's instructional applications in reading are limited by the available programming, computer, financial resources, curricula, and creativity of the users.

REFERENCES AND SUGGESTED READINGS

Anderson, J. R. Computer Simulation of a Language Acquisition System: A Second Report. *Basic Processing in Reading: Perception and Comprehension.* Hillsdale, New Jersey: Lawrence Erlbaum Publishers, 1977.

Atkinson, R., and Fletcher, J. D. An Evaluation of the Stanford CAI Program in Initial Reading. *Journal of Educational Psychology,* 1972, *63,* 597–602.

Baker, E. Improving Reading Instruction: The Use of Research Based Principles. *Educational Technology,* September 1973, *13*(9), 10–12

Baker, F. A Microcomputer Based Test Scoring System. *Educational Technology,* February 1978, *18*(2), p. 36.

Banet, B. Computers and Early Learning. *Creative Computing,* October 1978, 90–95.

Barry, J. G. Using a Computer to Calculate the Dale-Chall Formula. *Journal of Reading,* December 1975, 218–222.

Eisele, J. E. *Computer-Assisted Planning of Curriculum and Instruction.* Englewood Cliffs, N.J.: Educational Technology Publications, 1972.

Elliot, P., and Videleck, R. Reading Comprehension Materials for High School Equivalency Students on the PLATO-IV Computer Based Education System. *Educational Technology,* September 1973, *13*(9), 20–21.

Ellis, A. B. *The Use and Misuse of Computers in Education.* New York: McGraw-Hill, Inc., 1974.

Green, D. R. *et al.* Learning to Recognize Words and Letters on a CAI Terminal. Document No. ED02177, Office of Education, U.S. Department of Health, Education, and Welfare, Washington, D.C., April 1968.

Handier, K. The Computer Comes to the English Classroom: Computerized Monitoring of Pupil Progress in Reading. *Educational Technology,* November 1975, *15*(11), p. 34.

Hines, T. C., and Warren, J. A. A Computerized Technique for Producing Cloze Text Material. *Educational Technology,* September 1978, *18*(9), 56–68.

Jones, J. The Educational Technologist and the Reading Teacher. *Educational Technology,* September 1973, *13*(9), p. 19.

Kearsley, G. P. Some "Facts" About CAI: Trends 1970–76. *Journal of Educational Data Processing*, 1976, *13*, 1–12.

Kustar, A. Applications of Systems Analysis to a Spelling Program. *Educational Technology*, January 1975, *15*(1), p. 51.

Maeger, K. Computer Assisted Instruction and Reading. In W. E. Blanton and J. J. Tuninman (Eds.), *Reading Process and Pedagogy.* Bulletin of the School of Education, Indiana University, September 1972, 77–98.

Mattleman, M. Project Management to Improve Reading Instruction. *Educational Technology*, September 1973, *13*(9), 13–15.

Nelson, R. The First Literate Computers. *Psychology Today*, March 1978, p. 73.

Savage, J. F. A Reading Teacher Looks at Technology. *Educational Technology*, September 1973, *13*(9), 7–9.

Splittgerber, F. L. Computer Based Instruction: A Revolution in the Making? *Educational Technology*, January 1979, *19*(1), 20–26.

Steg, D. R. Intervention Through Technology: The Talking Typewriter Revisited. *Educational Technology*, October 1977, *17*(10), 45–47.

What Does Research on Computer-Based Instruction Have to Say to the Reading Teacher?

Ernest Balajthy

As computers became more accepted as an important aspect of reading instruction, there is concern about the effectiveness of this aspect of literacy education. Balajthy (1987) reviews the contemporary research on this important question noting some of the problems associated with this study and research. Consider his suggestions and recommendations for the use of computers and reading instruction.

Though the level of popularity of computer-based instruction in reading may vary, few doubt that computers have won a permanent place in the reading classroom. One of the most common related concerns of educators has to do with the effectiveness of computer-based education and the appropriateness of the many possible roles computers can play in reading instruction. Existing research offers the reading educator valuable insights, though even the most enthusiastic promoter of computer-based instruction must acknowledge that unexamined use of computers may not be the simple panacea some expect it to be.

IS COMPUTER-BASED INSTRUCTION EFFECTIVE?

There is no doubt that computer instruction is effective. A host of research studies, meta-analyses, and research reviews indicate clearly that computer instruction is effective for a wide variety of reading skill and concept areas (e.g., Alessi, Siegel, Silver and Barnes, 1986).

This, however, is not an important research question. There are many other "proven" methods of reading instruction. All of the methods *work*, in the sense that students learn from them.

IS COMPUTER-BASED INSTRUCTION MORE EFFECTIVE THAN OTHER METHODS?

Again, there is no doubt at all that computer-based instruction is more effective than other methods. There are many qualifications for this response, however. Before this research question becomes meaningful, one must ask three important questions:

1. What kind of computer-based instruction?
2. What kind of other methods?
3. What is meant by "effective"?

There are a host of computer-based instructional techniques, varying from rigid, behavioral computer-assisted instructional (CAI) programs to free-flowing, holistic "computer-as-a-tool" approaches. There are innumerable "other methods" to which we can compare computer-based instruction. Finally, "effectiveness" can be defined in a host of ways. For example, do we wish to be effective as demonstrated by measurement on a standardized reading test, or effective as demonstrated by development of a lifelong love of reading on the part of our students?

LIMITATIONS OF COMPUTER INSTRUCTIONAL RESEARCH

When examining the research on effectiveness of computer-based instruction which compares CBI to other methods, one must bear in mind a number of limiting factors.

1. Almost all CBI research is based on the programmed instruction model which, though it may be effective in some ways, is presently out of favor among reading researchers and teachers. Even during the heyday of conventional programmed instruction in the late 1950's and early 1960's, advocates were cautious about whether the techniques would lend themselves to reading instruction. These concerns have been carried over into applications of computer-assisted instruction to reading. Becker (1983) noted that CAI may have greater impact on mathematics instruction because it more closely simulates the practice of math than of reading or language use, though recent findings by Kulik, Kulik and Bangert-Drowns (1985) suggest that CAI in language arts is equally effective to CAI in mathematics instruction.

2. A variety of observers have indicated that the computer is not being well-used in the field of education (Burns & Bozeman, 1981; Holzman & Glazer, 1977; Snyder & Palmer, 1986). Research on inappropriate applications simply will not yield interesting findings. Thelen (1977) has noted that "computer-based education is a technological potential, not an educational guarantee" (p. 458).

3. The so-called *Hawthorne Effect* (also called the halo or novelty effect) makes it difficult to project today's results, when computers are new and therefore exciting, into a future when CBI is commonplace. The novelty of computers may result in increased student effort and persistence, but this effect may wear off with time. Kulik, Bangert and Williams' (1983) review of secondary computer instructional studies found that longer studies in which students became accustomed to computers resulted in significantly decreased learning improvement rate than shorter studies.

4. Much research has been carried out without a well-established theoretical framework for instruction, by experts in computers rather than content- or skill-area experts. Research reports often completely ignore the *reading* process and the software used to teach it. Instead they concentrate on the hardware used, as if the machine was the key component in instruction. A good example of this is the large body of material written about the effectiveness of PLATO, as if this system is uniform in quality. Only the hardware is uniform: Anyone familiar with the PLATO software will quickly realize that it varies tremendously in quality.

5. In addition, most research has been carried out by the designers of the computer software themselves, or by those who have personal or professional involvements in the CAI projects. Reports, for example, that PLATO can raise achievement by 5 years with only six months work, or that 12 hours of PLATO instruction raised reading achievement by 1.6 grade levels (Schneck, 1984), are of dubious validity to anyone familiar with the teaching of reading. The great danger in such research is that false hopes may be raised. Such unrealistic expectations may do instructional computing more harm than good (Slesnick, 1984; Roblyer, 1985) as people come to expect microcomputers to be "a veritable *deux ex machina* to put all things right" (Sloan, 1984, p. 541).

6. Scandura (1981) has suggested that lack of quality software which accurately reflects the cognitive processes it is attempting to teach is the major impediment to CAI implementation. This problem is severe both in research projects where software constructed specifically for the project does not have the finished appearance of top-notch commercial software and in commercial software for which publishers rarely support necessary basic research or even simple field-testing prior to production. In a survey of secondary reading teachers, Hague, Childers, and Olejnik (1986) found 61 percent indicating that they required improved software before increasing the amount of computer use in their classrooms.

7. Much research has been carried out with older readers rather than younger. There is some evidence (Kulik, Kulik, & Cohen, 1980) that computers may be more effective with younger students.

HOW CAN COMPUTER-BASED INSTRUCTION BE BEST USED?

Effectiveness of instructional methodology is dependent on a wide variety of factors, such as the characteristics of the learners, the learning activities, the nature of materials used, and the criterial tasks by which effectiveness is measured (Brown, Campione, & Day, 1980). Clark (1983) raises the valuable point that the medium itself (e.g., the teacher, computer, tape recorder or book) does not directly influence learning. It is

what the medium *does*—the teaching—that influences learning. Is a computer more effective than a workbook for drill and practice in word recognition? Yes, it is more effective because a computer gives immediate feedback. But a teacher *can* give immediate feedback on workbook activities if the class is small enough. If the teaching quality is the same—no matter what medium is being used to present that teaching—the achievement results will be similar.

As a result, the primary research question to be asked about computers and reading is the following:

> "What constitutes effective teaching of reading, and how can computers help provide this instruction?"

IS THE COMPUTER "JUST ANOTHER TEACHER TOOL"?

There are some who would say that computer-based instruction is not *better* than other techniques—it is *different*. It provides one more tool for the teacher to teach more effectively and the learner to learn more effectively. For example, Clark, in a 1983 article surveying educational media research, argued,

> *Most current summaries and meta-analyses of media comparison studies clearly suggest that media do not influence learning under any conditions . . . The best current evidence is that media are mere vehicles that deliver instruction but do not influence student achievement any more than the truck that delivers our groceries causes changes in our nutrition (p. 445).*

Clark's conclusions as to the effectiveness of media in enhancing achievement have been disputed on a variety of grounds (e.g., Petkovich & Tennyson, 1984). His proposition that media do not affect achievement ought not to be misinterpreted, however. Clark's meaning is that the format of instruction is the important factor: drill and practice is equally effective, whether administered by a teacher or by a computer. The advantage of the computer, according to Clark and Leonard (1985), lies in the possibility of its power and flexibility for increased efficiency and cost-effectiveness: human teachers *can* provide immediate and individualized feedback for drill and practice workbook activities—just as the computer can—but this is an extremely inefficient and expensive practice.

Clark may be correct in his argument that functions of the computer can be carried out in other ways. Each child could have a tutor to provide an "on-line" interactive session with workbooks or television. Each could be given a personal secretary to retype compositions as often as necessary. Each could be allowed to perform as many real-life scientific or social experiments as desired. None of these alternatives is at all realistic, however. The computer can give reality to highly effective—but hitherto difficult to achieve—learning environments, by providing tutorials, word processing, and electronic simulations.

The important point is not simply that the computer is effective. The point is that research on the effectiveness of the computer must address itself to each issue in turn, asking, "In what ways can the computer improve on conventional classroom effectiveness and efficiency?"

WHAT CONCLUSIONS CAN WE DRAW FROM THE RESEARCH?

The most comprehensive compilations of research studies on the effectiveness of computer-based instruction are those carried out by James Kulik and his colleagues at the University of Michigan (Kulik, Bangert, & Williams, 1983; Kulik, Kulik, & Bangert-Drowns, 1985; Kulik, Kulik & Cohen, 1980; Kulik, Kulik, & Schwalb, 1986). The results of these meta-analyses have indicated generally positive results from computer-based instruction.

Reading teachers must bear in mind the very damaging criticisms made of these meta-analyses before accepting their results at face value. Clark and Leonard (1985) examined a cross-section of the studies used in Kulik's analyses and found crippling experimental design weaknesses in the

majority. Many researchers had not used random assignment to treatments, for instance, or had not given the control group equivalent instruction while the experimental groups were receiving instruction on computers. Of the 15 studies which did meet Clark and Leonard's minimum standards for research design, only 2 resulted in significant effects in favor of computer-based instruction.

In addition, relatively few of the studies used by Kulik for his analyses had to do with language or reading instruction. Most were directed toward mathematics or science instruction. At best, therefore, these meta-analyses and the studies on which they are based can only be used as indicators for direction of future research.

Level of Students

One important finding had to do with a comparison of achievement between older students and younger students. Kulik, Kulik and Cohen (1980) reported that achievement gains were much more impressive with elementary age youngsters than with college age. It may be that the constraints of programmed instruction are better fitted to the subskill approaches characteristic of early instruction than to the more complex cognitive operations required of older students. Jamison, Supes and Welles (1974) reviewed research to find that computer-based instruction seems most effective with remedial students. The research on this issue, however, is scanty.

A variety of educators have expressed concern that computers will be used as justification for increase in low-level drill and practice exercises in instruction (Balajthy, 1984; Zaharias, 1983) rather than for increase in meaningful language activities.

Computers and the Affect

Jenkins and Dankert (1981) found that student acceptance of computers in education is positive. Computers cannot, however, be considered a magical motivational cure. Obertino (1974), among others, has noted that poorly designed software will be rejected by students as quickly, if not more quickly, than poorly designed conventional instruction. In fact, she has observed that the physically imposing presence of a human teacher has significantly more power to keep students on-task than a computer console.

Reinking (1984) has argued that the motivational value of some computer learning activities may actually work for students' harm rather than their good. If the motivational value is abused by subjecting students to irrelevant tasks (he offers as an example an arcade vocabulary game drill which is inappropriate due to level of words involved and to design of the activity), the computer work is actually harmful because students may be allowed to use the program extensively in the place of more useful activities.

Sex Differences

A variety of researchers have indicated that boys and girls respond differently to classroom use of computers. Hawkins (1984), for example, noted that, "Boys want to control it" (p. 12), that is, to command it to perform a variety of functions. Girls tend to "stay within the dictates of the established program rather than to explore the machine's capabilities" (Schrock, et al., 1985, p. 6). They are more likely to use software for drill and practice rather than engaging in programming activities of their own.

Schrock et al. (1985) also noted that boys tended to work longer at the computer than girls, with a mean of 20 minutes for boys and 13.6 for girls.

Motivation

Very little research has been carried out on motivating factors of computer-assisted instruction. Malone (1981) has carried out some research on computer instructional games, but his research stands in need of replication and elaboration. Clark's (1982) meta-analysis of motivational impact on instruction has suggested the rather surprising finding that students often learn the least from methods they enjoy the most. Balajthy, Bacon, and Hasby's 1985 study of computer-based vocabulary instruction indicated that, while students enjoyed video game activities, they benefited more from traditional worksheet drills and text computer activities.

Feedback

Despite the fact that feedback is an essential part of most computer drill and practice, the function of feedback in producing learning is poorly understood. For example, while most writers on CAI point to the computer's capability of providing immediate feedback as one of its great advantages, the fact of the matter is that research on feedback is not uniformly supportive of immediate feedback (Kulhavy & Anderson, 1972).

Students appear to learn best when they received detailed feedback as to which answers are incorrect and why they are incorrect (Gilman, 1968; Roper, 1977). Unfortunately, very little microcomputer instructional software provides such response-specific feedback.

Social Interaction in the Classroom

Fears that placing students into computer work stations would make them social outcasts with debilitated interpersonal skills have consistently been shown to be unfounded. Instead, a wide variety of researchers have reported increased social interaction revolving around the computer applications as students ask one another for help and advice. Hague, Childers, and Olejnik (1986), for example, found 75% of reading teachers surveyed disagreed with a statement that computers isolate students from one another.

Hawkins (1983) has suggested that the increased interaction noted in classroom computer applications has been due to the fact that microcomputers remain a new phenomenon in classrooms. The traditional taboos about doing one's own work have not yet begun to control teacher and student behaviors.

Early writings on computer applications in the classroom suggested that computers would have an almost magical effect in improving student interaction. Recent research in the quality of interactions among students using computers has raised new concerns. Much of the verbal behavior is not task oriented, and that which is relevant to the task may not be of satisfactory quality, involving such problems as hoarding of the keyboard, reprimands, and rude comments about others' abilities. True collaboration and mutual support among youngsters does not occur automatically with use of computers. Some concerns have also been noted about the development of "class experts" who tend to dominate use of computers and deny other students access to them.

Learner Control

Another possible advantage of computer-based instruction lies in the learner's control over instruction. Learners can, for instance, proceed at their own rates. There is some controversy, however, over whether learners benefit from all aspects of this control. Reinking and Schreiner (1986) found evidence that students' metacognitive controls—their ability to recognize when they have successfully learned from their reading—may not be sufficiently sophisticated to benefit from learner control in computer-presented textual readings. Steinberg (1977) reviewed research on learner control in CAI and found that motivation is increased by learner control but improved achievement is not. Benefits of learner control may be contingent on individual differences in students involving such factors as locus of control.

CONCLUSIONS

What, then, is the role of computer-based reading and language instruction? Future developments will certainly increase the computer's flexibility, but for now the following applications seem most powerful:

1. *Teacher tool.* Teachers can free themselves to spend more time in actual teaching by using the computer to manage grading, construct tests and exercises, and maintain student records.

2. *Management.* Computers greatly facilitate the administration and grading of reading subskill criterion tests. Grouping for instruction on the basis of test results can be carried out automatically, as can printing of diagnostic reports.

3. *Microcomputer laboratory drill and practice.* In instruction where practice exercises are considered essential for reinforcement and automaticity, groups of students can be sent to a microcomputer laboratory under the supervision of an aide or volunteer parent. This would free teachers to deal with higher-level instructional matters.

4. *Individualized microcomputer "learning center".* Microcomputers can be used to provide instruction to individual students on a host of reading-oriented topics, allowing them to investigate their interests or remediate weaknesses. In practice, however, it seems apparent that placing one or two microcomputers in a classroom is only useful when the teacher is committed to meeting such individual needs and desires. Unless a teacher is already using individualized techniques such as learning activity packets or learning centers, it is doubtful microcomputers will be used for that purpose if they are placed in the classroom.

5. *Student tool.* Few educational computer experts doubt that the major educational application of microcomputers in the next few years will be as tools, for word processing, data base research, and arithmetic calculations. In many colleges, word processing is the dominant application for microcomputers. This is already filtering down to the secondary and intermediate grades (Becker, 1985).

In summary then, results of research on computer-based instruction in reading are at best equivocal. There is no doubt that supplementing classroom instruction with CBI is effective. This, however, is true of virtually any kind of supplemental instruction, whether or not it is computer-based. Increased time-on-task leads to increased achievement. Before introducing computers into the reading classroom, educators should closely examine the variety of factors that influence effectiveness for the specific applications desired and in the specific contexts available.

REFERENCES

Alessi, S. M., Siegel, M., Silver, D., & Barnes, H. (1986). Effectiveness of a computer-based reading comprehension program for adults. *Journal of Educational Technology Systems, 11,* 43–57.

Balajthy, E. (1984). Reinforcement and drill by microcomputer. *The Reading Teacher, 37,* 490–495.

Balajthy, E., Bacon, L., & Hasby, P. (1985, November). *Introduction to computers and introduction to word processing: Integrating content area coursework into college reading/study skills curricula using microcomputers.* Paper presented at City University of New York Conference of Microcomputers and Basic Skills in College, New York.

Becker, H. J. (1983). *School uses of microcomputers: Reports from a national survey.* (Issue No. 1). Baltimore, MD: Center for Social Organization of Schools, Johns Hopkins University.

Becker, H. J. (1985, July). *The second national survey of instructional uses of school computers: A preliminary report.* Paper presented at World Conference on Computers in Education, Norfolk, Virginia.

Brown, A. L., Campione, J. C., & Day, J. D. (1980). *Learning to learn: On training students to learn from texts.* (Tech. Rep. No. 89). Urbana. IL: Center for the Study of Reading, University of Illinois.

Burns, P. K., & Bozeman, W. C. (1981). Computer-assisted instruction and math achievement: Is there a relationship? *Educational Leadership, 21,* 32–39.

Clark, R. E. (1982). Antagonism between achievement and enjoyment ATI studies. *Educational Psychologist, 17,* 92–101.

Clark, R. E. (1983). Reconsidering research from media. *Review of Educational Research, 53,* 445–459.

Clark, R. E., & Leonard, S. (1985, April). *Computer research confounding.* Paper presented at American Educational Research Association, Chicago.

Gilman, D. (1969). The effect of feedback on learners' certainty of response and attitude toward instruction in a computer-assisted instruction program for teaching science concepts. *Journal of Research in Science Teaching, 6,* 171–184.

Hague, S. A., Childers, N. R., & Olejnik, S. (1986), October). *Micros and reading: What do secondary reading teachers say?* Paper presented at College Reading Association, Knoxville.

Haven, R. N. (1985, April). *Researchers say?* Paper presented at College Reading Association, Knoxville.

Haven, R. N. (1985, April). *Instructional software, 1984: Trends and state of the art.* Paper presented at American Educational Research Association, Chicago.

Hawkins, J. (1983). *Learning LOGO together. The social context* (Tech. Rep. No. 13). New York: Center for Children and Technology, Bank Street College of Education.

Hawkins, J. (1984). *Computers and girls: Rethinking the issues.* (Tech. Rep. No. 24). New York: Center for Children and Technology, Bank Street College of Education.

Holzman, T. G., & Glaser, R. (1977). Developing a computer literacy in children, some observations and suggestions. *Educational Technology, 17,* 5–11.

Jamison, R. N., Suppes, P., & Wells, S. (1974). Effectiveness of alternative instructional media. *Review of Educational Research, 44,* 1–67.

Jenkins, T. M., & Dankert, E. J. (1981). Results of a three month PLATO trial in terms of utilization and student attitudes. *Educational Technology, 21,* 44–47.

Kulhavy, R. W., & Anderson, R. C. (1972). Delay-retention effect with multiple-choice tests. *Journal of Educational Psychology, 63,* 505–512.

Kulik, J. A., Bangert, R. L., and Williams, G. W. (1983). Effects of computer-based teaching on secondary school students. *Journal of Educational Psychology, 75,* 19–26.

Kulik, C., Kulik, J. A., & Bangert-Drowns, R. L. (1984, April). *Effects of computer based education on secondary school pupils.* Paper presented at American Educational Research Association, New Orleans.

Kulik, C. C., Kulik, J. A., & Schwalb, B. J. (1986). The effectiveness of computer-based adult education:

A meta-analysis. *Journal of Educational Computing Research, 2,* 235–252.

Kulik, J. A., Kulik, C. C., and Cohen, P. A. (1980). Effectiveness of computer-based college teaching: A meta-analysis of findings. *Review of Educational Research, 50,* 525–544.

Malone, T. W. (1981). Toward a theory of intrinsically motivational instruction. *Cognitive Science, 5,* 333–369.

Obertino, P. (1974). The PLATO reading project. *Educational Technology, 14,* 8–13.

Petkovich, M. D., & Tennyson, R. D. (1984). Clark's learning from media: A critique. *Educational Communications and Technology Journal, 30,* 240–250.

Reinking, D. (1984). *Reading software: Current limitations and future potential.* New Brunswick, NJ: Graduate School of Education, Rutgers University.

Reinking, D., & Schreiner, R. (1985). The effects of computer-mediated text on measures of reading comprehension and reading behavior. *Reading Research Quarterly, 20,* 536–552.

Roblyer, M. D. (1985). *Measuring the impact of computers in instruction.* Washington, DC: Association for Educational Data Systems.

Roper, A. L. (1977). Feedback in computer-assisted instruction. *Programmed Learning and Educational Technology, 14,* 43–49.

Scandura, J. M. (1981). Microcomputer systems for authoring, diagnosis, and instruction in rule-based subject matter. *Educational Technology, 21,* 13–19.

Schneck, M. A. (1984). PLATO implementations and evaluations: New behaviors and objectives for education. In *Proceedings of EdCompCon 84* (pp. 91–103). Silver Springs, MD: IEEE Computer Society Press.

Schrock, S., Matthias, M., Vensel, C., & Anastasoff, J. (1985, April). *Microcomputers and peer interaction: A naturalistic study of an elementary classroom.* Paper presented at American Educational Research Association, Chicago.

Slesnick, T. (1984). Computer education research: A blinder for the misguided. In D. T. Bonnette, (Ed.), *NECC 84 6th Annual National Computing Conference Proceedings.* Silver Spring, MD: IEEE Computer Society Press.

Sloan, D. (1984). On raising critical questions about the computer in education. *Teachers College Record, 85,* 539–548.

Snyder, T., & Palmer, J. (1986). *In search of the most amazing thing: Children, education, and computers.* Reading, MA: Addison-Wesley.

Steinberg, E. R. (1977). Review of student control in computer-assisted instruction. *Journal of Computer-Based Instruction, 3,* 84–90.

Thelen, H. A. (1977). Profit for the private sector. *Phi Delta Kappan, 58,* 458–459.

Zaharias, J. A. (1983). Microcomputers in the language arts classroom: Promises and pitfalls. *Language Arts, 8,* 990–998.

Becoming Literate in the Technological Age: New Responsibilities and Tools for Teachers

LOUANNE IONE SMOLIN AND KIMBERLY A. LAWLESS

The final article in this discussion of technology and reading, by Smolin and Lawless (2003), reflects the most current thinking on this subject. Of particular note here is the extended discussion of the importance of the knowledgeable classroom teacher in the effective use of these new technologies and literacy instruction.

Consider the following two scenarios (both teachers' names are pseudonyms):

Ms. Jones's first-grade students have been using computers to improve their spelling skills. Through the process of reading trade books, students keep a word bank containing the words with which they are unfamiliar. When in the computer lab, they use an electronic dictionary to look up the meaning of these words, which they enter into their word banks. Ms. Jones collects the students' word banks once a week and develops spelling and definition multiple-choice worksheets using her class computer. She prints out these worksheets and gives them to her students to complete during the language arts period.

Ms. Doyle is a second-grade teacher working in a bilingual classroom. She received digital cameras and video recorders through a curriculum grant and, with her students, has used them to interview bilingual business owners in the community surrounding their culturally diverse urban school. The purpose underlying the interviews was to discover insights on the question "What does it mean to be bilingual?" Ms. Doyle based the activities for this curriculum project around city and state standards in language arts, social studies, and technology. Together students wrote interview questions; practiced them on one another; took walking field trips into the community; and, armed with digital cameras, video cameras, and audiotapes, accomplished the interviews. Upon returning to their classroom, they reviewed their pictures, audiotapes, and videotapes and then used the five classroom computers to analyze and synthesize their information for a digital slide show, which they shared with their school community. They also e-mailed these slide shows to 'e-pals' with whom they had been communicating.

A PARADIGM SHIFT IN LITERACY INSTRUCTION

In both of these scenarios, the importance of teaching students to read and write in print remains an essential goal, yet in each the vision for doing so is different—each teacher's approach to instruction, as well as her use of technology, differs.

In the first scenario, Ms. Jones's notion of literacy is text based, and she is using a skill-building approach to develop her students' reading and writing abilities. In doing so, Ms. Jones lays out specific, directed tasks for her students to complete. These text-based tasks

target students' acquisition of spelling and vocabulary skills. Ms. Jones's use of technology stems from this skill-based approach to literacy instruction: Technologies are used for isolated skill development. Ms. Jones layered technologies on top of her established traditional curriculum and is merely replicating what is usually done with books and paper. As such, technology becomes nothing more than an electronic version of the classic student worksheet. Children accessed technology in much the same way that they engaged in individual seatwork.

The second scenario exemplifies a different, broader vision of literacy instruction. While Ms. Doyle's students are engaged in text-based literacy instruction, they are also involved in activities that move beyond text to include multiple literacies. Ms. Doyle designs her curriculum in a way that supports her students' abilities to use, question, and interact with a variety of media sources in order to communicate with an audience beyond the classroom. Ms. Doyle's curriculum project emphasizes a paradigm shift in literacy instruction from a reliance on alphabetic literacy to a more inclusive focus on media literacy (Honey & Tally, 2000). Using such a student-centered approach, Ms. Doyle's students are not only learning reading and writing but also developing other essential literacies. These include technological literacy, visual literacy, information literacy, and intertextuality. In the remainder of this article, we will discuss each of these new literacies in the context of the second scenario and conclude with suggestions of useful technologies to address these literacies in the classroom.

Technological Literacy

Technological literacy is defined as "the ability to use computers and other technology to improve learning, productivity and performance" (U.S. Department of Education, 1997). A technologically literate person is someone who understands what technology is and how it can be used and is comfortable with its use. For students, "technological literacy goes beyond *just* knowing how to use technology tools such as word processing and the internet. It is knowing how to use them *in conjunction* with school subjects to increase academic performance" (U.S. Department of Education).

Ms. Doyle's project exemplifies this marriage between technology and content instruction. In her classroom, students begin with a curriculum project and use a variety of technologies to accomplish it. These students not only use classroom and lab computers; they also use digital cameras, video cameras, and tape recorders. In "learning center" activities, Ms. Doyle teaches small groups of students how to use the equipment and asks them to teach another group. Students then move beyond operational skills to learn how to harness these powerful tools for effective interviewing. For example, they learn how "zooming" in and out for close-ups and focusing on different angles while videotaping can facilitate what an interviewee is trying to convey. The students don't learn these technology skills in isolation but rather in the context of a rich curriculum project aimed at developing their literacy.

Through this contextual approach of learning how to use technologies, Ms. Doyle's students are developing technological literacy. They are employing a variety of digital technologies as they are learning how to work in groups, how to express their ideas, and how to communicate with a diverse audience. These abilities are reflected in many language arts standards.

Visual Literacy

Visual literacy is defined as "the ability to understand and produce visual messages" (International Visual Literacy Association, 1998). Children acquire information and develop language through multiple sources. In order to be literate in this technological age, students must learn to make meaning not only out of text but also out of the vast amount of visual information conveyed to them through images. A visually literate child can "examine, extract meaning and interpret the visual actions, objects, and symbols that he/she encounters in the environment" (International Visual Literacy Association). Being visually literate also enables a child to use these abilities to communicate with others.

Ms. Doyle's students develop an understanding of "bilingualism" through a variety of sources, which include text and images. Using their digital pictures, they discuss what they have learned from their interviews. They then arrange these pictures and, along with text, communicate this newly acquired knowledge to members of the school community and e-pals.

Information Literacy

In today's world, we are bombarded with information. Information literacy is the ability to find, evaluate, analyze, and synthesize information. A teacher must help his or her students develop their abilities to use information to construct knowledge. Ms. Doyle effectively integrated information literacy into her instruction. In the process of developing their interview questions, her students used the World Wide Web to gather general information about businesses in their community. Using the websites that Ms. Doyle had preselected for age appropriateness, her students developed interview questions for community business owners. They did this by analyzing information contained in the websites and then synthesized it into what was most relevant for their interviews. Ms. Doyle's students were becoming "effective users of ideas and information" (American Association of School Librarians, 1998).

Ms. Doyle planned her curriculum to ensure that students were engaging in developmentally appropriate activities. She helped her students by preparing information resources prior to student use. She weeded out irrelevant and developmentally inappropriate resources. Ms. Doyle also provided her students with a plan and an authentic reason for using the resources. By pre-screening information resources, she ensured that her students were presented with only those that were appropriate to their ages and the task at hand. Then, she and her students viewed websites together and discussed what makes a good versus an ineffective information resource. The elements that Ms. Doyle and her students focused on were reliability or authenticity of an information source, its currency or recency, whether contact information is provided so that students have the potential to e-mail questions to information sources, and the ability to identify information as fact or opinion. In discussing these elements with her students, Ms. Doyle devised a rubric with them so that they could gauge the appropriateness of resources.

Ms. Doyle limited students' "free range" searching on the Internet to a few reliable search engines designed for young children, including Yahooligans and Ask Jeeves for Kids. By encouraging students to use these "safe" search engines and apply criteria for selection of resources, Ms. Doyle was not only encouraging her students to become autonomous learners but also increasing their developmental potential.

Intertextuality

Intertextuality is a term that was first coined by Kristeva (1984) to represent the process of comprehending one text by means of a previously encountered text. Orr (1986) further elaborated on the notion of intertextuality stating, "No literary text is written in a vacuum. Besides the general culture surrounding the text and the author's own horizon (i.e., his experiences, prejudices, uses of language system, 'worldview,' and so on), there are, perhaps more importantly, other texts" (p. 814).

As the number of information sources students have access to increases, the ability to synthesize and integrate information from a variety of resources and media based on important underlying principles of a content area versus surface details becomes critical. Students must have exposure to a number of text-based resources via books, CD-ROMs, and the Internet. This allows students to begin to understand that learning resources are not isolated from one another; rather,

they build on one another to help create a deeper understanding of the topic. Ms. Doyle's students encountered text from a variety of resources, including books, community business materials, and the Internet. They used these resources to develop a deeper understanding of what it means to be bilingual.

Technology played an important role in facilitating Ms. Doyle's ability to incorporate multiple literacies within her curriculum. Technology enabled the changes in classroom organizational structure, teacher and student roles, and use of resources that the paradigm shift required. Specifically, technology affords instructional methods that traditional methods do not. For example, it enables information to be presented in multiple ways. A teacher can use presentation software to introduce a new topic of study to the entire class. Then, moving into a small-group format, students can delve into key aspects of the information presented by engaging in technology-mediated research using the Internet or electronic databases.

Technology affords students nonlinear access to information. They can navigate a vast array of resources on the Internet or in electronic encyclopedias in a way that is based upon their particular interests or information needs rather than ways that are controlled by linear text formats. Electronic search engines enable students to access multiple resources on a given topic. Technology can also help students organize and synthesize information in different ways, facilitating their ability to construct and refine their knowledge. Finally, teachers can use technology to reconfigure information in a manner that is tailored to students' individual needs by using the cut, copy, paste, and highlight features of word-processing software programs.

WHAT THE PARADIGM SHIFT SIGNALS FOR TEACHERS

What specifically did Ms. Doyle do with her students that signals new responsibilities for teachers? She exposed her students to more than traditional texts for literacy learning. This required her to change the structure of her class so that her students could experience and use multiple literacies in the context of a rich, authentic curriculum project rather than during isolated skills instruction. Ms. Doyle chose a variety of technologies to help her students develop these multiple literacies and then folded specific technology skills instruction, such as the way to import digital pictures into a word-processing document, into the context of the curriculum.

Ms. Doyle's approach emphasizes a rich, complex use of technologies that facilitates change in the structure of the learning environment. While the project is teacher initiated, the activities underlying the unit are student centered. The arrangement of small-group activities supports the students' abilities to interact independently and learn from one another. The way in which the students interact with adults in the community provides a level of authenticity that helps the students develop lifelong literacies that will serve them well now and into the future.

This expanded vision of literacy, and the technological culture necessary to make such a vision a reality, has significant implications for teachers: It changes their roles and responsibilities. Teachers do not send their students to a computer teacher to learn how to use computers. Rather, teachers must begin to use a variety of technologies in their instruction and help students use them throughout their learning experiences. For example, in Ms. Doyle's classroom, digital and traditional cameras are used. The photos taken are easily transferred to classroom computers where they are analyzed and edited for use in e-mail communications and digital presentations. In this way, students are gaining comfort and familiarity with important tools and using them in ways that reflect their use in everyday life as opposed to their use in formalized, traditional school instruction.

This expanded vision of literacy brings a change in the quantity and quality of resources available, adding layers of new responsibilities for teachers. They must access a wider array of resources, including technology-based tools,

with the materials they evaluate for inclusion in a curriculum project. The quality of these resources is also a major issue. Technology enables teachers to widen the boundaries of their classroom to include the surrounding community as well as a global network. While this expansion has the potential to create a more authentic literacy environment for students, merely expanding opportunities does not ensure quality. For example, in an era of ubiquitous computing, most if not all teachers hunt the World Wide Web for resources, where there is little or no assurance of obtaining quality information. Anyone can post anything on the Web. Because of these changes in the quantity and quality of resources, it becomes imperative for teachers to find and evaluate technologies in a wider context that includes their curriculum, their students, and their community. They must then integrate these resources into the curriculum in a way that scaffolds the guidance their students will need to construct, represent, and communicate their knowledge.

TECHNOLOGIES TO SUPPORT THE PARADIGM SHIFT IN LITERACY INSTRUCTION

In a curricular space that has remained constant, how do we begin to undertake the responsibilities that address the necessary changes of technology? The vision is not manageable if we leave technology as a supplement to curriculum—we end up losing its richness and complexity, as well as the primacy of the curriculum. The way to implement the necessary classroom change is to avoid getting bogged down by technology and find existing technologies to facilitate our teaching. Technology professionals have already developed many useful tools; it becomes our role as educators to appropriate these tools in ways that nurture the paradigm shift in literacy instruction and to inform the developers of technology of the new tools we need to continue this mission.

A variety of technologies can be used to support this new vision of media literacy. Of particular support for teachers are technology tools that have been shaped into "templates." These tools are form driven, so specialized knowledge of programming languages isn't required. Because templates are easily customized and implemented, teachers can focus on the content of the curriculum and instructional planning rather than on learning esoteric, high-tech programming skills. The following are examples of templates that can be used within literacy instruction.

Digital imaging technologies. Pictures tell a thousand words. They also support what is being communicated with words. Slide-show programs such as Microsoft PowerPoint are traditionally used to create presentations, but they can also be used in the media development process. Once students have gathered visual images from digital pictures they have taken or traditional photos they have scanned, it becomes important for them to evaluate this "portfolio" and decide what pictures should be included in a particular presentation, story, or article. Slide-show tools benefit this process because they allow students to organize photos easily in order to evaluate how a certain display of pictures communicates an idea. Some of these tools also include special effects, which offer an array of artistic enhancements and borders. Slide-show templates include the following examples:

- Slide sorter view in Microsoft PowerPoint permits the easy organization of photos. Once photos are made into slides, they can be viewed on slide sorter, and their order can be easily manipulated. This enables students to gauge the way a particular order of pictures communicates an idea.
- Kid pix slide show enables very young students to organize and manipulate digital pictures.
- Ofoto (http://www.ofoto.com) sponsors an online photo album feature. Students can create themed photo albums or scrapbooks to share photos with others using the World Wide Web.
- Flaming Text (http://www.flamingtext.com) provides teachers and students with an on-line point-and-click mechanism to create individualized banners, buttons, and

bars to be used in a variety of multimedia projects such as newsletters and Web-based publications. For example, using this tool, students can communicate a particular message by creating images and text that convey the intended theme.

World Wide Web-based technologies. Often teachers have their students use the World Wide Web as an encyclopedia, gathering resources in ways similar to text-based sources. However, teachers can easily create Web-based files that engage students in a variety of active learning experiences. Teachers can use fill-in-the blank forms to create these files and post them on the World Wide Web. Filamentality (http://www.kn.pacbell.com/wired/fil) is an interactive website that helps a teacher turn Web resources into learning activities. Included are templates for creating five different Web-based instructional designs (Dodge, 2001; March, 2001). The following are descriptions of the instructional designs and the ways in which they can be used.

- A *hotlist* is a categorized list of websites that can be used to support a curriculum unit. Teachers can "mine," or search for and gather, websites that they want their students to explore. Once mined, Filamentality can be used to create and post the hotlist on the Web. Hotlists are an effective way to point students to Web-based resources. They can also be used to organize websites.
- A *scrapbook* enables an individual to organize Web-based media resources, such as images and sounds, and subject websites so that they can be integrated into a variety of multimedia products, including newsletters, desktop presentations, and webpages.
- A *hunt* poses a series of questions that can be answered by reading information found on key websites identified by a teacher. Once students have answered all questions, they are to respond to a larger question or concept that requires them to synthesize and analyze what they have learned. Internet hunts are an effective way for students to build their knowledge around a particular subject area.

• A *sampler* presents learners with a small number of interesting websites organized around a subject area or theme. These websites should be chosen based upon their ability to pique students' interests and invite their speculation about the topic. Once learners have perused the identified websites, they are encouraged to share their perspectives on the topic, share their experiences related to it, and discuss their interpretations.

• A *webquest* is a highly structured activity based upon cooperative learning strategies. For a webquest, students are presented with a challenging task and the Internet-based resources to accomplish it. Students must each adopt a role, share what they have learned based upon that role, and collaborate to create a product, such as a presentation, to share with others.

• TrackStar (http://trackstar.hprtec.org) helps instructors organize and annotate websites, which can then be used to shape lessons. A "track" consists of three areas. The first area contains a list of website addresses (URLs). As each URL is selected, another area describes the website, while a third area contains the actual URL link. Like hotlists (described earlier), teachers can use TrackStar to introduce students to a new topic of study. Students can also create tracks as part of a curriculum project requirement.

Webpage construction. A number of organizations host websites that allow teachers to create and post their own webpages. A teacher can use these templates to build a classroom presence on the Web. For example, many teachers use these websites to share student writing and artwork, list homework assignments, and encourage communication between home and school. The following websites offer fill-in-the-blank templates that teachers and students can use to create their own webpages. Because these created sites are given a Web address, they can be accessed via any computer that is connected to the Internet. The following webpages offer easy-to-create webpage models that are particularly useful for teachers.

• Homestead (http://www.homestead.com) enables teachers and students to create webpages for personal or organizational use. The personal site includes graphics libraries, design tutorials, and online support. While the professional site has many tools useful for business, it also offers individuals the ability to track who is using the website.

• Teacherweb (http://teacherweb.com) offers a template specifically designed for teachers and other school professionals. Teachers can create and post areas for homework, announcements, grades, calendars, links, and photos. Both Teacherweb and Homestead offer individuals the ability to create and post an unlimited number of webpages.

Global communication and collaboration. The World Wide Web gives students and teachers access to a global community. While students can accomplish the same literacy activities as they can on paper, such as creating poetry or writing fiction, the Web enables them to share this type of work with a wider authentic audience. This, in turn, positively influences their writing skills. The following websites can facilitate communication and collaboration across geographic boundaries:

• ePALS.com (http://www.epals.com) is labeled the "world's largest online classroom community." Using ePALS, teachers and students can find electronic pen pals and have the option to communicate in a variety of languages. Beyond e-mail writing, students can engage in online, themed group discussions and develop collaborative projects such as creating fiction and nonfiction books. This website offers an instant translation service, so students can communicate in their native language with individuals who may not share the same language.

• Collabo-write (http://library.thinkquest.org/2626) is a shared writing forum on the Internet. Using a fill-in-the-blank format, students can enter a story, add to an existing story, illustrate a story, or create a story from a variety of illustrations available on the website. Once created, all submissions appear on the Collabo-write website and can be accessed by a wide audience.

Global collaborative projects. The Internet has become a global classroom. Using technologies such as e-mail and the World Wide Web, teachers and their students can participate in curricular projects with other students and teachers from around the world. These projects offer students a variety of opportunities, including the ability to share and compare data, solve community-based problems, and learn from experts. For example, in the Square of Life project (http:// www.k12science.org/curriculum/squareproj/ smallworld_starthere.html), students collect data about plants, animals, and nonliving objects found in their schoolyard environment and share the information with students in other locations. The information gathered and compared facilitates students' observation and reporting skills, develops their effective communication abilities, and enhances their understanding of geography in a way that a textbook alone cannot.

Teachers can find collaborative projects across curriculum areas by using the Internet Projects Registry (http://gsh.lightspan.com/ pr/index.html). This service lists curriculum-based projects from a variety of organizations. Teachers can search for projects by subject area, age level, or project starting dates.

Student information searches. It is important for teachers to provide students with reference tools so that they can independently access, evaluate, and use information. The following resources provide students with tools to search safely for information and access references.

• Ask Jeeves (http://askjeeves.com) is a meta-search engine on the Internet. Students can search by questions, phrases, or terms. Based upon these queries, Ask Jeeves points students to information contained within multiple search engines such as AltaVista, Google, and Infoseek.

• Research Tools and Language Tools are part of the iTools website (http://www.itools.com), which offers students a variety of ways to research a topic in detail. These tools include dictionaries, a thesaurus, translation tools, biographical and quotation resources, maps, stock quotes, and a variety of other traditional research tools.

• When researching, students may have difficulty evaluating the authenticity of information provided within a website. Using Alta-Vista's search tool (http://www.altavista.com), students can place the prefix *link:* before a website URL to find websites that are "linked" together. This gives students the ability to see the types of organizations that host a particular link. Knowing that other well-known organizations such as the American Library Association use a particular website as a link can increase a student's confidence that the website he or she found is a reliable source of information.

Portals. The previous resources provide a starting point and a direction for teachers as they enact a paradigm shift in literacy instruction. However, teachers must also learn how to search independently for template resources so that they may continually shape their instruction. This can be a challenging task. Technology resources are endless and searching for them can take up much of a teacher's time. One strategy is to visit regularly a few educational portals that are posted on the Web. A portal is a categorized entryway to Web-based resources. The organizations that sponsor these portals continually search for and evaluate Internet resources, including those that they have found to be beneficial for teachers and students. Therefore, a good education portal is meaningfully categorized, evaluated by educators, and updated regularly. Following are examples of reliable education portals:

• Kathy Schrock's Guide for Educators (http://www.school.discovery.com/schrock guide)
• Education Planet (http://www.education planet.com)

A BROADER VISION OF LITERACY

In this technological age, teachers must expand their students' technological, visual, and information literacy as well as provide them with a sense of intertextuality, or the ability to make meaning from a variety of texts. This requires teachers to reshape their curricula and enhance students' abilities to understand and use multiple technologies in order to acquire, evaluate, and organize information.

The resources described in this article enable teachers to enact a broader vision of literacy instruction within their classrooms. In this way, technology, rather than being used as an engine for instructional delivery, can be used as a mass transit system to support student-centered learning and knowledge construction.

REFERENCES

American Association of School Librarians. (1998). *Information power: Building partnerships for learning.* Retrieved May 10, 2001, from http://www.ala.org aasl/ip_goals.html

Dodge, B. (2001). *The webquest page.* Retrieved September 25, 2001, from http://edweb.sdsu.edu/people/bdodge/Professional.html

Honey, M., & Tally, B. (2000). Digital literacy. Retrieved April 29, 2001, from http://www2.edc.org/CCT/cctweb/feature/art5.html

International Visual Literacy Association. (1998). *Frequently asked questions: What is visual literacy.* Retrieved May 9, 2001, from http://www.ivla.org/organization/whatis.htm

Kristeva, J. (1984). *Revolution in poetic language.* New York: Columbia University Press.

March, T. (2001, June). *Working the Web for education: Theory and practice on integrating the Web for learning.* Retrieved from http://www.ozline.com/learning/theory.html#Sampler

Orr, L. (1986). Intertextuality and the cultural text in recent semiotics. *College English*, 48, 811–823.

U.S. Department of Education. (1997). *President Clinton's call to action for American education in the 21st century: Technological literacy.* Retrieved May 10, 2001, from http://www.ed.gov/updates/PresEDPlan/part11.html

CHAPTER REFERENCES

Anderson, I. H. (1941). The Ophthalm-O-Graph and Metron-O-Scope evaluated in the light of recent research on the psychology of reading. *The Teachers College Journal*, 12, 60–65.

Balajthy, E. (1987). What does research on computer-based instruction have to say to the reading teacher? *Reading Research and Instruction*, 27, 54–65.

Berger, A. (1970). Speed reading: An annotated bibliography. Newark, DE: International Reading Association.

Dearborn, W. F. (1906). The psychology of reading: An experimental study of the reading pauses and movements of the eye. *Archives of Psychology, I*, 5–134.

Dodge, R. (1906). Recent studies in the correlation of eye-movement and visual perception. *Psychological Bulletin*, 85–92.

Gates, A. I. (1967). Programmed materials. *Teaching reading: What research says to the teacher, No. 1.* Washington, DC: National Educational Association, 25–27.

Huey, E. B. (1908). *The psychology and pedagogy of reading.* New York: Macmillan.

Integrating Literacy and Technology in the Curriculum. (2001). Newark, DE: International Reading Association.

Marrs, H., & Patrick, C. (2002). A return to eye-movement training? An evaluation of the Reading Plus Program. *Reading Psychology, 23,* 297–322.

McConkie, G. W. (1976). What the study of eye movements reveals about reading. (ERIC Document Reproduction Service, No. ED 155 651).

Palmatier, R. A. (1971). Machines in the reading program: What are their roles? (ERIC Document Reproduction Service, No. ED 051 980).

Rayner, K. (1997). Understanding eye movements in reading. *Scientific Studies in Reading, 1,* 317–339.

Smolin, L. I., & Lawless, K. A. (2003). Becoming literate in the technological age: New responsibilities and tools for teachers. *The Reading Teacher, 56,* 570–577.

Strickland, D. S., Feeley, J. T., & Wepner, S. B. (1987). Guidelines for computers and reading. In *Using computers in the teaching of reading.* New York: Teachers College, Columbia University, 9–11.

Thompson, B. J. (1980). Computers in reading: A review of applications and implications. *Educational Technology, 20,* 38–41.

Tinker, M. A. (1936). Reliability and validity of eye movement measures of reading. *Journal of Experimental Psychology, 19,* 732–746.

Townsend, A. (1964). What research says to the reading teacher. Programming in reading. *The Reading Teacher, 17,* 273–276.

ANNOTATED BIBLIOGRAPHY OF RELATED REFERENCES

Bibliography of materials published about the Edison Responsive Environmental Learning System: The talking typewriter. (1968). (ERIC Document Reproduction Service No. ED 028 648)

The "talking typewriter" was an early use of technology to teach reading. This bibliography includes references on this literacy machine and its uses to teach reading, particularly to the disadvantaged and physically handicapped student.

Blanchard, J. S., Mason, G. E., & Daniel, D. (1987). *Computer applications in reading* (3rd ed.). Newark, DE: International Reading Association.

Discusses the many possible uses of computers in the teaching of reading in the classroom. From a historical perspective, this discussion is an excellent description of the use of technology in literacy in the early 1980s.

Darter, C. L., & Phelps, L. N. (1990). The impact of the computer on the teaching of reading: A review of the literature. (ERIC Document Reproduction No. ED 326 836).

Notes the important impact technology has on the teaching of literacy, primarily through the use of the computer. Of particular note is the excellent list of related references.

Dearborn, W. F. (1906). *The psychology of reading: An experimental study of reading pauses and eye-movements.* New York: Science Press.

Dearborn, W. F. (1906). The psychology of reading: An experimental study of the reading pauses and movements of the eye. *Journal of Psychology, I,* 5–134.

These two references detail the early study of eye movements with particular emphasis on the existing methods and machines used in the study of this aspect of reading development.

Komoski, P. K., & Sohn, D. A. (1962). Programmed instruction in the field of reading. In J. A. Figurel (Ed.), *Challenge and experiment in reading: Conference proceedings, volume 7* (pp. 232–236). New York: Scholastic Magazines.

Discusses the development and use of programmed instruction in the teaching of reading in the classroom.

McKenna, M. C., Reinking, D., & Labbo, L. D. (1999). The role of technology in the reading clinic: Its past and potential. *Reading and Language Research, 6,* 347–364.

An important discussion of the influence of technology in the diagnosis and remediation of reading disabilities. The information presented on the past use of various types of technology in the treatment of reading disabilities is particularly useful.

Reinking, D., McKenna, M. C., Labbo, L. D., & Kieffer, R. D. (1998). *Handbook of literacy and technology: Transformations in a post-typographic world.* Mahwah, NJ: Lawrence Erlbaum.

A collection of readings reflecting ways in which all aspects of literacy are being changed by the new technologies, with emphasis on the impact of these developments on the teaching of reading and writing.

Spache, G. (1966). *Reading technology.* (ERIC Document Reproduction Service No. ED 013704).
Discusses the uses and potential of reading technology used in the early development of computer-assisted literacy instruction.

Townsend, A. (1964). What research says to the reading teacher. Programmed reading. *The Reading Teacher, 17,* 273–276.

This review of research is an important early discussion of contemporary studies on reading and technology. Of particular importance is the listing of thirteen related articles on this topic.

Yeager, R. F. (1977). *The reading machine.* (ERIC Document Reproduction Service No. ED 142 990).
Discusses the use of the PLATO Elementary Reading Curriculum Project, an early use of technology in teaching first-grade reading. The project illustrates some of the strengths and the weaknesses of the extended use of technology in literacy education.

YOU BECOME INVOLVED

The first article by Strickland, Feeley, and Wepner (1981) suggests some useful guidelines for the selection and use of technology in the literacy classroom. As you read these recommendations consider the following points.

- What are some of the problems you have had in the application of various types of technology in your literacy instruction?
- How might you apply these suggestions to decisions regarding the use, evaluation, selection, and future purchases of literacy technology?
- Which of these suggestions would you modify in light of recent developments in both literacy software and hardware today?

Gates (1967) was one of the pioneers in the use of technology for the teaching of reading. As you reflect on his article consider the following points.

- What are some of the pros and cons of using technology in literacy instruction that Gates discusses in this article?
- Are his concerns still relevant for today's use of various types of technology and reading instruction?

Thompson (1987) continues this discussion of the uses of technology as an important new development in the field of literacy education.

- In the twenty years between this article and that of Gates, what were some of the significant changes in the use of technology and reading?
- In this time span what were some similar, as well as new, problems that developed in the use of technology for literacy instruction?

Balajthy (1987) summarizes the contemporary research on computers and the teaching of reading.

- Summarize what research was saying at this time about the effectiveness of use of computers and literacy instruction.
- Note the specific problems Balajthy identifies with the use of computers for literacy instruction. Do we still have similar difficulties today?
- Review the conclusions provided in this article. Are these ideas still relevant when considering the current use of technology literacy for instruction?

The final article by Smolin and Lawless (2003) is an excellent summary of recent thinking on technology and literacy instruction. Consider the following points as you reflect back on the relatively brief history of the use of various types of technology to enhance literacy instruction.

- What does this article suggest should be the primary role of the classroom teacher in the use of technology in the teaching of literacy skills?
- Consider the article by Gates and those that follow it. What are some common problems that classroom teachers have faced in their uses of technology for literacy instruction? What have been some solutions teachers have used in this area?
- Based on what you have read in this chapter on the role of technology in reading instruction, how do you believe these ideas should be used in your classroom teaching of reading? What are the advantages and disadvantages of using technology for reading instruction?

CHAPTER 10

DEVELOPING A LOVE FOR READING

Whosoever therefore acknowledges himself to be a zealous follower of truth, of happiness, of wisdom, of science, or even of faith, must of necessity make himself a lover of books.

—Richard de Bury
The Philobiblon (1473)

It is the noblest of arts, the medium by which there still come to us the loftiest inspirations, the highest ideals, the purest feelings that have been allowed mankind. . . . Reading itself as a psycho-physiological process is almost as good as a miracle.

—Edmund Huey
Psychology and Pedagogy of Reading (1908)

I hope people will realize how important reading is and the most important thing is about reading to your own child. . . . It's really about enjoying that time together.

—Laura Bush
Interview with Harry Smith, The Early Show, June 15, 2003

The encouragement of a desire to read and to see it as being an important part of a person's life has always been the ultimate goal of effective reading instruction. As Francis Bacon noted almost 400 years ago, "Reading maketh a full man." Unfortunately, these ideals have not always been a priority for many reading programs. Almost from the beginning of reading education, teachers have struggled to find how best to encourage their students to read widely beyond the classroom. As you read these articles note how common many of the problems are both from a historical viewpoint and for today's educators. While a variety of solutions to the problems associated with voluntary reading have been attempted through the years, the results of these efforts have not always been successful. In this section the articles by Mangieri and Corboy (1981) and Block and Mangieri (2002) are related and thus are not included in chronological order.

AS YOU READ

In the following articles note the continuing emphasis on developing a love for reading as being the central goal of all effective reading instruction. As you read this material, reflect on your past experiences as a reader and consider what were the influences, positive or negative, that most shaped you and led you to become the reader you are today.

Pupils' Voluntary Reading

FRANKLIN ORION SMITH

This first article, written by Smith (1907), reflects the early concern of literacy teachers about the types and the amount of reading students were doing at this time. Note the questions about the relationship between school instruction and reading. The three suggestions at the end of this article on how schools can help improve voluntary reading are probably as relevant today as when they were made one hundred years ago.

How much do pupils in the grammar grades and high school read voluntarily? Is there any relation between the amount and character of voluntary reading done and the character of school work done by the same pupils? Is the course in English as presented in the schools vitally related to the pupils' voluntary reading? To what extent is the public library a determining factor in the formation of a good reading habit? These and similar questions form the basis of this study. To secure data, questions were submitted to the pupils in all grades above the fifth in the schools of Iowa City, Cedar Rapids, and Council Bluffs. Answers were received from 915 boys and 1,284 girls.

The report may be considered under three heads, viz., (1) as to the quantity of reading done, (2) as to the quality of reading done, and (3) conclusions and suggestions for further studies.

QUANTITY

1. About how many books of your own selection have you read since last September? Do not include books which have been assigned for reading, but those which you have selected voluntarily.
2. Do you read the daily papers?
3. What magazines do you read?

The following table is an analysis of the answers to the first question, combining the results of the three schools.

Pupils in the three grades (sixth, seventh and eighth) below the high school read on an average 19% more than do the pupils in the high school. Reference to the table shows that the highest average is in the seventh and eighth grades, which is due principally to the fact that the above-average readers and the excessive readers are more numerous in these grades than in any others. For example, the number of pupils reading more than 15 books, or two books a month, take rank in the following order by grades:

Eighth grade, 43.5%; twelfth grade, 38%; seventh grade, 35.5%; sixth grade, 28%; ninth grade, 25.5%; tenth grade, 24%; eleventh grade, 23.5%.

Grade.	No. pupils examined.		Av. No. books per pupil.		Total average.	% of pupils reading more than 15 books.		% of pupils reading less than 8 books.		% of pupils reading no books.		% of pupils reading from 8 to 15 books.	
	B.	G.	B.	G.		B.	G.	B.	G.	B.	G.	B.	G.
6	257	331	12.5	13	12.7	25	30	40	37	9	5	16	27
7	225	317	15.5	16.5	16	35	37	30	27	14	6	21	31
8	188	237	20	16	18	46	41	30	34	5	5	19	20
9	119	144	14.5	12	13	25	26	40	40	11	5	24	29
10	49	116	11.5	13	12	20	28	45	38	8	3	27	31
11	44	77	13	13	13	20	27	40	40	14	6	26	27
12	33	62	15	10	12.5	45	31	36	42	0	8	19	19

The high percentage of twelfth grade pupils who were above-average readers is accounted for by the fact that, although there were practically no excessive readers in this grade, there were very few who were below average.

Out of a total of 22 pupils who reported having read one hundred books during the eight months, 2 were in the seventh and eighth grades, 2 in the sixth grade, 4 in the ninth grade, and one each in the tenth and eleventh grades.

33% of the pupils in the grammar school and 40% of those in the high school read less than one book a month.

11% of the grades and 7% of the high school read nothing that was not required.

The percentage of pupils reading from 8 to 15 books, or from 1 to 2 books a month is slightly greater in the high school than in the grammar school. These are the average readers and constitute from about a fifth to a fourth of all the pupils.

The transition from the elementary to the high school is marked by a drop from an average of 18 books in the eighth grade to 13 in the ninth grade.

A number of causes may be assigned for the decline in the amount of voluntary reading done after the pupil enters the high school, viz., the ideals of the high school are usually radically different from those of the elementary school: more reference is made to the library in connection with school studies: new subjects, as algebra and rhetoric are often introduced in the ninth grade and methods of teaching high school subjects are frequently of such a nature as to require much more time in the preparation of lessons than was required in the grades. When we consider the amount of reference made to the library in the preparation of lessons in history and literature and the amount of collateral reading required by the English teachers it is quite probable that high school pupils read as much as seventh or eighth grade pupils.

If we compare the average amount of reading of boys with that of girls we find, on the whole, practically no difference. There is, however, a higher percentage both of excessive readers (those reading 40 or 50 to 100 books) and of delinquents (those reading no books), but a lower percentage of average readers among boys than among girls. 30% more boys than girls read excessively, and a proportionally large number read nothing voluntarily, while 23% of the boys and 20% of the girls read an average of 1 to 2 books a month.

Questions 2 and 3 refer to periodical reading. Fully 85% of all pupils, both boys and girls above the fifth grade, read the daily paper and quite as many read at least one magazine a month. The number of magazines increases noticeably from the sixth through the eighth grade where 50% of the pupils average 3 to 6 magazines a month. Above the eighth grade there is, at first, a slight decline and then a considerable increase. There is no noticeable difference between boys and girls with regard to quantity of periodical reading.

Data for studying the correlation between the number of books a pupil reads and the character of his school work was obtained from the register and from individual teachers. I compared the records of 85 pupils with their reports on reading and the result indicates practically no correlation between the amount of reading done and the character of school work. In a few cases fairly bright pupils were reported as doing poor school work at a time corresponding to a period of great reading.

"Excellent," "Good," "Medium," and "Poor" are equally distributed among the four groups of readers. If a pupil who reads little or nothing is graded good or excellent, one of two assumptions may be made, either that he is not interested in reading, or that his time and energy are all required to keep up his school work. Such cases should be studied individually and where proper incentives are wanting or opportunities insufficient these should be supplied. Pupils who read a great deal and are marked poor or medium form a variable class. A few may be educating themselves more truly than the school can do. Others are drifting in the current of aimless pastime and need the stimulus of sympathetic direction and inspiration. Only by studying individual cases can the problem be solved.

A comparison between pupils of the same grade and between boys and girls of the same and different grades shows two things, which will be of special interest to English teachers, and to all who attach a pedagogical significance to the study of individual differences. The first of these is the wide variation among pupils of the same grade with regard to the amount of voluntary reading done. The second is the close correspondence (1) between the boys and girls of the same grade, and (2) between the different grades.

Some of the data which should be considered cannot be tabulated. For example, some of the answers given by the pupils are significant. Some say they have no idea how many books they have read. One boy in the seventh grade says that his mother limits him to three books a week. Others say, "I read everything I can get my hands on." There are many negative answers, as "I have read very few books because my parents do not allow me to read at home." "I started three books this year." "I have read few books because I like magazine stories better." A frequent answer from girls in the high school is that their school work takes so much of their time that they are able to do very little reading except what is assigned. A few answered that they read nothing while school was in session, but read considerable during vacations.

QUALITY

4. Write the names of ten of those books which you like best, in the order of your preference. If you have not read ten, write the names of those you have read.

The following list includes all the books reported as "first choice" by 385 boys and 573 girls selected at random. This list, however, represents only about 1/4 to 1/3 of the total number of times that a large percentage of these books were mentioned. For they were included in the selections of other pupils, though not as "first choice." Following is the list:

Grammar School—Books marked "first choice" by both boys and girls.

	Boys	Girls
Black Beauty	2	23
Five Little Peppers	1	18
Uncle Tom's Cabin	4	15
Beautiful Joe	3	10
The Virginian	4	3
Ben Blair	4	3
Two Little Savages	4	3
The Jungle Book	4	1

Little Shepherd of Kingdom Come	1	4
Ben Hur	2	2
Life of Washington	2	2
Little Lame Prince	2	2
Man on the Box	1	3
Robinson Crusoe	2	2
Brewster's Millions	1	2
Graustark	1	2
Hope Loring	1	2
Lady of the Lake	1	2
Lorna Doone	1	2
Ramona	1	2
The Bishop's Shadow	1	1
Bound to Rise	1	1
David Copperfield	1	1
Editha's Burglar	1	1
Little Lord Fauntleroy	1	1
Man from Glengarry	1	1
Oliver Twist	1	1
Toby Tyler	1	1
Little Men	1	1

CONCLUSION

The importance of early forming a good reading habit can hardly be overestimated. Few other habits formed in school will operate more powerfully to influence the permanent conduct of the child than the habit of selective reading. It should be the chief aim of the English course to lay the foundation deep in the nature of the child for a permanent taste for the best in literature. It should be recognized that there are individual differences in matters of literary taste, and these differences should form the basis of instruction in English as in mathematics and science. It is a significant fact, and one that should be more often recognized by teachers and parents, that books appeal to children only in so far as they are translated into their own real experience. Hence there should be a close relation between the pupil's voluntary reading and the English, and especially so in the high school. In other swords the course in English ought to take its departure from the pupils' point of view. This would mean that, while Shakespeare, Milton, Burke, and Co-

leridge would still be read by most of the class and studied by a few, whose maturity, previous training, and environment has given them an apperceptive complex sufficient to appreciate the significance of these works, there would also be works by Henty, Stevenson, Ellis, Scott, Dickens, Alice Hegan Rice, Longfellow and a score of others so as to appeal to the various types of life and instinct found in the high school.

Curricula and courses in English will not alone produce desirable results. Much effort that is lost might be turned to good account if all teachers were more sympathetic in their methods of directing pupils' reading. To tell a pupil to read a certain book often inhibits the desire to read a very desirable book. A necessary prerequisite for intelligent and sympathetic direction in the matter of reading is a discriminating knowledge of books and a thorough acquaintance with the psychology of childhood and adolescence. And teachers who would assume this important and difficult task must be fitted by nature and training for this very special duty.

In concluding I will suggest three lines along which the school should endeavor to improve voluntary reading. These are:

1. That some definite plan of co-operation between teachers and pupils be organized whereby teachers may become acquainted with the reading habits of individual pupils and be able more efficiently to minister to their needs.
2. That the school be more vitally related to the public library by co-operating with the librarian to aid pupils in selecting books. A plan similar to this is already in vogue in some places.
3. That types of mental character and attitude as revealed in the quality of voluntary reading, should be carefully studied and the results correlated with the quality of school work accomplished, in order to aid both teacher and pupil to adjust the work of the school to the needs of the latter.

What Should We Teach in Reading?

Arthur I. Gates

The following article, written by Arthur Gates in 1951, is an excellent discussion of the importance of teaching the skills as well as the love of reading. As you read this article note his comments on the relationship between simply learning the mechanics of reading and the development of a desire to read.

During the past thirty years we have learned many important facts about the ways children learn to read, about the methods which are successful in teaching them to read, and about the skills which they need to establish sound reading habits. We have learned so much about the technicalities of learning to read that is seems we now face a real danger—the old one—of not being able to see the forest for the trees. For in our intense concentration, the mechanics of reading—on work analysis and word recognition skills, on phonics, on eye training and coordination, etc.—we have perhaps lost sight of the real goals of the teaching of reading.

There can be but two real goals toward which we aim in teaching reading—or, more precisely, a single goal with two aspects: to teach children to read well and to love to read. For unless they learn to read well, children will not love to read; and unless they love to read they will not read well.

WHAT IS ESSENTIAL?

Children must acquire sound techniques to read well, and ability to read well is essential to learning to love to read. But, to read well and to love it requires that the reading program provide an abundance of opportunity to read naturally and successfully. Every person has his limits within which he can read well. A typical sound third-grade reader can read well and enjoy reading material of modest difficulty, but a Shakespeare play is too difficult for him. Force him to do all or

most of his reading beyond the level at which he can read soundly with understanding and enjoyment, and you will soon destroy both interest and ability. You will also destroy the child's confidence and his sense of security. Both are essential to effective learning.

The regular basal reading program should provide the child with a wealth of enjoyable material on his own reading level. Over and above this, there should be available to him a library table or corner which abounds in interesting and lively stories and informational reading material *on the level at which he is able to read well,* and the day's schedule should provide time for him to enjoy these materials—to read freely and naturally with the same freedom from difficulty and the same smoothness which characterize an adult's personal reading.

This free reading, without stops to struggle with difficulties with unfamiliar words and constructions, is just as important, indeed it is probably more important, for the poor reader than for the superior reader. The poorer reader is precisely the one who is most readily bored by formal drill materials and who most seriously needs the assurance and satisfaction that can come only from reading really interesting stories.

We must give added emphasis to this matter of *interesting* children in reading. All the skills, all the techniques, all the mechanics, are only tools to use in learning to read well *so as to be able to enjoy reading.* We must not lose sight of the fact that they are only tools—useful, important, necessary tools, but still tools—means to the end but not the end itself. We must not so emphasize them that our pupils cease to enjoy reading. We must give children interesting material of suitable difficulty, provide them with simple but sound guidance, and give them ample opportunity to read by themselves and to learn to read better in the course of reading.

The reading teacher should never become so engrossed with mechanics or so intent on skill that she loses sight of this dual objective. Every day she should ask herself, "Are my pupils reading soundly and, most important, do they really love it?"

WHAT IS INVOLVED?

What is involved in reading well deserves a few words of explanation. First, to be able to read well the child must, from the beginning, read naturally and freely. He must have ample experience in reading as freely and naturally as an adult does when he relaxes after dinner and takes up his favorite book or newspaper or magazine. Many children have spent three or more years in school without ever having read this way. What they have been doing is laboriously translating printed words just as an adult does when he begins to read a foreign language in a series of hard lessons. A child may be average or superior in phonetic analysis or even able to "work out" more printed words than the average pupil in his class, and still be unable to really read well. Unless the conditions are provided which enable a child to really read freely and naturally from the earliest stages, he is unlikely to read well or to love to read.

Reading well is something very different from being able merely to recognize printed phonograms and words or even to pronounce the series of words in a sentence. The child who is adept at doing auditory gymnastics with phonetic elements may be a poor reader. Learning to recognize an unusually large number of words "by sight" in the first grade is likely to develop a distorted skill which is not reading and which, indeed, may even interfere with learning

to read well. The pupil who develops extraordinary skill in guessing words from context may have so neglected the ability to use the helpful usual and auditory clues in word forms as to become a word guesser instead of a well-rounded reader.

NEED ARRAY OF TECHNIQUES

No, learning to recognize words or to employ a series of word-analysis and other techniques is not learning to read well. Good, natural reading requires a properly balanced and unified array of techniques. It needs a highly co-coordinated unity of skills. No mere series or collection or sum of the particular techniques enables a child to read well. The test of success in teaching reading is not how well the pupil can perform in any of the component skills (such as sounding letters or phonograms, recognizing words, or moving the eyes along the line) but how well he really *reads* and how much he *enjoys* doing it.

This is not to say that techniques are unimportant. The contrary is true. Techniques must be taught. They must be the best ones. They must be neither over-taught nor undertaught and they must work together in such coordination to produce the smooth total activity which good reading is. To do this requires careful, shrewd guidance.

In learning any complex skill, there is the temptation to adopt the method which produces a quick display of results. For example, a person turned loose with a typewriter without expert guidance is likely to use only a few fingers in a hunt-and-hit procedure. This enables him to get obvious results quickly. He can hit off a paragraph right away. But he is not typing well nor is he learning to type well. If he persists, he will not only have to learn the whole sound process later, but also unlearn a lot of interfering techniques. And one sees very few hunt-and-hit typists who love to type.

Teachers of reading are faced with this temptation. The social pressure to make a quick showing of some kind of skill in reading is very great.

And there are numerous schemes offered to the teacher every year which are guaranteed to produce these quick results—usually some sort of highly formalized phonetic drill. But the final result of this kind of teaching is doomed to be the same as with hunt-and-hit typing. The flashy starter sooner or later falls behind those with sound techniques, and he either quits the activity or is relegated to the lowest group. The child with unsound reading techniques, however spectacular his beginning, eventually finds himself an inefficient and bored reader struggling along until remedial reading is provided.

The importance of developing the harmonious whole process involved in sound reading, and avoiding the distortions of overdeveloped isolated skills and techniques, however spectacular the stunts they make possible, can hardly be overestimated. Progress must be sound and sure even if it is slower and superficially less showy.

Given these basal things, they will learn to read soundly and to love it, and we will then have achieved the real goal of teaching reading.

From Reading to Literacy

Ethel L. Heins

Heins (1980) continues the discussion begun by Gates, which presents the seemingly endless arguments about reading approaches, materials, and literacy techniques but emphasizes the continued importance of encouraging students to see reading as a significant aspect of their lives both in and beyond school. As you read this article note the discussion of the stumbling blocks, often created in schools, that tend to hinder readers' appreciation of literature.

Research into reading has been a major industry in this country and abroad for many years. Thousands of words have been written on the subject— and often the jargon is baffling and obscure—but nothing has quite equaled the forthright, picturesque language used by Kenneth Goodman to state the undeniable truth:

> No quest among educational endeavors in America within the past century has been more diligently pursued with more energy, more resources, and more urgency than the search for universally effective reading instruction. Reading researchers, teachers, text au-

> thors have followed every promising path, explored every blind alley, turned every stone, rubbed every magic lamp, indulged every faith healer, bought every patent medicine. We've borrowed treatments from general medicine, psychiatry, physical therapy, industrial management.
>
> And when the dust settled, when the parade was over, when the band wagon lost a wheel, when the revival pulled down its tent and moved on, there we were with the same sobering truth: some kids learned to read easily and well and some didn't. And, if we were honest, we had to admit it was possible that some kids learned to read in spite of what we did to and for them rather than because of it.

Nowadays people scarcely need reminders of the clamor that has been raised over steadily declining *Scholastic Aptitude Test* scores and students' inability to read, write, speak, and even listen intelligently. A highly suspect educational back-to-basics movement, resulting in the adoption of competency testing programs for essential skills, has combined in unholy wedlock with the national stampede toward tax cuts and spending controls initiated by California's Proposition 13. As usual, young people, who are politically unattractive because they have neither voice nor vote, are the victims. But if a children's book specialist can be forgiven the temerity of talking about reading to professional educators, a few points can be made.

Ominous cries of dismay have been heard for a long time. In the January 1976 issue, the *Yale Alumni Magazine* let loose a stinging charge in a special section called "The Writing Gap."

> *Anyone who reads student writing today knows that students can't write. The students know it themselves—their eagerness to take writing courses is a desperate cry for help. It is easy to blame the schools and colleges for so fundamental a failure, and some of the blame is properly theirs. But the causes are rooted far more deeply in a society which rears its children on sentimental and shoddy reading matter, which bathes them in the linguistic sludge of television, and which debases the English language in the place where all learning begins: at home. Though the crisis of values that we explore on these pages is most harmful to the young, there is no hiding place for older generations in smugness or complacency. Many of the articles and letters sent to this magazine, for instance, are simply too fuzzy to be understood, and most are strewn with errors of grammar, syntax, usage, and spelling. The problem, in other words, belongs to us all. So does the solution.*

In 1975, *Newsweek* published an explosive article citing "a steady erosion of reading skills" and an appalling decline in verbal proficiency among students since the mid-sixties. Our country "is spawning a generation of semiliterates," said the magazine; and the criticisms were coming as loudly from industry, commerce, and the professions as they were from the universities. " 'The United States,' says poet Karl Shapiro, 'is in the midst of a literary breakdown.' "

Now this state of affairs seems all the more ironic to me when I think about our impressive library facilities for children; the brilliant, abundant array of books published for children; the enormous amount of money spent in this generation on educational research and special programs; and our modern scientific knowledge of childhood and its needs. So the blame for this verbal decrepitude must be distributed widely. Television, naturally, is a major culprit, not only because of the massive amount of time it absorbs from the lives of children but because of the passive nature of the viewing. Moreover, the total unsuitability of television to the minds of young children is well-known by now: the fleeting images that give them no opportunity to internalize or to respond to what they see and hear as well as the almost total lack of richness and originality in the use of language.

The *Newsweek* article claimed that one of the causes of the current crisis is that secondary schools no longer require the wide reading students need in order to write properly. Rather pathetically, it went on to say—

> *There is no question in the minds of educators that a student who cannot read with true comprehension will never learn to write well. . . . Very little improvement in writing skills . . . is likely unless the educational establishment recaptures the earlier conviction that the written language is important. . . . One thing that is clearly needed is a renewed emphasis on reading as both a discipline and a diversion.*

Now, American society has always managed to place the responsibility for its ills upon the schools. The cry for back to basics, which comes perilously close to throwing out the baby with the bath, is really a nostalgic yearning for a vanished era when life was less fraught with agonizing problems, when peace and order reigned, when teachers and parents were respected and supported one another, when science and technology were not threatening to betray the human race.

In the late fifties and early sixties, the hysteria after Sputnik resulted in a new stress on academic achievement; then the schools were charged with the crime of being cold institutions concerned not with human needs but only with test scores. So the schools responded again, this time with more humanistic approaches—the open classroom, education without walls, more emphasis on creativity, multimedia learning aids, and ever more innovation. And now the beleaguered schools are being called upon to return to so-called basics by a society that long ago turned its back on basics.

But there *are* some basic principles that I believe in rather passionately, and like most basic principles, they are actually rather simple.

Children, given the opportunity, respond spontaneously and joyously to books, for they have an inborn, primitive love of story. Narrative is not only a fundamental, primal form of expression—there's a *real* basic for you!—but it is also a print-oriented society's way of indulging in an ancient, universal practice. We put into stories the expression of our experiences in life. One immediately thinks of fables, parables, and moral tales; but all narrative subtly injects meaning into life, and stories contain so many more possibilities for each of us than does life itself.

The rightful heritage of children is story material, which will provide them with models, patterns, and symbolic figures for their own imaginative thinking. Stories help children make sense of the world—and of their own experiences. We all acknowledge by now that stories can promote sympathy and compassion; but they also enable children to detach themselves from their own personal preoccupations and, in seeing what happens to other people, to begin to universalize personal meanings. And, of course, the story content of television is pretty shoddy and watered-down—very far away from the great themes of folktales, myths, and, ultimately, of fiction.

Thus we must present to children the essence of literature and the literary experience—the ancient power of poets and storytellers. Start with nursery rhymes and simple folktales; go on to the marvelously vivid but economical prose of *Peter Rabbit* and then to the riches to be found in any good library. For here in literature is our link with undebased language.

Every day the child experiences so much that is new and confusing—events, feelings, ideas, information. Language helps to articulate the confusion; the writer's genius is that he uses the same tool everyone else uses, only he uses it more richly. Instead of struggling alone, the child, in reading, must meet the author halfway and thus becomes an autonomous learner.

And I am a great believer in the necessity—I almost said the urgency—of reaching out to the emotions of children and young people. Thoughtful and zealous teachers are all too frequently confronted by students whose sensibilities have been undernourished by the junk food of popular culture—students who are what George Leonard once called "emotional imbeciles, sensory ignoramuses, somatic dumbbells." Titillated and distracted by the superficiality and fragmentation of television programs, young people have become calloused, unreflective, and immunized against feeling.

Perhaps the greatest aim of education should be to turn children into humane human beings; and perhaps books that can arouse slumbering emotions—books that can make children *feel*—can help us with our jobs. I know that hundreds of children and teachers and librarians have been moved to unabashed tears by Katherine Paterson's *Bridge to Terabithia*. C. S. Lewis, in an essay on the teaching of English, said, "The task of the modern educator is not to cut down jungles but to irrigate deserts." We can surely try, through literature, to irrigate the deserts of young minds and to reclaim the wastelands of boredom in which so many children are hopelessly lost.

Let me go on and try to enunciate more of my basic principles—my eternal truths, you might call them, for they have been the underlying themes of the work that I have done all my life.

First, we must make available to children an abundance of books, and they must hear literature read aloud every day. Literary language is heard; then come the desire and the ability to read. It has been stated as axiomatic that children cannot begin to read what they have not heard spoken.

Our language is perhaps the richest in the world, and through daily reading aloud, children are introduced not only to an appreciation of literature but also to the heritage of their own tongue. For disabled readers the process is even more urgent, since they are normally cut off from the pleasures of literature and of literary language. Moreover, reading aloud to children is an act of sharing, and nothing more effectively binds generations together and bridges the gap between the adult and the child.

Margaret M. Clark of the University of Strathclyde in Glasgow wrote a fine book called *Young Fluent Readers* in which she explores the mystery of those children who magically arrive at reading early and spontaneously. Studying the children in a working-class community, she found that these children—the early readers— came from families in which visits to the public library were a vital, consistent part of a weekly schedule and that the parents, as children, had loved stories without intellectualizing the process; they simply read to their own children what they had loved themselves as readers.

Second, what happens when the child gets to school? We all know how faithfully teachers pursue "reading readiness"; but then they place before the child the most unexciting, bland, and flavorless prose illustrated with unexciting, bland, flavorless artwork—all packaged within shiny, washable, serviceable covers. Small wonder that nowadays, especially, young children eagerly turn to the activity and stimulation of the images on a television screen.

Schools can do a fairly good job of inhibiting and restricting young children's language. Compare their potential in language—or their ability to comprehend—with the language of a basal reader; observe the reduction in both quality and quantity. Think of the impoverished texts that are placed before small children, and see what constraints we place on their expectations and anticipations of the books and reading to come.

Connie Rosen in a remarkable book, *The Language of Primary School Children,* tells of a six-year-old who said she had discovered a quick way to read a page in her reader. She would read it *down*—vertically—and say, "Come, come, come; come, see, see, see, see, go, go, go, look, look, look," and so forth, picking out the words she saw repeated. The author says, "She had discovered the nonevent of the language on the page and her gobbledy-gook was just as good as the stuff that was printed. 'Reading a page' did not even remotely mean to her following someone else's thoughts."

If a reading series must be used, it is important to get on to trade books as quickly as possible. Take Pat Hutchins' *Rosie's Walk,* for example. So much happens in the pictures that is not indicated in the text, the child is drawn into the book and will talk about it. It is difficult to think of a child who would not be ensnared by Arnold Lobel's *Frog and Toad* stories in the Harper and Row *I Can Read* series; the language is simple but beautiful, the unfolding stories humorous and irresistible. Not to mention the pictures, which provide an early introduction to aesthetics and might well help to combat the debasing visual influences that surround young children today.

Now let's examine the teacher's role in the development of literate young readers. First of all, I know that many educators simply do not believe in the importance of imaginative literature—fiction, folktale, legend, poetry—and have never experienced this kind of reading themselves. I know reading specialists—good ones, conscientious ones—who admit that they almost never read for pleasure, that they know little about children's books or the reading interests of children. Obviously, the teaching of reading as a skill must be enhanced by adults—

teachers, librarians, and parents—whose fascination with reading for its own sake is contagious. The reading child depends upon the reading adult: it is as simple as that. Or to turn it around, as Aidan Chambers did in *The Horn Book:* "To put it crudely, illiterates are made by illiterates." Children must observe teachers who read for enjoyment, who give books an important place in their lives. Teachers must transmit themselves to children as *readers,* and they must also have a deep and broad knowledge of books for children.

How many people see literature as a substitute for the real business of living, a secondary, vicarious experience and not something for normal, active people? How many look upon books as mere resources—utilitarian commodities like globes or laboratory equipment or encyclopedias—using books as information banks?

I have found (and tripped over) various stumbling blocks in the way of making children into literate readers. Here are a few, seen entirely from the point of view of my own prejudices:

1. The gross misrepresentation of the art of literature in cheap, tawdry audiovisual form, especially in filmstrips, which repeat all the banalities of the worst television. I once wrote an article on this subject for *The Horn Book Magazine* called "Literature Bedeviled"; copies of it are still available.

2. The emphasis on speed in reading. I suggest that speed readers often fail to savor the full quality of a literary work and to comprehend the author's intentions. Experts recently have cast doubt on the advisability and the results of stressing speed reading.

3. The way literature is studied in schools. C. S. Lewis once said that he knew of no better way to turn children against books than to pull responses from them; we want to generate a positive pleasure in reading and not use the book as a tool for extracting from the child the answers to questions that ruin the whole process. Literary dissection and tortured analogies by children too young to engage in criticism can be terribly defeating. Helen Gardner, the Oxford professor, wrote, "The attempt to train young people in this kind of discrimination seems to me to be a folly, if not a crime. The young need, on the one hand, to be encouraged to read for themselves, widely, voraciously, and indiscriminately; and, on the other, to be helped to read with more enjoyment and understanding what their teachers have found to be of value." But this needs to be done without forcing pitifully inept judgments; the natural responses of children will grow more sophisticated as they mature.

Here are some questions that I have found in recent books dealing with children's literature for elementary schools:

Johnny Tremain: Was Johnny real or made up? Why do you think so? Is Boston an actual city? What leads you to think so? Is the main action physical or imaginary?

Harriet the Spy: Who is the main character? Is it someone who really lived? Or was made up for the story? Is the main action of the story physical or something that takes place in the imagination? Where does the action happen? Is it a real place? When does the story take place?

These insistent, nonproductive questions can absolutely stop the flow of the child's own ideas by circumscribing his or her thinking. Then there is the ever-present attempt to enliven the ubiquitous book report with old devices thinly disguised as new approaches. Just as ruinous are the pre-packaged, predigested kits—removing the teacher from the one responsibility he or she must never abdicate: the necessity of reading for himself or herself and sharing a living, vital work with children. And I have always suspected that the emphasis on creativity—endless dioramas, murals, posters, and book jackets inspired by stories—often leads to a deemphasis on the perception of literature, which can get bogged down in busywork. The teacher must be the vital factor in the connection between the child and the book. A child can talk about a book and enliven the talk with his or her knowledge of language and life; one can perceive the child projecting outward from the book into his or her own imaginings in order to penetrate inward into the book's meaning. And thus the story or the poem can be placed in the child's own world and made part of his or her life. Children cannot really engage in literary criticism, but they *can* express their responses in their own way. Most of us do the same thing, anyway.

4. The specter that haunts all lovers of literature is what is popularly known as bibliotherapy—not the legitimate clinical sort used by training therapists, but the practice of prescribing books like pills to help children solve specific personal problems and, indeed, to achieve many of the aims of general education. Just as our forebears produced a literature of piety and morality, designed to instruct, improve, and admonish the young, many adults now yield to similar temptations—which could send us straight back to the blighted children's literature of the early nineteenth century. For it is a cruel and futile misuse of literature to track down messages in children's books. No one would deny that books can be powerful instruments for moral and intellectual growth and for the development of awareness; but an imaginative work of art is not a political or a social tract, nor should its purpose be rhetorical persuasion or moral improvement. Authors cannot assume the roles of teacher, mentor, preacher; they are

artists, and books viewed as tools or as sugar-coated nostrums cease to exist in their own right and become simply the raw material from which lessons are hammered out. Any writer with conviction, who has something to say about life—about what it means to be human—cannot fail to reveal something of his or her views to the reader. Thus, for a child, circumscribed in a miniature world, books can open doors to an understanding of himself or herself, and, ultimately, of the universe.

We must return, finally, to the teacher and to his or her conviction of the educative power of literature. C. S. Lewis referred to the implicitly therapeutic function of literature when he wrote that it "admits us to experiences other than our own. . . . Those of us who have been true readers all our life seldom fully realize the enormous extension of our being which we owe to authors. . . . My own eyes are not enough for me, I will see through those of others. . . . Literary experience heals the wound, without undermining the privilege, of individuality." So teachers and librarians, from the wisdom born of a knowledge of children and of books, can invite the spontaneous responses of the young, encouraging them, by example, to seek for themselves the deep satisfactions of unlimited, unreluctant reading.

Making Reading Relevant for Adolescents

Thomas W. Bean

Bean (2002) discusses the role of recreational reading in today's classroom literacy programs. He notes that there is a continuing problem with teachers regarding how important they see the role of voluntary reading in a total literacy program. He cites a number of recent articles showing that factors such as high stakes testing have only increased this lack of emphasis on the role of literature reading in many programs. He notes a number of ways in which teachers can reverse this decline in voluntary reading.

Maria Sanchez is a high school sophomore in a large city. Her parents came to the United States from Mexico and she is the first member of her family to have career possibilities that extend beyond low-wage manufacturing jobs (Valle & Torres, 2000). Maria is a star student. She earns top grades, belongs to the pep squad, and holds down a part-time job to earn spending money. Maria achieves in school but has little time for recreational reading.

Dustin Rawlins, a middle school student living with a single parent in a small agricultural town, could not care less about school. He sees little connection between his classroom activities and his interest in becoming a professional skateboarder. Dustin earns low grades and daydreams about skateboarding near the California beaches. Recreational reading is not a part of Dustin's life, and few books are present at home. Dustin struggles in his classes and regards reading as a labor-intensive task to be avoided.

Should educators care that recreational reading plays a nearly nonexistent role in Maria and Dustin's lives?

At a time when adolescents are deeply engrossed in discovering their identities and life pathways, many students consider the middle and secondary school curriculums to be irrelevant. In a study of 1,700 6th grade students, Ivey and Broaddus (2001) found that it was difficult to identify in-school reading that students enjoyed. Students said that time to read and captivating material that reflected and suited their interests were important elements for motivating them to read, but that they did not view the classroom as a source of good reading materials. And, contrary to many homogenized views of teens, these students' interests were wide-ranging.

Despite a proliferation of excellent young adult novels that explore issues in adolescents' lives, schools often cling to badly outdated reading lists that convince adolescents that reading is boring and disconnected from their lives. Recreational reading among adolescents is in decline, with serious consequences for the development of a literate citizenry. Promising solutions to this

problem and useful resources exist, however, that can help educators encourage adolescent reading.

RECREATIONAL READING IN DECLINE

Educators often consider recreational reading to be an effective method of connecting to students' emotional and developmental needs. This "warm and fuzzy" conception of reading has been recently overshadowed by the realization that recreational reading has a number of other benefits. For example, time spent reading correlates with academic success, vocabulary development, standardized-test performance, attitudes toward additional reading, and the development of world knowledge (Moore, Bean, Birdyshaw, & Rycik, 1999). Unfortunately, the National Assessment of Educational Progress shows that 13-year-old students, such as Dustin, who never read for fun often have low reading ability and avoid recreational reading (National Institute for Literacy, 2002). Only 25 percent of 17-year-old students reported reading for enjoyment. Unfortunately, a decline in voluntary reading among struggling readers further aggravates their problems (Worthy, Patterson, Salas, Prater, & Turner, 2002).

In an era of high-stakes testing, there is an even greater danger that the curriculum is becoming more narrowly focused than in the past. Jessica, a 6th-grader, is bored by the highly structured and teacher-centered routines of her language arts class (Broughton & Fairbanks, 2002). Jessica experiences a curriculum that is largely divorced from her real interests, instead of one that treats reading as a valuable, lifelong social practice with direct connections to her life outside of school. She defines herself through connections with friends and family, not school, despite being able to follow the classroom routines and earn good grades. Outside of school, Jessica regularly writes in her personal journal to help her deal with her parents' divorce and her own depression. Jessica learned about the value of journal-writing from a cartoon character on television, however, and not in school. She also avidly reads young adult books on her own. In school, however, she feigns attention and completes tasks that are disconnected from her emotional needs.

Jessica's experience is hardly an isolated case. Fostering a lifelong love of reading will not happen if we simply allow high-stakes testing to drive curriculum design:

> *Teachers need to study the webs they have learned to create and in which they are suspended not only because they may differ from the webs of their students, but also because, as webs, they both support and ensnare. (Florio-Ruane, 2001, p. 29)*

Recognizing that teenage literacy has been largely ignored in this country, the International Reading Association formed the Adolescent Literacy Commission in 1998. The commission produced a position statement that advances key principles, one of which calls for attention to recreational reading: "Adolescents deserve access to a wide variety of reading material that they can and want to read" (Moore, Bean, Birdyshaw, & Rycik, 1999, p. 4).

IDEAS FOR THE CLASSROOM

One way in which educators can foster teenage literacy is to use young adult novels in the content areas. Teachers can pair classics, which typically center on adult issues, with the more accessible prose found in adolescent literature. For example, Shakespeare's *Romeo and Juliet* might be paired with Marie Lee's young adult novel *Finding My Voice* (Houghton Mifflin, 1992). Thematically, both works deal with tensions between two feuding families when their teenage children fall in love. Ninth graders can bridge nicely from the events in *Finding My Voice* to those in the more challenging *Romeo and Juliet*. As Gallo (2001) quipped,

> *The only two elements common in the classics that some contemporary young adult novels lack are plot complexity and dull, lengthy descriptions. (p. 342)*

A growing number of young adult novels span content-area topics in science, social stud-

ies, and physical education (Bean, 2000). Get to know these works by seeking out appropriate books and building a classroom library of young adult novels that relate to the curriculum. Although building a library sounds simple, teachers cannot simply visit their local chain bookstore and browse the young adult section for good novels; many of the best books must be ordered. Reviews in the *Journal of Adolescent & Adult Literacy, The English Journal*, and *In the Middle*, and on the Internet—including the readers' comments on booksellers' Web sites—are good sources for finding books. Such major publishers of young adult materials as Scholastic and HarperCollins and such esoteric multicultural publishing houses as Arte Publico Press are excellent resources. Including international young adult literature lets students see their peers in other countries grappling with such familiar issues as identity development, displacement, eating disorders, drugs, and suicide.

Once books are chosen, students need the opportunity to study them. Quiet time for extended reading and time for talking about books are both crucial elements in incorporating young adult novels in the classroom. Sustained silent reading is widely recommended, but depends on books that capture students' interests. If students do not connect to books, they become adept at staring blindly at the pages during the reading time or surreptitiously writing notes to friends (Broughton & Fairbanks, 2002). When sustained silent reading works, its impact is substantial. High school English teacher Steve Gardiner conducted action research on sustained silent reading for more than 20 years (Gardiner, 2001). He surveyed his students about their reading habits and learned that those students who read frequently had better literacy skills and earned higher grades in his classes. In addition, the central intent of sustained silent reading is to develop a lifelong love of reading for pleasure. Similar results have been apparent in international assessments of literacy. Higher-achieving students are more likely to hold positive attitudes toward reading, borrow library books at least once a month, and engage in moderate amounts of leisure reading:

> Variables such as attitude toward reading and frequency of leisure reading explained performance in reading literacy, even after school and student socioeconomic status had been accounted for. (Shiel & Cosgrove, 2002, p. 692)

Literature response journals give students a foundation for discussing novels that are connected to content-area concepts or are part of a sustained reading program (Readence, Bean, & Baldwin, 2001). Simply give students some time after their sustained reading period to record in their journals how they might deal with the situation that a fictional character is experiencing and provide time for follow-up discussion in small groups. My graduate students and I have been collaborating with a professor of English education and her preservice teachers in Australia to read and discuss online U.S. and Australian novels. Such a project allows the participants to challenge simple cultural interpretations and bring a fresh perspective to their reading and the discussion.

Venn diagrams can help students compare and contrast novel and text portrayals of events to be used in content areas. For example, in Walter Dean Meyer's *Monster* (Scholastic, 2000), readers experience the world of a county jail through the voice of Steve, a 16-year-old incarcerated for a robbery in which a storeowner was killed. A Venn diagram of Steve's view of his plight and society's view illuminates social justice and ethical issues that can be explored in a social studies class, for example.

Book clubs in content classrooms offer another means to engage students in reading and sharing their views about events in young adult literature related to concepts that they are studying (McMahon & Raphael, 1997). Create open-ended discussions that prompt questions to get the process rolling. In a social studies classroom, students might consider the older Korean cultural values expressed in Marie Lee's *Necessary Roughness* (HarperCollins, 1997), and how those

values clash in the main character's life as a teenage football player in a small, largely white Minnesota town.

Readers' theater (Young & Vardell, 1993) and dinner party (Vogt, 2000) are two approaches to help students interpret and discuss young adult novels. In readers' theater, key passages that propel the novel are selected and noncritical lines are eliminated so that it may be read aloud effectively. Two or more readers deliver a dramatic reading of the passages to be followed by group discussion.

Dinner party involves a group of six to eight students who are interviewed by a commentator. Each student plays a character from a novel that they have all read. For example, in Gary Soto's *Buried Onions* (Scholastic, 1997), Eddie is a Latino community college student who is down on his luck. His former athletic coach helps him plot a more promising future against a backdrop of gang vendettas and violence. The novel's characters help or hinder Eddie's quest for a better future, and students can role-play the different characters as though they are attending a dinner together. Dinner party is a culminating activity following reading, journal-writing, and book club responses to sections of a young adult novel.

KEEPING IT REAL

Throughout the classroom activities used to explore young adult literature, it is important to avoid superficial student responses. Students are so accustomed to trying to figure out what the teacher thinks is the correct interpretation that in-depth responding may take some time (Lewis, 2001). In a 5-year observational study of 25 high schools and related English classes, Langer (2001) found striking contrasts between effective and superficial literature instruction. In highly orchestrated discussions with a high degree of teacher control, student responses were often predetermined and shallow. In contrast, during effective in-depth literature discussions, teachers provided a framework for students' creativity and rich responses. In one class, for example, when students were preparing to read Elie Wiesel's *Night* (Bantam Books, 1982), they first looked at photos from concentration camps and jotted down words or phrases the photos called to mind. Students used these words and phrases to create poems. While they were studying the novel, students visited the Museum of Tolerance in Los Angeles, California, and wrote letters from different points of view. As a result,

> the reading of *Night became not merely an under-standing and critique of the work itself (though this was done), but rather an integrated opportunity to contemplate historical, ethical, political, and personal issues raised by the reading. (Langer, p. 871)*

Students were challenged to go beyond pat responses to create rich mosaics of interpretation and understanding in their reading.

If educators are serious about developing students' lifelong love of reading, they need to incorporate in the curriculum literature that is captivating and issue-based. The extensive and evolving genre of young adult literature offers an array of books that appeal to adolescents' interests and experiences. To exclude this literature from the classroom is to do a disservice to our youth. Young adults struggle, often in isolation, with postmodern identity issues, family displacement, globalization, cultural and ethnic issues, job losses, and other problems that schools need to address.

As the examples of Jessica, Maria, and Dustin suggest, the disconnect between adolescents' lives in school and outside of school is too often the norm. Educators need to disrupt this status quo, using both high-powered young adult literature linked to content-area concepts and interpretive activities and discussions that engage students. Until educators stem the tide of adolescents' declining recreational reading, we will continue to produce a nation of people who can read but choose not to.

REFERENCES

Bean, T. W. (2000). Reading in the content areas: Social constructivist dimensions. In M. L. Kamil, P. B. Mosenthal, P. D. Pearson, & R. Barr (Eds.), *Handbook of reading research: Volume III* (pp. 629–644). Mahwah, NJ: Lawrence Erlbaum.

Broughton, M. A., & Fairbanks, C. M. (2002). Stances and dances: The negotiation of subjectivities in a reading/language arts classroom. *Language Arts, 79,* 288–296.

Florio-Ruane, S. (2001). *Teacher education and the cultural imagination: Autobiography, conversation, and narrative.* Mahwah, NJ: Lawrence Erlbaum.

Gallo, D. R (2001). How classics create an alliterate society. *English Journal, 90,* 337–345.

Gardiner, S. (2001). Ten minutes a day for silent reading. *Educational Leadership, 59*(2), 32–35.

Ivey, G., & Broaddus, K. (2001). "Just plain reading": A survey of what makes students want to read in middle school classrooms. *Reading Research Quarterly, 36,* 350–377.

Langer, J. (2001). Beating the odds: Teaching middle and secondary school students to read and write well. *American Educational Research Journal, 38,* 837–880.

Lewis, C. (2001). *Literacy practices as social acts: Power, status, and cultural norms in the classroom.* Mahwah, NJ: Lawrence Erlbaum.

McMahon, S. I., & Raphael, T. E. (1997). *The book club connection.* New York: Teachers College Press.

Moore, D. W., Bean, T. W., Birdyshaw, D., & Rycik, J. A. (1999). *Adolescent literacy: A position statement.* Newark, DE: International Reading Association.

National Institute for Literacy. (2002). *Literary Fact Sheet: National Assessment of Educational Progress (NAEP).* Retrieved from: www.nifl.gov/nifl/facts/NAEP.html

Readence, J. E., Bean, T. W., & Baldwin, R. S. (2001). *Content area literacy: An integrated approach* (7th ed.). Dubuque, IA: Kendall/Hunt.

Shiel, G., & Cosgrove, J. (2002). International perspectives on literacy: International assessments of reading literacy. *The Reading Teacher, 55,* 690–692.

Valle, V. M., & Torres, R. D. (2000). *Latino metropolis.* Minneapolis, MN: The University of Minnesota Press.

Vogt, M. (2000). Active learning: Dramatic play in the content areas. In M. McLaughlin & M. Vogt (Eds.), *Creativity and innovation in content area Teaching* (pp. 73–90). Norwood, MA: Christopher-Gordon.

Worthy, J., Patterson, E., Salas, R., Prater, S., & Turner, M. (2002). More than just reading: The human factor in reaching resistant readers. *Reading Research and Instruction, 41,* 177–202.

Young, T. A., & Vardell, S. (1993). Weaving readers' theater and nonfiction into the curriculum. *The Reading Teacher, 46,* 396–406.

Recreational Reading: Do We Practice What Is Preached?

JOHN N. MANGIERI AND MARGARET RIEDELL CORBOY

The following two articles are directly related. The first by Mangieri and Corboy (1981) reports on the results of a survey of teachers on their knowledge of children's literature resources and encouragement of recreational reading in their students. The results are rather discouraging, to say the least. Some twenty years later, Block and Mangieri (2002) replicate the original study. This second study, while much more in depth than the first, unfortunately had much the same results regarding the continuing lack of attention classroom teachers give to the promotion of voluntary reading in their students.

"Our educational goal is children who will read rather than children who can read." Although this statement was made by Smith and Dechant (1961, p. 289) nearly two decades ago, it is relevant to the goals of today's reading programs. Current literature and basal programs both emphasize the importance of recreational reading.

However, emphasis by reading authorities does not automatically entice students to read. It is the teacher who must translate the advice of the experts into practice by exposing children to books and providing opportunities for recreational reading. In the words of Charlotte Huck (1979, p. 748), "It lies within the power of every teacher and librarian to give children a rich experience with literature. We must do more than teach children to read; we must help them to become readers, to find a lifetime of pleasure in the reading of good books."

An important ingredient of recreational reading is children's literature, and since teachers play such a vital role in the development of recreational reading habits, their knowledge of children's literature is primary. To use literature effectively, teachers must be cognizant of recently published children's books in addition to the classics and able to use these books effectively with students.

To assess the degree to which both of these conditions are being met, the following study was conducted.

QUESTIONNAIRE SURVEY

We gave a questionnaire to 571 elementary school teachers and administrators in Ohio, South Carolina, and Pennsylvania. The sample included urban, suburban and rural areas, and school districts having both majority and minor-

Percentage of Elementary School Educators Who Named a Children's Book Written in the Past Seven Years in a Designated Category

CATEGORY	ABLE	UNABLE
Biography	2%	98%
Fantasy/science fiction	9%	91%
Fiction	21%	79%
Mystery/adventure	8%	92%
Picture books	19%	81%
Poetry anthologies	3%	97%

ity group populations, thus encompassing the full range of socioeconomic levels.

The primary purpose was to determine elementary school educators' knowledge of children's literature and their recreational reading activities. The three items teachers responded to were:

1. Name three children's books written in the past five years.
2. Name a children's book written in the past seven years in each of the following areas or genres: fiction, biography, poetry anthology, fantasy/science fiction, picture books, and mystery/adventure.
3. Name three or more activities which promote recreational reading on the part of children.

The correctness of answers provided to questions 1 and 2 was determined from the annual compilations of *Children's Books in Print.* For question 3, the respondents' answers were compared to a compilation of recreational reading activities suggested in the literature by reading authorities.

SHOCKING RESULTS

With regard to question 1, 91% of the respondents could not name three children's books written in the past five years; 71% could not list even a single book. Of the 9% who did successfully respond to the statement, many named appreciably more than the requested three books.

The Table indicates the response to question 2, the percentage of participants who were able and unable to name one children's book written in the past seven years in each of six categories. Again, few of the teachers succeeded, although 1 out of 5 was able to name a children's fiction book and a picture book.

Of the 571 participants, 11 could name three or more activities which promote recreational reading on the part of the children; the remaining 89% could not. Most popular responses were reading stories to children, sustained silent reading, and designing or acting out plays.

NEEDED FOR A GOOD PROGRAM

When we initiated this study, we had two questions in mind. We wanted to determine what elementary educators know about recent children's books and the range of recreational reading practices being employed in elementary classrooms. The data suggest answers.

First, based upon our representative sample of over 500 elementary educators, it appears that the majority do *not* possess a knowledge of recent children's books. We had anticipated that many teachers would have a limited acquaintance with children's books, but we were genuinely shocked when only 9% of our study's population could name three children's books written in the past five years. When one considers the vast number of children's books produced annually, the results are disheartening. For whatever reason, these educators simply are not staying abreast of children's books.

Our second question showed that only a small percentage of educators could identify a children's book written in the past seven years in six designated categories. These areas were not of our own creation; children's literature authorities maintain the six are ingredients of a balanced literature program. An examination of the Table shows that a mere 2%, 3%, and 8% of the respondents were able to identify a biography, poetry anthology, and mystery/adventure book, respectively, written in the past seven years; only

19% and 21% could name a picture book and a fictional book. These findings suggest that the respondents were deficient not only in their knowledge of recently published books but also in terms of the salient elements of a children's literature program.

Finally, although virtually every reading authority espouses the merits of recreational reading, serious questions arise about its practice in the classrooms. Eighty-nine percent of the respondents could not name three or more activities which promote children's recreational reading. Over half were unable to list more than one such activity. Thus, we now have doubts regarding elementary educators' knowledge of recreational reading, and the extent and diversity to which it is occurring in classrooms.

SOURCE OF CONCERN

If elementary teachers are not familiar with recent children's books, then either children's books are not being used in the classroom or somewhat outdated ones are being used. Where funds are limited, of course, the use of older books is understandable. What is worrisome is the possibility that recreational books simply are not being used. The deficiency of teachers' knowledge regarding recreational reading practices suggests this fear may be a reality: If teachers are not aware of such practices, recreational reading must have a low priority in classroom practice.

Ask yourself the three questions contained in our questionnaire. If you are unable to respond to one or more of the items, what will you do to overcome this deficiency? The answer will be important to your effectiveness as a teacher of reading and your students' future love of reading.

Mangieri heads the Reading Department at the University of South Carolina in Columbia. Corboy is particularly interested in recreational reading and teaches at the Fort Jackson Elementary School in Fort Jackson, South Carolina.

REFERENCES

Children's Books in Print. New York: NY. R.R. Bowker Company

Huck, Charlotte *Children's Literature in the Elementary School.* New York: NY. Holt Rinehart and Winston, 1979

Smith, Henry P and Emerato V Dechant *Psychology in Teaching Reading.* Englewood Cliffs: NJ. Prentice-Hall, 1961

Recreational Reading: 20 Years Later

CATHY COLLINS BLOCK AND JOHN N. MANGIERI

In 1981, an article entitled "Recreational Reading: Do We Practice What Is Preached?" appeared in *The Reading Teacher* (Mangieri & Corboy, 1981). It reported data from a survey administered to 571 elementary educators from three states during the 1979–1980 school year. The sample represented urban, suburban, and rural areas of the United States; school districts that served majority and minority populations; and the full range of socioeconomic levels. This study sought to determine elementary teachers' knowledge of (a) current children's literature, (b) children's books in six literary genres, and (c) activities that they could use to promote students' recreational reading. We decided to replicate the 1981 study to determine the level of knowledge possessed by today's teachers concerning children's literature and methods of increasing students' reading for pleasure. We did so to update the database about contemporary literacy practices.

Since the 1981 recreational reading article appeared, several significant events have occurred that could have increased or decreased teachers' use of children's literature and classroom recreational reading activities. For example, many school districts have provided funds to create classroom libraries. In New York City, 300 books for each elementary classroom were purchased to augment centralized school libraries ("Books are purchased" 2001). Since the publication of *Becoming a Nation of Readers* (Anderson, Hiebert, Scott, & Wilkinson, 1986), the practice of reading children's literature aloud has been endorsed as one of the most important activities that educators can do to enhance students' achievement and pleasure in reading.

During this same time period, however, in response to the plethora of state-mandated, criterion-referenced high-stakes literacy tests, many teachers have been asked to spend more time teaching isolated skills and strategies. In addition, parents and teachers reported that today's students spend less time in leisure reading activities at home and school than those adults did when they were children (Mahiri & Godley, 1998). The number of children's books published each year has increased significantly during the last quarter century. Has teachers' knowledge of quality children's literature kept pace? Have computers and other forms of technology reduced or increased teachers' knowledge of current children's literature? Has the greater volume of information to be included in elementary content disciplines increased or decreased the amount of time that teachers allocate to recreational reading activities at school? The purpose of this article was to address these questions.

THEORETICAL BACKGROUND

During the past 25 years, several studies have demonstrated the benefits of providing more opportunities at school for students to read for pleasure and to develop their recreational, self-selected literacy habits. To illustrate, students who spent more time in recreational reading activities (a) scored higher on comprehension tests in grades 2, 4, 8, and 12; (b) had significantly higher grade-point averages; and (c) developed more sophisticated writing styles than peers who did not engage in recreational reading (Block, 2001a; Gallik, 1999). Researchers also documented the effects of recreational reading on vocabulary development. Students who had opportunities to read recreationally over extended periods of time learned significantly more words, without direct instruction, than control subjects, due to the former group's numerous experiences of decoding unknown words during recreational reading (Burgess, 1984; Krashen, 1993).

Moreover, Smith and Joyner (1990) reported that students who engaged in ongoing recreational literacy activities during school hours read books out of school more frequently and significantly increased their independent reading levels on informal reading inventories. Even when elementary students read for only 15 minutes a day, they significantly increased their reading abilities. Average and below-average readers experienced the greatest gains (Collins, 1980; Taylor, Frye, & Maruyama, 1990; Wiesendanger & Bader, 1989).

During the past 25 years, researchers have also examined the effects of various methods used to increase the amount of time students spent in recreational reading. These methods included the following:

- sustained silent reading periods (Burgess, 1987; Collins, 1980; Dully, 1989; Dymock, 2000; Halpern, 1981; West, 1995);
- daily recreational reading with a buddy (Barron, 1990; Block & Dellamura, 2000/2001; Libsch & Breslow, 1996);
- reading to children daily (Langford & Allen, 1983; Morrow, 1986, 1991);
- incorporating children's books into content area lessons (Duke, 2000; Pressley, Allington, Wharton-McDonald, Block, & Morrow, 2001);
- sharing and discussing books read (Smith & Joyner, 1990; Widdowson, Moore, & Dixon, 1999);
- replacing regular reading instruction with free reading of trade books once a week (Morrow, 1991, Strickland, Morrow, & Pelovitz, 1991);
- increasing parents' knowledge of the importance of recreational reading (Block 2001b, in press; Pressley et al., 2001);
- teachers' modeling of the pleasure that they receive from reading pursuits (Krashen, 1993; Strickland et al., 1991);
- cross-age tutoring (Baumann, 1995; Block & Dellamura, 2000/2001);
- continuously making newly published books available to students (Barron, 1990; Pressley et al., 2001); and;
- exposing students to a wide variety of genres in classroom-based and schoolwide libraries (Barron, 1990; Duke, 2000).

These practices significantly increased the amount of time that students spend reading. The amount of time that students spend in recreational reading is a predictor of students' academic success (Gallik, 1999).

Other investigators have focused upon the amount of time that teachers and students allot to reading for pleasure. These data were not as positive (Dwyer & Reed, 1989; Halpern, 1981). The time spent in sustained silent reading in school has declined over the past 2 decades, as has students' interest in reading for pleasure (Morrow & Weinstein, 1986; West, 1995). Equally important are data that recreational reading habits and appreciation for a wide variety of genres must be acquired early in children's lives (Block, 2001b; Widdowson et al., 1999). For instance, today's primary children often received as few as 3.6 minutes a day of exposure to literary genres beyond fiction or textbooks (Duke, 2000). Further, the number of college-bound seniors who report reading *no books* during their last year of high school has doubled since 1976 (Mahiri & Godley, 1998).

Students' positive attitudes toward literacy decline continuously as they progress from kindergarten through Grade 5 (Kush & Watkins, 1996; Morrow, 1986). Teachers' attempts to alter this trend by allowing students to visit the school library more frequently have failed (Morrow, 1996). Similarly, principals, teachers, and parents have stated that the promotion of recreational reading was a lower priority in daily classroom schedules than comprehension instruction, word recognition skills, and study skills programs (Morrow, 1986). Silent reading experience may increase an individual's ability to sustain attention and concentration, which are necessary for many types of academic and professional success (Block & Mangieri, 1996). Based on these data, as new literacy challenges emerge in the 21st century, a need exists to examine teacher's knowledge concerning children's literature and recreational reading.

METHODS AND PROCEDURE

In this study we replicated the procedures and methods followed in the 1981 study. We administered a survey to 549 elementary school teachers engaged in professional development activities in Georgia, Missouri, New York, and Texas during the 1999–2000 school year. These educators were chosen because their school district profiles were comparable to the sample in the 1981 investigation. Of the 549 surveys that were distributed, 514 were fully and accurately completed by the teachers who took part in the present study. This was a successful completion rate of 93%. Educators responded to the same three questions that were administered to those who took part in the 1981 study. Specifically, elementary teachers were to complete the following tasks:

1. List three children's books written in the past 5 years.
2. Name a children's book written in the past 7 years in each of the following areas:
   a. Fiction
   b. Biography
   c. Poetry
   d. Fantasy/science fiction
   e. Picture book
   f. Mystery/adventure
3. Identify three or more activities used to promote recreational reading for students.

We allowed participants to spend as much time as required to answer these questions. The average number of minutes spent in completing the survey was 23 minutes as compared with 18 minutes in the 1981 study. For both the original and current studies, the criterion used to determine the correctness of answers to questions 1 and 2 was the appearance of a cited title in the annual compilations of *Books in Print* during the designated years. In order for a teacher's answer to be judged correct, the title had to either be an exact match, or all words cited by the teacher had to be derivatives of the original words in that book's title.

For question 3, the correctness of respondents' answers was measured through a comparison of cited items to a compilation of recreational reading activities. To be correct, the content of an answer had to appear in the most widely used literacy methods textbooks (e.g., Block, 2001c; Burns, Roe, and Smith, 2002; Tompkins, 2001). An exact match of words was not necessary. The content had to be consistent with the purpose of the activity advocated by contemporary literacy authorities.

When teachers turned in their surveys, we interviewed those who provided three or more recreational reading activities in response to question 3. We asked interviewees to suggest methods by which the profession could increase educators' use of recreational reading activities and availability of recent selections of children's literature in elementary classrooms.

RESULTS

With regard to question 1, in the 1981 investigation only 9% of the respondents could name three children's books published in the past 5 years. Seventy-one percent of the respondents could not identify even a single book.

In the current study, 36% of the participants could correctly name three children's books written in the past 5 years. As shown in Table 1, this increase relative to elementary teachers' knowledge is significant. However, 17% of the investigation's population was unable to cite even one book. This was more than expected, as almost 1 in 5 of the surveyed elementary teachers could not recommend recently published literature to their students.

For question 2, data from the two studies are presented in Table 2. Current elementary teachers' knowledge of recently published selections of children's literature in all six categories is greater than peers' knowledge in 1981. The differences in knowledge levels ranged from 18% to 39% higher

TABLE 1 **Percentage of Respondents Who Could Name Three Children's Books Published within the Last 5 Years**

Educators who named three or more books published within the last 5 years	Educators who could not name a single book published within the last 5 years
1981 study	
9%	71%
Current study	
36%	17%

TABLE 2 Percentage of Respondents Who Named a Children's Book Written in the Past 7 years in a Designated Category

CATEGORY	1981 STUDY	CURRENT STUDY
Fiction	21%	56%
Biography	2%	41%
Poetry	3%	27%
Fantasy/Science fiction	9%	48%
Picture books	19%	37%
Mystery/adventure	8%	38%

for each of the six genres by the current sample when compared with that of peers in 1981.

With regard to question 3, of the 571 participants in the 1981 investigation only 11% could name three activities that promoted children's recreational reading. In the present study, 65 different responses were given by participants that were considered to be correct. Twenty percent (20%) of current teachers correctly identified three such activities.

Similarly, when the percentage of educators in the original 1981 investigation who could cite more than one recreational reading activity was compared with that of peers in the 1999–2000 study, a slightly higher percentage of today's educators could identify an activity that could be used to promote reading for pleasure (68% compared with the previous 50%). These growths in a positive direction are encouraging, yet diminished when cast against a 20-year period of professional development advancements. See Sidebar for teachers' responses by grade.

DISCUSSION

When we initiated this study, we sought to determine the knowledge of elementary educators concerning recently published children's books as well as their knowledge of practices that promote students' desires to read. We also wished to see how these figures compared with the ones in the study published in 1981.

On each of the three questions, current participants outperformed their 1981 counterparts. For question 1, four times (36%) as many teachers today could successfully name three children's books written in the past 5 years as their peers in 1981.

Today's educators' responses to question 2 were equally positive when compared with those in the prior study. In all six genres, the current group of educators knew more titles than the 1981 study's participants. The percentages by which they outperformed the prior sample ranged from 18% to 39%. Similarly, in response to question 3, more current teachers could identify three activities that promote recreational reading on the part of children than the 1981 participants. Also, more of the present group of educators could cite more than one of the aforementioned activities than their prior counterparts.

While the percentages of correct responses to all three questions exceeded those of the prior study, the percentages of elementary school teachers who are knowledgeable about children's literature published within the last 5 years, as well as activities that promote recreational reading for students, are still relatively low. More teachers (36%) were able to name three current children's books titles when compared with the 1981 study participants. However, 64% of the sample could not name three recently published books, and 11% could not identify a single title.

In the 1981 article (Mangieri & Corboy, 1981) it was said that "When one considers the vast number of children's books produced annually, the inability of most respondents to name three of these materials was disheartening. For whatever the reason(s), these educators simply were not staying abreast of recently published children's books" (p. 925). Regrettably, these words are still true today for many teachers.

In a similar vein, even though significant gains were shown in current teachers' knowledge of specific titles in each of the six designated genres (question 2), the percentages of

Commonly Cited Recreational Reading Activities

Recreational reading activities cited
by 88 kindergarten teachers

DEAR (Drop Everything And Read), SSR (Sustained Silent Reading), NIBS (Nose In Books Silent Reading)	52
Family reading, parents read as model, bedtime stories	43
Book-It	29
Library time	28
Teacher gives exciting introduction to books/ Teacher models that reading is pleasurable	28
Book Buddies and partner reading	24
Book sharing, group share time, Author's Chair	21
Choice and variety in reading tasks	20
Computer/interactive books	16
Discussion/teacher read-alouds	16
Listening centers	16
Acting out the parts of stories	12
Book bags	12
Guided reading	12
Incentive charts for home reading	12
Incentives	12
Bookmobile	8
Book pets and reading to a stuffed animal	8
Book raffle	8
Books on audiotape	8
Field trip to a bookstore	8
Puppet shows	7
Story cards	7
Class activities/games	4
Classroom read-around	4
Contests	4
Contracts	4
Free time to read while others finish their work	4
Homework activity sheets	4
Making new book covers	4
Reading newspapers	4
Poems	4
"Read Book" series	4
Book clubs or reading clubs	3
Reading score cards	2
Rereading	1

Recreational reading activities cited
by 84 first-grade teachers

DEAR, SSR, Silent Reading	50
Book Buddies and partner reading	43

Incentives and stickers	31
Book sharing and teacher read-alouds	26
Discussion	20
PJ party/Read-in/book party/book brunch	17
Accelerated Reader program	14
Reading and listening	12
Library time	10
Students' interests and topic choice	10
Author of the month/Author studies	8
Book swap	8
Contracts	8
Family reading	7
Reading newspaper and writing headlines	7
Book clubs	6
Books on audiotape	6
Book reports	5
Book-It	5
Contests and raffles	5
Parents read as role models	5
Bookmobile	4
Computer books	4
Folk tales	4
Read-a-grams	3
Big Books	2
Building "reading trains" around the room	2
Choral reading	2
Comfortable area in which to read	2
Home Club Accelerated Reader program	2
Homework	2
Plays about readings	2
Read-around	1
Reader of the week	1
Weekly poems	1

Recreational reading activities cited
by 93 second-grade teachers

Incentives—free restaurant meals, amusement park tickets	57
DEAR and SSR	49
Book discussions, teacher read-alouds, and book talks	43
Book Buddies and partner reading	37
Book-It	20
Accelerated Reader program	18
Library time	13
Contracts for books and reading	12
Centers	10

(continued)

Commonly Cited Recreational Reading Activities *continued*

*Recreational reading activities cited
by 93 second-grade teachers (continued)*

Parents reading as a model	10
Family reading time and no TV at home for 20 minutes	9
Contests/STAR program	8
Buying new books to disperse	6
Comfortable reading area and bean bag time to read	6
TV characters/book characters enacted	5
Reading in areas of interest	4
Book fairs	4
Books on audiotape	3
Games to reinforce books	3
Homework	2
Writing journal for reading responses	2
Read-In	1
Book clubs	1
Book reports	1
Free choice activities	1
Reading magazines	1
Reading "Mystery Readers" series	1
Reading newspaper clippings	1
Read-a-thon	1
Read to stuffed animal	1
Reader of the week—student gets to read to teacher, parents, class, and with a partner throughout the week	1
Reading Rainbow	1
Weekly reader	1

*Recreational reading activities cited
by 82 third-grade teachers*

SSR and DEAR	50
Incentives, 600 minutes reading to receive free tickets to amusement park	26
Accelerated Reader Program	24
Book-It	22
Teacher read-alouds, discussions, and book talks	21
Book Buddies, partner reading, and reading to lower grade-level schoolmates	19
School library time	18
Book sharing/Author's Chair	17
Computer interactive books	15
Read-In	12
Reading, writing, and ravioli	10
Students reading out loud	10

Book clubs and reading clubs	9
Bookmobiles	8
Contests, such as Read-a-thon	8
Family reading and parents reading to be role models	8
Homework	7
Readers Theatre	7
Summer programs	7
Book orders/gifts	6
Choice	6
Contracts	5
Centers	4
"Story clips"—students read aloud favorite parts of a book	3
Book box time	3
Book fairs	2
Books on audiotape	2
Comfortable settings in which to read	2
Field trip to bookstores	2
Hooked on books program	2
In-class library	2
Reading newspapers	2
Poetry	2
Popcorn reading	2
Puppet show	2
Read-a-grams	1
Reading *Time for Kids* magazines	1
Reader of the week	1
Journal writing	1

*Recreational reading activities cited
by 85 fourth-grade teachers*

Discussions	61
SSR and DEAR	56
Family reading and parents read as role models	42
Readers Theatre	32
Book orders from Scholastic Book Clubs	25
Book-It	25
Reading, writing, & ravioli	23
Accelerated Reader Program	22
Incentives	22
Guided reading	19
Book Buddies and partner reading	16
Read-Ins	14
Book clubs	13
In-class library	13
Library time	13
Homework	11

Commonly Cited Recreational Reading Activities *continued*

Recreational reading activities cited by 76 fifth-grade teachers		
DEAR; SSR; Stop, Drop, and Read	50	
Incentives (e.g., 600 minutes of reading to receive free amusement park tickets)	48	
Book sharing, book talks, and discussions	46	
Teacher reads to model that reading is pleasurable	24	
Accelerated Reader Program	21	
Family reading and parents read as role models	19	
Book Buddies and partner reading	12	
Book-It	9	
Book clubs	8	
Comfortable setting	8	
Choice	7	
Readers Theatre	7	
Library time	4	
Reading newspapers	4	
Snacks	4	
Visit a bookstore	4	
Book fairs	3	
Contracts	2	
Reading a series of trade books	1	

We want to express our gratitude to Celina Goss, graduate assistant, Texas Christian University, for the tabulation of data.

educators who could name a children's book that had been written in the past 7 years was still low. In only a single category, fiction, did the percentage of teachers exceed 50% (56%). In addition, 11% of the respondents in the current study could not cite even a single book in any of the six genres. Another 18% of the participants were able to correctly identify a book in only one of the six genres.

What makes these data important was that children's literature and language arts have long maintained that the six genres included in this and the prior investigation are necessary components of a balanced literacy program (e.g., Barron, 1990; Huck, Hepler, Hickman, & Kiefer, 2001). These findings suggest that many respondents did not have knowledge of recently published books and did not know current works that compose important parts of a children's literature program.

Moreover, two patterns emerged from these data. It appeared that a bimodal distribution existed in our profession. Eighty-eight percent of current teachers could be placed at opposite ends of the spectrum of knowledge concerning recreational reading activities and children's literature. Current teachers were either (a) very knowledgeable about recently published children's literature and diverse activities that can be used to develop lifelong leisure reading habits

for their students, or (b) not knowledgeable regarding recent children's literature titles, especially outside of the fiction genre. Teachers in the latter group were also most often unable to list any recreational reading activities.

Finally, although literacy research has demonstrated the merits of recreational reading for decades, we can raise questions as to its actual implementation. Seventeen percent of current educators could not name even one activity that promoted recreational reading on the part of children (question 3). An additional 33% of these respondents were able to cite only one. Kindergarten- through second-grade teachers cited, in order of frequency, (a) SSR and discussion of books read; (b) reading aloud by teachers, parents, or students; and (c) self-selected partner or buddy reading for pleasure. The three activities cited most frequently by teachers at grade levels 3–5 were (a) SSR, (b) discussions of books read; and (c) reading incentive programs.

CONCLUDING COMMENTS

Few would argue that one of the major goals of literacy instruction is to create lifelong readers. For some children, this love of reading develops innately. In other children, it is nurtured in the home. For still others, it results from pleasurable and diverse experiences with a cadre of enjoyable books and recreational reading activities in elementary classrooms.

When we questioned many of those teachers who cited three or more responses to question 3 in our study, one finding emerged consistently. Teachers who had a high knowledge of children's literature and recreational reading activities were lifelong readers themselves. They provided their students with a rich and wide array of pleasurable experiences with books, and engaged students in books of diverse content, styles, and formats. These teachers routinely (a) offer numerous opportunities for children to read books of choice silently, (b) provide incentives to read at home, and (c) ask for pupils' responses to books read during recreational reading activities in class. They reported that they did so in spite of the pressures to prepare for state-mandated literacy assessments.

Today's educators also agreed that it is important to develop students' basic literacy skills. They recommended that we, as a profession, not forget to include a healthy dose of children's books and recreational reading activities in daily classroom instruction. They suggested that we accomplish these objectives through new types of professional development sessions. One suggestion was to provide teachers with opportunities to bring their favorite recently published selection of children's literature to districtwide inservice professional development meetings to share with others. At these meetings, grade-level teacher teams could discuss methods that they used to increase the time that students spend reading books recreationally at school.

While time has been allocated in many schools for teachers to hold book clubs with professional books, none of the campuses in our study provided time to share favorite recently published children's books in similar book club meetings. Teachers were not provided professional development time to update their knowledge about recently published children's literature and how these books could be used to increase students' desire to read for pleasure.

We enacted one of the study's recommendations, to provide time for teachers to meet to discuss how to use current selections of children's literature, during the 2000–2001 school year. In four school districts in Missouri, New Jersey, and Texas, 347 teachers conducted 45-minute book sharings of six recently published children's books that they had read and used with their students to promote recreational reading. Principals observed all the teachers' literacy instructional periods three times during the 6-week grading period following the sessions, which occurred from September 2000 through February 2001. During that time period, 75% of the teachers who attended the book-sharing sessions used the books discussed in their classrooms. Teachers who did not attend these professional development sessions were not observed using current selections of children's literature or the activities for recreational reading. By contrast, teachers who participated in the book sharing created 2 hours in their classroom schedules (during the first 2 weeks following the professional development sessions) to engage students in recreational reading activities. These activities had never been used by these teachers prior to the professional training session, according to self-report data and observations of administrators and researchers.

Moreover, some of the educators that we interviewed in our study stated that they increased their awareness of children's literature by attending author sessions at annual state, regional, and international meetings of the International Reading Association. Many participants also mentioned that they have found that the fastest way to fall in love with and invent exciting ways to use current literature in recreational reading activities was to literally hold new children's books in their hands. As they read, new ideas emerge as to how these books could be used to enhance the recreational reading experiences that they planned for their students. One method of placing books in teachers' hands (and subsequently of enhancing their students' use of current children's literature) is by committing to visit the children's section at bookstores or libraries at least once a year.

We have developed a method of doing this that has become a pleasurable and habitual professional activity in our lives. Each year we compose a holiday gift-giving list, and we select one person on the list to receive a book as a present. On the day that we purchase this gift, we allocate time to bestow a prize upon ourselves as well. We spend one half to a full hour every holiday season seated in a child's chair in the bookstore's youth division, enthralled with the year's newest selections of children's literature.

Participants in our study proposed two additional methods to build colleagues' knowledge of current children's literature and recreational reading activities. The first was created by a former fifth-grade teacher. She developed the "one-minute pass around." Each year she brought the most recently published children's literature to the opening-of-school professional development session for elementary literacy teachers in her district. She distributed one book to everyone. Each teacher had one minute to read and scan that book, noting ideas as to when it could be used with content to be addressed that year. At the end of that minute, each book is passed to the left. Teachers thus have the opportunity to hold in their hands, and become familiar with, 30 recently published selections in 30 minutes. This teacher has also used the "one-minute pass around" with reluctant fifth-grade readers on the first day of school.

Several participants offered another suggestion. It was to hold children's literature Author's Chairs. At monthly team meetings, a selected teacher reads a recently published, high-quality selection of children's literature to the rest of the team and presents ways that the book can be used to foster a love of reading. If a different genre was shared each month, by the end of each school year teachers at that grade level would have knowledge of several books in nine varied genres, as well as methods of using these books to promote children's recreational reading.

Teachers in our study also suggested that librarians be scheduled to attend classes regularly to read selections of recently published books to students. As librarians read, teachers could hear new selections of children's literature with their students. Librarians could also route books to teachers, and as schools focused on a specific genre in particular months, recently published books in that genre could be displayed atop the library's bookcases and tables. In this way, teachers could peruse new titles easily in the library as they assisted their students in selecting and reading a wide variety of genres.

This study attested to the lack of attention that recreational reading is receiving in schools today. In most classrooms, the time and priority that teachers placed upon the promotion of voluntary reading is not significantly higher than it was 20 years ago (Mangieri & Corboy, 1981; Morrow, 1986). Because recreational reading and the use of high-quality literature has been shown to increase student achievement and develop avid literacy users, we should revisit the amount of time and level of effort that we invest in reaching that goal each day, each week, and each year of our students' schooling experiences. We can begin today, and we must.

REFERENCES

Anderson, R. C., Hiebert, E. H., Scott, J. A., & Wilkinson, I. A. (1985). *Becoming a nation of readers: The report of the Commission on Reading.* Washington, DC: National Institute of Education.

Barron, B. G. (1990). Make room for children's literature. *Reading Improvement, 27,* 282–283.

Baumann, N. L. (1995). Reading millionaires—It works! *The Reading Teacher, 48,* 730–732.

Block, C. C. (in press). Improving thinking abilities through reading instruction. In A. L. Costa (Ed.), *Developing minds: A resource book for teaching think-* *ing* (3rd ed.). Alexandria, VA: Association for Supervision and Curriculum Development.

Block, C. C. (2001a). Case for exemplary instruction especially for students who begin school without the precursors for literacy success. *National Reading Conference Yearbook, 49,* 110–122.

Block, C. C. (2001b). Missy Allen. In M. Pressley, R. Allington, R. Wharton-McDonald, C. C. Block, and L. M. Morrow (Eds.), *Learning to read: Lessons from exemplary first-grade classrooms* (pp. 162–183). New York: Guilford.

Block, C. C. (2001c). *Teaching language arts: Expanding thinking through student-centered instruction* (3rd ed.). Boston: Allyn & Bacon.

Block, C. C., & Dellamura, R. (2000/2001). Better book buddies. *The Reading Teacher, 54,* 364–370.

Block, C. C., & Mangieri, J. N. (1996). *Reason to read: Thinking strategies for life through learning: Volumes 1, 2, and 3.* Boston: Pearson.

Books are purchased for New York City public schools. (2001, January 7). *The New York Times,* p. 16A.

Burgess, A. (1987). *A clockwork orange.* New York: W. W. Norton.

Burns, P., & Roe, B. D., & Smith, S. H. (2002). *Teaching reading in today's elementary schools* (8th ed.). Boston: Houghton Mifflin.

Collins, C. (1980). Sustained silent reading periods: Effects on teachers' behaviors and students' achievement. *The Elementary School Journal, 81,* 109–117.

Duke, N. K. (2000). 3.6 minutes per day: The scarcity of informational texts in first grade. *Reading Research Quarterly, 35,* 202–224.

Dully, M. (1989). *The relationships among sustained silent reading to reading achievement, and attitudes of the at-risk student.* (ERIC Document Reproduction Service No. ED 312 631)

Dwyer, E., & Reed, V. (1989). Effects of sustained silent reading on attitudes toward reading. *Reading Horizons, 29,* 283–293.

Dymock, S. J. (2000, December). *The effect of sustained silent reading on reading comprehension: A review of the research.* Paper presented at the National Reading Conference Annual Meeting, Scottsdale, Arizona.

Gallik, J. D. (1999). Do they read for pleasure? Recreational reading habits of college students. *Journal of Adolescent & Adult Literacy, 42,* 480–488.

Halpern, H. (1981). An attitude survey of uninterrupted sustained silent reading. *Reading Horizons, 21,* 272–279.

Huck, C. S., Hepler, S., Hickman, J., & Kiefer, B. Z. (2001). *Children's literature in the elementary school* (7th ed.). New York: McGraw Hill.

Krashen, S. (1993). *The power of reading: Insights from the research.* Englewood, CO: Libraries Unlimited.

Kush, J. C., & Watkins, M. W. (1996). Long-term stability of children's attitudes toward reading. *Journal of Educational Research, 89,* 315–319.

Langford, J. C., & Allen, E. G. (1983). The effects of U.S.S.R. on students' attitudes and achievement. *Reading Horizons, 23,* 194–200.

Libsch, M. K., & Breslow, M. (1996). Trends in non-assigned reading by high school seniors. *NASSP Bulletin, 80,* 111–116.

Mahiri, J., & Godley, A. J. (1998). Rewriting identity: Social meanings of literacy and "re-visions" of self. *Reading Research Quarterly, 33,* 416–433.

Mangieri, J. N., & Corboy, M. R. (1981). Recreational reading: Do we practice what is preached? *The Reading Teacher, 24,* 923–925.

Morrow, L. M. (1986). Attitudes of teachers, principals, and parents toward promoting voluntary reading in the elementary school. *Reading Research & Instruction, 25,* 116–130.

Morrow, L. M. (1991). Promoting voluntary reading. In J. Flood, J. M. Jensen, D. Lapp, & J. R. Squire (Eds.). *Handbook of research on teaching the English language arts* (pp. 681–690). New York: Macmillan.

Morrow, L. M., & Weinstein, C. S. (1986). Encouraging voluntary reading: The impact of a literature program on children's use of library centers. *Reading Research Quarterly, 21,* 330–346.

Pressley, M., Allington, R., Wharton-McDonald, R., Block, C. C., & Morrow, L. M. (2001). *Learning to read: Lessons from exemplary first-grade classrooms.* New York: Guilford.

Smith, L. L., & Joyner, C. R. (1990). Comparing recreational reading levels with reading levels from an informal reading inventory. *Reading Horizons, 30,* 293–299.

Strickland, D. S., Morrow, L. M., & Pelovitz, T. M. (1991). Cooperative, collaborative learning for children and teachers. *The Reading Teacher, 44,* 600–602.

Taylor, B., Frye, M., & Maruyama, K. (1990). Time spent reading and reading growth. *American Educational Research Journal, 27,* 351–362.

Tompkins, G. E. (2001). *Literacy for the 21st century: A balanced approach* (2nd ed.). Columbus, OH: Merrill Education/Prentice Hall.

West, K. M. (1995). *Silent reading: What the research says.* Unpublished masters' thesis, Texas Woman's University, Denton, TX.

Widdowson, D. A., Moore, A. W., & Dixon, R. S. (1999). Engaging in recreational reading. In G. B. Thompson & T. Nicholson (Eds.), *Learning to read: Beyond phonics and whole language* (pp. 215–226). New York: Teachers College Press.

Wiesendanger, K. D., & Bader, L. (1989). SSR: Its effects on students' reading habits after they complete the program. *Reading Horizons, 29,* 162–166.

CHAPTER REFERENCES

Bean, T. W. (2002). Making reading relevant for adolescents. *Educational Leadership, 60,* 34–37.

Block, C. C., & Mangieri, J. N. (2002). Recreational reading: 20 years later. *The Reading Teacher, 55,* 572–580.

Gates, A. I. (1951). What should we teach in reading? *School and Community, 37,* 13–14.

Heins, E. L. (1980). From reading to literacy. *Today's Education, 69,* 41–46.

Mangieri, J. N., & Corboy, M. R. (1981). Recreational reading: Do we practice what is preached? *The Reading Teacher, 34,* 923–925.

Smith, F. O. (1907). Pupils' voluntary reading. *The Pedagogical Seminary, 14,* 208–222.

ANNOTATED BIBLIOGRAPHY OF RELATED REFERENCES

Cutright, P., & Brueckner, L. J. (1928). A measurement of the effect of the teaching of recreational reading. *The Elementary School Journal, 29,* 132–137.
Describes the development of a procedure for measuring the effects of classroom literacy instruction on the voluntary reading of students.

Dearborn, W. F. (1906). The psychology of reading: An experimental study of the reading pauses and movements of the eye. *Journal of Psychology, I,* 5–134.
These two references detail the early study of eye movements with particular emphasis on the existing methods and machines used in the study of this aspect of reading development.

Du Breuil, A. J. (1928). Checking outside reading. *English Journal, 17,* 559–566.
Describes a procedure for the evaluation of the outside reading activities of students.

Gardiner, S. (2001). Ten minutes a day for silent reading. *Educational Leadership, 59,* 32–35.
This reference suggests a school program that describes the extensive use of "sustained silent reading" as a basis for the development of a love for reading in students.

Green, J. L. (1923). When children read for fun. *School and Society, 17,* 390–392.
An early discussion of a research report on why children read and how they select the materials they read.

Irving, A. P. (1900). Home reading of school children. *The Pedagogical Seminary, 7,* 138–140.
Describes the results of a survey of the reading habits and interests of a group of 600 children at the turn of the last century.

Lasswell, A. (1967). Reading group placement: Its effects on enjoyment of reading and perception of self as a reader. (ERIC Document Reproduction Service, No. ED 011 816).
Investigates the effects of early reading instruction, particularly that related to group placement, on the eventual enjoyment of reading.

Lehman, H. C. (1926). Reading books "Just for fun." *School Review, 34,* 357–364.
Discusses the role of recreational reading as an important aspect of a total reading program.

Lockledge, A., & Matheny, C. (1987). Looking toward the family: Case studies of lifelong readers. (ERIC Document Reproduction Service, No. ED 283 140).
Reports on the results of interviewing over two-hundred adults regarding what educational efforts encouraged them to be lifelong readers or caused them not to enjoy reading throughout their lives.

Sancore, J. (2002). Questions often asked about promoting lifetime literacy efforts. *Intervention in School and Clinic, 37,* 163–167.
This article describes a program that encourages teachers and administrators to develop in students not only skills in reading but also a love for reading that will extend beyond formal education.

Worthy, J. (1996). Removing barriers to voluntary reading for reluctant readers: The role of school and classroom libraries. *Language Arts, 73,* 483–492.
This discussion presents information on a school-wide effort to help struggling readers to see the importance of voluntary reading, especially through the resources of the library.

Recall your own personal background as a reader and the specific influences, both positive and negative, that shaped your reading activities. What are some ways that classroom teachers can help students see reading as being an important aspect of their lives, both in and out of school?

As you answer these questions, recall what you have read in this chapter. Even though Smith's article (1907) is now almost one hundred years old, the reading information gathered on students of the past can be compared to today's students.

- Compare the interesting list of leisure books being read by these students to a similar list of more recent books. Are there any on this list still being read by students today?
- Are any of the concluding suggestions on how schools might help students improve their voluntary reading relevant today?

Donald Durrell (1939) expands on this discussion of voluntary reading.

- At the beginning of his remarks, the author sets forth a number of goals or ambitions that most of us as literacy teachers would support and encourage. Based on his survey of students' reading, why do you think these desired objectives are not always met? What are the implications of these results for today's teachers?
- What are some of Durrell's suggestions how we might help students see leisure time reading as being important in their lives beyond the classroom setting?

For the author of this book, the article by Arthur Gates (1951) is one of the most important references included in this collection of materials. In a very straightforward manner he establishes what he considers to be the important goals in reading education. Reflect on his comments, then answer the following questions.

- What does Gates believe are the two most important goals of an effective reading program? How do you believe you might realize these ideals in your own classroom literacy activities?
- In achieving these ideals, how do literacy issues such as specific teaching techniques and the use of materials help or hinder in this process?

- What is your role as a classroom teacher in balancing fundamental reading instruction and developing a love for reading?

Heims's (1980) discussion, despite being written some twenty-five years ago, speaks to us today about a number of relevant issues still faced by literacy teachers.

- Heims notes that we as literacy teachers at times seem to be overly involved in the latest fads and approaches to the teaching of reading rather than just simply encouraging our students to be readers. What can you do as a classroom teacher to help students see reading as being an important part of their lives?
- What specific suggestions does Heims make on how we can encourage our students to become better readers in the face of the seemingly endless debates over new approaches and materials in literacy education?

Bean's (2002) article reflects the current thinking on the issues related to helping students value leisure reading.

- What are some of the specific ways Bean suggests for teachers to help their students see reading as relevant?
- In this discussion what does the term "keeping it real" mean in terms of current reading instruction?

The final two articles in this chapter by Mangieri and Corboy (1981) and Block and Mangieri (2002) present a bittersweet summary of the progress that has been made in helping students see reading as being more than just a school subject.

- Briefly summarize what each of these two articles details about students' thoughts concerning recreational reading.
- Why do you believe there has been so little progress made in the area of recreational reading between the writing of these two articles?
- What specific ways can you as a literacy teacher reverse this continuing trend of lack of interest by students in recreational reading?

INDEX

Prior knowledge, 33, 110
Problem-solving
    components of, 212–213
    computers and, 230
    in content area reading, 172–173
    parallels with diagnostic process, 213
    in remedial instruction, 211–217
Product discriminators, 217
Professional development
    children's literature and, 279
    for content area reading, 174
Programmed materials, 226–228
    nature of, 226–227
    types of, 227–228
Progressive Education movement, 5, 232
Pronouns
    as relational words, 92
    in sight-word vocabulary, 185–186
Protheroe, N., 218–220, 222
Psychology
    behaviorism, 134, 213, 216–217
    cognitive psychology, 33, 101
    spelling and, 127, 128

Questions, in reading comprehension, 103–104, 105–108

Raphael, T. I., 106–108
Read, C., 31
Readability formulas, 4, 28
Readence, J. E., 176
Readers' theater, 266
Reader-text transactions, 114
Reading aloud. *See* Oral reading
Reading assessment, 37–59. *See also* Standardized tests
    comparisons across grades, 39–40
    of comprehension, 40, 45–46
    diagnosis of disabilities in, 42–43, 47, 206–207, 211–217
    future of, 49–57
    informal, 28, 54–55
    interests of children and, 40–41
    types of reading and, 40
Reading comprehension, 8, 14, 28, 32–33, 86–121
    assessment of, 40, 45–46
    changing face of, 100–113
    changing questions in, 102–104
    changing role for teachers in, 111–112

composing and, 109–111
comprehension skill instruction and, 105–111
for content area reading, 163, 165, 171, 172
historical perspective on, 87–88, 101–102
importance of teaching reading skills, 256–258
kinds of instruction needed for, 115–117
mistakes in paragraph reading, 88–96
ongoing challenge of, 118
phonics instruction and, 62
problems of meaning in reading, 96–99
teaching strategies for, 113–118
techniques for, 257–258, 265–266, 271–272, 275–277
vocabulary development and, 192–194
vocabulary instruction in, 104–105
Reading disabilities, 41–43
    diagnosis of, 42–43, 47, 206–207, 211–217
    multiple causation of, 42
Reading level, 39–40, 42–43
Reading readiness, 10, 27, 32, 261
Reading Recovery program, 31, 137, 144
Reading research, 1–36
    comprehensive instruction, 20–21
    computers and, 231–232, 233–240
    on content area reading, 162–167
    gender differences in classroom use of computers, 237
    gender differences in reading development, 19–20, 209
    hypothesis for improving reading achievement, 21
    influence on classroom practice, 10–12, 29–34
    instructional changes and, 27–29
    IQ and reading, 9, 15–18, 45–46
    literacy research, 24–35
    on pacing reading instruction, 18
    possible future research, 5
    on student voluntary reading, 252–255
    supplemental reading instruction, 19
    on teacher knowledge of children's literature, 268–280

that made a difference but shouldn't have, 9, 15
that makes a difference, 2–6, 7, 13–14
that should make a difference, 6–24
word recognition strategies, 18–19
Reading speed, 45
Reading-to-learn, 171–172, 173–174
Reciprocal teaching, 108–109
Recreational reading, 161–162
    of adolescents, 264–265
    commonly cited activities in, 275–277
    teacher knowledge of children's literature, 268–280
    vocabulary development and, 271–272
    voluntary reading, 252–255
Reinking, D., 237, 238, 249–250
Relational words, 92
Remedial instruction, 41–43, 47, 99, 205–222
    action plan for, 220
    basic principles of, 205–206
    diagnosis and treatment in, 42–43, 47, 206–207, 211–217
    effective reading instruction and, 218–219
    factors in reading success, 208–211
    identifying effective and struggling readers, 218
    problem-solving approach to, 211–217
    suggestions concerning, 207
    support systems in, 219
    teacher analysis of reading disabilities, 207–211
Research. *See* Reading research
Research Program on First Grade Reading Instruction, 8, 21, 32
Research Tools and Language Tools, 247
Rickleman, R. J., 176
Riley, J. D., 211–217, 222
Rime, 141
Robinson, H. A., 36
Robinson, H. M., 58, 205, 221
Robinson, R. D., 36, 167–170, 177
Roblyer, M. D., 235
Roper, A. L., 237
Rose, A., 219
Rosen, C., 261

CREDITS

Chapter 1

p. 2: David H. Russell, "Reading Research That Makes a Difference." *Elementary English, 38,* 74–78. Copyright © 1961 by the National Council of Teachers of English. Reprinted with permission.

p. 6: Harry Singer, "Research That Should Have Made a Difference." *Elementary English, 47,* pp. 27–34. Copyright © 1970 by the National Council of Teachers of English. Reprinted with permission.

p. 13: Harry Singer, "Research in Reading That Should Make a Difference in Classroom Instruction." In S. J. Samuels (Ed.), *What Research Has to Say About Reading Instruction* (1st ed., pp. 55–71). Copyright © 1978 by the International Reading Association. Reprinted with permission of the International Reading Association. All rights reserved.

p. 24: Timothy Shanahan and Susan B. Neuman, "Literacy Research That Makes a Difference." *Reading Research Quarterly, 32,* pp. 202–210. Copyright © by the International Reading Association. Reprinted with permission of Timothy Shanahan and the International Reading Association. All rights reserved.

Chapter 2

p. 41: Marion Monroe, "General Principles of Diagnosis of Reading Disabilities." From *Remedial Reading.* Copyright © 1937 by Houghton Mifflin Company.

p. 43: Arthur E. Traxler, "Values and Limitations of Standardized Reading Tests." In H. M. Robinson (Ed.), *Evaluation of Reading* (pp. 111–117). Copyright © 1958 by University of Chicago Press. Reprinted by permission.

p. 49: Robert J. Tierney, David W. Moore, Sheila W. Valencia, and Peter Johnston, "How Will Literacy Be Assessed in the Next Millenium?" *Reading Research Quarterly, 35,* pp. 244–250. Copyright © 2000 by the International Reading Association. Reprinted by permission of Robert J. Tierney and the International Reading Association. All rights reserved.

Chapter 3

p. 63: Nila Banton Smith, "The Present Situation in Phonics." *The Elementary English Review, 4,* 278–281, pp. 303–307. Copyright © 1927 with the National Council of Teachers of English. Reprinted by permission.

p. 66: Theodore Clymer, "The Utility of Phonics Generalizations in the Primary Grades." *The Reading Teacher, 56,* pp. 478–482. Copyright © 1996 by the International Reading Association. Reprinted with permission of Theodore Clymer and the International Reading Association. All rights reserved.

p. 72: A. Sterl Artley, "Phonics Revisited." *Language Arts, 54,* pp. 121–126. Copyright © 1977 by the National Council of Teachers of English. Reprinted with permission.

p. 77: Susan Kidd Villaume and Edna Greene Brabham, "Phonics Instruction: Beyond the Debate." *The Reading Teacher, 56,* pp. 478–482. Copyright © 2003 by the International Reading Association. Reprinted with permission of Susan Kidd Villaume and the International Reading Association. All rights reserved.

Chapter 4

p. 96: Paul McKee, "The Problem of Meaning in Reading." *English Journal, 30,* pp. 219–224.

National Council of Teachers of English. Reprinted with permission.

p. 211: James D. Riley and Jon Shapiro, "Diagnosis and Correction of Reading Problems as a Problem Solving Process." *Clearing House, 62,* pp. 250–255, 1989. Reprinted with permission of the Helen Dwight Reid Educational Foundation. Published by Heldref Publications, 1319 Eighteenth St., NW, Washington, DC 20036-1802. Copyright © 1989.

p. 218: Nancy Protheroe, "Helping Struggling Readers." *Principal, 82,* pp. 44–47. Reprinted with permission from *Principal,* September/October 2003. Copyright © 2003, National Association of Elementary School Principals. All rights reserved.

Chapter 9

p. 224: From Strickland, D., Feeley, J., and Wepner, S. (1987). *Using Computers in the Teaching of Reading.* New York: Teacher's College Press, pp. 9–11.

p. 226: Arthur I. Gates, "Programed Materials." From *Teaching Reading: What Research Says to the Teacher, No. 1* (pp. 25–27). Washington, DC: National Education Association.

p. 228: Barbara J. Thompson, "Computers in Reading: A Review of Applications and Implications." *Educational Technology, 20,* pp. 38–41. Copyright © 1980 by Educational Technology Publications. Reprinted with permission.

p. 233: Ernest Balajthy, "What Does Research on Computer-Based Instruction Have to Say to the Reading Teacher?" *Reading Research and Instruction, 27,* pp. 54–65. Copyright © 1987 by Ernest Balajthy. Reprinted with permission of the author.

p. 240: Louanne Ione Smolin and Kimberly A. Lawless, "Becoming Literate in the Technological Age: New Responsibilities and Tools for Teachers." *The Reading Teacher, 56,* pp. 570–577. Copyright © 2003 by the International Reading Association. Reprinted with permission of Louanne Smolin and the International Reading Association. All rights reserved.

Chapter 10

p. 256: Arthur I. Gates, "What Should We Teach in Reading?" *School and Community, 3,* pp. 13–14. Copyright © 1951. Reprinted by permission.

p. 258: Ethel L. Heins, "From Reading to Literacy." *Today's Education, 69,* pp. 41–46. Copyright © 1980 by the National Education Association. Reprinted with permission.

p. 263: Thomas W. Bean, "Making Reading Relevant for Adolescents." *Educational Leadership, 60,* pp. 34–37. Alexandria, VA: Association for Supervision and Curriculum Development. Copyright © 2002 by ASCD. Reprinted by permission. All rights reserved.

p. 268: John N. Mangieri and Margaret Riedell Corboy, "Recreational Reading: Do We Practice What Is Preached?" *The Reading Teacher, 34,* pp. 923–925. Copyright © 1981 by the International Reading Association. Reprinted with permission of John N. Mangieri and the International Reading Association. All rights reserved.

p. 270: Cathy Collins Block and John N. Mangieri, "Recreational Reading: 20 Years Later." *The Reading Teacher, 55,* pp. 572–580. Copyright © 2002 by the International Reading Association. Reprinted with permission of Cathy Collins Block and the International Reading Association. All rights reserved.